This book tells the story of the truly f... John Redekop and is written in ... the story behind his volumin... lic lecturing, preaching, political ... en and broader communities a... Dr. Redekop's many worldwide ... by motorcycle to meeting with high-level of... Union, making the case for greater freedoms for Christi... ...re. Readers will be not only informed but inspired to answer their own calls to serve through reading this book. It is well worth the read.
Paul Chamberlain, Ph.D. *Professor, Ethics & Leadership, Trinity Western University*

Mennonite in Motion is an engrossing and delightful read. John Redekop has written a truly epic autobiography from his parents emigrating from Ukraine to his thoughts on the chaotic departure of the US military from Afghanistan. Christians will be interested in John's spiritual development. Others will engage with his tales of an epic journey on a motorcycle across the Sahara in the 1950s! John is always insightful in his political and cultural analysis.
Janet Epp-Buckingham, Ph.D., *Professor, Trinity Western University; Director, Global Advocacy, World Evangelical Alliance*

John Redekop reminds me of the servant in Jesus's parable to whom five talents had been given. Much was expected of him. He didn't disappoint. We know it is God who rewards in the end and that is still to come. But from the many years observing this highly gifted man and now reading *Mennonite in Motion*, I see again how well John put his many gifts to good use in a multitude of settings.
Harold Jantz, former editor of the *Mennonite Brethren Herald* and *ChristianWeek*

Here's a Mennonite on a rocket. Whatever quality of leadership interests you: natural gifting, discipline, tenacity, ingenuity, it's here in riveting style. Dr. Redekop is the Mennonite equivalent of Elon Musk and Richard Branson. It reads like fiction but it's a real story of a great man of faith.
Dr Peter W. Nikkel, *pastor*

I always admired John's thoughtful and often challenging critique of issues within the church and around the world. His level of activity in terms of travel, writing, organizational work and fund-raising is quite astonishing. He has been an intellectual gift to our church community and beyond. Congratulations on a life productively lived and a great book.
Art DeFehr*: businessman, entrepreneur, philanthropist*

I've known John Redekop for over 40 years, at least I thought I did. In *Mennonite in Motion* my friend, John, tells of his amazing and expansive range of involvements and interests. The story is much more, however, than a recital of the many things he has done. It is also about who he is and how he sought to live and serve as a passionate follower of Jesus. He is courageously and sensitively transparent in his candid observations and reflections, even as he describes the challenging and painful times of his life. I am confident that you will find yourself drawn in to this fascinating and inspirational story of a dedicated and faithful servant of Christ.
Dr. Larry Martens, *retired pastor and former Professor and President of Fresno Pacific Biblical Seminary*

Mennonite in Motion is the fast-moving story of Dr. John Redekop, born to a Mennonite immigrant family, pioneering on the Canadian prairies during the "dirty thirties". As an outstanding scholar and university professor, he has been widely recognized for his impact on thousands of students and peers. As a skilled writer, John boldly addressed contemporary issues — informing, provoking, and entertaining his readers. His insights and skills as a leader greatly impacted the health and success of numerous organizations, including his own Mennonite Brethren denomination and the larger Canadian church community. Most noteworthy, is John`s modelling of integrity, marked by his uncompromising commitment to Jesus as Lord, and his example of untiring service. It is not surprising that many recognize him as one of the most informed, and trusted Canadian Christian leaders. Mennonite Brethren readers will especially find interesting his analysis of recent unwise changes, and current challenges facing their denomination. ***Mennonite in Motion*** will inspire, and inform. It is a book you will greatly enjoy and highly value.
Herb Neufeld, *Mennonite Brethren pastor and Church Growth leader*

To say that John Redekop has been involved in church work, politics, social issues, charitable organizations, education, and writing at the local, national, and international levels is an understatement. John was not just involved, he was more like a powerful engine driving forward in many directions all at once. This detailed, almost encyclopedic autobiography chronicles the impacts he has made in all of these areas, includes some unique and interesting stories, and offers insights into what in turn has driven him.
Dr. James R. Coggins, *former editor of the Mennonite Brethren Herald*

Mennonite in Motion is beyond a book; it is an expression and summary of a unique life. John Redekop has been a diligent and faithful servant, devoted to causes bigger than himself, able to sense the importance of the big picture, and working for the greater good of his Mennonite constituency, the larger Christian community, and Canadian society as a whole. This book is a valuable summary of his life and lessons. He is a man of action: he has always jumped in to help and make a difference, he has led and enlisted many others in his sundry causes, and he is finishing well. He is irrepressible; his default position is to act and organize. This autobiography accurately reflects the ethos of the man and should prompt readers to reflect on their own.
Richard (Rick) J. Goossen, JD, Ph.D., *Chairman, Entrepreneurial LeadersOrganization and Adjunct Instructor, Wycliffe Hall, University of Oxford*

Mennonite in Motion should be on every MB pastor's reading list. Serving alongside John on the MB Global Mission Board was an education in boardsmanship, leadership, and Kingdom commitment. John's wealth of experience and education alone make this a worthy read. Only a short list of brothers and sisters remain who have been eyewitnesses to the growth and development of our contemporary MB Church. John has lived it and viewed it through the lens of a scholar who didn't lose his love for the Body of Christ. True to his character, he writes with candor and courage. Read and learn.
Dennis Fast, *Mennonite Brethren Pastor and Conference leader*

ACKNOWLEDGMENTS AND THANKS

It is my privilege to thank key people who helped bring this book to completion. My wife, Doris, assisted with substantial research, proof-reading, and provided encouragement and continuous support. Peter Nikkel and Herb Neufeld offered valuable critiques on my first draft.

Win Wachsmann, with HeartBeat Productions, Inc., did the formatting of this complex project. He patiently carried out my numerous requests for text revision and the placement and replacement of pictures. He also masterfully restored more than a few badly aged, poor quality pictures. Thanks, Win. Carrie Wachsmann deserves much credit for her painstaking colour restoration and enhancement.

A special word of thanks goes to the former member of the British Columbia Mennonite Brethren Executive Board who wrote an exceptionally candid and important statement about his experiences on that Board when my Stillwood ministry was being discussed. He kindly permitted me to quote at length from his statement. David Leis, the renowned investigator hired by the Reconciliation Advocates, kindly allowed me to use his name and quote from his report.

To Dr. James Nikkel I express my sincere thanks for his fine Introduction to this book. I am also deeply grateful to the friends, colleagues, and former students who provided statements of affirmation in Appendix A. Similar thanks go to my associates, in various arenas, who wrote the endorsements found in the first pages of this autobiography. My special gratitude goes to the four Canadian authors who wrote the endorsements found on the back cover, and particularly to Brian Stiller who also provided the words found on the front cover.

For the top photo on the cover I am indebted to the Special Collection and Archives Department at the University of Waterloo. The middle portrait, as well as the picture of the three Conference leaders on page 227, was provided by Jon Isaak, director at the Centre for Mennonite Brethren Studies in Winnipeg, assisted by Harold Jantz. The recent bottom photo was taken by Win Wachsman who also took the Sumas Prairie-Mt. Baker photo. Barb Draper, at the office of *The Canadian Mennonite,* provided several key pictures of the 1986 Mennonite Brethren apology to Mennonite Church Canada.

Numerous other friends offered encouragement and, on occasion, counsel. I thank them all.

John H. Redekop Ph.D.
Abbotsford, British Columbia
December 17, 2021

TABLE OF CONTENTS

Acknowledgments 7
Foreword 9
1 Introduction 11
2 My Forebears: Grandparents and Parents 15
    My Redekopp Heritage 16
    My Wiebe Heritage 20
    My Parents 25
3 Childhood 1932 – 1946 35
    We were Poor but Always had Good Food 37
    Farm Life, Crop Failures, Poverty 39
    Lobetal School 45
    Relevant Political and Public Affairs 47
    Church Life; My Spiritual Pilgrimage 48
    Reflections and Memories of my childhood years in Saskatchewan 50
    Our First Winter in British Columbia 55
    Grade Seven 56
4 The High School Years 1946 – 1951 57
    The Mennonite Educational Institute 57
    Church Life; My Faith Pilgrimage 67
    Relevant Political and Public Affairs 69
5 Post-Secondary Education Part I 1951 – 1955 71
    Abbotsford Mennonite Brethren Bible School 1951 – 1952 71
    My Railway Career 73
    The University of British Columbia 1952 – 1955 75
    Reflections on my Time at the University of British Columbia 79
    The Beginning of a Writing Career – *The Canadian Mennonite* 82
    Relevant Political and Public Affairs 83
6 The Adventures of a Two-Month Teacher 85
7 Heidelberg University and Travel in Europe 1955 – 1956 ... 89
    Travel and the Fall Semester 89
    Three Holiday Celebrations 95

8 Travel in Africa, Asia and Europe **99**
    Italy 100
    Tunisia and Libya; A Sandstorm 102
    Egypt 111
    Lebanon, Syria and Jordan 115
    Israel 119
    Sailing Back to Europe, Yugoslavia, Italy, Austria 123
    The Second Semester in Heidelberg 128

9 Romance and Marriage **133**

10 My Four-Year High School Teaching Career 1956 – 1960 .... **141**
    Teaching High School 141
    Church Life; My Spiritual Pilgrimage; The Death of My Father 147

11 Post-Secondary Education Part II 1960 – 1964 .... **155**
    The University of California, Berkeley 1960 – 1961 156
    The University of Washington 1961 – 1964 162
    Church and Spiritual Matters 167
    Relevant Political and Public Affairs 169

12 Living in Fresno 1964 – 1968 .... **171**
    Living in Fresno; Pacific College 171
    Scholarly Research and Writing; My First Book 179
    Church Life and Christian Ministries 180
    Relevant Political and Public Affairs 181

13 Living in Waterloo 1968 – 1980 .... **183**
    Moving to Waterloo 1968 183
    Living in Waterloo 184
    Wilfrid Laurier University 190
    Scholarly Research and Writing; Books 192
    Writing for the Christian Community 193
    Addressing Christian Audiences 195
    Ministries in Mennonite Brethren Conferences 196
    Other Christian Ministries 199
    Writing for the General Public 200
    General Speaking Engagements 201
    Church Matters and my Spiritual Pilgrimage 201

Relevant Religious Developments in the Larger Arenas 203
Relevant Political and Public Affairs 204

14 Living in Waterloo 1981 – 1994 .... **207**
Living in Waterloo.. 207
Wilfrid Laurier University 218
Scholarly Research and Writing; Books 219
Writing for the Christian Community 222
Addressing Christian Audiences 224
Ministries in Mennonite Brethren Conferences 226
Mennonite Central Committee Canada 229
Evangelical Fellowship of Canada 232
Additional Involvements 232
Writing for the General Public 233
General speaking Engagements 234
The Debates: Marxism versus Christianity 235
Activity in the Political Arena 239
The 1984 Trip to the Soviet Union 239
The 1986 Trip to the Soviet Union 244
The 1987 Trip to the Soviet Union 252
Awards and Affirmation 253
Relevant Political and Public Affairs 257
My Spiritual Pilgrimage 258

15 Living in Abbotsford 1994 – 2010 .... **259**
Returning to a Burgeoning City 259
Bakerview Church 266
Scholarly Research and Writing; Books 268
Writing for the Christian Community 270
Addressing Christian Audiences 275
Ministries in Mennonite Brethren Conferences 277
Mennonite Brethren Missions and Services International 278
Mennonite Brethren Biblical Seminary. 282
A Missions Trip to Congo (Kinshasa) 284
Columbia Bible College 288
Mennonite Faith and Learning Society 291

Stillwood Camp and Conference Centre	292
Other Christian Ministries	301
Activity in Political Arenas	302
Writing for the General Public	306
General Speaking Engagements	307
Awards and Affirmation	308
Stillwood Fundraiser Fund	309
Relevant Religious Developments in the Larger Arenas	311
Relevant Political and Public Affairs	313
My Spiritual Pilgrimage	315
16 Living in Abbotsford 2011 – 2021	**317**
Living in Abbotsford	317
Stillwood – Later Developments	323
Scholarly Research and Writing; Books	334
Writing for the Christian Community	336
Addressing the Christian Community	337
Ministries in Mennonite Brethren Conferences	338
A Mission Trip to Paraguay 2011	338
Music Mission Kiev	341
Tabor Home Society	342
Writing for the General Public	343
General Speaking Engagements	343
Awards and Affirmations	344
Developments in the Larger Religious Arenas	347
Relevant Political and Public Affairs	349
My Spiritual Pilgrimage	351
A Concluding Statement	352
Our Family	**353**
Appendix A Statements by Others	**357**
Appendix B Publications	**367**
Appendix C Stillwood Development	**377**
Appendix D Honorary Degree Citations	**383**
Stillwood Memories	**386**
Index	**387**

DEDICATION

I dedicate this memoir to Doris,

a faithful, humble, and diligent

disciple in the Kingdom, a loving

and self-giving mother, an altogether

devoted, loving and lovable wife,

a wonderful life partner and the love of my life.

John

FOREWORD

John Redekop begins his memoir with an account of his forebears migrating from Russia in 1913. The story continues with a description of their impoverished farming years in Saskatchewan where John was born. His family endured dust storms and drought in the 1930s, and then settled on a farm in British Columbia which required blasting tree stumps in order to bring virgin land into production. The book follows the chronology of his life.

Dr. James Nikkel

I am greatly honoured that John Redekop, whom I have known for most of his professional life, asked me to write this Introduction which I hope will encourage many to read about this exceptional Mennonite leader. My comments are based on John's memoir and from my relationship with him over many decades. This introduction reflects on the character traits and values of John that have resulted in this important story.

John is part of the 20th century Mennonite pioneers who homesteaded in Canada during an era of dramatic social change. His family knew how to live without electricity, farm with horses, and use the well as a refrigerator. John attended a one-room school. Later John's schooling included skipping a grade and winning awards. Before Junior High he was already reading the political columns in newspapers and listening to radio talk shows on public affairs. It is no surprize that John's early interest in political life ultimately led to a career of teaching Political Science.

University education was important to John. He even delayed his marriage to Doris to accept a one-year scholarship to Heidelberg University in Germany. John's educational journey to his PhD took them to three other universities, and finally to the University of Washington. Part of John's ongoing international education included travels to various parts of the world. He had a passion to see and understand the world.

Alongside John's teaching career at Wilfred Laurier University, he pursued his writing passion. For many years he contributed to a wide variety of journals, including his own denominational paper, the **Mennonite Brethren Herald,** which for four decades carried his weekly Personal Opinion Column. For fifteen years he also wrote a column for *The Canadian Mennonite*, the Mennonite Church Canada journal of record. John's writing generated much response, a testimony to a fertile and illuminating mind. Readers of this memoir will be inspired by John's extensive and varied community involvements, which included television panels, university debates, radio interviews and many speaking assignments. He generously contributed his time to serve on Church Conference and Mennonite Central Committee Canada Boards. These many involvements speak of his healthy motivation and work ethic. Another value for John that generated public involvement was his reputation for excellence and attention to details, as noted in the detailed table of Contents and the comprehensive Index in this book.

This memoir gives evidence that John is a team player. In the Evangelical Fellowship of Canada, his ministry partner was Brian Stiller. While volunteering at Stillwood Camp and Conference Center, it was Harry Edwards, and in several recent projects I have worked with him. In many regards John is seen as a professional "go to person" for political opinions, research that is waiting to be done, or raising financial support for charitable causes. He is often invited as an event speaker, widely considered to be a voice for Anabaptists.

Although John's memoir operates mostly as an autobiography, it also includes significant historic content regarding contemporary church life. For example, he details how the Mennonite Brethren Conference developed in recent generations. He also describes the 1984 account of the Quebec Association of Churches joining the Canadian MB Conference during the time when John was the Canadian Conference moderator.

John is an eminent scholar, a deep thinker and an exceptional researcher. Besides his many decades of Personal Opinion Columns, he has produced ten books, as well as contributed chapters to many others. Over the span of his professional life, John was awarded numerous research grants which covered costs for his assistants and related expenses.

John is a deeply spiritual person, committed to the disciplines of Bible study, daily prayer, and Sunday worship. He has often been called on to preach and is widely known as a church statesman. It was during his university years that he settled many of his faith questions. He credits InterVarsity Christian Fellowship for helping him develop a Christian world-view. He is sensitive to injustices, and when necessary, has the courage to facilitate public apologies. As moderator of the Canadians Conference of Mennonite Brethren Churches he arranged an apology to the Mennonite General Conference (GC) for the Mennonite Brethren practice, in some churches, of excommunicating those who married GC members. As a board member for Mennonite Central Committee Canada, he led in an apology to First Nations people for the mistreatment visited upon them by fellow Canadians. John also led in addressing the injustices practiced against Japanese-Canadians. Most important was his determination to settle the discord between himself and the BC Mennonite Brethren Conference regarding his role as fundraiser for Stillwood. John's life is an example of Christ-like discipleship.

I conclude this introduction with some of the awards John was granted for his rich contribution to public life. With John's retirement from Wilfrid Laurier University in Waterloo, he was awarded the distinction, Professor Emeritus. The *Vancouver Sun* named him among BC's fifty most noted intellectuals. Further, John was included in Harold Jantz's book, Leaders That Shaped Us, which lists him as one of twenty-five Mennonite Brethren that were most influential during the 20th Century. It is noteworthy that Trinity Western University recognized John's public contributions with an honorary Doctorate of Humanities degree. These honours speak of the blessing of God on John's life.

John Redekop's memoir, *Mennonite in Motion*, is a reflection of what a purpose-driven life looks like. It is a story of servant leadership that deserves to be read widely.

James Nikkel, Abbotsford, British Columbia, November 2021

CHAPTER 1

INTRODUCTION

Writing one's autobiography is both enjoyable and challenging. It is enjoyable because of the many good memories that come with reviewing the wonderful times and the many blessings in one's life. It is challenging for at least four reasons. First, is one's memory accurate? Second, which experiences should be included and which left out? Third, how much detail should be included? Fourth, how can one best deal with bias?

My response to these challenges is as follows. First, I have tried to be as accurate as possible, to recount history to the best of my ability. I have been guided by the best available sources and my recollections. Second, deciding what should be included involves making judgment calls. I have sought to include content that would likely interest readers. Third, my intent has been to include enough detail to make the recounting interesting. Fourth, concerning bias I have tried to be trustworthy and fair.

Perhaps some readers think that certain sections of this book should have been left out. I included those matters that were an important part of my life. Some readers may think that the sections on Awards and Affirmation should have been omitted. Those realities were significant in my pilgrimage. They greatly encouraged me to continue to work hard in service to God and others. All readers are, of course, at liberty to skip any section of less interest to them. Any reader not interested in my forebears may want to begin with *My Parents,* although I would encourage readers to read the preceding pages.

Since my profession as well as much of my other ministry and service has involved writing and speaking, it should not be surprising that in recounting my life, I give extensive examples of both. It is simply a reality that much of my life was taken up with writing and speaking. As I reflect on more than seven decades of activity, it seems there was almost always some speaking or writing responsibility for which I was preparing, some deadline to meet. But I have no complaints about busyness. Every decision to write or speak was, of course, mine.

I should add this clarification. When I cite or count speaking engagements, I do not include Sunday School teaching, care group lessons, or worship service preaching other than a few exceptions, such as at the 50th anniversary of the Central Heights Church.

I trust that one of the strengths of this autobiography is the abundance of pictures. Photos convey realism, detail, immediacy, and authenticity.

Several times I have included brief sections on selected political and religious events of the day. They help us to understand the milieu in which I, my family, my faith community, my social community, and my academic community functioned. The realities noted have all had major significance for me.

Readers will note that the subheadings are not consistent from chapter to chapter. The scope and nature of the content warranted such deviation.

Writing my autobiography is, for me, an important exercise in reminding myself that I am but a link in a long chain. When we ignore or forget our past, when we lose our memory and traditions, then we weaken our sense of significance, starve our self-image, and lose some of the light that illuminates the pathway of the future. The light of our past falls over our shoulder. We are wise if we learn from it and let it guide us.

At this point, it seems right to introduce what could be called a *leitmotif,* an occurrence with continuing significance, an event which has had a huge impact in shaping my life. Until recently, as far as I can recall, I have not mentioned this surprising realization to anyone except Doris.

I do not remember exactly when, but many years ago, one of my older sisters decided to inform me about a certain event in our family history. She simply told me that when my father had discovered that my mother was pregnant with me, he had cried. I was stunned! Who wants to be an unwanted child? Who wants to realize that his father wished he had never been born? My self-esteem plummeted. Then, as I reflected on what I had been told, I realized that in 1932, at the height of the Great Depression, my father, having experienced three financially devastating crop failures, was already having an incredibly difficult time providing for his family. With my birth, he would have another mouth to feed, another person to clothe.

I left that conversation in very deep thought. It was painful to discover that my father had cried because of my eventual birth. Once I got over the initial shock, I reminded myself that all along, my father had loved me and cared for me. I knew enough about the hard times our family had experienced to understand why my father had cried. I wanted to believe that he had cried not so much because of me but because of his tough situation. That made me feel a little better.

I decided that instead of humiliating my father, I would, instead, do my very best to excel in whatever I did so that even though I was initially an unwelcome addition to the family, he would increasingly feel good about me. From that time onward, both consciously and I am sure also subconsciously, I have done my best to impress my father, to prove my worthiness. While there are doubtless other personality factors which shaped my desire to succeed and excel, as I assess myself my deep desire to give my father as much reason as I could to feel good about me greatly influenced my entire life. I believe this deep motivation became so ingrained that it continued to influence me long after my father had passed away. What my sister told me and my reaction to it have played a significant role in what I did and who I became.

In writing this life story, I often sensed waves of gratitude engulf me. First of all, I am deeply grateful to my parents. Although my father was not much given to verbalizing his feelings, I always knew that he loved me. He certainly always did his best to provide for his family. I was also impressed from my early years by how he treated my mother with love, respect, and admiration. I do not recall that he ever belittled her or spoke unkindly to her. My mother, not surprisingly, was more emotional and outgoing about her sentiments. I never doubted her deep love for all of her six children.

Not many years ago, probably when my sister Clara was already in her 80s, she said that she wanted to tell me something. She said that when I was probably six or seven years old, my mother, on a Mother's Day, called all six of us children together and told us the following. She said that she was privileged to be the mother of each one of us, and she wanted us all to know that. If I recall Clara's words correctly, my mother then gave us each two gifts: something she had baked and something she had crafted, probably sewed. She was an excellent cook. Quite apart from that special occasion, if putting herself out for her family is a measure of a mother's love, then my mother deserves an A+.

As the youngest in the family I am also, of course, deeply grateful to my siblings for helping to raise me and to my many friends down through the years who have enriched my life and have often supported me and at times corrected me. I am thankful for some exceptional teachers and professors who mentored me and modelled a good life and good character for me. Many a preacher and Sunday School teacher increased my knowledge and helped me to progress spiritually. A particular word of thanks goes to my dear wife, Doris, who has been a wonderful partner for 65 years. Our children have also played a significant part in shaping me. Parents raise their children but children, in turn, help shape their parents.

I am grateful for my Mennonite heritage. Only after considerable travel and some maturing did I come to appreciate that for me, it was a great gift. Our past shapes us. The German proverb is apt: *"Keine Herkunft; keine Zukunft."* (No story of the past; no story in the future)

I am deeply thankful to God for the fact that I was born in a free country and have lived almost all of my years in this fine land. Many a time when I returned from travels to certain countries, I have felt like kneeling down and kissing the ground of this unassuming but intrinsically good country. I think I actually did that once.

Up to a point, my autobiography can be summarized in one long sentence. I am a Canadian by citizenship; a Mennonite by birth; an Anabaptist Christian by choice and conviction; a professor by vocation; a fortunate husband by marital status; a privileged retiree by divine providence; and a happy and very grateful resident in a prosperous and free country by circumstance – all by the grace of God.

My purpose in writing this life story is three-fold: to describe as accurately as possible significant experiences of my life; to transmit values and whatever understanding my life has brought me, and to express gratitude. Several biblical statements apply. "Look to the rock from which you were cut and to the quarry from which you were hewn." (*Isaiah 51: 1b*) "The boundary lines have fallen for me in pleasant places; surely I have a delightful inheritance." (*Psalm 16: 6*)

Finally, I express my most sincere and deep gratitude to God for accepting me as a flawed and sometimes failing person who was, nevertheless, accepted by salvation into Christian sonship. I have sometimes failed my Lord; He has never failed me. My hope and prayer is that in these sunset years, I might continue to be guided by my motto, **To serve God and Others**, and by my desire to end well.

I take no credit for the many opportunities and amazing experiences that happened in my life. Credit goes to many people but fundamentally to God. If my life's work, as described in these pages, has been of benefit to others, in smaller or greater measure, I give God the glory.

Every person has a story to tell; this is my story.

CHAPTER 2

MY FOREBEARS: GRANDPARENTS AND PARENTS

Jacob F. Redekop and Agnes (nee Wiebe) Redekop, October 15, 1918, John's parents.

It was my good fortune, by divine grace, to be born into a fine family. My parents, Jacob Frank Redekop and Agnes (Wiebe) Redekop were godly people who placed great emphasis on eternal values. They were traditional folk who thought and talked much about earthly life as preparation for heaven but they also considered this life as an opportunity to live rightly and a journey to be enjoyed. Even though during many years their life was difficult, even extremely difficult, they enjoyed leisure and happy times. They stressed nurturing relationships, developing one's abilities and talents, making the most of every opportunity, and helping others. Fundamentally they saw this life as preparation for eternity. In fact, one of my father's favourite sayings, also the title of one of his favourite hymns, was, *Die Zeit ist kurz.* (The time is short.)

My Redekopp Heritage

Franz B. Redekopp and Elizabeth Redekopp, John's paternal grand-parents.

My father, together with his parents and some siblings, migrated to Canada from the Ukrainian steppes of Imperial Russia in April 2013. Because the lives of parents and grandparents impact any person's life, it is worthwhile to summarize the major events which led to this obviously very consequential migration.

My father's parents, Franz Benjamin Redekopp (March 15, 1857 - June 3, 1920) [my father dropped the second "p"] and Elizabeth (Friesen) Redekopp (October 18, 1858 - July 26, 1938), had relocated together with some other Mennonites from the village Neuendorf in the province of Ekaterinaslav in 1889 to settle in a newly developing area in the neighbouring province of Kharkov.

Together with other Mennonites seeking available land and new economic opportunities, they established the village of Petrofka. Although the first two years were very difficult, they soon prospered and developed impressive estates. Within a few years, largely because of their innovative methods of farming, they were growing large amounts of grain, which was milled and the flour sold to local bakeries. Before long, there was too much flour for that market.

Being resourceful as well as entrepreneurial, grandfather Franz Redekopp, in partnership with two others, built two large flour mills, one in the neighbouring town of Kamenskaya and a second at another nearby location. As is evident from both the size of the buildings and the number of employees, this was no small undertaking. Additional markets were found.

The flour mill owned and operated by Franz Redekopp, and partners Hiebert and Rempel in Kamenskya in 1908.

Employees of the Franz Redekopp mill. Benjamin in white shirt, left end of second row, was the older brother of John's father.

Even though times were good, there were political clouds on the horizon. One major challenge was the growing Russification of immigrant peoples and, with that, the loss, for Mennonites, of their exemption from military service. Family lore also has it that grandfather Franz, an informed and aware gentleman of the day had remarked that the June 1907 Russian Revolution had not gone far enough in bringing about badly needed reforms to Russian society, especially concerning the mistreatment of the peasants, and that there would surely be a greater revolution in the future. Maybe I inherited my political interests from him.

Because of these concerns and also because he had become aware of new economic opportunities in western Canada, grandfather Franz, who was at the time well off financially, traveled to western Canada in 1908 to check out the land grant and settlement opportunities being offered by the Canadian Pacific Railway. Although doubtless impressed by the freedoms in this Dominion, he saw the great financial challenges which the Mennonite pioneers faced. He returned to his estate in Russia and decided not to emigrate.

Times changed. By early 1913 several major factors brought about the decision to leave the Ukrainian steppes of Russia for the prairies in Canada. Perhaps the most important reality was that the Redekopp flour mill business had overextended itself in the purchase of wheat to be milled. At the same time, the price of flour dropped sharply.

There is also subdued talk about the firm's bookkeeper, anticipating financial trouble, somehow seriously mishandled funds to his advantage. In any event, grandfather Franz was forced to sell his estate to cover debts.

I would be remiss if I did mention one other relevant development. Already before Franz and his family relocated to Petrofka, likely in 1884, Franz, together with his brother Benjamin (February 8, 1855 - July 6, 1923), had left the very traditional, very theologically conservative and not very inspiring main Mennonite Church and joined the reformist, more contemporary, and more theologically vibrant Mennonite Brethren movement which had arisen in 1860. Both brothers took their new religious commitment very seriously. This also created serious tensions for them.

Although their parents, Benjamin Redekopp (March 15, 1833 - May 9, 1907) and Anna (nee Wiebe, Berg) Redekopp (1819 - September 24, 1899), remained with their traditional church, the two sons, ignoring the Czarist directives against such endeavours by the Mennonites, initiated significant missionary and evangelistic activity. They, together with some associates who had also experienced spiritual revitalization, established several new churches. The main, traditional Mennonite Church strongly opposed such activities. This evangelization was also strongly opposed by both the Russian government and the Orthodox Church. After two of the new evangelists, A. H. Unruh and Gerhard Froese, were imprisoned for 20 days for their religious zeal and after both Benjamin and Franz Redekopp had been summoned to appear before a representative of the Russian Duma (parliament) about their proselytizing among Ukrainians and threatened with deportation, fear of what might happen because of their religious activity became another major reason to leave Russia.

> *"Clearly, the strong reaction to the Redekopp brothers' missionary zeal was important. A relative who remained in Russia until after World War 11 and who remembers those early days believes that one of the reasons for the unusual dates [1913] for the emigration of Benjamin and Franz Redekopp was the opposition and anger they had aroused by their missionary work; hence it is reasonable to suppose that they decided to leave while they still had the freedom to do so."* (**The Redekop(p) Book,** (RB) 1984**,** p. 9)

Doubtless, the fear of religious persecution, especially what that would mean for their families, weighed heavily on the Redekopp brothers.

Franz Redekopp and his family left for Canada in February 1913, having paid all debts but with very little cash in hand. Initially renting some land in Gouldtown, some 20 miles (30 kilometres) north of Herbert, Saskatchewan, they soon acquired a homestead in the Main Centre area, a few miles southwest of Gouldtown. That is my father's homestead, where we visited many times.

I have distinct memories of visiting my grandmother Elizabeth Redekopp, likely in 1937 or early 1938, when I was four or five. I remember her as a reserved but kind and generous lady. I obviously never got to see my grandfather Franz Redekopp who died 12 years before I was born.

Fortunately, we have some records of the Franz Redekopp's settlement in Canada. One important fact is that having lost his substantial wealth, Franz did not hesitate to work hard to re-establish his family during the six years he lived as a pioneer in the Canadian frontier. Some sentences from the 1984 volume, **The Redekop(p) Book**, [RB] offer a glimpse into the life of the Franz Redekopp family after arriving in Saskatchewan.

> *"When the Redekopp family came to Canada in the spring of 1913, they began their life here in very difficult financial circumstances. They had approximately $100, which even then was a pittance with which to set up a farming operation. They had brought dishes and bedding such as quilts and pillows, but at first, all family members slept on straw sacks on the floor. As soon as they could afford it, they bought folding cots for the parents. The many prairie chickens and wild ducks helped to supply some meat and eggs. Father Redekopp was concerned that children beyond school age should be able to adjust to the language and in this new land. During the first winter, a young lady was engaged as a live-in teacher to help the Redekopps learn the basic use of the English language.* (**RB** p. 117)

My Wiebe Heritage

My mother's parents, Johann Paul Wiebe (November 29, 1868 - June 9, 1956) and Aganeta (Martens) Wiebe (January 15, 1873 - January 19, 1952), were also Mennonites who migrated from the Ukrainian steppes of Russia to Canada.

I have always been keenly interested in the background and early Canadian experiences of the Wiebes, not only because they were my grandparents and I grew up on the homestead they developed, but also because I was born on my grandfather's birthday, November 29, and was named after him. Beyond that, he had a significant relationship with me.

In his biographical account, grandpa Wiebe relates some significant experiences in Russia, especially concerning his and his parents' spiritual heritage and pilgrimage. We shall review some of this history.

In his short autobiography, translated into English, grandpa Wiebe makes it clear that his father, Paul Wiebe (? - January 19, 1904) and mother Katherine (nee Schellenberg) Wiebe, (? - 1904) had a great influence on him. He reports that while his parents were active in their Mennonite community, they did not have what he called a "saving faith." Concerning his father's pilgrimage, he recounts several interesting events:

Paul and Katherine Wiebe,
John's maternal great-grand-parents.

> *"In those days, it was, of course, customary that every family scheduled a [hog]-butchering day. Our siblings and other relatives were invited to our butchering day. On one such day, when father announced to the table guests that now, since he had given his life to God, he would no longer put a bottle of brandy on the table but instead the Bible,...one of my uncles stood up and said, "Well, now it has gone far enough." He looked at his wife, my aunt. The two of them then left for their home."* (p. 1, *typed manuscript* JPW)

This family division was very difficult for grandpa's mother, who had not yet experienced the spiritual renewal of which her husband spoke. Grandpa writes that she asked, "Is this the way to tear the family apart?" He adds, "She cried."

Shortly after this tension-filled mealtime altercation, grandpa's father decided he must be baptized. The form would be by immersion which was the new practice of the reformist Mennonite Brethren Church. My great-grandpa Paul Wiebe was not inclined to wait for warmer weather:

> *"The place of baptism was cleared of three inches of ice. The baptismal candidates changed clothes in a warm room and, bundled in fur, walked towards the water."* (JPW p. 2)

There they were immersed. That same day they were accepted into the church at a membership service. Grandpa Wiebe adds an interesting note:

> *"Father, the baptismal candidate, from time to time experienced such severe bouts of lumbago in his back that he had to lie down and could not move. Thus it happened that he was in that state on a Saturday, the day before the Sunday when he was to be baptized. My mother feared that if in this condition he would go ahead with his baptism, he might actually cause his own death."* (JPW p. 2)

Somehow, great grandfather Paul Wiebe dragged himself to the icy baptism. Grandpa John Wiebe writes that "A consequence of this step of obedience, in addition to many other blessings, was that our father, for the rest of his life, never again experienced an attack of lumbago. This result had a convicting impact on my mother." (p. 2)

Before long, great-grandmother Wiebe came to what was called "saving faith." Continuing his story, grandpa John P. Wiebe states that he was very much aware of his own "lost condition." He writes that one day:

> *"I went into the darkened barn and threw myself on my knees and began to pray.... I began earnestly to pray for grace and forgiveness and.... I soon found myself in a mode of thankfulness.... A voice then spoke to me very clearly, 'Your sins have been forgiven. Your faith has brought you salvation.... Go forth in peace.'... This experience gave me complete assurance of salvation.... How great was the joy when I shared this experience with my parents."*

Grandfather Johann P. Wiebe's written account makes it clear that he firmly believed that the Lord Jesus had specifically spoken to him in that darkened barn. He needed that strengthening confidence because his life at school was a real challenge. He writes that:

> "One day, during the noon recess, I was sitting in my usual place and reading the Bible. Then a student came in and shouted to me rudely, 'There sits the holy dog again with his Bible.' and gave me a powerful slap on my ear. I sat in quiet bewilderment. I remained silent and did not look around to see who had done this to me."

Before long grandpa Wiebe was recognized for his several talents. Already as a young adult in Russia, he began a life-long ministry as a preacher, a choir director, and a teacher of choral and other musical activities.

The Johan P. Wiebe family before leaving Russia in 1904. John's mother, Agnes, stands next to her father.

Johann P. Wiebe's autobiography recounts that:
> "In the year 1891 the Lord gave me a faithful life's partner in Aganeta Martens, daughter of brother and sister (Geschwister) [Jacob] Martens in Petrofka. Her older sister, Elizabeth, was engaged to Abraham Buhler who lived in Adelsheim and therefore, we had a double wedding. The next year we moved back to No. 5 [village] and built a small house on our half farm."

It should be noted here, that the parents of Johann Wiebe, Paul and Katherine Wiebe, had already emigrated from Russia in 1903 and settled near Osler in what became northern Saskatchewan when Saskatchewan and Alberta were carved out of the Northwest Territories in 1905. They arrived with their two younger sons, Jacob and Paul.

> "Very suddenly and unexpectedly, Paul Wiebe [the father] passed away within his first year in Canada. He died on January 19, 1904, at the age of 57 years.... Katherine was grief-stricken. She was in a new country with two teenage sons. One to two months after her husband died, she also died. The medical doctor claimed that she died of a broken heart."

Thus it happened that before the Johann P. Wiebes arrived in Canada to be reunited with his parents, both had already passed away.

We have little information about why Johann and Aganeta Wiebe left Imperial Russia. It appears that the main reasons were the Russification of the educational system, the termination of exemption from military service, the shortage of available farmland in Russia, and the availability of virtually free farmland in Canada.

Johann and Aganeta Wiebe left Russia on March 17, 1904. Their travel, with various delays, across Russia, across the Atlantic and to the prairies in Canada was time-consuming. They arrived in Winkler, Manitoba, on April 17. Because the area to which they would relocate was totally undeveloped, it was decided to leave the family in Manitoba while Johann, with his father-in-law Jacob Martens, who with his wife, had left Russia with the Wiebes, and another immigrant, Adam Quiring, would travel by train to Herbert to scout out the new homesteads. An unknown writer of that time has left us the following account.

> "Early in May, they arrived in Herbert - a post with a board with Herbert on it and an old railway car, flat on the earth. That constituted the station building. Numerous tents had already been erected, and quite a lot of construction had already begun. In the town, they met a man who offered to be their guide and drive them to find their land.

'Thus we set out into the north. An almost treeless prairie, one almost without any human population, stretched before us. Repeatedly whole herds of frolicking antelope crossed our path.'

Eventually, having traveled more than 15 miles north and several miles west, their guide "showed them the number on the marker for their quarter [section] of land." [160 acres] They were impressed. "As they looked over the expanse of prairie with grass up to the horses' stomach, indicating good soil beneath, their 'hearts overflowed with feelings of thankfulness to God.' The three men then returned to Manitoba to get their families. The whole entourage returned to their new lands on June 4, 1904.

'Their first job was erecting temporary living accommodations - canvas put around their wagons to provide shelter. Then the virgin prairie had to be broken and planted....'"

John's grandfather Rev. Johann P. Wiebe.

Grandpa Wiebe was 35 years old when he arrived at his Canadian homestead, for which he paid $10.

It took several years but eventually the homestead buildings were all erected and the trees planted. We have no picture of this homestead in its early years, but the following picture taken by me in 1959 indicates how I remember it from my childhood.

This is where my mother grew up. When my grandparents relocated to Herbert for early retirement, my parents moved into their homestead. This is the place where I was raised.

In October 1945, Johann and Aganeta Wiebe retired to a small home in Clearbrook, B.C., across the road from where the Mennonite Educational Institute, which I attended for five years, was built.

The Johann P. Wiebe homestead where John grew up.

During my high school years, I had numerous occasions to have lunch with my grandparents, in part because grandpa and I were both greatly interested in politics. Despite the 64-year age difference, we had some significant political discussions.

My grandfather was particularly interested in the rise and fall of Adolf Hitler and the Nazi era in Germany. I soon got the impression that he had initially supported Hitler because of his strong anti-communist stance and, to a lesser extent, because of his amazing economic redevelopment of Germany in the 1930s, while much of the world was languishing in the Great Depression. It seemed to me that disillusionment and sorrow ran deep when grandfather learned of the horrible antisemitism, the pogroms, and especially the death camps. My grandfather was a wise saint who raised important questions and made insightful observations.

My Parents

My father, **Jacob Frank Redekop** (July 23, 1895 - May 23, 1959), was born in Petrofka, in the province of Kharkov, Russia. My dad was baptized on July 20, 1909, and joined the Petrofka Mennonite Brethren Church. He, his parents and his siblings arrived in Canada in 1913. They settled first near Gouldtown and then in the Main Centre area of Saskatchewan. Dad attended the Mennonite Collegiate Institute in Gretna, Manitoba, in 1916-17 and 1917-18, where he completed two more high school years to learn English. The fact that his father had hired a young lady in the first year to teach the family English stood him in very good stead.

John's mother, Agnes Wiebe, before marriage.

My mother, Agnes Wiebe (May 28, 1897 - February 25, 1965), was born in Nikolayevka, in South Russia. She migrated to Canada with her parents and siblings in 1904, settling in the Main Centre area in what would become the province of Saskatchewan in 1905. She was baptized on September 27, 1914, and joined the Main Centre Mennonite Brethren Church.

About four months after my father completed his studies in Gretna, my parents were married in the Main Centre MB Church on October 15, 1918. The marriage ceremony was conducted by the bride's father, Rev. Johann P. Wiebe. Family lore has it that, in part, their matrimony was an arranged marriage. We know that their courtship, cut short because in those days a Bible School teacher needed to be married, lasted three weeks.

Very soon after the wedding, my father began his Bible School teaching career by teaching in the Herbert Bible School. He sensed that he needed additional education. Dad and mom then moved to Hillsboro, Kansas, where dad studied for three years at Tabor College, completing a Bachelor of Arts degree in 1922.

For the next four years, from the fall of 1922 until the end of the school year in June 1926, dad taught at the Rosthern Academy, a high school in Rosthern, Saskatchewan. During that time, dad earned his permanent teaching certificate. Beginning in September 1926, dad taught at the Main Centre High School until June 1929. This was followed by one year of teaching at

John's father, Jacob F. Redekop, B.A. Tabor College, 1922.

Bethany Bible Institute in Hepburn, Saskatchewan. He returned to Main Centre in the summer of 1930 and returned to teaching at the Herbert Bible School, where he taught until the spring of 1944. That fall, our family moved to Abbotsford, BC, for a trial year, 1944-45.

My overarching statement about my father, Jacob Frank Redekop, is that he was a godly man who pursued two careers; he was a preacher and an educator. He greatly enjoyed both and was good at both. For economic reasons he also undertook farming although that was never a preferred vocation. For some years he taught high school classes, but his real love was to teach in Bible Schools and Bible Institutes.

As stated, because teaching provided very meagre income and preaching generally none, dad and mom took up mixed farming while dad continued with his teaching and preaching. The fact that he spoke Russian, Ukrainian, High German, Low German and English enabled him to preach in many venues and locations.

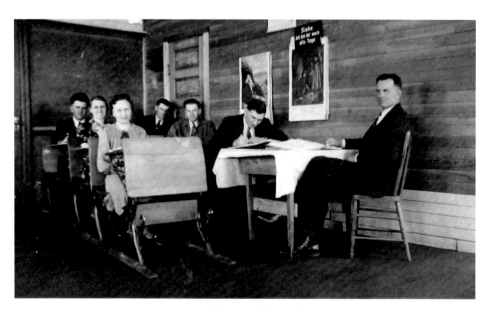

Jacob F. Redekop, Bible teacher.

We are not sure when dad and mom took up residence in the Johann P. Wiebe homestead, but that event probably happened in the summer of 1926 when dad began teaching in the Main Centre School. In any case, for many years my parents rented the two quarters of land, 320 acres, from the Johann P. Wiebes, my mother's parents. The rental arrangement was that the Wiebe grandparents would get a fraction of the income from the crops. We don't know the details of this share-cropping arrangement, but we know that for some years in the 1930s there was no crop for the owner and the renter to share.

Having completed another year of teaching at the Herbert Bible School in the spring of 1944, dad and mom decided that after completing the harvest in the fall, dad would accept the invitation to teach for a year in the newly-established Bible School in Abbotsford, British Columbia. The five of us made the trip. That trip west created problems. We did not have enough war-time gas-rationing coupons to drive all the way to the West Coast. I recall that some special arrangements had to be made.

Our rather modest mixed-farm operation was left in the hands of my brother Paul and his wife Rosella, very recently married. With their regular letters Paul and Rose kept us informed about how things were progressing on the farm. I was particularly interested in how my pigeons were doing. Paul kept me informed. In spring we moved back to Main Centre to resume farming.

As it happened, dad then received an invitation to come back to Abbotsford to serve as principal of the Bible School. For him, that was not a difficult decision. Accordingly, after the crops had been harvested in the early fall of 1945, dad and mom and we three youngest children made the final move to Abbotsford. This second move to Abbotsford was more complicated. Just before we left, we had an auction sale. Farm implements, most of the furniture, most of the household effects, and most of our animals were sold. For me that was a very sad day; I loved our farm, especially all the birds and animals.

That summer, dad and mother, with Abbotsford friends assisting, purchased a 10-acre farm on King Road, site unseen, which had a small house and a small barn. It was decided to ship our basic household effects, some animals, and some farm tools and smaller equipment items to Abbotsford by railway. My parents hired a young man, Ernie Stelting, to ride with the animals and look after them in a CPR rail car. In those days this could still be done at a low cost by applying to have farm-related items shipped in what was called a Settler's Car.

While we gradually built up this small acreage into a mixed-farm operation, dad's real interest was leading and teaching at the Bible School. He served faithfully at that school, for ten years as principal and four more as regular faculty member, until his untimely death of a coronary occlusion on May 23, 1959.

My father loved to teach and preach, especially doing a series of services in which he did Biblical exposition. He was good at what he did. Even now, in 2021, I still encounter some older folk who remember dad's preaching and comment favourably on it. I also still meet some couples whom he married.

I have no recollection of my parents ever arguing about dad's work or, for that matter, about anything else, but I vividly recall one time when mom ruefully said that some scarce dollars that she had hoped to spend on something, perhaps it was some rare new garments for children, had been spent "*für die Bücher*" (for the books).

My father was always kind and fair toward us children, at least in my experience. Doubtless in keeping with his own home experiences, he was not given to much verbal or emotional expression of love or tender feelings. In that sense he was very traditional. I do not recall him ever telling me that he loved me but, of course, throughout my childhood years and later, I experienced extensive instances of his love in action.

Perhaps it goes without saying that dad was not perfect. No human parent meets that standard. What I can say with sincerity is that in my experience, I observed that dad personally practiced and clearly taught us his strong Christian convictions. These included truthfulness, honesty, reliability, kindness, a readiness to help others, generosity, thrift, optimism, gratitude, willingness to rise to a challenge, the importance of hard work, and especially having a right relationship with God. I remember several times when one of the children would be getting ready to work for someone else he would say, "*Erwerb dir Kredit,*" [earn a good reputation for yourself]. I also recall that at various times when one of his grown-up or almost grown-up children was to leave for a longer period of time he would read the third chapter of Colossians for such an occasion. I sensed in later years that he took considerable pride in the various achievements of his children but I do not recall him ever expressing such sentiments.

Dad never earned a significant salary. I do not, however, recall him ever complaining about his meagre earnings although I do recall hearing about one rather telling comment. He observed that when my brother Ernie began his elementary school teaching career, he earned more in that first year than dad was earning after his approximately 30 years of teaching experience.

This may be the time to do a little complaining. As I clearly remember, for quite a few years in the late 1940s my father was paid $50 a month as a Bible School teacher during the 7 or 8-month school year and another $50 for being the principal, doing all the administration [there was no secretary], doing the financial bookkeeping, and doing school promotion and student recruitment in the summer months. That extra $50 must surely be the least money for the most work that I have ever seen.

The salaries improved only slightly in the early 1950s. I thought then, and I think now, that as the economic well-being of church members was improving markedly, the Bible School teachers should have been treated better. The boards of that day seriously exploited dad and our family and all the other Bible School teachers. The only reasoning I can imagine is that since the pastors and preachers were paid nothing, and since the Bible School teachers were something akin to the preachers, they should be paid only a partial salary. Such reasoning, of course, made no sense given that the Bible School teachers taught five days a week. In retrospect, I consider the treatment of the Bible School teachers in those years to have been truly lamentable and unchristian. Maybe they should have formed a union!

If I had to make one general comment about my father it would be that although he served his God and other people with diligence and to the best of his ability, and generally with very positive results, he was, in part or at times, a frustrated person. He was frustrated because the economic situations in which he perpetually found himself not only created huge challenges for him but also did not allow him to apply his considerable intellect to further studies. He would have been a first-rate graduate student. True, in later years at Abbotsford he enrolled in a graduate school, unfortunately not an accredited institution, and fulfilled the reading and research requirements for a doctorate in theology. Much as he enjoyed those studies, he knew that they were essentially a substitute endeavour. As stated, dad also farmed, both while living near Main Centre and later in Abbotsford, but I always sensed that he never enjoyed those pursuits the way true farmers do.

My mother was in many respects a remarkable woman. As I reflect on those pioneer years, I have come to realize how hard she worked at trying to look after all of us children and her husband to the very best of her ability with the incredibly little money available. I remember her bleaching flour sacks and other items to get white fabric to sew. I recall how she resized clothing for the younger children. She taught other children and me how to use a wooden foot to darn socks to make them last longer and how to patch clothes. All the while, she spent very little on herself.

My mother was a talented woman. Unfortunately, she never had the opportunity to attend school beyond Grade six, but she had learned much in an often-hard life. She knew how to organize her time, how to stretch very limited resources, how to make wise decisions, how to be grateful for what you have, how important it is to think of others, and how to make do when you do not have what you need. In terms of how to live and how to manage one's life, I probably learned more from her than from my much more schooled father.

Although I think that she nor anyone else in our family ever used the word craft, she was skilled in many crafts. Her embroidery, using a variety of stitches, was outstanding, and her crocheting was impressive. Especially in the long winter evenings, she sewed much and even taught me several embroidery stitches. I still have a small quilt in which I embroidered all the squares. She also taught me how to darn socks, using a wooden foot, and some other types of sewing. I recall her kneeling on the floor drawing rather impressive geometric designs on the floorboards and then painstakingly painting them individually in various shades. As a seamstress she was remarkable. Not only did she complete reams of sewing, she developed an uncanny ability to size up someone from all angles, rather slowly, and then proceed, as I recall, often without taking any measurements, to make a garment for that person that fitted perfectly. Doubtless, sometimes she used her tape measure, but I think sometimes not.

A particular skill my mother developed was to look at a doll carefully and then sew a variety of clothes for that little doll.

This skill developed into something quite significant. Not only did she sew doll clothes for her children, grandchildren and others but after retiring to the Peardonville Street home in 1956, also for the orphan girls in a mission compound in India, Ramabai Mukti Mission, run by her relative Lillian Doerksen. The picture shows one shipment of such clothes, maybe to be displayed in a craft fair, before they were eventually sent to India.

Mother's doll clothes

My mother loved to sing. Although we never had a piano and later on the Main Centre farm only a rather overly-experienced pedal-powered organ, she somehow managed to get instruments for most of us. I clearly recall her saying on many Sunday afternoons or summer evenings, *"Wollen musizieren"* (Let's make music). As the picture shows, my sisters and brothers all had a musical instrument. I do not recall that I ever acquired one. I do, however, recall being taught how to put tissue paper against a large comb and, after some training, to play various notes on this contraption which we called a kazoo.

Back Row L to R: Paul, Sophie, Ernest.
Front Row L to R: Frieda, John, Clara.

One of my mother's special gifts was gardening. For as long as I can remember, she had a huge garden. Aside from an abundance of beautiful flowers, her large garden produced mounds of vegetables which she canned or stored in root cellars. Her well-tended garden also produced fruits such as strawberries, gooseberries, currants, and rhubarb, from which she made jam for the whole year. Watermelon pickles and chokecherry jelly were specialty preserves. Early on she taught me how to plant the seeds correctly and then how to develop a system of small irrigation canals which, together with some appropriately aged barnyard fertilizer, produced bounteous yields.

My mother was a very godly woman. I know that she prayed a lot. She also took Bible reading seriously and was a very regular church attender.

Although she always let dad take the lead in family devotions, she made sure that we children heard Bible stories, said our prayers, and generally were taught the truths of the Christian faith. Although the summer and especially the winter conditions could be daunting, I do recall that only rarely did mother stay home from church services.

As far back as I can remember, mom had some fairly serious health problems but, amazingly, these hardly kept her from her extensive work or from her church activities. Perhaps most significantly, I do not recall hearing her complain about her ailments.

Although children can never be sure that they assess their parents' marriage accurately, my strong impression is that my parents had a good marriage. In keeping with the habits of the times, there was little display of emotion but I do recall hearing some statements in which they encouraged and thanked one another, a reality which became much more common in the latter years of their life together. I distinctly remember dad repeatedly saying that the food mom prepared tasted so good. He also insisted that at all times we children must be loving, kind, respectful, and courteous to mother. Dad modelled such behaviour.

My mother, Agnes Redekop   My father, Jacob F. Redekop

Key remembered traits and qualities

kind	a wise counsellor	kind	a strong preacher
talented	a great hostess	talented	a good listener
grateful	interested in others	grateful	interested in others
congenial	a devout Christian	collegial	a devout Christian
resourceful	a hard worker	knowledgeable	a hard worker
innovative	had a servant heart	organized	a student of the Word
organized	non-complaining	disciplined	an effective teacher
loving	a praying parent	generous	a praying parent
generous	habitually optimistic	loving	generally optimistic
friendly	a fine role model	friendly	a fine role model

John's maternal grandparents
Johann P. and Aganeta Wiebe

CHAPTER 3

CHILDHOOD, 1932-1946

John, left and Sophie

I was born in a private home in Herbert, Saskatchewan, on November 29, 1932. A midwife assisted my entry into the world. My parents had moved to that town, about 18 miles south of Main Centre, for the winter months so that father could teach in the Herbert Bible School. Because there simply was very little money for bought clothes, mother did an amazing job of getting her family dressed properly. Hand-me-downs were the rule of the day.

Maybe that is why one of the earliest pictures of me has me wearing a dress which was probably handed down from my sister Sophie.

Some years at least part of our family would move to Herbert for the winter months; other years, dad would commute, leaving the Main Centre home in time for classes Monday morning in Herbert and returning Friday evening. I clearly remember at least two winters when we moved to Herbert for the winter. I think one year I was in Grade 2 and the other in Grade 4. I don't recall who looked after our farm animals during those times. Interestingly, for one of those winters, as I vividly recall, we also took some animals with us. I remember that we loaded chickens and hogs and feed for the animals on what we called a hay-rack wagon, drawn by two horses, and selected a few cattle to follow behind, guided by one of my brothers on horseback. That must have been quite a sight as that odd caravan slowly made its way the 18 miles or so to the small hobby farm dad had rented on the western edge of Herbert.

Those 14 years, from the fall of 1930 until the spring of 1944, must have been very difficult for mother. Either dad would be away during the week, which happened most years, or she would have to relocate her household to Herbert in fall, and back to Main Centre in spring.

The Redekop family (c. 1941). Back Row L to R: Frieda, Paul, Ernest, Clara. Sophie and John between the parents.

My parents' economic situation was very difficult in the 1930s. Since virtually everyone else in our circle of relatives and neighbours was in a similar predicament, I was unaware of our poverty and enjoyed a mostly very happy childhood. With my arrival on the scene, we were then a family with six children. According to prevailing contemporary criteria, I was doubtless underprivileged. I, however, considered then and still consider myself privileged and blest.

We were Poor but Always had Good Food

I am pleased to say that we always had adequate food. Mom's huge irrigated garden was very productive and allowed us to enjoy a wide array of produce, and to store large amounts of potatoes, turnips, carrots and probably beets in a deep, frost-free root cellar. In addition, mom canned copious amounts of vegetables and made many jars of jam and fruit preserves. We also always had chickens, milk cows, and, as I vividly recall, each year we slaughtered a hog which gave us excellent sausage, ham, and other pork products.

All of our food, of course, was organic although we never used or heard of that term. Incidentally, in recent decades I have heard parents telling young children what nice boys or girls they are for eating the food on their plates. It never occurred to me at that time that eating the food served on our plates was virtuous. For us it was a great privilege to have food on our plates and we knew that. We were aware of severe poverty in other parts of the globe. At each meal our dad and sometimes others thanked God for the food we were privileged to have.

A vivid memory comes to mind. One winter day, when I was about six, dad somehow came into possession of a very large red apple. I think it was a Red Delicious variety. This was a significant occasion. I remember we were seated around our table, all eight of us, and we each received one-eighth of the most delicious large apple you have ever tasted.

In those pre-electric days on our farm our parents, of course, had no refrigerator. Nor did anyone else we knew. Those pioneers developed two ingenious ways to keep food from spoiling during the hot summer months. One way was to lower food in a bucket down our perhaps 40-foot well. This could work well if you did not give the rope too much slack, which could cause the bucket to tip when it hit the water. Also, if you put too much weight into the bucket, it might sink into the well water. Such a mishap would not only cause loss of food but, more significantly, serious drinking water pollution. Also, of course, the outside of the bucket needed to be very clean because the well provided our drinking water.

A second and main method of cooling food in summer involved digging a pit, perhaps 10 feet by 6 feet and about 6 feet deep. During the winter this pit would be filled with slabs of ice brought in on a skid, called a stone boat, from a frozen pond. Alternatively, it could also be filled by pouring some inches of water into the pit, letting it freeze and then gradually adding more until the pit was filled with one large block of ice. The ice cellar was then covered with a thick layer of straw. A low roof, perhaps with sods of grass on it, covered the pit. An entrance was built partly below the surface at one end. If properly constructed, such an ice cellar retained some ice throughout the spring and summer. By placing pails of hot water on the ice we created good-sized spaces in the ice into which we could then place food containers which would be cooled on all sides. One consequence of this strategy was that we could enjoy homemade ice cream during the summer.

Our dietary indulgences included puffed wheat or corn flakes on Sunday – on other days we had porridge. I actually enjoyed my porridge even though, at times, it got rather cool when dad's Bible reading was lengthy, and his truly significant prayer seemed to address many of the world's problems. I have no recollection of my parents buying any prepackaged food. Of course, we had to buy sugar and other supplies but, with very little exception, we ate what was grown or made on the farm.

Both mom and dad were very conscious of our health needs. Because we generally lacked fresh fruits in wintertime and also most fresh vegetables, we

A prairie dust storm

were required to consume what struck me then as copious amounts of truly foul-tasting cod liver oil. It was drilled into us that this medication would ward off rickets. Presumably, it did. I should mention here that we had very little medical or dental care. Although mother suffered from several health problems, I do not recall ever having a physician come to our family home or any of us going to Herbert for medical help.

Wonder Oil, bought from a travelling salesman, was another popular medication. I remember hearing something like this: "A teaspoon for a child; a tablespoon for an adult; a tablespoon for a calf; a quarter cup for a cow; and a half cup for a horse." As a young child I had great faith in Wonder Oil. I never did find out what it was. If one has enough faith in it, Wonder Oil can do wonders.

Farm Life, Crop Failures, Poverty

From 1930 until 1939 we did not have even one decent crop on our 320-acre farm. Every year drought or grasshoppers or dust storms or hail destroyed what had been seeded. I clearly recall a time when the billows of dust clouds were so high that semi-darkness set in during the daytime and oil lamps were lit. Dust penetrated everywhere.

It was probably in 1938 that I practiced my printing on the dust-covered windowsill before mom or an older sibling did the quick cleaning. I also remember a time when the air was filled with an ominous hum, almost a roar, of millions of grasshoppers destroying our crops. Within a few hours, our standing grain, such as it was, had become mere hay. At that time there was no crop insurance. My recollection is that at least one time dad and mom stood in the doorway and quietly wept. Unfortunately, the drought persisted. Some years the summers were so dry that either the seeded grain did not even sprout or quickly withered. Those were the years when hardy farm folk had to remind themselves that for them farming was not only a means of livelihood but a worthwhile way of life.

One year, probably 1937, the first year about which I have very clear memories, our financial situation must have been especially desperate. As it happened, the federal government arranged for help which was called Relief. I think such assistance was provided for several years. I remember riding with someone older in a horse-drawn buggy to the small Main Centre railway station, about three kilometres south of our farm, to pick up a box or two of delicious MacIntosh apples, some salted cod, and bags of chicken feed. We had some difficulty coming to terms with the very salty dried fish but were grateful for whatever assistance we could get. The Macs were great.

John at the Main Centre train station, 1959.

Understandably, we children did not have many bought toys. Fortunately, at Christmastime and for birthdays, we got useful gifts including colouring books, crayons, clothes, and inexpensive toys. Our parents did their best to make our life enjoyable. In summer we played various games outside. We always had pet dogs and cats.

Sophie and John with pets

We also greatly valued our horses. I had a special horse called Charlie. At an early age, probably 7, I learned to ride him. As I recall, he would come when called and even followed me around.

John with his pets

For a while we had two bicycles, but only one of them had rubber tires.

Sophie and John on bicycles, one without tires.

One of the springtime and summer pursuits which we boys undertook was to develop an egg collection. We would take an egg from the bird nest, gently make small holes at each end of the egg and carefully blow out the inside. If the chick was already developing, this could become complicated. Soon we had an amazing collection carefully stored in a drawer. As I recall, our collection had at least the following kinds of eggs: sparrow, robin, crow, magpie, killdeer, wild duck, sandpiper, gull, owl (various types), hawk, prairie chicken, partridge, oriole, warbler, blackbird, plover, woodpecker, thrush, tanager, cardinal, chickadee, curlew, barn swallow, meadowlark, eagle, sparrow hawk, and others.

Beginning in 1939 we began having decent crops and the economic situation improved markedly. Also, the onset of World War II brought major increases in prices and high demand for virtually everything that farmers produced. I remember dad and mom happily shoveling grain from a box wagon into a granary. I also recall them contentedly sitting on a box-wagon seat taking grain to one of the two Main Centre elevators. There they probably picked up the weekly mail placed in our mailbox.

Dad and Mom driving to Main Centre.

A particularly happy occasion was the day we got our first tractor. It did not have rubber tires and was not very large, but we took great pride in our Massey Harris and took turns sitting on this wonderful addition to our farming enterprise.

Sophie on our new tractor.

One of the consequences of an increase in farm income was that we got our first radio, a small battery-operated Philco, if my memory serves me correctly. I remember all of us sitting around this marvel and listening to what for us were distant programs from Regina and Moose Jaw, even Saskatoon! When darkness had set in we could even pick up some US stations. That was really exciting for me. Before long, dad announced some very specific guidelines. We could listen to the news. We could listen to hockey games if they were broadcast when we were not required to work. We could listen to *The Happy Gang*. We could listen to religious programs. Weather forecasts were, of course, approved, as were "farm broadcasts." Some entertainment programs were marginally acceptable, but we could not listen to "the soap stories." I recall that dad avidly followed newscasts, especially if there were reports about Hitler, the Nazis, or the war.

As I recall we had good family relationships. We worked together well. We often laughed and played together. We readily helped one another. We all had clearly assigned chores. As the youngest of six, I probably had the easiest assignments. I think that my oldest brother Paul, who was a big and strong fellow, carried the biggest load. I know that sometimes he had to miss school, lots of school, to help on the farm. I don't think my parents realized at the time how disadvantageous this was for him.

I might add here that I do not recall ever being spanked by my parents but it probably did happen. In any case, I am sure it should have. I do recall that from time to time I was disciplined by being sent to our parlour to sit out my punishment. Actually, I rather quickly came to enjoy this type of detention but told no one. What I enjoyed was reading some books in dad's modest library which was located in our parlour.

I spent a lot of time trying to understand Clarence Larkin's well-illustrated big book **Dispensational Truth.** I became a very young dispensationalist - for some years! When my father passed away I acquired that copy. We also had some very interesting **Books of Knowledge** which I thoroughly enjoyed. I even gained some spiritual information from some of dad's more basic theology books. He had a good dictionary where I could look up new words. Those times of detention greatly expanded my elementary knowledge of the animal kingdom, other lands, famous people, religious history, theology and especially end times. Sometimes I quietly went into the parlour to read without a detention having been pronounced - except on Saturdays because then the parlour must be kept in unsullied condition for likely visitors on Sunday. A housewife's housekeeping reputation depended on that.

As a young lad I greatly enjoyed interaction with our animals and birds. One of my jobs was to look after the hens and gather the eggs. At the time there must have been a young biologist within me because I enjoyed going to the hen house, sitting on a stool, and observing individual chicken behaviour. I sometimes spent an hour or two trying to understand why chickens did what they did. Why did they make certain sounds? Why did they scratch the floor when food was available in a low feeder? Were any hen noises related to egg-laying? Why did the rooster crow at certain times?

One of my other jobs was to get the newborn calves to learn to drink milk from a pail. When calves are born, their instinct is to turn their heads up to their mother's udder. It can be quite difficult, even painful, to put your fingers into a calve's mouth and with the palm of the hand, push its nose down into the bucket. More than a little milk was spilled and a few days of frustration ensued before the newborn calf caught on. My fingers were also sometimes sore because they were slightly chewed.

On a typical mixed farm such as ours, all of the children learned to work hard even in their early childhood years. As I look back, I am amazed how much was entrusted to us. By the time I was eleven I would walk all day, except for the lunch break, behind a harrow, about 20 feet wide, drawn by slowly plodding horses. On a hot day they were not inclined to work too hard. I found it interesting to follow the horses as they seemed to know exactly when to start turning when we came to the end of the field.

Although I got very tired, I actually enjoyed this activity, especially studying the movement and gradual vaporization of the clouds and the habits of birds, especially the worm-gouging Franklin gulls plucking worms from the freshly tilled soil right behind the harrows. Sometimes I could almost touch the flapping gulls.

Later we acquired a two-wheeled cart which enabled me to sit while doing such fieldwork. That was real progress, almost luxury for me! Henceforth only the horses needed to walk. The burlap-wrapped brown water jug at the end of the field provided a most welcome and enjoyable pause. Evaporation from the soaked burlap helped keep the water cool.

I also recall that before we finally left the Main Centre farm in October of 1945, I had learned how to cut the umbilical cord when our sow gave birth, how to stook sheaves of grain in the field, how to help load the sheaves of grain onto hay-racks to be taken to the threshing machine, how to slaughter and clean chickens, how to patch a tire tube, and how to milk cows. As a 12-year-old, I once milked five cows during threshing time. My hands were very tired. Also, by age 12 I knew how to drive a tractor. When I was not yet 13 I was assigned to ride, whether it was on horseback or by bicycle I cannot recall, to the Henry Siemens farm about five kilometres away to work there all day stooking sheaves of grain. Any money thus earned was, of course, put into the family kitty. I was proud to be treated almost like an adult. No one where we lived had heard the words "child abuse." As far as I am concerned, there was none, only good child training.

By the time I was going to school, the older siblings were required to help at home in ways not required of me. In fact, after I was born there was a great need for help at home, so that my oldest sister, Frieda, had to drop out of school after Grade 8 and help look after me and help my mother who was not well. Ever since I was informed of that reality, I have always been deeply grateful to Frieda for what she did and have tried to repay her by helping her, especially when she needed help in her later years.

Lobetal School

Before we moved to Abbotsford I generally attended Lobetal School, about three kilometres northeast of our farm. In those days the farms were relatively small and most families relatively large, which meant that the one-room school was a full and busy place.

I recall that one year the teacher was responsible for teaching all the subjects to the pupils in grades 1 to 8 and for supervising a few high school students doing correspondence work in grades 9 to 11. Grade 12 was offered only in the Main Centre School. That year Lobetal had 38 pupils.

Lobetal School

How any teacher could carry out such an incredible assignment still boggles my mind. In addition, the teacher was required to keep the school furnace going in winter and keep the school tidy. I had two amazing teachers. For grades 1 and 2, I had Mr. Adolph Janz, a member of the famous Janz Team family. For grades 4 to 6 I had Mr. Jake Neufeld, a brother of Walter and Menno Neufeld, two famous musicians and music teachers in BC's Fraser Valley. During grades 2 and 4, if my memory serves me correctly, I spent about six winter months attending the multi-classroom Herbert School.

Upon reflection I can only marvel at what Mr. Janz and Mr. Neufeld undertook and what they achieved. Somehow they did an excellent job of getting the children to progress through the grades. They had to assign work, relying heavily on the blackboard, to all other grades while they explained algebra or grammar or literature or world history to one grade or, at times, combined grades. I learned much by listening to what was being taught to higher grades. Current educationists would call that pedagogical enrichment. All of this happened in one crowded room.

We also had additional activities for the entire school. These included a Friday afternoon Christian worship service, spelling bees, preparation for school concerts, Christmas programs for the entire community, daily outdoor sports, softball games at other schools, and preparation for the annual multi-school sports day at Main Centre. On one of those occasions, I saw my first ice cream cone and hot dog. I had arrived. How those teachers survived the demands placed on them defies explanation. What is especially noteworthy is that this incredibly multifarious teaching milieu produced many very successful entrepreneurs, teachers, professors, musicians, missionaries, clergy, and a variety of other professional people. Some, of course, became farmers. Such success was probably the result of strong parental encouragement, early cultivation of good work habits, learning to work on your own, learning much from the instruction given to higher grades, and the teachers' skill.

In summer, we usually rode to school in our horse-drawn buggy, or walked, probably a mile and a half. In winter we usually rode in a covered horse-drawn sleigh, called a cutter. I recall that both in summer and winter our horse became so familiar with the route that we could virtually ignore the reins and let the horse make the needed turns. Sometimes the horse cut corners too sharply and we almost tipped into the ditch. Those trips to and from school could be rather interesting in their own right. I recall once when my brothers Paul and Ernie did some friendly wrestling in the buggy, I got thrown off the front. Fortunately, the horse's hoofs did not strike me, nor was I injured by the wheels which fortunately rolled beside me. As I clearly recall, I was offered the princely sum of 25 cents, the equivalent of more than $10 today, if I would not tell our parents. I never did!

The Jahnke Cattle Ranch was located in the region. I remember vividly that the teacher announced to his pupils that on that day some Jahnke Ranch cattle would be herded along the road running past the school. We were then allowed to watch the large herd of Herefords slowly making its way along the fairly narrow roadway with several cowboys making sure that no cattle wandered off onto a field or into a homestead driveway. I quite enjoyed the constant low mooing of the cattle and the skillful herding of the cowboys.

I greatly enjoyed my years attending Lobetal School. I often tried to finish my assignments early so that I could get a library book from our small school library or listen to the lessons being taught to the higher grades. I learned much from both.

I must mention one other aspect of my grade school education. When I was a pupil at Lobetal, all of the students were Mennonite except Kenneth and Velva Hallett, who were of British stock and, as far as I know, not church-attending folk. How they put up with all of the Mennonite and Christian aspects of school, including many ethnic German folkways and Mennonite assumptions, remains a puzzle. They deserved gold medals for toleration and goodwill.

These were the structured pillars of my childhood: family, church, and school in that order. They gave me identity, community and purpose.

Political and Public Affairs

Although politics was never a dominant interest for my parents, they took their Canadian citizenship seriously, kept themselves informed of political developments, discussed politics with friends, and practiced good citizenship. They voted and prayed for "those in authority." Politically my parents were supporters of the Liberal Party, mostly because the Liberals were in office when the Wiebe clan arrived in 1904 and also because they were in a coalition government when the Redekopps came in 1913.

In the late 1930s and early 1940s, it happened that the democratic socialist party, the Cooperative Commonwealth Federation (CCF), became quite popular in Saskatchewan. Rather incorrectly, my parents and many other Mennonites in the region were suspicious of the CCF. They wondered to what extent that new party shared policies and goals with the hated communists in Russia. After all, Communist Russia did call itself the Union of Soviet Socialist Republics. At least one storekeeper in Main Centre, Mr. Peter Sawatzky, was a strong CCF supporter arguing that the new party, led by a Baptist pastor, Rev. T. C. Douglas, would help meet the needs of the poorest folk. I recall some heated political conversation about the growing popularity of the CCF. They were elected provincially in 1944, the first democratic socialist government in North America.

At this point, I should note the initiation by the Canadian government of a major assistance program on January 1, 1945, the Family Allowance payments. Under this program, mothers got a monthly cheque incorporating funds for each child. The rates ranged from $5 for children under 5 to $8 for children 13 to 15. This was Canada's first universal welfare program. I clearly remember when it was launched. For the first time in her life, my mother received a monthly cheque issued specifically to her. The amounts might now seem very modest. It must be remembered, however, that the purchasing power of those $8 in 1944 was equivalent to what about $120 would buy in 2021.

It was noted by some observers at that time that the evangelical Christian folk who were in the main antithetical to socialism were quite pleased with the establishment of this program. Somehow democratic socialism sheds its negative aura if one is a beneficiary.

I also recall that even though times were financially desperate, dad somehow found funds to subscribe to the *Winnipeg Free Press* and later also the *Country Guide*. I think it was when I was in grade three that I began spending hours reading both publications. Right from my earliest reading experience, I particularly liked the column in the *Country Guide* called *Under the Peace Tower*. I'm not quite sure how or why it happened, but I soon became somewhat familiar with Canadian political affairs and avidly followed the leaders' exploits. I also have vivid memories of how I would carefully read casualty lists in the *Free Press*. At times I would virtually cry as I slowly and with respect read the names of those killed. My interest in politics, especially matters dealing with war and peace, developed early in life.

World War II gained prominence in our area when some Mennonite boys joined the Army or Air Force and attended church services in their uniforms. When VE Day, victory in Europe, was announced on May 8, 1945, there was celebration in Main Centre. When Japan's military effort collapsed on August 13, there was further rejoicing. In both instances, the celebration focused not so much on the military victories but on the end of the terrible slaughter, suffering, and destruction.

Church Life; My Spiritual Pilgrimage

Church life loomed large in our immigrant Mennonite community. Family devotions were taken very seriously by my parents. We had Bible reading with comments by my father at the breakfast table. Dad seemed to have lots of time for this even though the porridge would be cooling.

Then we all stood around the table for prayer. It was considered disrespectful to God to pray while seated. We, of course, also had table grace at the other meals. At the close of the day the family assembled for evening devotions. Again we would have Bible reading with comments followed by prayer. For those prayers we knelt at our chairs. I recall that more than once I fell asleep while kneeling and waiting for rather lengthy prayers to end.

In retrospect, it seems that even on the hottest summer days and in severe winter weather, except in the most extreme conditions, our family would go to church, the Main Centre Mennonite Brethren Church, about five kilometres south of our farm.

I recall that in summer, if dad could afford the gas, we would sometimes drive our 1928 Oldsmobile. That was a thrill for us. For much of the time the Olds was put on blocks because we could not afford the gas to drive it. For those times we went by horse and buggy, eight people crowding onto a fairly small buggy. There was no room for all of us in the buggy, so Paul and Ernie stood on the back axle and held on to the back of the back seat. I remember that in winter we sometimes had a charcoal foot-warmer to counteract the severe frost even in our sleigh. I also remember that sometimes some of us took turns running behind the cutter.

Main Centre Mennonite Brethren Church.

In addition to the usual Sunday services, including Sunday School classes on the main floor in curtained sections for adults and in the basement in curtained small rooms for children, we often also had Sunday evening services. Those were of interest to me for various reasons, including watching custodian Mr. Corny Wiebe trying, with a long wooden rod, to hang gas lanterns on ceiling hooks. In retrospect, I consider that action to have been a huge fire hazard.

We also had special events. I remember that annually we had a Sunday forenoon Thanksgiving Service, then lunch at the church with cold coffee in glass jars, followed by an afternoon Missions Fest Service. We had this Thanksgiving Service even when we had just had an almost total crop failure. If no sheaves of grain were available, these dear saints would display garden produce. These deeply pious country folk always felt that they had sufficient reasons to thank God. Even in the most difficult times financially, and they were truly difficult, these hardy and frugal pioneers always found occasion to have a Missions Fest and to donate scarce money for foreign missions. Such selfless commitment impressed me deeply. I am reminded of St. Paul's comments about certain Macedonian Christians: "They gave as much as they were able, and even beyond their ability." (*II Corinthians 8:2*)

At virtually all of our services we had an excellent choir. On occasion we had a regional Song Fest at our church. At such times the churchyard was filled with horses and buggies and a few cars. The church was packed with happy worshipers. According to my recollection, none of our preachers, all unpaid, had more than Bible School training in theology but they were all schooled in the Word and in practical Christian living. They were convincing because they lived what they preached.

My extensive exposure to Christian teaching, first at home, also somewhat at school, and repeatedly in Sunday School and the preaching and singing at church made a deep impression on me, confirming authenticity, and greatly influenced my spiritual pilgrimage. Although, at the time, my understanding of a personal commitment was limited, the grounding I received in those formative years never left me. At about age seven, at my parents' bedside during one stormy night, I made a child's acceptance of salvation. While the plow of faith was not set deeply at that time, I never doubted who God is and what the Holy Bible says about him. My Main Centre religious experience has stood me in very good stead.

Reflections and Memories of my Childhood Years in Saskatchewan

In this section, I shall briefly describe several additional events or experiences which were part of my childhood. One of my earliest memories is accompanying either dad or an older brother heading out in a horse-drawn box wagon into some pasture lands to collect buffalo bones. These were still sufficiently plentiful so that we could collect a pile perhaps four feet high. These bones, then sold to make fertilizer, brought a few much-needed dollars.

One year in the late thirties, dad heard of a way to save on fuel costs. Behind the barn he levelled an area about 50 feet by 50 feet and erected planks all around it. He then had the area filled to about 4 inches with manure from our large manure piles. Then water was added. One of my sisters and I were then instructed to trample barefoot in it so that everything was fully mixed. This composite was then allowed to dry in the sun. It was then cut into roughly 8-inch squares and stacked as furnace fuel for winter. At that point, it was no longer smelly. We did use it. It burned but did not generate much heat. Thankfully for us manure tramplers, dad did not repeat this experimental undertaking.

From the earliest years, we had a telephone. In those days, about six to ten families shared a party line. Each home had its special ring. I think ours was two short and one long or something similar. The system worked quite well except for the fact that almost always, when someone's particular ring was heard, then, upon lifting your own receiver, you could hear a series of other receivers being lifted by fellow-party liners listening in. There were thus few secrets in our community.

The Main Centre phone system had perhaps 60 or more households. All but a few were Mennonite. On occasion, the central phone operator, Miss Schroeder, would sound a special ring, perhaps one long ring, to indicate that she would be making a general announcement. These announcements could cover almost any issue, from roads and weather to deaths and mail service.

As I reflected on this phenomenon in later years, it seemed very strange to me that these announcements by Central, as we called the lady, were usually made in Low German and some in High German. I am amazed that the few non-Mennonite families in the region put up with such insensitivity.

A small quilt John embroidered.

On Saturdays our family of eight had a bath-time ritual. We had a long tub: brass outside, tin inside, in which an adult could sit very comfortably but not lie down. This tub was placed near the kitchen stove with chairs between it and the rest of the room. A sheet or blanket was then draped over the chairs to provide some privacy. Several buckets of water, which had been heated on the stove were then emptied into the tub until it reached a depth of perhaps 4 inches. Cold water was added as needed. We took turns. As I recall, mom bathed first, then dad, then the oldest of the six children, followed by the other five according to age. As needed, additional hot water was added. I, the youngest, bathed last. I might have the deepest water but it was clearly the least transparent. I don't recall that the water was changed somewhere down the line. Be that as it may, we were clean, ready for Sunday.

One year we somehow acquired a gramophone with perhaps 40 to 50 records. The records were cylindrical, lined with thick ceramic. The record was slipped onto an arm. The contraption was hand-cranked. Another arm with a needle was then lowered onto the cylinder. The sound was not fully natural but quite enjoyable. Clearly, this was a time for parental guidance. I remember that some of us children, I think Sophie and I, sat with mom around the gramophone and played each of the records, at least in part. After each performance mom announced her verdict, whether we could keep it or not. As I recall, most records did not measure up to her level of moral appropriateness. Many were rejected because mom announced, "*Dass sind nur Liebeslieder.*" [Those are only love songs.] As I remember it, *Beautiful Isle of Somewhere* made the cut although nobody there knew what "the isle" really meant. I know that many fine recordings bit the dust that day. Most of the collection was country and western. The garbage container was soon filled with discards.

The annual fall hog-butchering ritual was a delightful event, not because we children stayed home from school to help - I actually liked going to school - but because of all the excitement. Also, the meals were always special. Generally, some three or four neighbouring couples arrived to help. Such help was reciprocated when hog-slaughtering was done by them.

The well-fed hog, weighing about 350 pounds, was brought from its pen quite oblivious to its imminent demise. It was shot. I watched with great interest as its legs buckled. Then its throat was slit to drain the blood. A few minutes later the carcass was strung up from the high hay hook so it hung about 6 feet up in front of the barn. It was then dunked into a large barrel of very hot water which, after the barrel was removed, enabled us to scrape off the bristles quite easily. Next, the carcass, still hanging from the hay hook, was sliced open on the stomach side. This intrigued me. The entrails were carefully removed. The carcass was then sorted and cut, some while still hanging and some after the quarters were put on a table. The liver became part of liverwurst. The heart was its own meat dish. The various parts of the hog became the usual pork options.

What fascinated me, in particular, was that the intestines were carefully set aside. They were then taken to a remote part of the yard where they were emptied, then repeatedly rinsed on the inside, washed on the outside, and eventually taken to the sausage-making table where certain parts of the carcass had been cut, spiced, and mixed waiting to be put through the grinder to make the popular farmer sausage. I developed some skill at jamming the intestine casing onto the protruding spout of the sausage machine. This had to be done very carefully because a tear in the gut was a minor catastrophe. The many coils of sausage then were hung on a long rod, probably metal, and carefully smoked. The result was delectable!

For some years, as I recall, my task was to stir a very large vat, hung over a fire, where various cuttings were heated and stirred to become lard with layers of cracklings being formed. Later there was a similar undertaking with lye added to that particular mixture to produce soap. I enjoyed cutting the bricks of soap later.

This cooperative pioneer ritual, with its high-voltage comradeship, with everyone knowing exactly what to do and with obvious joy doing everything expertly, left a deep impression on me.

The last six years, when we had had good grain crops, we had interesting harvest days. In preparation for threshing, the sheaves of grain, generally four to six, were stood on end so that they were leaning to the centre. This was called a stook. The stooked sheaves dried, after which they were ready for the threshing day. Threshing day was another day when we children stayed home from school to help. The harvesting crew arrived at our house early. Typically the crew consisted of about six workmen plus an expert to operate the complicated threshing machine and the stationary tractor, which, by means of a long belt around a power drive on the tractor, provided the power to operate the big unit.

The six or so workmen, often bringing their own team of horses and hay-rack, had the task of loading the stooked sheaves onto their hay-racks, driving alongside the threshing machine intake deck, and then with a hayfork tossing them onto the belt-driven machine. To help the hard-working stook-loaders to get their load done as quickly as possible, there was also a "field-pitcher" to help load the hay-racks. Before there were trucks to carry the grain, there would be at least one horse-drawn box-wagon, which would be parked next to the threshing machine to receive and then take away the grain.

For several years my job, about 6:30 or 7:00 AM, was to provide a wash basin outside for the men, help feed the horses and drive a buggy out to the threshing crew to provide what we called a second "small breakfast" at about 10 in the forenoon. I greatly enjoyed contributing in even a small way to the entire operation. I knew that selling the grain provided the family with money. I also greatly enjoyed watching the straw being blown out to form a strawstack.

Harvesting with a threshing machine.

The constant conviviality of the crew during mealtime was a delight to hear. Some of those earthy farmhands had obviously developed skill in telling stories and jokes, especially in Low German. I still remember one humorous tale.

As was common practice in those times, all of us children were put to work at an early age. I think I was 9 when I got the assignment to keep some cattle from wandering away from an unfenced grazing pasture about a mile away. Our dog and I kept the cows in line. My pay, as I recall, was 5 cents for the day, not per hour. In today's purchasing power that would be about one dollar. I was very grateful for the income.

I remember that on quite a few occasions, I was assigned to work in a field by myself, maybe stooking or piling up stones or guiding a team of horses. Since we could not afford watches for the children, my instructions, at least a few times as I recall, were that I was to come in for supper when the sun was four fingers from the horizon. The idea was that I would stretch out my arm to determine quitting time. I must confess that at times I fudged a bit by bending my arm. That shortened the workday a little. I may not have confessed that childhood transgression.

I clearly remember the day that World War II broke out in September 1939. But, of course, it was not then known by that name. As I recall, my father and I were picking up stones in a plowed field - plowing always brought out more stones. I knew what war was, probably from lessons taught in Sunday School. I remember asking dad if the war would come to Canada. He informed me that the war was taking place in Europe. I knew that Europe was far away. He assured me that he did not think that war would come to Canada. The conversation we had that day launched my immediate and continuing interest in that war and then later in wars and politics generally. I listened very intently to the CBC news reports on our little radio. As I recall, I learned to read before I started in Grade 1. Probably a year or two later, I began reading the political commentaries and the war reports in the *Winnipeg Free Press* and the *Country Guide* with intense interest.

Our First Winter in British Columbia

As already stated, in October 1944 my parents and the three youngest children traveled by car to Abbotsford where dad would teach at the newly-established Bible School. The trip itself was memorable for several reasons. First, we barely had enough wartime gasoline ration coupons to make it to Abbotsford. As I recall, some selective but legal bartering happened. Second, because of a money shortage we brought most of our food with us. I don't think we ate in a cafe or restaurant even once. Near our destination we encountered very dense fog on the US highway. Near Mt. Vernon, Washington, we either slowed down greatly or even stopped to make sure we were still on the roadway. Suddenly a large transport truck struck the back of our car. No police were called. When we arrived in Abbotsford, we had to proceed from inside the car to get at our possessions. For some months, until dad could scrounge up repair funds, we drove with the badly indented rear end.

During that year I took some grade six Saskatchewan correspondence courses. For some reason, I did not take those assignments very seriously. Maybe they were insufficiently challenging. To keep me occupied I took large numbers of books from the South Abbotsford Church library and did much reading. I then completed grade 6 in Lobetal when we returned to the farm in late April.

Grade Seven

I remember taking the first six weeks or so of grade seven in Lobetal School in the early fall of 1945. After travelling to Abbotsford and getting settled there, my parents enrolled me in the local school system. Because of the great increase in the local population consisting largely of Mennonites coming from the prairies, the local Abbotsford schools were all crowded. It therefore became necessary for me to take an early school bus to the Philip Sheffield High School in downtown Abbotsford and then another bus to the not-crowded multi-classroom Matsqui Elementary School in Matsqui Village, located about five kilometres to the north, close to the Fraser River.

Although I had to adjust in mid-term to a totally new curriculum, the overall educational experience that year was a good one. Several memories remain vivid. My primary teacher, Mrs. Ruby Brown Shand, was a good teacher and took considerable interest in each pupil. I remember that she even had at least some of us pupils visit her in her home. I do recall some specifics. Mrs. Shand was quite the anglophile with a particular fondness for British royalty. As I recall, we spent almost the entire social studies course learning about the kings and queens of England and Scotland and then of Great Britain and the United Kingdom. Already then, this struck me as rather odd.

Although I was never strapped in school, I came perilously close to such a misadventure one day in grade seven. On that day, not for the first time, someone in our class threw what was called a spit-ball, a half-egg-sized ball of tightly-wrapped wet paper, across the room, targeting some unsuspecting classmate. The challenge was to do that, look innocent, and not get caught. This time the teacher spotted the projectile. I had not done the dastardly launching but my neighbour had. For some reason Mrs. Shand assumed that I was the guilty party. She had not known me to be a misbehaving pupil but now, I think reluctantly, she decided that I had seriously misbehaved. I was told to go stand in the corner, which I did. She then called the principal, Mr. Jim Reid. He came, proceeded to the desk and got the strap to administer the punishment. I then, for probably the first time, drew upon my ability to think on my feet and to argue. I did not plead for mercy but calmly stated that I had not done the dastardly deed and that he would not want to punish an innocent pupil, and as a totally innocent observer, I did not deserve to be punished. I remember that Principal Reid pondered the matter briefly and then walked back to the front of the room, returned the strap to its place of storage, and left. I quickly resumed my seat. I think that some fellow pupils admired me not only for talking my way out of a strapping but for not telling Principal Reid which pupil had launched the projectile.

CHAPTER 4

THE HIGH SCHOOL YEARS 1946-1951

The Mennonite Educational Institute

A strange thing happened in the summer of 1946. Since the recently-established Mennonite Educational Institute (MEI) offered courses only in grades 9 to 13, I knew I would not yet be able to attend the school which my siblings Sophie and Ernie had already attended the previous year, 1945-46. I would need to return to Matsqui School for Grade 8 and wait another year. Then in late summer I was told by my father, I was not consulted about the matter, that in September, I would be attending the MEI and taking grade 9. For some reason, probably including a desire to have me attend a Christian school as soon as possible, I would be skipping grade 8. As it happened, the same decision had been made by the parents of several of my church friends. Presumably the parents communicated with one another. Thus, in September 1946 some three or four of us boys skipped grade 8 and began taking grade 9 at the MEI. Five years later, we all graduated together.

The original MEI at the corner of Old Yale and Clearbrook roads.

I already knew most of the teachers from my church involvement and looked forward to this new experience. Unfortunately, it did not start well. During the first day of grade 9 mathematics, our very fine teacher, Mr. A. B. Voth, who later became a medical doctor in Saskatoon, administered a math test reviewing grade 8 math. I think I got about 55%. I was generally good at math, but I did not know how to calculate the volume of a cylinder nor some other formulas. Within not many weeks those of us who had skipped grade 8 managed to catch up on what we had missed.

I consider my education at the MEI to have been first class. The teachers were competent and highly motivated to make the new school as successful as possible. Most significantly, they were all impressive Christians who lived out their faith. Without exception, they focused not only on teaching their academic lessons but teaching us students. Not surprisingly, I probably learned as much from them as individuals as from their teaching.

Mr. Bill A. Wiebe was an excellent math and science instructor. Also noteworthy were Mr. William Neufeld, history and English; Principal I. J. Dyck, mathematics; Mr. Dan Froese, biology; Mr. Franz Thiessen, German and music, Mr. Walfried Klassen, health; Miss Susan Krahn, English and German, and Mr. C. D. Toews, music and religion.

We need to remember that the MEI offered the standard BC curriculum plus courses in religion and Mennonite history as well as extensive non-course-related music and community program preparation involving virtually the entire student body. The fact that the MEI was offering a high-quality educational experience was soon confirmed by the disproportionate number of provincial scholarships that its senior students won. We were an immigrant school still needing to prove ourselves to ourselves and to the general public.

Several extra-curricular activities stand out in my memory. Each noon hour the student body would assemble on the central steps and in the hallway to sing a Table Grace in German. I still recall them. Every Friday afternoon we had a Christian assembly at which teachers or guest speakers challenged us to make wises decisions, to live ethically, and to cultivate our Christian faith. Importantly, students were always encouraged to talk about the concerns, challenges, blessings, etc., in their life and especially their Christian pilgrimage. Many students spoke in these assemblies. We had no gym in the early years but we had excellent outdoor sports activities in all seasons.

Even with a small student body of between 300 and 400, gradually increasing, we had major community impact, especially academically, but also musically and with dramas. The school choir was an important community presence and presented various outstanding and well-attended concerts during the year.

In 1948-49 I was in Grade 11. I have many memories of excellent teaching by gifted teachers, a tremendous school spirit, and a rapidly growing impact of the MEI on the Mennonite as well as the larger community. It happened that a Canadian general election was called for June 27 of that year. By 1949 the Mennonite community in Abbotsford had developed in socioeconomic status to the degree that not only were the people greatly interested in economic and other policies that impacted them, but also some had become active politically. Several even became candidates for elected office.

Responding to this surge of political interest, the MEI teachers decided to stage an evening meeting to inform the community about political issues. They selected three students to present the ideologies and platforms of the three main political parties - Liberal, Conservative and the democratic socialist Co-operative Commonwealth Federation (CCF), renamed the New Democratic Party in 1961. Partly because I had expressed interest in the Christian roots of democratic socialism in the Canadian prairies and, I suppose, partly because I am by nature not hesitant to express controversial views, I was asked to make the case for the CCF. That excited me. I did considerable research, and as part of my presentation to a packed auditorium, I recited, with considerable gusto, the entire CCF Regina Manifesto. I don't think I convinced any of my Mennonite audience but I think many were impressed by my memorization and my enthusiasm. I thoroughly enjoyed the event.

But that was not the end of the story. Shortly after that evening there was an event at the MEI dealing mainly with refugees and immigration. The speaker that evening, again with a packed auditorium, was Peter Dyck, later of MCC fame and an acclaimed author and Christian statesman. Someone had informed him of my CCF presentation. For reasons that still seem puzzling, he publicly expressed great criticism of my recent CCF presentation. As I recall, he greatly embarrassed me. Peter Dyck was an American preacher. What I had not yet discovered at that time was the extent to which in the US, much different than in Canada, democratic socialism was outside of the legitimate political spectrum. In fact, it was widely preached and believed, as it still is, that socialism is close to communism.

A day or two after Mr. Dyck's public criticism of me, I tracked him down in the home where he was staying. We had an amicable discussion. Although I was obviously much younger, I told him, as I quite clearly recall, that I thought he was in error on two counts. First, there were elements of socialism that were related to Christian teaching and, second, that I was embarrassed and offended by his public criticism of me when all that I had done was carry out an assignment given me by teachers.

Unfortunately, I do not recall his response but I do recall that it greatly disappointed me. That day I lost some respect for prominent people who are not sensitive about what they say about lesser folk and who are not willing to make amends when they have clearly done something very unwise or blatantly wrong.

There was no shortage of optional activities for all students. Perhaps the most ambitious undertaking was the production of the student newspaper, *The Students' Call*. It published many student submissions and carried commercial advertising to cover production costs. It was my privilege to serve as the editor of *The Students' Call* in 1949-1950 when I was in grade 12.

STAFF OF THE "STUDENTS' CALL"

Standing: Mr. W. Neufeld, H. Janzen, M. Lenzman, H. Wiebe, H. Janzen, G. Schroeder, M. Esau, L. Pankratz, D. Nikkel.

Seated: E. Suderman, A. Konrad, H. Penner, J. Redekop (editor), B. Suderman (assistant editor), A. Wiens.

The Students' Call committee.
Standing L to R: Mr. W. Neufeld, H. Janzen, M. Lenzman. H. Wiebe, H. Janzen, G. Schroeder, M. Esau, L. Pankratz, D. Nikkel.
Seated: E. Suderman, A. Konrad, H. Penner, J. Redekop (editor), B. Suderman (Assistant Editor), A. Wiens.

The following year, my graduating year, I was privileged to serve as editor of *The Evergreen*, the student-produced yearbook.

The Staff of the "Evergreen"

Back Row:
Ernie Dyck,
Betty Balzer,
Henry Esau,
John Dyck.

Front Row:
John Redekop,
(editor)
Mr. Dyck
(sponsor),
Leona Siemens
(secretary).

• • •

ADVERTISING
COMMITTEE:
John Isaak,
Dave Harder,
Ernie Dyck,
Jake Janzen.

The Evergreen committee.
Standing L to R: Ernie Dyck, Betty Balzer, Henry Esau.
Seated: John Redekop (editor), Mr. Dyck (Sponsor), Leona Siemens (Secretary).

Each year MEI students produced a major theatre production. In those days we called them dramas. These productions were offered to the entire community in the new gymnasium-auditorium built, as I recall, when I was in Grade 10. The large auditorium, seating about 600 people, was typically filled for several evenings, if my memory serves me correctly. During my Grade 12 year, 1949-50, the major production was a fairly long drama, *Esther*, which depicted the life of this major biblical heroine. I was asked to play the part of Mordecai.

John as Mordecai

While my assignment was not as long as Esther's, played powerfully by Hilda Janzen, I recall spending many hours memorizing lines. For several nights the auditorium was packed. The drama was very well received. As I learned and then recited my many passages, the entire story became very meaningful to me. That intense involvement in an Old Testament story helped shape my spiritual pilgrimage.

In those days MEI students put on what were called Literary Evenings for the general public. These well-attended events consisted of musical and literary offerings, generally presented with considerable skill by students. When I was in Grade 13, 1950-51, one of the Literary Evenings had special meaning for me. During that year, classes in religion and literature had set me thinking a lot about ethics and parent-child relationships.

I began doing some writing and ended up writing a play which I entitled *Sir Cecil's Gold*.

The plot of the play, set in the early 17th century as I recall, was as follows. A prominent British chemist had won accolades for his chemical discoveries, mostly alchemy. Ere long he was knighted, hence Sir Cecil. Toward the end of his career, Sir Cecil set himself a very specific goal. He hoped that just as carbon and some other elements can exist in disparate forms, it ought to be possible to create gold through innovative chemistry. He spent months working at this dream. He worked such long hours that his health suffered.

Sir Cecil's daughter, who loved her father dearly, observed her father's determination and also his deteriorating health. She struggled with the tension between living honestly or doing some cheating to help her father. She finally

The cast of Sir Cecil's Gold.

decided that love for her father trumped her ethics. Her emotion trumped both her reason and her ethical conviction. Very skillfully she cheated. She slipped a little gold dust into one of the very complicated concoctions her father was creating. He was overjoyed. At last he had achieved success! Amidst all of the accolades and praise her father was receiving, his poor daughter was almost overcome with guilt. Should she confess and destroy her father's special achievement? Should she let him celebrate while she struggled with her guilt? Would he get caught? What would she do if he did get caught? How was God evaluating her praiseworthy motive which resulted in a wrongful action? Would God give her credit for the honourable motive of a loving daughter or would he simply condemn her for deceit? Sir Cecil's daughter was in agony.

Sir Cecil's daughter in agony.

As I recall, I left the dilemma unresolved and with a clear challenge to the audience to decide for themselves.

Unfortunately, the script of my foray into drama writing is lost. I have often thought that if I still had it, I would like to develop its basic themes more fully, but that is not possible. In retrospect, I can say that the entire experience was, for me, very stretching and rewarding. How many high school students have an audience of perhaps 600 people come to see their effort at writing a play and addressing some basic human ethical dilemmas? I am deeply grateful that the teachers, especially Mr. William Neufeld, allowed a novice such as me to present some inner tensions to a large audience.

Years later, in 2002, when the MEI asked me to write a short statement for a promotional booklet I provided this summary:

> "MEI has been a very significant part of my life. During my five years as a student in that school, I learned life-long habits. I learned how to think critically, and I learned the importance of establishing priorities. The excellent modelling by the teachers played a key role in the development of my personal values. Equally important, by observing teachers and senior students, I learned how to apply my Christian beliefs in practical ways to daily life and how to integrate the various areas of my life."

At this juncture in my story I must acknowledge a significant misdeed. Unfortunately, I have no recollection of making things right at that time as I should have. For a long time it virtually disappeared from my memory. In recent years it has come back to haunt me. Given that it now bothers me, I must deal with it. I do not recall the details but sometime during my MEI years, I submitted a poem, I think for publication in the student newspaper, that I had not written. After more than 70 years my memory is hazy, and I have no existing evidence. There may be none. Be that as it may, whether needed or not, I take this occasion to confess my wrongdoing even though I cannot direct it to anyone in particular. I have confessed to God and now to the larger community and feel forgiven.

I must note several additional experiences during my high school years, experiences not related to the MEI. During the first few summers I picked strawberries, then raspberries. If the fruit was abundant, I actually enjoyed picking berries. I generally challenged myself to be as good a picker as I could possibly be and tried to pick more pounds or flats than the other pickers. As it turned out, on several occasions I did quite well. One summer, I think it was in 1947, I managed to pick 500 pounds of strawberries in one day. The British Sovereign berries that year were large. The local paper, as I recall, carried a brief note that I was the champion picker. I think it was also in 1947 that I managed to pick 312 pounds of Newburg raspberries at the Peter Block farm in Yarrow. The Newburg crop that year was truly bounteous. Dad and mom allowed me to keep enough of my earnings to buy my first new bicycle.

Hop-picking, which came next, was much less pleasant. Our mother and several of us children moved into picker cabins at the John I. Haas Hop Company near Chilliwack. The cabins were very primitive. We had to get up very early, have breakfast, pack lunch and then were taken out to the hopyards. As it happens, the sticky hop blossoms seemed to weigh almost nothing. It took a lot of picking to acquire a significant number of pounds. As I recall, anyone who earned $5 in one day did very well. Even though the pay was low, if our family unit worked there for a few weeks, we could make enough money to help augment the rather slim family income. Our hops, we reassured ourselves, all went into baking yeast, not beer.

During my high school years we were able to clear the last remaining stumps from our 7.5-acre very modest farming project. (Dad and mom had sold 2.5 of our 10 acres to Abe and Frieda Wieler, my oldest sister and her husband.) As I recall, we had perhaps 10 to 15 large stumps remaining in the pasture. Some were probably 5 feet or more in diameter. This entire region was once wooded with very impressive old-growth timber. We would pick up cases of dynamite from the local reeve's home. Each case had perhaps 50 sticks of dynamite packed in sawdust. We also bought cord and fuses. My brother Ernie and I were in charge of the blasting. We would dig a hole under the stump, then we put the cord, with a fuse squeezed onto its end, into one of the sticks. Then we very carefully put in about 10 to 20 more sticks of dynamite, depending on the size of the stump. Then the hole was filled with dirt and tamped as hard as possible. With the fuse sticking out we cut it so that perhaps four to five feet protruded. Then we would light the cord which then sputtered noisily, and run some 200 feet away to await the blast.

Generally, the procedure worked well. The stump would be blown apart so that a bulldozer could easily maneuver the larger pieces onto a pile to be burned. One time, however, we had a problem. Dealing with a very large stump we put more than the usual number of dynamite sticks under it, maybe 35. The resulting blast blew the stump apart as we had hoped. As usual, standing about 200 feet away, we could duck when any smaller parts of the stump came flying through the air. Unfortunately, one piece, weighing about 100 pounds, went sailing into the air to the north. It crossed our property, went over the road, over the Nick Toews' dairy barn and landed in a pasture about 100 feet beyond the barn. I estimate it sailed at least 500 feet. We were indeed fortunate that this heavy part of the old stump had not struck a cow or crashed into the barn's roof.

On June 8, 1948, the mighty Fraser River was at flood stage, threatening many thousands of acres of Matsqui flatland. For several weeks news reports had warned of a possible flood resulting from the very rapid melting of the unusually heavy snowpack in the mountains. One evening there was an emergency call for help. Our dairy-farming neighbour, Nick Toews, loaded up a carful of volunteers and hurriedly drove to the Matsqui flats. As I recall, the high-water Fraser had just started seeping through the south shore dyke. My brother Ernie joined the crew trying to prevent the dyke from giving way. As it turned out, some hours later the softened dyke succumbed.

I was assigned with others to get dairy cattle onto trucks. We worked feverishly all night. Together with many other crews we managed to get all of the thousands of dairy cattle out of their barns and safely trucked to the large green fields at the Abbotsford Airport. There must have been many thousands of cattle, mostly Holstein cows and young stock, taken there during the night. The farmers must have had quite the challenge sorting out their herds the next day to have them trucked to some highland farms for the essential milking.

One other event should be mentioned. On Saturday, February 18, 1950, I was having a bath in the mid-afternoon when I heard a very loud scream. I jumped out of the tub, quickly put on clothes and shoes and ran, heading east toward the scream. About 600 feet down the road, hidden behind some buildings, was a man in fairly deep water, hanging onto the ice and screaming loudly. I was puzzled why a grown man apparently walked out onto thin ice. I also wondered then, as even now, why no one else had shown up at the lake. I was sure that other neighbours must have heard the man's desperate screams. I believe that the small lake was not deep enough for the man to drown, but the weather was cold and hypothermia might set in quickly. Try as he would, the desperate man was unable to scramble onto the ice.

Having no rescue equipment at hand, I ran to the Paul Neufelds' home across the road and quickly found a strong rope. As the *Abbotsford News* reported the event on February 22, "the quick-thinking son of Mr. and Mrs. J. F. Redekop threw a rope to Mr. Ingwersen." By then, more help had arrived. We managed to get Cornelius out. He was totally soaked, very cold and truly grateful.

One other very interesting event happened in the winter of 1950. The Fraser Valley experienced the heaviest snowfall on record. Except for main thoroughfares, the roads became impassable. Schools were closed for many weeks. The MEI was closed for five weeks. When classes eventually resumed it was a huge challenge for teachers and students to make up for the lost time. Where we lived, dairy farmers were forced to dump their milk; even the big milk trucks could not get through. To deal with some growing shortages I walked the three to four miles to the village of Abbotsford to buy some badly needed groceries. On Sumas prairie the snow had drifted so high that, as the newspapers reported, some people were stepping over telephone wires.

Church Life; My Faith Pilgrimage

From the time we arrived in the Fraser Valley, first for the school year 1944-45 and then permanently in the early fall of 1945, we attended the South Abbotsford MB Church until the daughter church, now known as Central Heights on McCallum Road, began its services in January 1950. Those five years, 1945 to 1950, were very important in my faith formation. In the first place, I had excellent Sunday School teachers, notably Les Schmidt, who not only taught us well but took an interest in each boy in his class. He mentored us before I knew what the word meant.

Beginning in late 1948, if my memory serves me correctly, I sang in the South Abbotsford Church Junior Choir. That was an excellent experience. Not only did I develop many good friendships, but I also benefited from instruction in singing and the many times we served in church services.

A particularly significant experience for me was the first time, when I was 16 or 17, I was asked, together with two other young men, to preach a short sermon Sunday evening. As I recall, we were each asked to speak on three of the nine fruits of the spirit as described in Galatians 5:22. I know I did not do very well, although I did the best I could at the time. In any event, since then I have had the opportunity to deliver hundreds of sermons in at least ten countries. I have always valued the fact that some older people cared enough about us young fellows to give us a start.

During those South Abbotsford years, when I was in my teens, we had many social activities which we organized by ourselves. There was no youth pastor. We had numerous evening wiener roasts, some sports events, and also lots of group meetings in homes. Every home had a radio and some had a record player. There was, of course, no television. More than a few times a group would assemble in a home to listen to a variety of records. They were not called albums then, only by their correct name as records. We listened to a lot of good classical, religious and some western music. We knew that there were charts plotting the popularity of pop singers but somehow none of us seemed interested in that genre.

As I reflect on those important and formative teen years, I am grateful for the fact that we had vibrant, very active and interesting church choirs. Also, often we young folk simply formed impromptu groups. We sang at homes on Christmas Eve and sometimes also at Easter-time. Easter Monday we often hiked up a nearby mountain. Cultus Lake provided excellent boating and swimming. We had parties and socials. We were the children and grandchildren of ethnic immigrants who had earned some money, who were enjoying a newfound freedom and independence, and who were building our own collegial community but in a milieu of new opportunities and experiences.

My personal life did not change much after we left the South Abbotsford Church and on January 1, 1950 became part of the new Abbotsford Mennonite Brethren Church with its 204 charter members. It was commonly called the McCallum Road Church. About 1961 that church was renamed as the Central Heights Church. My future father-in-law, Rev. Henry H. Nikkel, was the founding pastor. My father was the founding assistant pastor. The third ordained preacher in that church in the 1950s was Rev. Abraham H. Wieler, the husband of my oldest sister, Frieda, and also a Bible School teacher.

Those were the years when I consciously began evaluating the tenets of Christianity and my own beliefs. I had many questions on my mind. These dealt mostly with big issues about eternity, God's justice, creation, inherent guilt, God's ability to know what billions of people are thinking and doing, what God's love meant for people who never heard the Gospel, the immensity of the universe, the evidence of geology, the blurred distinction between love and lust, the place of situation ethics, an eternity without a beginning or end, and a host of other issues. Two were perhaps the most difficult for me. First, how could a just God punish anyone endlessly? Surely, at some point, the terrible suffering would be sufficient. Second, how could God always have existed? I spent many hours reading, thinking, and trying to process such questions in my mind.

Naturally, given that I already believed the Christian gospel to be true, I thought much about my own spiritual well-being. I heard various individuals talk of a crisis event. Such personal testimonies impressed me. My problem, if that is the right word, was that I could honestly say that I had always believed the biblical teaching to be true. I had always believed in Jesus and his atonement for human sins. I had no memory of not believing. I had always had a measure of faith. Thus I could not identify a time when I came to a saving belief. What I did lack was a complete assurance about my eternal state. I must stress, however, that throughout these formative years, as also throughout the rest of my life, even though I had many questions,. I never doubted the inherent veracity of the Christian gospel. Whatever questions I might have, I have always been fully convinced that Christianity is true. I do not recall ever being without faith, only without commitment.

Finally, on November 24, 1949, while in Grade 12, I decided that if I ever needed to settle on a date when I knew what I believed and in whom I believed, then that was the date. Eventually, I came to understand that, as one might put it, the existence of a birth certificate is not the best confirmation that one is alive. I needed to demonstrate in my life what it meant to be a

Christian. I gradually also realized that simply believing the Jesus story was insufficient. The Bible tells us that the evil one also believes; in fact, he and his minions "believe and shudder." *(James 2: 19)*

Believing the facts is not enough. One needs to move beyond mental affirmation to making a decision, a personal commitment. One needs to accept personal salvation and then to grow in the knowledge that Jesus is not only one's Saviour but also one's Lord. That is what creates a changed life. I gradually came to understand that truth. Such development continues throughout life - I am still on that pilgrimage. As I became more firm in my beliefs and commitment, I decided that the time had come for me to be baptized. I was asked to recount my spiritual pilgrimage to the church members which I did gladly. I was then baptized, on September 3, 1950, in a small lake in what is now called Albert Dyck Park off Clearbrook Road. The baptizing minister was Rev. H. H. Nikkel, my future father-in-law.

Relevant Political and Public Affairs 1946 - 1951

Although I had read political news and columns in the *Country Guide* and *Winnipeg Free Press* probably since I was in Grade 2 or 3, I really became interested in political affairs when I enrolled in Grade 9 at MEI. We could not afford a daily newspaper so I listened as much as I could to radio broadcasts. This was not easy given that we had only one radio and other members of the household also had listening preferences. I also had chores to do and lots of homework. Even so, I looked forward to the various newscasts. In particular, I was intrigued by a 15-minute daily news program called *The UN Today***.** In those days, the United Nations was a new international agency in which masses of people placed great hope. I eagerly followed numerous developments around the world. I followed as closely as I could the early phases of the developing Cold War between the Allied West and the USSR. The 1948-49 Allied Airlift to save West Berlin from communist conquest was of great interest. The 1949 Canadian election also provided exciting drama.

Some time, probably when I was in Grade 11, I became fascinated by American politics. Earlier, in 1944, while attending Lobetal School, I heard of the death of US president Franklin Delano Roosevelt. That left a great impression on me. I had already learned that he had done much to bring the US out of the Great Depression. Later, in 1948, I followed the presidential election campaign between president Harry Truman and Republican Thomas Dewey. As I recall, at my bedtime it was announced that Dewey had won. In the morning it was announced that Truman had won. As we know, some news reporters and some headline writers were greatly embarrassed by their hasty pronouncements.

What truly got my attention in 1950 was the drama of Wisconsin Senator Joseph McCarthy's witch-hunting of alleged communists in the US State Department and elsewhere. His main accusation, made in February 1950 was that 205 communists had infiltrated the US State Department and were subverting US government operations and shaping US policies. That allegation fascinated me. The sometimes-raucous hearings conducted by the House Un-American Activities Committee added to my interest. I remember at times rushing home after school to get some live coverage. Already then I sensed that Senator McCarthy was a dangerous demagogue who was being believed by millions, especially in the US hinterlands. He seemed invulnerable. He ruined many reputations. About 2,000 government employees lost their jobs because of him. After 1951 the senator's popularity gradually declined. He died on May 2, 1957, in disgrace.

Other political developments that fascinated me in my years at MEI were the Chinese Civil War which finally ended with Communist victory in 1949, the Soviet explosion of its first atomic bomb in August 1949; and the outbreak of the Korean War on June 25, 1950. I vividly recall how, after hearing the news on the radio that day, I walked slowly back to my strawberry-picking, wondering whether the North Korean attack on South Korea would expand to become World War III, wondering if there would be another military draft in Canada and how I would react if, at age 18, I would be drafted!

Politics had become my hobby. Some twelve years later, the study of politics was to become my career.

Before I close this section, I should mention a contemporary political development that significantly affected my home community and, indeed, all of Canada. In 1952 the Canadian government created the Old Age Security Plan, a policy still in effect. An earlier plan which required a "means test" had been implemented back in 1927. In contrast to the American Social Security system, in which benefits are received according to contributions made by individuals, the Canadian OAS system is universal. Its benefits are based on age and residency in Canada, not on any contributions. With the initiation of these substantial monthly payments, caring for seniors became a much easier task in Mennonite homes and communities as also elsewhere in this country.

CHAPTER 5

POST-SECONDARY EDUCATION PART 1 1951-1955

The last year of high school includes thinking about next steps. During my grade 13 year I rather enjoyed envisioning various careers. Without a doubt, my preference was to go into law. This, however, was problematic because I knew that my parents would not want me to go that route. For various reasons they, like most of the folk in our sphere of relationships, considered a career in law somewhat suspect. In retrospect I think I may have been too submissive to my parents' wishes in making a career choice. Be that as it may, I decided to wait before making any career decision and to spend one year in some serious Bible education which I knew I needed. As I recall, mostly for financial reasons I decided to enroll at the local Bible School in Abbotsford.

Abbotsford Mennonite Brethren Bible School, September 1951 - April 1952

The Abbotsford Mennonite Brethren Bible School, a precursor to Columbia Bible College, was a denominational institution located in a building on the same grounds as the original South Abbotsford Church. The enrollment would have been about 130. The school offered a four-year program. The first two years were considered to be equivalent to grades 12 and 13 in terms of academic rigour. Years three and four were deemed to constitute post-secondary education. Because I had completed Grade 13 and had had some Bible studies in all my five years at MEI, I was registered as a third-year student.

For me it was both a plus and a minus that the principal was my father, Rev. Jacob F. Redekop, that another teacher was my brother-in-law, Rev. Abraham Wieler, and that another teacher, Rev. Henry H. Nikkel, was my future father-in-law. Fortunately, they were all fine instructors. Also, fortunately, there were two other fine instructors, Rev. Herman Voth and Mr. H. P. Neufeld.

The courses were wide-ranging and included Introduction to the Old

Testament, Introduction to the New Testament, Doctrine, Life of Christ, and a variety of practical offerings. While the courses were not as intellectually demanding as my senior math and sciences courses had been at MEI, they were all beneficial, although I did not apply myself to them as studiously as I should have.

Highlights for me were the choral concerts which we offered the larger community, gaining a better understanding of how to read and study Scripture, and simply a greater knowledge and a better understanding of Christianity. I also formed some important and lasting friendships.

One of my extra-curricular undertakings deserves special mention. My brother Ernie was teaching in a remote area in north-central British Columbia, some 200 kilometres west of Williams Lake. He let me know that if I could get myself to his location he, together with a guide, would take me hunting. I first had to get permission from my father. Rather reluctantly he said I could go. I had no gun. My friend Abe Warkentin said I could borrow his 303 rifle.

How could I get to that rather distant and remote place? I decided I would take the gun apart, package it unobtrusively, pack only the absolutely essential items into (I think) a rucksack, and hitchhike. That's what I did. Perhaps surprisingly, I got rides quickly. Maybe I had to buy a bus ticket for the last distance - my memory has faded on that detail.

Ernie was boarding with a Mrs. French. She hosted me royally. Within a day or so we set out. The guide took the two of us and, as I recall, two other men further west into moose country. It did not take us long to spot some moose. With the aid of the guide I bagged a large bull. The other hunters were also successful. It did not take us long to clean out the animals. The carcasses were trucked out. Since the weather was cold, they could be stored outside without the meat spoiling. I think it was the next day that I managed to arrange for two American hunters who were headed back home via Sumas, near Abbotsford, to take my moose and me on their large truck with their own moose and drop us off in Abbotsford. To say that my parents were surprised that Sunday evening is to put it mildly. Fortunately, it was cold when we arrived in Abbotsford so we could hang the rather bulky moose in the garage.

Next day I was back in class. I think I had missed three days. When I told my friends that I had gone hunting and had bagged a moose, they smiled in disbelief. I then asked dad for the use of the car during the lunch hour and drove my doubting friends to see the evidence. I opened the garage door. They were surprised, impressed, and silenced.

That evening I had to tend to the carcass. Even though temperatures were quite low, the meat was not frozen. I needed to act. That evening my parents got all the moose meat they could freeze or can. As I recall, some of my teachers got lots of meat - a sort of peace offering for missed classes. So did others, including my future in-laws. Rather quickly a lot of people learned how to cure moose meat to get the "wild taste" out of it and how to prepare it well. In our family we had a unique source of protein for quite a long time. We had lots of moose steaks and moose-burgers.

A related item should be mentioned. It was while on the moose-hunting trip that my brother Ernie asked me to do him a favour. He had developed a strong romantic relationship with a lovely young lady, Jean Sawatzky, then working at Woodward's in Vancouver. He very much wanted to send her a romantic Christmas card but had no way of buying one. He asked me to buy one and write an affectionate statement and not only a few words. He provided the postal address. I agreed and followed through on the request. I learned how to duplicate Ernie's handwriting and signature. I wrote a very romantic statement of love, signed it as *Ernie*. The scheme worked. Doubtless, for many other reasons, the romance flourished. I never revealed the truth and I don't think Ernie did. I guess Jean was so excited about getting this outstanding card from Ernie that she never noticed that the postmark showed it was mailed from Abbotsford, not Big Creek. Hopefully, the good Lord overlooked my well-intentioned duplicity. I might say that this undertaking was the first of various experiences as a ghostwriter. In one case, many years later, a prominent national politician paid me $500 to write a major speech for him.

My Railway Career

Shortly after the Bible School classes ended I landed a very interesting job. I became a third cook for the Canadian Pacific Railway Dining Service. After some on-site training and a training trip on the Kettle Valley run to BC's southern interior, I was ready to get to work. I greatly enjoyed that work. My responsibility lay mostly in the areas of soups and pies. I made many a trip to Banff, Winnipeg, and St. Paul/Minneapolis. The work in the small, hot galley was hard but we had various breaks. Unless we were deadheading, that is taking an empty train to pick up a load or returning empty, the routine was as follows. After dinner, we would clean up the dining car and bring out the cots. We would try to get to bed by 9:30 or 10. Because I was the third cook, it was my job to get up about 3:45 AM and get breakfast ready for the entire dining car crew. We had breakfast around 4:30 AM.

Then we removed our cots, set up the tables, put on the linens and silverware and the decorations. The kitchen crew then did advance preparation of hot cereals, bacon, ham, and sausages, varieties of toasts and hotcakes, and whatever else on the menu which we could prepare in advance. I was surprised to see the passengers generally line up by 6:30 or even at 6:00 AM. I think we allowed them in at 7:00.

I particularly enjoyed the several times that we took a trainload of soldiers from Winnipeg to Vancouver where they would depart for action in the Korean War. Well before mealtime the commanding officer would come in and announce which items he had selected from our menu, and everyone, except perhaps the officers, got the same fare. That made cooking easy for the hundreds of troops. The troops were jovial but at times also very serious. They knew that some of them would not come back and that some would return seriously maimed.

The first cook usually prepared very fine noon lunches and dinners for the crew. During mid-afternoon we had about an hour and a half of free time. I really enjoyed those hours travelling through the mountains and also the prairies. I never got tired of the sights. Sometimes, with the top half of the galley intake door open, I would lean out and enjoy the smell of hay.

There were also some unpleasant experiences. Early on, I noticed that just before leaving Vancouver, the first cook was handing meats to someone outside the galley intake door. He would then wire or phone back for "missing" meats to be supplied at some stop. I remember mentioning this theft. The second cook then poured hot grease over my shoes and warned me not to talk. I heard later that the first cook's thievery was discovered and he was fired. Sadly, I have no picture of my summertime career in a tall white hat.

John on his 1951 moose-hunting trip in central British Columbia.

The University of British Columbia   September 1952 - April 1955; also Summer 1957 and Extension Studies 1957 - 1958 for my B. Ed. (Grad. Prog.)

After my first summer as a third cook in a CPR dining car which generated substantial funds for me, I enrolled at UBC. I had not yet decided on a career path, so I took a variety of social science, science, and humanity courses. Having reluctantly set aside law, I had thought of a career in medicine but soon discovered that I did not like even the elementary lab work and decided to complete majors in history and science. By taking an extra course in 1952-53 as well as in 1953-54 and summer school, 1953 and 1954, I managed to complete the requirements for the three-year Bachelor of Arts in two years.

Tuition costs were low in those days. I believe that I paid $250 for each of the two semesters. The additional Alma Matter Society fees and my book costs added perhaps another $150 per term. Given that I had saved most of my summer earnings, I managed to get by financially provided that I practiced serious frugality.

At that time UBC, the only university in the province - there were a few two-year colleges - had a student population of only about 5,500. There had been a surge of veterans moving through the programs after World War II but they were gone by 1952.

In those days it was customary to post a notice on the appropriate campus bulletin board requesting a ride from your location to campus. Living near 12th and Cambie streets I did that. Before long I had arranged for a fellow student to pick me up in time for 8:30 AM classes and bring me home later in the afternoon. I think I traveled with him for a modest fee five days a week. There were probably four of us in his small British car. What struck me even then was that as we traveled, the driver would turn to the CBC station so that we all listened to *Morning Devotions* with its theme song, Handel's Water Music. Times have changed.

The first year I roomed with my long-time friend and MEI classmate, John Isaak, a student in the Normal School as the teacher training school was then called. We rented a room which was really part of an attic. We shared a double bed. As I recall, we had a hotplate but, to the best of my recollection, not a refrigerator. This seriously limited how we could cook for ourselves. Even so, we had a great time. I don't recall who washed the linens or how often.

Sometime in the second term, our situation became somewhat complicated. My friend Neil Toews, then dating my sister Sophie, needed a place to stay for some months if my memory serves me right. He had a night-shift job and needed a place to sleep during the day. John Isaak and I decided that since we were both away from our room for each weekday, he could sleep in our bed during the day. Neil would go home weekends, as I recall. At that time I was guilty of one of my many shortcomings. John Isaak and I had not checked with our landlady, living on the first floor, about having another person sleep in our bed during the daytime. I recall that one day she stopped me and asked about this other fellow who frequently came to our room. Sheepishly I had to acknowledge the unusual arrangement we had made. The good landlady very kindly forgave us and allowed our bed-sharing enterprise to continue. I don't recall how we handled the linens.

During the summer of 1953 I took a full load of summer classes because I wanted to complete my Bachelor of Arts degree as quickly as possible. I still, however, had the months of May and June and the last two weeks of August to be employed. As I recall, I worked on the train in those times.

The second year, 1953-54, I roomed with Ed Bauman, another former MEI classmate. That, too, was a good year. By that time I had more or less decided that I would become a high school teacher. Finances were a little tight but I managed to work some Saturdays for my brother-in-law, Abe Wieler, who was a master carpenter, cabinet maker, and house builder. I actually learned some valuable carpentry skills that stood me in very good stead later. My parents would very much have wanted to provide financial help but they had no spare funds. They wished me well and, I am sure, prayed diligently for me. As I recall, my dad once gave me $10 during my UBC years. I remember that once I pawned my signet ring to get funds for food but I did manage to redeem it.

Although I always took a full load of courses, there were many other aspects to campus life. I got involved in student politics and became president of a campus politics club. A major interest was the Letters Club which consisted of students with high marks who wanted to probe various topics and met every two weeks or so to hear each other's special research papers. After a student was admitted to the club, the practice was for each student to make as strong a case as possible for a perspective on some important topic and then be subjected to vigorous questioning by the other students. I think we met mostly in professors' homes. On March 23, 1954, I somewhat hesitatingly presented my research paper on *The Book of Genesis*. There were many questions from some smart students who did not consider Genesis to be inspired Scripture. That was a very challenging evening for me, a real trial by fire, but I think it went well.

Another major interest of mine was being part of the UBC debating team for two years. We represented UBC locally but also at tournaments in the US.

One year a fellow student, Walter Young, and I won the Legion Cup for which teams from various locations contended.

The impromptu speaking contests were the ones that I enjoyed the most. The contestant stands behind a lectern, is then given a topic and has, as I recall, 10 minutes to speak on it. I relished those challenges. What fun it was to wax eloquent about some city, world leader, tribal custom, the Great Pyramid, an extinct bird, a political party, a war, some food, or the origin of a word. Never before or since have I spoken so enthusiastically, complete with gestures and deep emotion, concerning a topic about which I actually knew very little and sometimes nothing.

Bachelor of Arts, 1954.

The purpose was to impress the judges with what you claimed to know and how you expressed it. In writing this, I am reminded of a note a UN delegate allegedly left on the lectern in the UN General Assembly Hall. It would have applied to some of my impromptu speaking: "Weak point, shout here."

During the summer of 1954, I attended summer school in July and part of August but again cooked on a CPR dining car in May and June and part of August. Because the shifts on the train were so long, about 16 hours a day, I had about as many weekdays at home as on the train. This enabled me to do other work, typically picking berries or working for my brother-in-law as a carpenter's helper.

In August, 1954, I completed My Bachelor of Arts degree with First Class Honours with majors in history and science. By that time, I had decided to take the Graduate Teacher Training Program at UBC the following year.

In September 1954 I again enrolled at UBC. This time I roomed with John Dueck whom I also knew from MEI days. He later became a medical doctor with a practice in Chilliwack. Again we batched, this time in a small basement room near UBC, but we also ate out more. Money was not quite as tight as previously. To augment my resources, I found a job teaching an evening class at a private school catering mostly to adults who wanted to complete high school. Located on 10th Avenue near the UBC gates, it was called the BC School of Science and Matriculation. Teaching there allowed me to discover that I really enjoyed that profession.

In fall 1954, near the beginning of the academic year, I was surprised to be asked by university officials to be the coach of the UBC debating team. We actually had a very successful year. In fall our team went to a tournament at the College of Puget Sound in Tacoma, WA. Teams from 25 universities competed. A postcard I sent to Doris states that on one day my team debated four times and that we were scheduled to have seven debates the next day. As I recall, our UBC team came second in debating and ranked high in impromptu speaking and in the other categories.

A very important development happened in the latter part of the second term, probably in early March 1955. Various scholarship and exchange programs were advertised on campus. One that particularly appealed to me was offered by the *Deutsche Academische Austausch Dienst*, the DAAD, the German Academic Exchange Program. It offered several awards. The top one paid for room, board, some train travel, and tuition at any German university. I applied and was interviewed, as I recall, by the German Consul for Vancouver and two professors. I must have met their expectations because in late March I received word that I had received the top award. I was given perhaps a few weeks to confirm my acceptance.

Now I faced a problem, a very serious personal dilemma. Doris and I had planned to be married in the summer of 1955, shortly before I would be starting my high school teaching career. At this time Doris was working for the Royal Bank in Abbotsford. We faced a difficult choice. Should I accept the excellent DAAD award which meant we would postpone our wedding for a year, or should we stay with our existing plan, get married, and settle down to work at our jobs. We decided we would take a drive to Mt. Baker and spend some hours there weighing all the factors and then make a decision. I am sure we both prayed about this matter.

That day, in a delightful spot on the slopes of Mt. Baker, was a very challenging one. In the final analysis Doris played a key role in our decision. She would be the one most disappointed if our wedding were delayed a year. I give her full credit for looking at the long-term consequences and deciding with me that I should accept the scholarship award and go to Germany. As I recall, there were tears. I was and remain profoundly indebted to Doris for allowing me to pursue this dream. We made the right decision. I happily informed the Awards Committee that I would accept the DAAD award. I also stated that I had selected Heidelberg University as the location for my studies. Now many kinds of preparations lay ahead.

I should add here that during my last year at UBC I did take a modest student loan, I think about $250, which I managed to repay reasonably soon. I do not remember exactly when.

Reflections on My Time at the University of British Columbia

Because my years at UBC were years of finding myself spiritually and intellectually and had a profound effect in shaping my vocational choice, my life values, and my world view, I shall review that experience in some detail.

The challenges at the university were substantial. I had sound study habits, was well prepared academically, and was highly motivated. I had not, however, been adequately prepared intellectually. Concerning university studies I had received more warnings than preparation.

UBC was an entirely new world—socially, ethically, and intellectually. My traditional ethics were challenged, my worldview was questioned, and the prevailing perspectives on faith were decidedly antithetical. Moreover, almost all my brilliant and personable professors brought into question what my other role models had preached and practiced in "the Valley." I observed that on campus the spiritual dimension of life was routinely trumped by the intellectual. The neat categories and fixed boundaries I had acquired as a child and which had been carefully nurtured in later years became less evidently right.

As I interacted with professors and students, I found it difficult to feel part of a community that was definitely more inclined to reject evangelicalism than to understand it. It was painful to hear, sometimes in thinly veiled words, that smart people outgrow God. At the time I had neither the knowledge nor the courage to reply with something like Charles Malik's perceptive and cogent assertion that "The universities would not have come into being in the first place without Christ." While few professors took advantage of their status to belittle students' beliefs, those who did so illustrate a phenomenon I have since encountered in many academic situations, namely, that anti-evangelicalism is the antisemitism of intellectuals. I am also reminded of a comment in a *Times* editorial: "A blinkered secularism is no better than theological dogmatism."

Some of us Mennonite students from "the Valley" suddenly found ourselves living in two worlds: the university and the home community. This bifurcation was a function of time and location. During the week we were immersed in the partly daunting, partly liberating ,UBC milieu. But weekends we usually retreated to the familiar and psychologically supportive sanctuaries of our staunchly conservative Mennonite home communities. There our traditional values and worldview were reinforced. "Care packages" from home strengthened these family and community ties.

The bifurcation was also intellectual. Part of us clung to the fixed notions of the past, but another part accepted the new values we encountered. This geographical and situational duality became increasingly frustrating as we matured intellectually in the university setting.

Christians, we had been taught, were to see the university campus as a place to witness about their faith. I concurred with that view, but how? My first foray was not successful. I recall asking a new friend whether he believed that the Bible was inspired. He thought a bit, then said, "Yes, just like Shakespeare." Unprepared for that reply, I had no appropriate response.

As young adults we faced the challenge of how to develop greater autonomy of thought without becoming, or being perceived as, rebellious. We had to learn how to question some things without questioning all things. Indeed, the habit of questioning is quickly learned and easily applied. At times it was difficult to decide what issues fell within the boundaries of responsible dialogue and questioning and which did not. The distinction between merely holding differing views and rejecting some as wrong became blurred. On the one hand, we still believed that God's Word is truth and that the Spirit guides us to truth but, on the other hand, we were investing heavily in alternate paths to truth. More than a few of us struggled with the dilemma of how to develop an inquiring mind without setting aside religious commitments. Initially, I was reluctant to set aside anything of what I had learned. I would have been far less anxious about such questions had I known James Russell Lowell's maxim: "The foolish and the dead alone never change their opinions."

We quickly learned to focus on questions but we did not want to question all things, nor did we want to elevate questioning to the rank of the highest intellectual virtue. We tried to reconcile our faith in Christ with our growing commitment to abstract reasoning. We had yet to learn that there is no inherent contradiction between Christian faith and God-given reason. Also, eventually, I came to realize that faith and doubt can co-exist. John Donne's famous 17th-century axiom was helpful: "doubt wisely."

The idea that a thoroughly committed Christian can have lingering doubts, especially about details, was for me a releasing realization.

Put another way, it was a struggle to reconcile deep faith with an inquiring mind. Can a person offer confident answers to ultimate questions while cultivating a critical mind? And what do we do if our search for truth threatens to undermine the truth we know by faith? Unfortunately, some professors intimated or even stated that religious faith requires the suspension of the mind. Fortunately, reading great Christian thinkers such as C. S. Lewis and Reinhold Niebuhr helped me to understand that brilliant people can be people of great faith and that faith often guides and transcends reason. I also found it helpful to understand that "faith is not belief without proof but trust without reservation."

Those of us taking a heavy load of science courses usually (in my case all as far as I know) had professors who held no religious beliefs. They assumed the validity of the theory of evolution and rejected all notions of creation. This left us scrambling to find a way to subscribe to the validity of scientific research without accepting the belief that the scientific method is the only road to truth.

We also had to learn tolerance for other people's views, whatever they might be. We came to realize the value of understanding other religions and even learning from them instead of simply refuting them. I still believed that certain faiths were not based on truth but I now had friends who belonged to them!

InterVarsity Christian Fellowship (IVCF) became our most significant spiritual support. It helped bridge Christian and academic communities, provided campus-based spiritual nurture, constituted a network of Christian friends, offered excellent social events, and functioned as a supportive Christian community. Recent scholarship has shown that the need for community looms large for university students not living at home, particularly if they are struggling with how to maintain a connection with a traditional community or grappling with the consequences of gradually losing or rejecting it.

During our university years, most of us retained memberships in the Valley churches where we were baptized. Beyond stoking nostalgia for simpler times, this connection provided a sense of still belonging to a faith community and strong affirmation from our families. Nevertheless, the challenge of functioning in two ethically distinct, intellectually disparate and, in the main, religiously antithetical communities was a major one for me and many other Christian UBC students in the 1950s.

As I see it now, we students had not yet learned that tension is a goal in learning, that challenges and friction and questioning can make a Christian a better student as well as a more mature believer

My UBC years were especially significant because I had not yet developed my own *Weltanschauung.* I was still in the early stages of integrating my Christian commitment with academics. Later, after four years of high school teaching and progressing in graduate studies, I was more fixed in my orientation and the tensions I encountered had fewer consequences.

During my UBC studies I was sustained by family, personal faith, supportive friends, and excellent books. While the winds of secular humanism buffeted me, I can say with integrity that eventually they merely drove the roots of my faith deeper into my being. I am grateful to God, parents and to many friends for supporting me. What also helped to stabilize and sustain me was the realization that the students and professors who challenged my spiritual convictions and way of life had nothing of substance to put in their place. Their ethical relativism and lack of spiritual telos simply did not appeal to me. They focused mainly on questions. What I needed were answers. The preachers back home offered me much more of a credible purpose in life than they did.

In fact, it strikes me that there is an inherent illogic in much academic activity in the past and still today. Many a professor has stressed that the central pursuit of academic research is the pursuit of truth. So far, so good. But most of these same people also say or imply that they will not be committed to any dogmatic truth. In fact, many say that apart from the hard sciences and math, there is no truth that they will ever affirm, no absolute truth which they will accept and by which they will live. If they will not accept the truth for which they are searching and researching, then why search and research? Why pursue such truth?

Looking back on more than 60 years of academic involvement on various campuses, I can say with conviction that a Christian's experience of higher education can be strongly positive. Pursuing a college or university education need not involve a Faustian bargain of selling one's soul for academic success. Nurturing the soul and seeking intellectual understanding can complement and enhance one another.

All things considered, my university student experiences in the 1950s and 1960s were a challenging but positive, liberating, mind-expanding, and definitely faith-deepening time.

The Beginning of a Writing Career - *The Canadian Mennonite*

Although I had a few minor items published previously and in high school was the editor for one year of the student paper, *The Student's Call,* my first article written for a newspaper appeared in *The Canadian Mennonite* on December 10, 1954. After he published this article, editor Frank Epp expressed interest in having me write for that weekly paper. The result was a 15-year association with him and his paper. My files, which are not complete, contain 87 articles written for *The Canadian Mennonite* between 1954 and 1969. This number does not include the various articles I wrote for the 1956 special issue of his paper which is described in Chapter 10. These 87 articles fall into four categories. During those years I wrote at least 24 feature articles including the following. "Should Traditional Church Auctions be Re-Evaluated?" (February 17, 1956); "We Must Evaluate What We Believe." (July 6, 1956); "Why are Mennonites disliked in Canada?" (July 27, 1956); "Mode of Baptism - How Important?" (March 3, 1961); and "Guidelines for a Christian Response to Revolution." (January 21, 1969).

During 1955-1956 I wrote 30 columns entitled *This Is The World Today*. Most of them dealt with my experiences overseas as a student. Here are two examples. "Christianity and the Cold War" (January 13, 1956) and "A glimpse at Yugoslavia." (May 18, 1956).

In late 1959 it occurred to me that it might be useful to write some perhaps more controversial columns using a pseudonym. Frank let me proceed. From October 1959 until July 1960 I wrote 30 columns entitled *As I see It* by *Depictu*s. Some were statements of my opinion. Some were items by others on a theme. They generated interesting responses. Here are two examples. "Idle worship leads to idol worship" (October 9, 1959); "The essence of non-conformity" (June 24, 1960).

Three times Frank had me write guest editorials. For me, a neophyte writer, that was a special privilege and honour. They were: *A Critical Spirit* (August 26, 1960); *Silent Participation* (September 21, 1960); and *Christianity and Capitalism* (July 7, 1961).

Frank's trust in me, his helpful comments, and his encouragement of me as a writer played a major role in launching me as a writer of columns and articles for the next six decades. I am deeply indebted to him.

Relevant Political and Public Affairs 1951 - 1955

Although my university years were filled with studies, work, and as much romance as I could fit in, I continued to be greatly interested in politics. On campus I was active in several political clubs and served as president of the Social Credit Club, which was actually a conservative club. Given that the Socreds were in office in Victoria, we had major speakers visit us. Some members of our club were invited to the legislature in Victoria and were introduced to the members and the media.

I also became involved in the Abbotsford Social Credit Constituency Association as much as time would permit. I remember that, at the age of 20, I was given the privilege of nominating Rev. Alex Patterson to be the Social Credit candidate for the Fraser Valley riding for the August 10, 1953, Canadian election. He won easily and served several terms with distinction. At this time many Mennonites and other conservative Christians were switching their political support to Social Credit.

National and world affairs continued to hold much interest for me. Canada's involvement in the Korean War became very important, partly because I had some interaction with troops and officers while working on the train. The perpetual question was whether the Korean conflict would expand to become World War III. As it turned out, the Allied and communist forces fought to a stand-off and a cease-fire line was negotiated which remains the border today between The Republic of Korea and the communist Democratic People's Republic of Korea.

John and Harvey Dyck on their DKW motorcycle, 1956.

CHAPTER 6

THE ADVENTURES OF A TWO-MONTH TEACHER

Some weeks before the completion of my teacher-training year, we student-teachers were informed that numerous BC schools were desperately in need of teachers for May and June. We were strongly encouraged to help. I applied for a position and very quickly found myself hired to teach a class of 33 pupils in grades 4, 5, 6, and 7 in one room in a three-room school, Narcosli Creek School, about 70 kilometres south of Quesnel, on the west side of the Fraser River. I think my salary was about $300 a month. This seems very low but we must remember that in 1955 the price of gasoline in BC was about 29 cents per gallon, not per litre. I also wrote Doris that my food costs consisting of groceries bought at the one local store came to about $20 a month.

The bus trip from Abbotsford to Quesnel and then Narcosli took me through the beautiful Fraser Canyon and other scenery and would have been quite delightful had it not been for the fact that I had just had my tonsils removed and despite whatever pain killer I took, my throat felt like a ball of fire. As we got closer to my destination, I was preoccupied with the thought of how I would handle the first day when, with almost no preparation time, I would face a class of four grades, each grade waiting for me to teach them 7 or 8 lessons per day.

My accommodation was a small cabin for which I paid $25 a month. I had a sawdust stove for cooking and heat but no refrigerator. This made cooking a little difficult. There was only one store with a garage and post office. If the owner of the store and garage was thus inclined, he started up his generator which gave me electricity some evenings. That enabled me to pick up some stations on my little radio during those hours. Mail arrived on Fridays if the roads were passable.

A few weeks after arriving at Narcosli, my Abbotsford mail was forwarded to me and I received my marks for the 1954-55 year at UBC. I was pleased to see that my graduate year of teacher training had resulted in First Class Honors. I thank God that he has always given me the health and motivation to work hard at my studies.

The Narcosli School situation was challenging. Because their previous teacher had gone on maternity leave, these grades had missed about five weeks of school. This situation created a huge challenge for me. I had to prepare lessons for four grades while also trying to catch up on the month of missed classes. The situation was further complicated by the fact that many pupils, decent and likable though they were, had very little interest in school. Some seemed to be anticipating the time when they reached the age where they could drop out. They were more interested in ranching, hunting, fishing, logging and the outdoors generally than in studies. I spent long hours preparing lessons in arithmetic, language, spelling, art, social studies, literature, health and reading. On top of that, there was the marking of many assignments. I think that I earned my salary. My initial impressions were mixed. In my first letter back to Doris, written May 2, a few days after my arrival, I wrote, "I wouldn't teach here for a year even if they paid me $500 a month. but for two months, it will be all right."

The children loved sports. I was also in charge of athletics and organized various games. We soon developed a fine softball team and actually played games with at least one other school. The fact that this area was indeed part of BC's hinterland was impressed upon me one day when a moose sauntered across the softball diamond.

Of all my memories of my short stint as an elementary teacher, the following event is perhaps most vividly remembered. During one of the last days in June, the school superintendent, Mr. Mouat, arrived to carry out his inspection. He visited classes and interviewed us three teachers. For some reason, after his visits he met with principal Gordon and me in one of the classrooms. While he was talking to the principal and me seated in that classroom, a pupil threw a mudball through the open-top transit window. It splattered noisily against the blackboard. There was silence - embarrassing silence. Mr. Mouat then turned to the principal and calmly said, "You're fired!" or words to that effect. He then turned to me and asked if I would accept an appointment to be principal for the coming year. I must say here that Mr. Mouat had been a school superintendent in a district where my brothers Paul and Ernie were teachers and obviously thought very highly of them. I think that I benefited from their stellar reputations.

I told Mr. Mouat that I was greatly honoured by his offer but that I had been awarded a scholarship to study in Germany for the coming year and was thus not in a position to consider his very generous offer. My walk, alongside the principal, back to our cabins that day was not a happy time, even if it was the last or virtually the last day of the school year.

One other important experience must be recounted. Given that there was no religious service held in the area, I typically spent part of Sundays in the nearby woods. That was a good time to enjoy the outdoors, relax, daydream, meditate, dream of Doris, and plan. One Sunday, deep in the woods, I sat down and leaned against a tree. As time passed I was close to falling asleep and shifted my body a little lower on the tree. At almost the same second, a bullet slammed into the tree just above my head. I saw the shooter but not very clearly. In the thickly-treed forest he must have mistaken my clothing for an animal. He must then have suddenly realized what his target actually was, and immediately hurried away. I wonder if he ever knew whether he had hit me. Thank you God, for sparing my life!

I almost certainly came within seconds or inches of being shot. This was the first of at least four times when I firmly believe that divine or angelic intervention spared my life. Each such occurrence reminded me that my days are numbered and that God spared my life for a purpose. Increasingly I have tried to live by my motto, "To serve God and others." I believe that serving others is a way of thanking God.

After the Narcosli Creek School employment ended, I again took up employment as the third cook in a CPR dining car. My focus at that point was to prepare for my trip to Europe and to earn money which I would need for the travel to some countries in northern Europe, which I planned to do before classes began in Heidelberg in late October.

Doris and John in the Fraser River Canyon.

CHAPTER 7

HEIDELBERG AND TRAVEL IN EUROPE 1955-1956

Travel and the Fall Semester

On September 5, 1955, I set out for Europe. I had decided that before classes began at Heidelberg University in October, I would travel in northern Europe. This would involve a lot of hitch-hiking as well as some bus and train travel. What would I take with me? Clearly, not much. I acquired a middle-sized suitcase that I could easily carry with me and filled it with several sets of clothes, my Bible, a few other books, a camera, and some personal effects. As I recall, my suitcase weighed about 25 pounds. It traveled with me for many a mile when hitch-hiking, on a bus or train, on plane rides, and on ferries. In retrospect it is amazing that I could get by for almost a year with what I could carry in my trusty brown suitcase.

My DAAD scholarship covered all my student expenses, including travel in Europe to Heidelberg, but obviously not the additional travel that I planned to undertake. My first challenge was to get to Montreal, from where I would board an ocean liner for Europe.

As it happened, my aunt and her husband, Nora and Peter Warkentin, were planning to travel to Waterloo, Ontario by car in early September so Peter could enroll at a university there. Unfortunately, he had broken his leg and had a major cast which meant he could not drive. Nora did not want to drive that distance by herself. Thus I got a free ride all the way to Waterloo. Peter sat in the back of the Volkswagen Beetle with his leg stretched out. All things considered, we had a good trip and managed to visit many relatives and see the homestead where I was raised. In my correspondence to Doris I mentioned that one evening in Minnesota, we paid $6 for a two-bedroom motel unit. Rates have changed.

At this point I should probably note the following reality. Before I left Doris I told myself, not her, that I would write her a card or letter for every day that I was away. I think I kept that commitment. Doris received a card or letter for every day I was away except for the last few days when I would arrive before any mail sent to her. Those cards and letters are extremely useful now as I recreate and summarize almost a full year's activities overseas.

On September 12 I took the train from Kitchener to Ottawa where I visited Doris's brother Ruben and his wife Mavis, relatively newlyweds. From Ottawa I traveled by train to Montreal.

On September 13, 1955, I boarded the Cunard Steamship liner *Ascania*. I was truly impressed with all its amenities, the outstanding cuisine, and the beautiful rooms and lounges on the ship. All went very well until we encountered a huge storm in the North Atlantic. The fierce winds created waves about 30 feet high, which caused some water to wash onto the first two decks. As a totally uninitiated land person, I was a bit frightened but the crew seemed fully at ease and in control. As I recall, at the height of the storm, only six of us passengers showed up for a certain meal. At times I felt queasy, but I never got seasick. After the storm subsided, the ship suddenly encountered some huge icebergs. As I recall, the navigators had to make some quick directional adjustments to avoid them. Looking at those beautiful, huge hulks on the horizon it was easy to envision what happened to the Titanic.

After a one-night stop in La Havre, France, our ship docked at Southampton, September 23. Following a train ride to London I spent my first night on British soil in a hotel room for which I paid $2.

After three amazing days seeing the sights of London, I left for Heidelberg, arriving there on September 27. Although fall classes at Heidelberg University did not begin until late October, I needed to get there well in advance to

Trafalgar Square, London

John viewing Heidelberg from the *Philosophen Weg* (Philosopher's Path).

report to the DAAD officials and to arrange for accommodation. Although the DAAD paid for my accommodation and meals, I still needed to apply to stay in a university residence or make arrangements elsewhere.

I spent September 28, 29, and 30 getting established in Heidelberg. My first choice for accommodation was a four-story former monastery called *Collegium Academicum*, located only a block or so from the main campus. This residence had its own food service although it provided no breakfasts. Fortunately, my monthly DAAD grant more than covered my costs, including breakfast. Covering my own breakfast costs was worth it to me because of other advantages. I immediately submitted my application to the residence officials. Then I spent a few days familiarizing myself with the absolutely beautiful and very old city, the surrounding hills, and the Neckar River, which flows through the city.

After some interviews I was invited to become a *Collegiate* and thus a resident in the very desirable *Collegium Academicum*. There were many advantages and benefits in living in that building. The place offered numerous activities and presentations by residents and invited experts. The students living there formed numerous interest groups and clubs. There was always a lot happening. The meals were generally quite good especially given the fact that finances were very tight for this residence. One thing that I had to get used to was the great respect and deference that the servants at the residence extended to us, mostly graduate and professional school students.

Given my generous monthly allowance from the DAAD in Bonn, I was able to live well on that allowance and managed to put aside some funds for future travel.

Heidelberg is located in that part of Germany liberated by the US Army in World War II. It was not bombed during the war. The Americans had announced their plan in a German ditty: *"Heidelberg werden wir schonen weil dort wollen wir wohnen."* (We will spare Heidelberg because that is where we want to live.) True to their word, the US Army officials established a large headquarters just outside the city. I was privileged to visit there on occasion as a guest of a military person and could then buy North American goods at the PX store. I might add here that during all of World War II only one bomb was accidentally dropped on Heidelberg. That bomb reportedly killed one person, the only daughter of an industrialist from the Ruhr area who had placed his daughter in Heidelberg to keep her safe during the war.

On October 1, 1955, I set out on a major sightseeing trip to parts of northern Europe, now carrying only the essentials I would need for almost a month. Most of the time I hitch-hiked which was usually successful. Sometimes I took the train or bus. At times, of course, I took ferries.

For this 22-year-old who, prior to this trip, had never before been further afield than the three western provinces in Canada and the northern areas of a few northern states, the sights were almost overwhelming. Having joined the Youth Hostel Society, I stayed at youth hostels most nights. When no hostel was available, or it had no space, I stayed at the YMCA or some very low-cost alternative. As I recall, one night I found myself fairly late in a rural area of the Netherlands and, there being no other alternative at hand and the weather being mild, I wandered into a farmer's field and slept on the ground. Jacob of old rested his head on a stone. I had my little carrying case. I actually slept well.

For the next 24 days I toured some amazing sights in north Germany, spent a few days in Copenhagen and, after a delightful ferry ride, toured Malmo and Lund in Sweden. Turning back, I traveled to Hamburg where I met a gentleman who, upon discovering that I was a Canadian, expressed his profound gratitude to Canada for liberating that coastal region by giving me a truly impressive tour of the city. I spent several days touring areas of The Netherlands and Belgium and then took a ship back to the United Kingdom. Having spent some days in London previously, I hitch-hiked to Scotland. I was fortunate to get a long ride, as I recall, from the northern limits of London all the way into southern Scotland. The gentleman who picked me up was very kind. Unfortunately, his little old car, it was probably an Austin or Hillman, was in poor condition. I noticed as I sat on the front seat beside the driver that I could look down through a fairly large hole in the floor and see the road surface. Clearly, I needed to be careful.

After a few days touring several beautiful cities and the highlands of Scotland, I took the ferry from Stranraer, Scotland, to Northern Ireland. The Emerald Isle did not disappoint. At times I did have difficulty understanding the heavy Irish brogue but the people were absolutely delightful, helpful, and kind. After returning to Stranraer, I toured western England and Wales. By October 19, I was back in London. Crossing to the continent I then toured parts of northern France, spending a few delightful days in Paris. What a city! After a day in the small country of Luxembourg I headed back to Heidelberg, arriving late on October 24

It is not possible to provide the pictures I have of the incredible spectrum of inspiring, amazing, and sometimes surprising sights I was privileged to see during that trip. Suffice it to say that no one can experience such a mind-stretching trip without becoming a grateful and different person. Previous assumptions of what was normal and usual were permanently expanded.

I believe it was on my first day back in Heidelberg, right after the evening meal, that all of us new *Collegiaten*, seated in a large room, were invited to find roommates. The policy was that we would live two in each of the fairly large rooms. I, of course, knew no one. I waited a short while and then noticed a handsome German, also sitting more or less alone. I walked over to him, introduced myself and began a conversation. It turned out that he also was unfamiliar with Heidelberg. He had come from communist East Germany and was a medical student. He, too, was a new *Collegiate*. Hermann Krieg and I struck it off immediately. We agreed to become roommates and registered as such. That arrangement turned out to be mutually beneficial. We became close friends.

John and Hermann Krieg, his roommate.

I must note, here, that while I had learned a reasonable amount of German at home, for two years as I recall at a Saturday German School, and had done well studying German at UBC, my conversational German was distinctly dated and totally lacked many of the changed meaning of words. I think it was during the initiation of *Neu*

Collegiaten that I had my first serious embarrassment. In the German I learned at home, the word *blöd,* meant shy. Therefore, when I was asked to introduce myself, I knew that I could do that quite well but I also wanted to say that I was somewhat shy. I therefore said that I was a little *blöd.* The entire assembly of *Neu Collegiaten* burst into laughter. I had no idea why. After the session I asked Hermann why they had all laughed so much at my statement of shyness. He said that the meaning of *blöd* was "slightly insane."

Hermann and I had many very interesting and important conversations. He told me about his experiences in the *Hitler Jugend* (Hitler Youth) and his experiences during World War II. He told me how he escaped from East Germany and that he probably would never see his family again. I wondered if he and his family had been aware of the Holocaust against the Jews. He was quiet and then said that when he and his father, if my memory is accurate, needed to go in an open wagon, I think drawn by horses, past a certain establishment, apparently one of the extermination camps, the stench was so bad that they turned away. But nobody spoke much, not even to family members. Everyone feared what the SS might do if negative reports surfaced. Hermann and I enjoyed short walks to the famous Heidelberg *Schloss* (castle) ruins where concerts were given. There was much else to see and do in beautiful Heidelberg

My university courses included history, politics and sociology dealing with Germany and Europe generally. Since I would be in attendance for only one year, I did not attempt to qualify for any degree. The German university offerings, especially at that time, were very unstructured. Other than in professional programs such as medicine, law, teacher training, social work, nursing and engineering, students simply enrolled in courses and did extensive reading in preparation for a set of exams which they were generally allowed to take when they considered themselves ready to do so.

I also enrolled in the *Dolmetscher Institut*, the Translation School. There I took instruction in speaking German and in translation, both sequential and simultaneous, from German to English and English to German. At the end of the first term I sat for the exams and passed them. Now, in 2021, I would not trust myself to do a very good job of translating from English to German, especially in technical matters, but I am still comfortable translating from German to English.

A goal that I set for myself was to learn to speak German in a manner that would allow me to pass as a German. I had such a test near Christmastime. I attended a social gathering of students, and to my total delight during the entire evening, as far as I could tell, no one detected that I was not a German. Of course, I also had to dress like a German, which required some attention, especially because my wardrobe budget was almost non-existent.

I should perhaps add here that while, at times, I attended church services in one of the cathedrals, especially the *Heilige Geist Kirche*, I actually became part of a fairly small German Baptist congregation. Here, again, the people welcomed me warmly and were very hospitable and friendly.

As Christmas approached, my thoughts turned to home and especially to Doris whom I missed greatly. Although students could stay in their rooms and meals were available, the university itself closed down for holidays from December 23 until January 9. Since my intention for the entire year abroad was to learn and experience as much as I could, I decided to take advantage of the offer to spend Christmas with a German family.

Three Holiday Celebrations

The administrators in the *Collegium Academicum* worked very hard to make the German experience as beneficial and interesting for foreign students as they could. Among the many things they did was to arrange for us to spend Christmas in the home of a German family. I happily accepted their first recommendation.

On December 23 I was up real early to catch a fast train to Offenburg and then a truly slow train up the beautiful hills of the Black Forest to the old town of Koenigsfeld.

My host family was the Heinz Schmidt family. Heinz was the pastor of the local Moravian church. The Schmidts had seven children, with the oldest 18. I was impressed by the fact that this large family, obviously not well-off financially, had declared themselves willing to accept this Canadian student to celebrate Christmas with them. Pastor Schmidt and his family were amazing hosts.

On December 24 the congregation of about 200 to 300 assembled at 7:00 AM for an hour-long candlelight service to start the official Christmas celebration. I was told this is standard Moravian practice. The service consisted of small group and congregational singing, poems, readings, and violin music. It might be noted here that everything in the church, even the window drapes, was in white.

At 3:30 PM the congregation assembled again for the children's Christmas service which consisted almost entirely of children reciting their Christmas verses.

Following this service, families had their *Bescherung*, the giving of gifts. Obviously, the Schmidts were not well off. The children, as I recall, received almost no toys or games. They received fruit and books.

After that, the congregation assembled again for a very fine Christmas

Eve service with choir, orchestra, band, and pipe organ. Three Christmas services that day. On Christmas Day the congregation assembled again for another fine forenoon service.

I gained three valuable impressions from this visit. First, one does not need to eat exceptionally well in order to celebrate Christmas. Second, people do not need to be well-off to practice authentic hospitality. Third, children need not be showered with gifts to sense parental love. On December 26 I returned to Heidelberg.

On the 27th, after dealing with mail and other essentials, I packed a few things and began hitchhiking north. I got as far as Frankfurt and then, because there were 12 others hitchhiking at the same place, I decided to spend the money and travel by train to Detmold and Bielefeld where a Canadian-style Christmas awaited me. We celebrated at both locations.

The Canadian group, hosted by Canadians studying music in the *Detmold Musik Academie,* included Vic and Dorothy Martens, William and Lydia Reimer, John Wiebe, Wanda Dyck, Harvey Dyck, and theologian Clarence Bauman and Alice. Clarence was a doctoral student at the Bethel Seminary. Wanda came from Manitoba. All the rest of us came from the Fraser Valley in BC. I should note here that Harvey, son of principal Mr. I. J. Dyck, had won a DAAD scholarship to study at Hamburg University.

Canadian Students' Christmas Retreat.
Back row L to R: John Webe, Alice Bauman, Wanda Dyck, guest, Bill Reimer, Dorothy Martens.
Front row: Clarence Bauman, John Redekop, Lydia Reimer, Victor Martens.
Harvey Dyck took the picture.

I should also state that during these days Harvey and I began planning a major trip south at the end of the winter term.

The Canadian Student Retreat, as we named it, was simultaneously relaxing, inspiring, stimulating, and educational. We talked, hiked, slept, shared experiences, laughed, sang, prayed and ate. Dorothy and Lydia worked incredibly hard to provide Canadian meals like we had not had since we left home. Everyone pitched in. The overall hosting by the music students deserved an A+. Together we had several days of another great Christmas celebration.

On December 30 I took the train back to Heidelberg. Again my stay in the *Collegium Academicum* was brief. Before Christmas, the foreign students at Heidelberg University were informed that some generous German businessmen, probably alumni, had funded a major retreat for about 30 foreign students and about 30 students who had fled the communist *Deutsche Demokratische Republik* (East Germany). I applied and was accepted.

By noon on December 31, I embarked on my third holiday celebration. A two and a half-hour train ride into the beautiful mountains to the south took me to a castle. *Burg Liebenzoll*, located deep in the Black Forest, was built in the 12th century but has been somewhat, I stress somewhat, modernized. The large edifice was truly impressive.

This was a memorable New Year's celebration. I heard so many fascinating reports that I could hardly absorb all that I heard. I heard students from about 20 countries tell their stories. All spoke German well enough to be understood.

Although it was not announced as a Christian event, we sang in the New Year with *Nun Danket Alle Gott* ("Now thank we all our God"). On Sunday, January 1, a Protestant church service was held for everyone.

We played many games and sports, including a ping-pong tournament. Table tennis is a very popular sport among the students. In the final set of games I was to play an American student who had an amazing serve. He had defeated me previously. I practiced hard. In the final set I was fortunate to win all games.

As the lone Canadian I was invited to speak about Canada. I projected a set of slides and also projected a map. The students were impressed by the size and diversity of the country, especially the wide reaches of the north, and the various vistas. They had many questions.

On January 6 I returned to Heidelberg. This six-day third retreat capped a holiday season I shall not forget. Thank you *Deutsche Academische Austausch Dienst* for making all of this possible.

The Winter Term at Heidelberg ran from the end of October to the end of February. The weeks after the long Christmas holiday break required the completion of lectures and preparation for exams in my nine courses. As I reflect on those courses a few impressions should be noted. It struck me how many professors managed to bring the World Wars and the Nazi Era into their presentations even if the course content did not include these topics. While there was a spectrum of perspectives presented, all professors attributed significant guilt to German political leaders. Some, however, took the view that because of economic tensions and rivalries, the Allies would have started World War II if Hitler had not done so. It is very difficult for students and professors to be both very critical of their country's past and also to be proud citizens of a country with the amazing cultural tradition and current economic achievement of which Germans can boast.

I must mention one humorous event. One day one of the professors failed to show up for a class. An American friend, Paul Froman, and I were both taking that course. We suddenly had the idea that we would tell the class that we would together offer to teach the lesson. Perhaps surprisingly, our fellow students agreed to our proposal. Since both Paul and I were quite familiar with the general content of the course, we held forth, without planning or rehearsal, in full form. The class went well. We never found out how the professor felt about it but, as I recall, he must have heard that the topic of the day was adequately taught because he moved on to the next topic in the course.

A distinctive reality that deserves comment is that while some professors delivered outstanding lectures, others simply read from some book or academic article they had written. It is not surprising that where we speak of lectures, the common German word is *Vorlesungen* (readings). Presumably, there was a time, some centuries ago, when readings were needed because books were not available.

My nine exams, I think five of them were oral, were spread over one week. The oral exams, obviously not a very efficient way of examining a class of students, were a new experience for me. In one course the oral exams involved questioning two students at the same time. I found this a more favourable approach because it often gave me more time to think. Never having taken German university exams previously, I had no idea what the results might be. Fortunately, my studying proved worthwhile. I received 6 A marks, 3 B marks and one C. I was one of six students in that division who achieved an A average. As I recall, the C was given in a course of advanced German grammar and composition. I had had difficulty using the various German moods correctly.

All things considered, my first term of German university classes was very beneficial. I am indebted to several brilliant professors who took time to assist this *Ausländer* (foreigner).

Fortunately for Harvey and me, the second semester at Heidelberg and also at Hamburg did not begin until May 2. We would have time for major travelling.

CHAPTER 8

TRAVEL IN AFRICA AND EUROPE

During our Christmas celebrations in Bielefeld and Detmold, Harvey Dyck and I began planning a major motorcycle trip through Switzerland and Italy to North Africa, across the Sahara, and some Middle Eastern countries. In January Harvey bought the type of motorcycle we planned to get. A 1954 two-cycle 225cc DKW. It was rather small for a major trip but it was all we could afford. It had about 10,000 kms on it. The price was DM 850 or about CD $250. Neither of us had ever driven a motorcycle. We both learned rather quickly.

Harvey Dyck and John on their DKW (Deutsche Kraftwagen) 225 cc.

We planned to leave right after exams. Because of the heavy snow and the icy conditions, Harvey shipped the motorcycle by train to Heidelberg. The road conditions were better in this more southerly part of Germany. We bought two sleeping bags, appropriate side-bags given that the motorcycle had no enclosed carrying units, some spare parts, and assorted other items for our trip. We were excited.

We left Heidelberg on March 2, 1956. Although the Autobahn was still partly covered with snow, we made it to Basel, Switzerland, the first day. There we learned that the Alps passes were closed so we shipped the motorcycle with us by train through the Gotthard Pass. After that we had no other road closures.

Italy

Travelling down the southern Alps by motorcycle was both breathtaking and inspiring. Touring southern Italy down to its toe and across Sicily brought us several unusual and interesting experiences. They started in Milan. While we stopped, waiting for a street light to change, a man ran out from the sidewalk, cut some cords and stole one of our sleeping bags. From that time on, when on our own, one of us had a sleeping bag and the other slept under our jackets. In Milan also we had the following experience. One of my student friends in Heidelberg was an Italian girl, Rosi Lausch. Her parents were

John and the DKW.

wealthy, I believe owners of a major newspaper. She had arranged for us to visit them. We were treated royally in their mansion. At one point Harvey and I were ushered into their fancy dining room where a waiter brought us the food. After some hors d'oeuvres and salads we were served excellent pasta. We really filled up on that. What we did not know is that in high-class Italian dining pasta is a standard preliminary dish. Then came the main course.

Unfortunately, we could not do justice to that outstanding fare. Also, we could only sample the fine desserts.

In Genoa we toured the house where Christopher Columbus lived. In Pisa, we scaled the Leaning Tower.

Rome was impressive but also brought us unusual experiences. Upon arrival we stopped at the Canadian Embassy to pick up letters from our sweethearts. Doris had written me several and Harvey got some from Anne Konrad. The embassy staff were very accommodating and helpful. Before we left they offered us each a Coke in a glass which we enjoyed. After driving around for perhaps 15 minutes we both began laughing and feeling light-headed. Then we realized that the embassy staff had spiked the Cokes and not only a little. We may not have been fully inebriated but with some alcohol on an empty stomach, we were definitely "under the influence." We were slightly drunk! We therefore decided, wisely, that we would not drive until we regained sobriety. We then simply parked the motorcycle right where we were, near the huge white monument of Victor Emmanuel the Second, sat down and laughed at our own predicament. It was some time, perhaps an hour or two, until we trusted ourselves to drive to the youth hostel.

Among the many exciting aspects of our several days in Rome, several stand out. First, we spent some unforgettable hours in the huge catacombs. The main one we toured had many side extensions. We were told that the total length of this main catacomb with all of its side branches was 8 miles. What particularly impressed me were the huge underground burial crypts. It is almost unbelievable. We heard that during the centuries of most severe persecution of Christians, the third to the sixth century, a total of 150,000 people were buried underground. This must be seen to be believed.

In a sense our visit to St. Peter's Basilica constitutes the key highlight. After listening to an address by Pope Pius XII we managed to get tickets to attend what was called a private session with the pope. Sometime later we were ushered to an upstairs reception hall.

The invitation to a papal audience.

As I recall, there were at least 30 in our group. I happened to be at the front and, according to my notes, stood about three feet from the pope. As I recall, he addressed us in several languages. Not surprisingly, he gave us very good counsel. It was an unforgettable experience.

Another definite Italian highlight was seeing the extensive excavations of Pompeii, a city totally buried under lava after the eruption of Mt. Vesuvius in 79 AD. It is estimated at least 2,000 people were buried alive.

The farther south we drove, the more primitive the farming methods were. I had not been aware of the huge difference in living standards between northern and southern Italy. It is not that southern Italians are less happy or less civilized. They are simply much poorer. One time, when we stopped to take in the scenery and lifestyle, I counted 18 yokes of oxen working in the fields.

After touring some very picturesque areas in Sicily we embarked on a good-sized ship for Tunis. We were exhausted but also hungry. After a brief rest we got out our usual bread, margarine and jam. We may have had some fruit. As we were eating, we heard a bell. Upon checking what it meant we discovered that our tickets covered a dinner on board. Being naive students and still inexperienced ship passengers, we missed a fine dinner and could do no more than eat at least a little of the excellent fare.

Tunisia and Libya - A Sandstorm

Disembarking in Tunis brought us to the Muslim and Arab world. Our few phrases of Italian and French were helpful, but mostly we relied on sign language. At that time tourists were infrequent and English and German did not get us very far. The totally different and very colourful garb, the many women with only their eyes visible, the food, the chaotic, crooked, narrow, crowded streets, and the endless calling out by the many merchants was a huge culture shock.

We slowly navigated our way, carefully avoiding the many street vendors hawking their wares right on the street and the trinket barkers sometimes coming right close to us. When we decided to buy something, we got involved, as we knew we would, with high-pressure bartering. We managed that rather well. There were many beggars, some severely handicapped. When we stopped for a traffic light or for some other reason, many people, especially children, surrounded our motorcycle. That was truly a new experience, almost overwhelming. We were very careful. If one person entered a shop or began bartering with a vendor, the other person guarded the motorcycle and everything on it. We had learned our lesson in Milan.

The Sahara Highway

Fortunately, in Tunis and later also in some other towns, we had addresses of youth hostels where we could relax, prepare our meals, store our motorcycle safely, and sleep. In some places we could rent sheets and blankets. Our one sleeping bag was obviously inadequate for such times. In this warmer region we could, however, get by with the one sleeping bag and our jackets.

Leaving the teeming crowds of Tunis, we headed southeast into the Sahara Desert. From Tunis until about 100 miles west of Cairo the Sahara at times runs close to the shores of the Mediterranean Sea. At other places the Sahara limits are many miles inland. Similarly, this road, the Sahara Highway, sometimes also runs quite close to the Mediterranean coast and sometimes many miles inland. It is paved but with some very poorly maintained sections.

The worst aspect, however, was that in several places the bridges were out. Obviously, we needed to watch very carefully. In at least one place, there was no barrier to prevent traffic from simply going over the edge and landing on the dry wadi about 15 to 25 feet below. In some places, there were tracks to be followed as vehicles bypassed the missing bridge by going down the embankment to the wadi and then back up the other side.

The weather was warm and sunny as we headed out of Tunis. Some hours later, however, we encountered a wind, and shortly after that a vicious sandstorm. We battled the sandstorm all day. Our progress was very slow. At times we pushed sand aside to determine if we were still on the highway.

No bridge over the wadi.

It soon became clear to us why, until about noon, we had not encountered a single vehicle. In some instances the drifts of sand on the highway were already so high that we could get through them only by pushing the motorcycle through the drift to the other side. It was also the case, of course, that given the dense sandstorm we were proceeding in something close to perpetual twilight. Everything looked a dusty yellow.

Already during our first day in the sandstorm trouble hit. The very tiny grains of sand got into virtually everything. The first problem was that sand got into our handlebar speed control so that we could go only about 30 kilometres an hour or nothing.

Motocycle on the Sahara Highway in a sandstorm.

We could coast into oases and towns but getting started created a mini-crisis – or worse. When it was parked, the back wheel of our DKW was raised off the ground. So, when we started the motor it would now race ahead to about 30 kms an hour. You can imagine what happened when the rider or riders lurched forward, which is how one gets underway, and the back tire hit the road. We took off with instant and incredible acceleration. We had to hang on tightly while gravel, sand, stones and sparks flew! I think the Arabs must have thought we were truly stupid. Or maybe they figured out what the problem was. I should add that if this phenomenon of a real jump-start happened on a paved road in a town, then we unintentionally really "laid rubber" as race drivers put it.

Removing sandrifts from the Sahara Highway.

The other problem hit us one afternoon in the middle of the sand blizzard. The sand got into the gas feed and plugged the fuel filter. We had brought tools. Although we had never before done so, we took the carburetor apart. We removed the sand which had plugged the filter and set out again. We had to do this repeatedly. In my later letter to Doris I wrote that on one day, March 23, we had to carry out this process five times, once in near darkness. During a fairly long day of driving that day we covered, as I recall, barely 200 miles (300 kms).

I need to say something about the distinctive sand we encountered in the Sahara. After millennia of blowing, the grains of sand are so small that one should probably speak of sand dust. We had not previously seen anything like it. The sand dust penetrated everything we wore. It got into all of our clothes which caused a lot of itching. We got sand dust behind our goggles and even into our eyes. In fact, later we noticed that it had managed to get into a writing pen with the top screwed in place and in an inside pocket. It took us days to get rid of the penetrating sand. This phenomenon has to be experienced to be understood.

Throughout our many hours of challenging travel through the sand blizzard we saw quite a few single camels, heavily loaded. With each camel there was an Arab, seemingly Bedouins, either on the camel or walking alongside. We also saw camel caravans with loads heading in various directions. It seemed like medieval times. These men seemed to know where they were going, even though not on the highway. I might add here that to the best of my recollection, during the entire day's travel through blowing sand and growing sand drifts on the road, we encountered not a single car and only one or two trucks.

Sometimes the winds died down and we could see wrecked tanks and fuel cans lying around. There were, in fact, still many signs of the great World War II battles fought there more than a decade earlier. It was surprising to us that a decade after the North African campaign ended and German General Erwin Rommel's *Afrika Korps* had been defeated by British General Bernard Montgomery, the ruins of war were still abundantly evident. We spent some time at the famous battle sites at Tobruk and El Alamein.

Harvey on a reminder of World War II.

At an oasis in the Sahara.

One evening, when the sandstorm was over, we realized that we would not make it to the next town for the night and decided to bed down as best we could in the desert. The air was warm and we thought that we should be able to get some decent sleep. As we proceeded down the road we saw various signs but only in Arabic. Obviously, they did not mean much to us. We also saw bones on the sand. We assumed they were camel bones but gave the matter no further thought. We should have. We pushed the motorcycle perhaps 100 feet off the highway and bedded down under the stars. We slept well.

In the morning we were awakened by the sound of a truck nearby. It turned out that we had bedded down in the middle of a wartime minefield. Both the Allies and the Germans had planted many mines in this area during World War II. Many were still in place and very dangerous. The truck we heard was operated by some Americans whose task it was to find the hidden mines in this area not far from the great Battle of Tobruk. With their Geiger counters, they were very carefully proceeding to clean out this area. They were very cautious. Apparently the crew of 4 or 5 men made a good living finding the mines, disarming them and selling the components. As I recall, we were told that it would take six pounds of pressure to detonate a sand-covered mine. I then became firmly convinced, as I think Harvey was also, that God spared our lives that evening. We had selected a sleeping spot right among the active mines. After we had been spotted by the mine-sweeping crew, we remained where we were. Then, together with our motorcycle, we were loaded onto the truck. That was doubly advantageous given the mine danger and the fact that our motorcycle had a somewhat deflated tire with which we would have had to make our way quite a few miles to the next town. Thank you, God, for sparing our lives! The truckers delivered us safely to the next town.

Several times during those Sahara days we needed to drive into fairly small oasis villages. Clearly, we were a great novelty. Crowds gathered quickly. Given that there was a very strong anti-French sentiment in North Africa, and since we knew that at least some of the Arabs might mistake us for Frenchmen, we did not stay too long in such places. In one oasis, however, we were invited to have Arabic tea with some friendly Arab men, probably Bedouins. The utensils and cups didn't look overly clean but we knew that to reject such an overture might be very disadvantageous, even dangerous. We drank the tea and hoped for the best. That unusual tea-time may, however, have been the cause of serious illness later in Damascus.

We encountered various checkpoints. Some were well-staffed, and we were questioned. At others, the attendant official seemed rather lackadaisical.

A Sahara Highway checkpoint.

Given that we had already twice run out of gas and that our gas tank was rather small, and given that we never knew how far it might be to the next filling station, we tried to keep the motorcycle tank filled as much as possible. One time, while still in Libya, we were informed at a checkpoint that fuel was available in a town six miles to the south of the main highway. We made our way to the town of perhaps 15,000. The streets were mostly deserted except for soldiers presumably needed because of the Egyptian border. We noticed, in passing, that there was no sign of any electricity anywhere.

Arab herdsmen in Libya.

Oil lamps provided whatever light was needed. At first the soldiers we met were very friendly. One even asked if I would exchange hats with him temporarily so that he could be photographed wearing a motorcycle helmet. Soldiers tend to carry cameras. They also carry guns. I was agreeable.

We were again offered strong tea. This time the situation seemed quite sanitary so we drank it. Suddenly a soldier arrived with an urgent message. Translated, it said that the two motorcyclists were to report immediately to the commanding officer. There was serious tension in the air. We had no idea why we were being summoned or what awaited us. In such situations compliance is the only option.

We entered the commander's quarters. The commander and his assistant, who both spoke English, questioned us for more than an hour. We soon realized that they thought we might be spies, likely Jewish spies.

We drew their attention to the German license plate but that reality was considered of no consequence. Such a plate is easy to get and could be nothing more than a decoy. Our student identification papers and our hostel memberships also did not impress the officers. Our other documents did not help us either. Any document, as these officers knew, could be forged very easily. We were suspect.

At one point we told the commander that we were both history students. As I recall, he smiled. My letter to Doris recounts the following.

"Possibly he didn't believe us. When we started discussing ancient Egyptian history figures I thought I would impress him. I quoted a fair amount of Egyptian history and asked him questions about them. I now realize that was a risky thing to do. Possibly that convinced him of the truth of our stories."

My Old Testament knowledge and some studies at UBC suddenly were of great practical value. After a considerable pause the commander ordered that we be given some fuel and allowed to proceed on our way to Egypt.

Repairs needed.

A food store in the Sahara.

A rest stop on the Sahara Highway.

Only later did we fully realize that we might have been in very serious trouble. I mean big trouble. Libya, along with several other Arab counties, considered Israel to be an enemy state. Suspected spies had been known to disappear. I recall how we patiently observed the commanding officer think for a while about us and our situation. It did not occur to me then that he was probably asking himself whether he should take us into "permanent custody" and then deal with us in whatever manner he deemed right. Only after additional rather scary situations in that region did we realize how close we were to disappearing in the Sahara. Thank you, God, for delivering us that day!

Egypt

We had emerged from the Sahara sandstorm several hours before we crossed from Libya into Egypt. In Egypt the roads were better and we could make better time. That is, we might have done so had it not been for the very frequent military checkpoints. Sometimes we were delayed for quite a few minutes.

To be in Egypt, the land of Abraham and Moses, to see some of the sights these patriarchs saw makes deep and lasting impressions. The country teems with fascinating history and present reality. I shall allow myself only a few observations. When a dictatorship is in a state of war, as Egypt still was with Israel, military commanders are not preoccupied with niceties when checking out possible spies. We had several additional unpleasant encounters. Eventually, we arrived at the ancient city of Alexandria at the mouth of the mighty Nile River.

From Alexandria, we headed south to Cairo, one of the oldest cities in the world. I thought of Abraham and Moses, who centuries ago had also viewed the Nile and this great city. Cairo struck me as being distinctive for two reasons. First, never before or since have I experienced such crowded and noisy streets. Amidst the oxen, donkeys, camels, and water buffalo and crowds of pedestrians, one sees an almost endless variety of bicycles, motorcycles, three-wheeled vehicles, cars and trucks, tiny to very large. It seemed to me that all of the drivers were honking loudly all the time.

Fortunately, everything, animate and inanimate, moved very slowly. So did we - moving along slowly with surging people, animals, and sundry vehicles. Most accidents that seemed clearly about to happen didn't. Maybe the continuous honking helped! The second thing that struck me was that for the first time, but not the last, I observed hundreds of passengers clinging to the outside of buses, sitting on top of buses, and hanging on to the back of buses. My immediate thought was, "Did they pay?" My second and more consequential thought was, "Are they safe?"

One cannot ignore the pyramids. To the best of my knowledge no scholar or engineer has been able to explain how the ancient experts achieved all the excavating, shaping, hauling and raising of the almost countless huge slabs of stone. The giant pyramid, Cheops, in particular, remains a puzzling marvel of human ingenuity, creativity, engineering, and resourcefulness. Everyone is incredibly impressed by the precise way in which all the stones fit into the pyramid. The Great Pyramid contains an estimated 2.3 million stone blocks, each weighing approximately 1 to 1.5 tons. The entire reality is almost unbelievable. Nobody knows how, about 2,500 BC, these massive building blocks, hewn of rock, shaped very precisely, were raised to amazing heights. Cheops, or Khufu, rises in the Al Ghiza Desert to a height of 479 feet (150 metres) and covers 13.1 acres (5.3 hectares). When I was a young teenager my parents bought a 10-acre farm on King Road in Abbotsford, BC. It boggles my mind to think that this one pyramid would extend well beyond our farm's boundaries.

The 13-acre Khufu pyramid.

In 1956 it was still possible, for a reasonable fee, to crawl into Cheops and investigate its inside tunnels and tombs. That was in itself a fascinating adventure. Harvey and I crawled along a maze of tunnels for what seemed very long distances. One battles claustrophobia. The intricacies of the inner parts, the marble walls, the complex labyrinths, the impressive and beautiful crypts, the huge stone caskets, the very long and connected tunnels, and the clever ducting to facilitate air circulation all defy explanation. Today such inside exploration is no longer permitted. We, of course, also climbed to the top.

We had planned to spend Easter Sunday at the famous Garden Tomb in Jerusalem. Instead, because of sandstorm delays and the numerous security checkpoints, we spent Easter Sunday, April 1, 1956, checking out an ancient Pharaoh's tomb. This Egyptian tomb was fascinating but not a resurrection site.

John on Khufu.

After several days in Egypt we were scheduled to sail from Alexandria to Beirut, Lebanon. On April 5, having had the motorcycle checked and fueled, we were ready to head north to Alexandria except for one more important engagement. Before I left Canada, *The Canadian Mennonite,* for which I was a columnist and also a certified correspondent, arranged for me to get a Press Card. At various times it came in real handy. Here, in Cairo, it enabled me to schedule a one-on-one interview with President Gamal Abdul Nasser. My editor would be delighted, I told myself, especially given the growing tension between President Nasser and the United Kingdom over the Suez Canal and the existence of Israel. My schedule, given our sailing time from Alexandria, was tight, but that could not be changed.

I arrived at the President's suite in lots of time and waited. If he arrived on time, we would still have enough time to board our ship in Alexandria. The president was late. I should have anticipated that. I was getting restless. The President's secretary assured me that he would come as soon as he could. Finally, I could wait no longer. I must leave or we would miss our sailing. Reluctantly I excused myself and Harvey and I headed north along the Nile. We drove as fast as the posted limit permitted. It looked like we would just make it. Then, about 35 miles south of Alexandria, our motorcycle stopped.

We were stunned. We quickly spotted the problem. In Cairo the mechanic had either intentionally or unintentionally oiled the clutch pad so that it slipped. We were burning much more fuel than we should. We were now out of fuel. What could be done? No amount of trip planning could ever prepare one for this! We were stranded, late, and seemingly helpless.

Typically we would be carrying some oil and gas since our two-cycle motor needed a blended mixture to operate. This time, because we should have had much more than enough in the tank to get us to our destination, we carried no extra gas or oil. Almost immediately a car stopped. A very kind gentleman, who fortunately spoke English, said he would try to help. Unbelievably the kind gentleman, as I recall he was an Arab, allowed us to get some gas from his gas tank, I think by siphoning it. Then, even more surprisingly, he allowed us to drain some oil from his car's crankcase. We probably required about half a litre. That was an incredible act of kindness. I doubt if anyone else has ever done that. Of course, this all took some time. We then carefully poured both the gas and the oil into our fuel tank. Typically, the gas and oil must be mixed in a precise ratio but the DKW motor cooperated, and we got away with whatever the ratio turned out to be. Thank you, God, for bringing us another truly amazing Good Samaritan!

We drove off, incredibly indebted to a total stranger. We now were much behind schedule. According to my memory, we had lost almost an hour. Then a series of military checkpoints, which we had anticipated, slowed our travel even more. The speed limits are at times enforced on this superhighway so we could not make up much time. Eventually we arrived in Alexandria and though we were really late because of the fuel problem, probably about an hour, we decided to check out the harbour. We didn't say much but my guess is that we both hoped there would be some other ship that would take us to Beirut.

When we approached the harbor, we could hardly believe our eyes. To our utter amazement, the fairly large ship, the *Asperia,* we knew the name, was still lying at anchor. For reasons that violate any ship's protocol and logical thinking, the captain had decided to delay the ship's departure until the two Canadians arrived. Can you believe that? The captain of a fairly large ship had waited for us! Hearts pounding with excitement and gratitude, we boarded, got the motorcycle in place, proceeded to our quarters and flopped down on our beds. We were both incredibly grateful and emotionally exhausted.

In Old Testament times God hardened the heart of a prominent but evil Egyptian. In 1956 God softened the heart of another, for me only somewhat less prominent, Egyptian - this one truly virtuous – or was he an angel?

There are still Good Samaritans in the Middle East. Miracles still happen. Twice that day!

Lebanon, Syria and Jordan

Upon arrival in Lebanon after an all-night passage across the eastern Mediterranean Sea, we needed to be processed by the Lebanese authorities. Perplexing as it may seem now, and as it was to us then, we had to go through five customs and entry procedures and had to pay five different fees. It seems that in some of these countries' unemployment numbers are brought down by appointing the unemployed to unneeded bureaucratic posts. Eventually, we and our motorcycle were free to leave. Incidentally, at one of the disembarking registration places, both Harvey and I needed to be present. While we temporarily left our motorcycle by itself, our driver's goggles, which we had locked to the frame, were stolen.

We could spend only three days in Lebanon. What struck us immediately was that Beirut was easily the cleanest and most orderly of all the Arab cities we had visited. This fine city was aptly called, *The Paris of the East* and *The Mediterranean Jewel*. It was an amazing and very friendly city, clean and largely modern. What we encountered almost immediately, however, was the deep-seated hatred against Israel, only about 70 miles to the south, an emotion that was expressed freely almost everywhere.

There was much to see and do in Lebanon, but I shall mention only two experiences. We had a fine but somewhat challenging drive up to the ancient Cedars of Lebanon. By my estimate there were at that time only about 500 trees left. Clearly, there had been much harvesting of timber apparently without any reforestation. I saw no young growth.

Our second main event was our visit to the American University of Beirut. This school functions much like a North American university but has somehow managed to accommodate both the mostly Muslim population and the minority Christian sector. I found it to be a rare example of how the West and the East have managed to cooperate for the benefit of all. Such mutual accommodation for mutual benefit was and is still very rare in the entire Middle East.

Perhaps it may be of interest in my chronicling of experiences to incorporate a few sentences of a letter I wrote Doris at that time. Clearly, thinking and planning for our future together was on both our minds. While in Beirut I responded to one of Doris' letters by saying,

"Also, I was very happy to have you write that we want to really live for God. That shall indeed be the purpose of our life."

Writing a few days later from Damascus and focusing on more earthly matters, I wrote:

"Although we are quite occupied these days, I spend a good part of my time daydreaming about you and our future. I'm anticipating our reunion,

marriage, honeymoon and life together. I am as happy as a child before Christmas. Things will be happening fast after I get back."

Fortunately, distances in the Middle East are not great. On the afternoon of Saturday, April 7, Harvey and I drove the 100 miles or so to Damascus, one of the oldest cities in the world. It has been inhabited continuously since ancient Biblical times. This city, of course, contains many sites of Christian significance. Tourists are readily directed to the street called Straight. It is a straight street, a rarity in most of the Arab cities we have seen. Whether it dates back to St. Paul's day is unsure. Similarly, tourists can visit the House of Ananias and the wall from which St. Paul was lowered in a basket.

Although we took all the precautions we reasonably could, dysentery, the scourge of tourists in this region of the world, did hit us. By early Sunday morning Harvey had a fairly mild case. Only a few hours later I was hit hard. We wondered whether this was the result of the tea break we had in the Sahara. Fortunately, we had, as I recall, a low-priced but comfortable hotel room in Damascus. For a while I was totally delirious. Even now I recall that my mind drifted off into another realm of unknown sounds and colours swirling around me that made no sense. The hallucination lasted several hours. The high fever and stomach ache lasted longer. I think it was late Sunday afternoon that we got medical help. Sulfa drugs helped the most. Although I was weak and still dizzy, my fever had subsided by Monday morning. Clearly, I was not yet fit to drive but Harvey was - barely. We were on a tight schedule. On Monday afternoon, April 9, with me still very weak, although strong enough to sit on the back seat and hang on, we left Damascus for Amman, the capital city of the Hashamite Kingdom of Jordan. That was for us a unique Damascus Road experience.

The tourist promoters in Amman said that this city was named millennia ago as the capital of the Ammonites with whom the ancient Israelites struggled. Who can say whether this is true? This was one of many stories which we heard, most of which seemed plausible. By Tuesday I felt much better. For the next five days we had a truly fascinating time visiting scores of biblical sites, but first I shall relate another tourist experience.

It did not take us long to discover a basic problem tourists encounter in this city, namely, that many streets have no name and many buildings have no number. Presumably, this shortcoming was corrected in later years but for us it was a huge problem. Streets and buildings are identified in various ways. A building might be identified as "red-brick, a block south of the Post Office but on the other side of the street." The British Embassy was identified by its flag. To find a bank, one might be told to go north one block, then east for two blocks and then look for two brass doors.

Not only was it very hard to find the right street and building in Amman, but also the situation was further complicated by the fact that donkeys, mules, ox-carts, camels, scooters and bicycles filled the streets with virtually no sense of staying on one side in order to go in a certain direction. One soon learns that one must be very alert, one must beep the horn a lot even if for no reason, and one must at all times be prepared either to swerve sharply or stop. One also prays.

Try as we might, we could not find the local YMCA where we hoped to be able to stay for the night. We discovered that sometimes the Y rates are only slightly higher than youth hostel rates and offer better facilities. Fortunately, because of the British colonial past, some people here spoke English. Also fortunately, we found a policeman who understood what we wanted. In fact, he said he knew exactly where the Y was and offered to escort us there. Off we went with a police escort. How fortunate! We arrived at the destination and thanked the officer. The policeman smiled, waved, and left. As we turned to enter the building we suddenly realized that this was the YWCA, a facility for women only. After scouting around for a while longer, cruising unnamed streets, we eventually found not the YMCA but a low-cost hotel.

In 1956 the Hashamite Kingdom of Jordan extended west beyond the Jordan River all the way to Jerusalem and south and north to take in many of the Old and New Testament sites. During the next days we visited literally scores of so-called holy places. These included Jericho, the Garden of Gethsemane, the Mount of Olives, the narrow Kidron Valley, the Garden Tomb, Golgotha, Pilate's House, Bethany, Bethphage, Dome of the Rock, the Mount of Temptation, the Jordan section of Jerusalem, the Church of the Nativity, the Shepherd's Field, Jacob's Well (75 feet deep and 7.5 feet wide), Mt. Ebal, Mt. Gerazim, Ai, the fields of Dothan, Bethel, Mizpah where Saul was crowned, and much more.

We also visited a very interesting UNWRA (United Nations Relief and Works Agency) Palestine refugee camp. Let me add a comment about the UNRWA camps. When we were in the Middle East these camps, housing hundreds of thousands of Palestinians who fled or were driven out by the Israelis when that country was created in 1948, had been established as emergency centres by the UN in Lebanon, Syria, Jordan, and Gaza. When we visited the large one near Jericho, we were told that officially no one ever died in that camp. In fact, we were told, the dead are secretly buried on site so that their ration cards can continue to be used by others. I did not blame them. As I observed the throngs of people in their dry and dusty setting with virtually no employment for anyone, I could only muster great pity.

Writing now, in 2021, I must point out the sad reality that virtually all of these emergency camps created in the 1940s still exist.

Several times, especially when we wanted to take pictures, we were accosted as being Jewish spies. Sometimes groups assembled quickly when we parked the motorcycle. More than a few times some people, especially the young men, became quite hostile. In fact, in Bethlehem we were taken into custody by the police. We spent quite a long time convincing them that we were who we said we were. In some places, however, the local folk were very friendly, especially when they discovered who we were. In one town, a friendly Arab, upon discovering that we were Canadians, told us, with tears in his eyes, that he had learned that Canada had sold planes to Israel. He said, "May God forgive you." There was nothing suitable that I could say. I should perhaps add here that throughout our days in Greater Palestine, we heard gunshots from the Jordan-Israeli border, especially in the Jerusalem sector, virtually every night.

Clearly, a highlight was going for a swim in the Dead Sea situated 1,200 feet below sea level. This, we were told, is the lowest spot on the earth's surface.

The Dead Sea, we learned, is about seven times saltier than any ocean. It feels very strange floating while reading the newspaper as I did. The experience is actually quite enjoyable. However, we discovered that if you bend your knees in the water, you will flip over. Not pleasant. Getting all the salt out of one's hair and elsewhere turned out to be difficult.

John floating on the Dead Sea.

Among the sights that remain etched in my memory is a small field in which turbaned Arabs were cutting ripe grain with a hand scythe and tying the bundles by hand. That reminded me of Sunday school pictures. As we slowly took the old steep Jericho Road up from Jericho to Jerusalem, we encountered a shepherd with his mixed herd of sheep and goats. Obviously, many a Biblical image and parable took on a new meaning for us. Jesus had obviously used his environment when he taught.

In the late afternoon on Sunday, April 15, we crossed from Jordan into Israeli Jerusalem through the famous Mandelbaum Gate. This transition could be difficult for the simple reason that Jordan and the other nearby Muslim countries did not accept tourists whose passport has an Israeli stamp and Israel did not accept a passport with a stamp from a Muslim country. We had been warned of this conundrum and, on good advice, had arranged to get second passports. I think these were issued to us by the Canadian Embassy in Cairo. In any event, in order to leave Jordan legally, we had to show our regular passports indicating when and where we entered. When we got to the Israeli side of No-Man's Land in Jerusalem, we showed them our new passports with no entries. This whole arrangement made no sense. The Israeli officials had watched us as we pushed the motorcycle from one country to the other but we could not enter Israel if we had been to any adjacent Muslim country. In this make-believe absurdity, the Israeli guards welcomed us because our passports showed that we had not been to any enemy country. This ludicrous arrangement must be the height of bureaucratic idiocy.

Israel

We had done significant preparation for our trip and were not too surprised to see that Israel was much like a western democracy. Also, with English and German we had no difficulty communicating with officials and some of the common folk. Pushing our motorcycle to the Israeli side of No-Man's Land immediately gave us the sense that we were re-entering the western world.

Having completed the two-passport entry we needed to find a place to spend the night. We quickly found a low-cost but reasonably inviting one-star hotel. As was the custom, one of us stayed with the motorcycle and our belongings while the other checked a store, inquired at an information centre, or scouted out whatever we were investigating. In this instance I was the one to check out the hotel.

The concierge at the desk was most helpful. He inquired what I wanted. I replied I needed a bed for two. He indicated that would be fine. In keeping with our practice, I asked to see the room. He then took me down the hall and opened the door to what immediately struck me as a rather fine place.

I glanced around the room and then looked at the double bed. There, to my immense astonishment, was a smiling young woman in the bed. Sensing my utter surprise, the concierge, as I recall, reminded me that I had asked for a bed for two. I explained. Rather quickly he took me to a different room, one in which the double bed did not have an attractive young lady in it when I checked. Maybe the smiling girl thought I didn't like what I saw. I made no further inquiries.

At this point, aside from wanting to see as many holy sites as possible, our pressing concern was to arrange for a sailing back to Europe, preferably to Greece. Because of the lost days in the Sahara, we were behind schedule and might have only three days to see the sights of Israel. Fortunately, distances in that country are short. We decided to proceed to Haifa and make that our base for the rest of our stay. Haifa is the main port city and being there would enable us to check out sailing options easily.

We found a low-cost hotel. The hotels were advantageous for us because, in contrast to most youth hostels, they provided linens and blankets. This was important because, as will be recalled, we had only one sleeping bag.

Having settled into our hotel room we immediately inquired about sailings either to western Turkey or to the mainland of Greece. Our initial plan had us motorcycling through those regions with stops for sightseeing. We applied at various sailing companies but with no indication of success. Despite this disappointment we proceeded with our tourist agenda.

Israel contains a large number of religious sites. We were fortunate to visit many, including Nazareth, where we saw what a tourist booster insisted was the workbench Joseph and Jesus used, Mt. Tabor, Nain, Capernaum, Tiberius, the Wailing Wall and many other sites. We also saw Megiddo (Armageddon), Cana, where Jesus turned water into wine, and Mt. Carmel where Elijah produced a fire that burned water and

The Elijah statue

the nearby Kishon Valley where he then somehow single-handedly dispatched 450 prophets of Baal. A highlight was to get up early on April 20, drive to the Sea of Galilee, have breakfast at its shore and take a swim in the lake where Jesus, and briefly Peter, walked on water.

Sunrise over the Sea of Galilee.

One day we visited an Israeli kibbutz. A kibbutz is a cluster of perhaps 20 families living in a tight community. They function as one economy. All participants are looked after very well but they do not own private property except for personal effects. Typically, the children are with their parents a few hours each evening and on the Sabbath. Otherwise they live in a residential school on the property. Based on our observation, the children seemed not to mind leaving their parents for the night. The Kibbutz we visited had a large dairy operation. We were hosted very well. Today Israel has many Kibbutzim.

Because of the delay in finding passage, our plan to drive through western Turkey and Greece had to be set aside. Early one morning, after we had already been in Israel six days, I walked out on some errand. I will not forget that morning, Sunday, April 22, 1956. As I glanced along the street I stopped short - our motorcycle was gone. Harvey and I scoured the nearby streets. It would have been impossible to drive the DKW away. The front wheel was locked at a very sharp angle so that the motorcycle could move forward in only a tight circle. We had the key and without a key no one could start the motor unless some battery shortcut could be rigged.

The missing motorcycle created a double problem. Not only was our transportation gone but a second serious problem was created. At that time, in order to take any vehicle out of Germany without an export permit, the owner had to put on deposit a sum equal to the value of the vehicle. We had therefore deposited as a surety some of the money we would need to buy our tickets to fly home. A further complication was that our insurance did not cover theft in Israel. Perhaps the insurance company had concluded that such coverage was not needed in that almost Western country.

It was hard not to be anxious. We were. We, of course, immediately went to the local Haifa police office and reported the theft. The officer assigned to us checked with his associates. We had a long conversation about what might have happened. No constable had any knowledge of the missing motorcycle. As I recall, the nearby detachment with which we connected consisted of perhaps 15 officers. Some listened in to our conversation with the officer assigned to us. The police officers all seemed to feel very bad about our loss but they could not offer us any helpful information. Our officer then accompanied us to the spot where we had parked the DKW. He was very helpful and supportive. Together with the police officer, we returned to the police station. We discussed what might have happened. Again, nobody had an explanation other than simple theft. We left. We prayed fervently and hoped for the best.

It became clear to us that we would have to leave Haifa without our motorcycle. As I recall, it was later on Sunday, April 22, the day before we were hoping to find a ship to take us to Europe, when we again went to the police station to give the police forwarding addresses and phone numbers. We left the police building slowly, obviously dejected.

At the entrance to the police compound was a large gate. Just as we were walking out through the gate I sensed what seemed like a firm hand on my left shoulder. I turned. There was nobody near me. But as I glanced back I suddenly saw something that immediately caught my attention. I saw a small part of the front wheel of a motorcycle protruding from behind a building. It was only from a certain vantage point that one might notice it. If it had been parked a few feet farther back, I could not have seen it. We rushed over to check it out. Could it be? It was. The DKW had been found! Our hearts were pounding. Was it the hand of an angel on my shoulder? It must have been! Thank you, angel! Thank you God!

What a feeling of relief to see our beloved DKW again and to know that we would not be forfeiting our deposit money in Germany. Harvey and I rushed in to tell the police officers that our stolen vehicle had been found - right on their property. It was leaning against one of their buildings. They all expressed total surprise. Nobody could explain how our motorcycle came to be where it was nor how, apparently, not a single officer had seen it parked there. It turned out that the front wheel had been forced and thus the locking mechanism was broken. With the key a person could drive it that way but the vehicle could not be locked.

Aside from the broken lock mechanism there was no damage. Perhaps some officer had always wanted a small German motorbike. My reasonable conclusion was that the thieving police officer broke the lock and then simply pushed our DKW the perhaps four or five blocks to the police station. Presumably he planned to find some locksmith who could make a new key.

We had the key with us. We started the motorcycle and drove away. Never before had a muffled roar sounded so beautiful! The locking mechanism was repaired. We imagined that there was some heated conversation in the police building after we left. Or maybe they all simply had to acknowledge that they had bungled their theft. They had been caught. They should have parked the DKW in a different place. Thus ended the saga of how our stolen DKW was found at a police station in Haifa. Was one officer guilty? Were they all in on the theft?

Later that day we again toured the waterfront, checking with the various ship companies. By now it was clear that there would be very little, if any, time even to drive right across Greece, let alone tour it. Because of academic and insurance reasons we needed to be back in Germany some days before classes resumed. We still hoped to find a ship that would take us to a Greek port, about a two-day ocean voyage, and then we could travel north through Greece and Yugoslavia for four or five days before entering Austria.

As I recall, that Sunday night we managed somehow to get the unlocked DKW right into the hotel.

Sailing Back to Europe, Yugoslavia, Italy, Austria

Finally, on Monday, April 23, we found a possibility. A fairly small and slow Israeli freighter, the ***Nahkshon***, was leaving port that evening bound for Trieste, the eastern-most city at the top of Italy, almost adjacent to the Yugoslav border. That was not our preferred destination but with no other option in sight, we were glad for this opportunity.

This ship was a true freighter. It had no accommodation for passengers. The management agreed to take us but only with the proviso that we might not have bunks, only mattresses laid out somewhere. An advantage was that the cost was very reasonable. At 9:30 PM on the 23rd, we boarded the ship and set sail. We were the passenger list of two.

Although we lost some touring days, the five days aboard the ***Nahkshon***

Our ship, the Nakhshon.

were actually a very delightful holiday. The weather was sunny and warm. The Mediterranean was mostly smooth as glass. The crew of about 25 men treated us very well. In fact, we generally ate excellent meals with the senior officers.

We read a lot, played a lot of chess, and had long discussions with the officers often about the Arab-Israeli situation. The Arab and Israeli perspectives were polar opposites. While the officers told us how the brave and outnumbered Irgun Gang and other brave fighters had "liberated" various villages and helped create Israel in the land God promised to Abraham, the Arab spokespersons had related how the Israeli thugs, such as the Irgun Gang, had driven them from lands which they had occupied for almost 1,800 years. Mutual hatred ran very deep. I recall one day, while playing chess with the Second Mate, an officer in the "War of Liberation" with whom I developed a fine relationship, simply asked out of the blue, "What is better than a dead Arab?" I was taken aback and remained silent. He answered his own question: "Two" and kept on playing.

During this delightful but time-consuming voyage, Harvey and I had time to write detailed journals and various letters. In a letter to Doris, I wrote:

"It will be almost 11 months from the day I left till the day I return....I shall never leave you alone like this again. Life without you is incomplete. I was not born to be a bachelor."

During our voyage we discovered that we would be docking in Rijeka, Yugoslavia, far north on the Adriatic coast, before proceeding on to Trieste in Italy. We arrived in Rijeka on the evening of April 28. Although we did not yet have our Yugoslav visas, the customs authorities kindly let us tour the city during the evening. This was my first visit to a communist country. Harvey and I were immediately struck by the fact that almost every building, it seemed, displayed a picture of the dictator, Marshall Tito, partly because May 1 would see the big communist May Day celebration. We also noticed that once again, the pedestrians wandered all over the street. In a sense, it didn't matter because during the entire evening in the city of about 100,000 we saw exactly three cars. We also noted that there seemed to be no traffic lights. While food was cheap, widespread poverty was obvious. We learned, for example, that more than a month's wages was needed to buy a dress shirt, assuming that it was available. Significantly, all incomes were roughly the same.

We returned to the **Nahkshon** for night and during the night sailed across the Adriatic Sea to nearby Trieste. From there Harvey and I drove to Venice and greatly enjoyed that distinctive and charming city on stilts. The next morning we drove back to Trieste and because the kind and friendly captain had invited us to do so, we returned to the **Nahkshon** for supper, a night's rest, and breakfast.

After further touring, we drove back to Yugoslavia on May 4. We had no difficulty getting the needed papers. Again we noticed that there are no billboards, other than for the communist cause, and no advertising anywhere. We traveled to Ljubljana. We were surprised to see that even in a fairly large city much of the transportation involved ox-carts. That evening we happened to find a Greek Orthodox church and took in the service. We noticed that no children were present and that the congregation consisted almost entirely of older women.

We rightly concluded that because of the policies of the communist government, children were not allowed to attend and that for men and also for employed women, it could be very counter-productive vocationally and professionally to attend a church service.

On May 5, we drove the connecting highway to Zagreb. We were surprised to discover that this significant highway was actually a dirt road. We also noted in driving through the countryside that not only were oxen still widely used but also that some of the plows were made of wood.

In Zagreb we fortunately met a very friendly medical student who invited us to come to his student residence and meet some of his fellow students. We went with him. That evening was amazing. As I wrote in a letter to Doris,

"For several hours tonight, I answered questions about the free world. One of the students who speaks English translated for the others. They have some very strange concepts of our way of life and Western politics."

We stayed at our guiding student's residence for the night.

The hospitality extended to us by these Yugoslavians was truly surprising.

For the next day, Sunday, we were given an English-speaking guide who gave us a very interesting and informative tour of this ancient city. Although the population, generally speaking, is relatively poor, they have much to offer us. They have learned how to live meaningful lives despite their poverty and their oppressive government. Although the communist government claimed to allow for considerable religious freedom, the reality was different. Practicing Christians had a very difficult time finding a government job and almost all jobs are government jobs. We encountered another very unusual government practice to discourage people from attending a Sunday worship service.

During our escorted Sunday tour we came to a large city square. It was a beautiful sunny Sunday forenoon. The large area was filled with vendors selling a huge variety of items. There must have been a hundred tables and stalls. Apparently all of these vendors represented government enterprises or were fully controlled by the government. Adjacent to this large square was a cathedral, probably the largest in the city. People, mostly older folk, were making their way to the church. We stayed to watch. As I recall, the church bells began to ring. There was excitement in the air. Upon inquiry we discovered that when the church service begins, prices in the huge market square are significantly reduced. As soon as the church service ends, the prices revert to their earlier higher levels. This the people had to choose - price reduction or piety.

On May 7, we reached the border between Yugoslavia and Austria. We

Market square in Zagreb, Yugoslavia.

had intentionally chosen to cross at a fairly quiet border customs and immigration port of entry. The crossing process might be simpler there. When we got to the border we encountered the following situation. On the Yugoslav side the customs office was apparently staffed by one person. He was a soldier sitting on a chair or bench outside, within a few yards of the international border. He happened to be asleep with a rifle resting on his lap. Should we wake him? Does one wake a man with a gun?

Rightly or wrongly we decided on the following plan. I would remain standing near the sleeping sentry while Harvey quietly pushed the DKW the few yards across the border into democratic, safe and free Austria. If the soldier awoke, I would explain what happened, and Harvey might have to come back with the DKW into Yugoslavia. If the border guard did not wake up by the time Harvey was safely in Austria, then I would quietly follow. Harvey crossed into Austria. The border guard did not wake up. I then quietly walked into non-communist Europe. I suppose that on the official customs records, Harvey and I are still in Yugoslavia.

Vienna in springtime must be one of the most beautiful cities in Europe. It is a blend of old-world charm and modernity. It offers amazing architecture, a distinctive culture, and beautiful parks, gardens, and hills. The famous Vienna Woods were at their late spring best. Vienna struck us also as having a bustling economy and shops laden with an abundance of goods. Doubtless this amalgam of factors impressed us, given what we had just observed in Yugoslavia.

One of the many sites we visited in Vienna was its world-famous opera house. Fortunately, a major production was being offered so we bought tickets for an evening performance on May 8. We appeared that evening in plenty of time. Then we ran into a problem. At first it was difficult to know what it was but then the truth came out. The ticket attendant rather hesitatingly informed us that we were not properly dressed for the occasion. She had a valid point. In comparison to the fine-dressed other patrons now coming in large numbers, we were obvious misfits. Unfortunately, we had no other clothes. We had only our scruffy motorcycle trousers and altogether weathered and not attractive leather jackets.

One does not come to Vienna often so we were not prepared to simply walk away. After some diplomatic persistence we negotiated the following arrangement. We would disappear off to the side somewhere. Then, after all the proper, in some cases elegantly, garbed guests had entered we would be ushered to a back corner on the most distant balcony where we would have two seats. I think that we had to promise to stay there until all of the attendees had left. The plan worked. We greatly enjoyed the excellent performance.

The time for us to return to our university cities was drawing near. All along, we had planned to be back in Heidelberg by the 10th of May, at the latest by the 11th. Harvey would need one more day to travel to Hamburg. Because of our scholarship requirements, we needed to be home for the advance course registration for the spring semester. In my case, I also needed to be back for the special events at the *Collegium Academicum* which take place in the early days of every term. Although the term started sooner, lectures for the spring term were scheduled to begin on May 14.

On May 9, after touring the incredible Schoenbrunn Castle, we left beautiful Vienna at 1:30 and headed west. The Autobahn, which follows the blue Danube for many miles, was fast, the scenery spectacular, and the mountain air invigorating. It was exciting. We were headed home. Letters from our sweethearts awaited us. We decided to drive until quite late. It should not be too difficult to find a youth hostel for the night. Then we suddenly had a change of heart. We decided that we would drive through the night. In retrospect that was probably unwise but after all that we had experienced, we were eager to get home.

With very little traffic at night, we made very good time. We took turns driving, as we typically did, and stopped quite a few times for coffee and some rest at the *Autobahn Raststätte*. The caffeine worked. The excitement helped. Neither of us got sleepy. We arrived at the *Collegium Academicum* in Heidelberg about 8:30 AM on May 10.

A truly eventful, enjoyable, exceedingly enriching, incredibly educational, genuinely mind-stretching and altogether memorable motorcycle trip had come to an end. I would end up having a sheaf of notes and about 350 slides to remind me of all that had happened. It was for me the experience of a lifetime! Thank you, DAAD! Thank you, Doris, for agreeing to let me have this fabulous adventure. Thank you, God for keeping me safe, even miraculously so, and healthy, except for one human-caused reversal in Damascus!

The Second Semester in Heidelberg

Because of space limitations I can report only briefly about my second semester in Heidelberg. I again enrolled in university courses; however, Harvey and I had both decided that we would miss some classes and make several more motorcycle trips, two to the south and several to the north. Fortunately, professors tend not to take attendance. True, I missed quite a few classes but my education was not interrupted. I shall highlight a few experiences.

The first of our planned trips began on Saturday, May 19. It took us north.

We toured around Hamburg and then took a flight to the beleaguered city of West Berlin, surrounded by the communist East Zone, the *Deutsche Demokratische Republik* (DDR). Berlin survived, indeed flourished economically because of its one Autobahn, a lone rail line, and its airline connections to West Germany. During the 1940s Berlin airlift, of course, it had only airplane connections. Although the financial and business districts had been rebuilt, much of Berlin still lay in ruins. We toured the amazing 100,000-seat Olympic Stadium built by Hitler. It was not destroyed by bombs. It is truly impressive. We saw many historic sites, including the place where Hitler's family committed suicide.

A special highlight was our travelling to East Berlin. The contrast was stark; political suppression and financial doldrums versus political freedom and prosperity. In East Berlin we took in a movie which turned out to be a feature film on the Protestant Reformation. We could hardly believe our eyes and ears. The film described the Reformation as an uprising by the oppressed peasants against their capitalist oppressors and the religious aristocracy who camouflaged their oppression by religious trappings.

On May 24 we took the short flight from Berlin's famous *Tempelhof Flughafen* to Hanover. For the next 10 days we visited many historic sites. Virtually everywhere, we saw evidence of Germany's *Wirtschaftswunder*, its miraculous economic recovery.

Speaking of economic recovery, let me recount this experience. One day I saw some men get off the bus and start running. This seemed strange. I asked someone nearby what this meant. He said that the men were running to get to their jobs as quickly as possible so they could help rebuild Germany's economy.

In Wolfsburg we had a tour of the huge Volkswagen factory. Its 35,000 employees, working several assembly lines, produced 1,540 cars every day in the two 8-hour shifts. On June 9 I headed back to Heidelberg for some classes.

Our next trip took us south. Visiting the ancient city of Nuremberg was a highlight. Harvey and I visited the courtroom where the Nazis were tried and convicted. I spent some time sitting in the chair in which *Reichsmarschall* (Imperial Commander) Hermann Goering, Nazi Germany's second most powerful leader, sat when he was tried, convicted and sentenced to death. He committed suicide on October 15, 1946, a few days before he was to be hanged. Nearby we visited the small building where 10 Nazi war criminals were executed. My grandfather, Johann P. Wiebe, would have been excited to hear me report about this experience.

We spent several days in Munich as well as in Berchtesgaden in the magnificent Alps where the famous *Alpenstrasse* is especially beautiful. Nearby is the delightful retreat centre that was Hitler's favourite spot. No wonder that the local youth hostel where we stayed several nights is huge, apparently the largest in Europe. We shared that modern facility with more than 400 other youthful travellers. Other highlights in this trip were our visit to Bern, Zurich and Basel in Switzerland. It was sobering to stand at Lake Zurich and remember the early Anabaptist martyrs who were drowned there.

After some more classes, our next trip was to take us to northern Germany and Denmark. Since Harvey now had our DKW I needed to get to Hamburg. I decided to save money by hitch-hiking. Usually, this worked out well. All went well for me heading north until I found myself left by the roadside in a rural area about halfway to Hamburg. In a July 1, 1956, letter, I recounted my experience to Doris as follows

"Fortunately, the air was not too cold. As long as I kept walking, I was warm, but I didn't want to walk all night. I soon came across a hayfield. The hay had already been pitched into little piles. I warmed myself by running around a bit and then crawled into a pile of hay. I slept only a little but rested for about two hours. By 3:30, the sky was getting lighter again, so I got up. There was practically no traffic, so I walked to keep warm. I quite enjoyed the early Sunday morning out in creation. By 4 o'clock, the cuckoos were cuckooing everywhere. I love to hear them. Then there was the thrill of a beautiful sunrise."

I soon got rides which took me right into Hamburg. This was my most unusual celebration of Canada Day.

This trip took us to several very interesting German cities, including Bremen, Luebeck, and Kiel. Denmark, with its typical thatched roofs and distinctive culture, offered another enriching experience complete with the sampling of many of the famous Danish pastries.

Harvey had to leave for an academic activity so, alone, I toured the historic Mennonite sites in Witmarsum and Pingjum in The Netherlands. In the small church in Pingjum, the oldest continuously operating Mennonite Church in the world, I stood where Menno Simons preached after his conversion. That experience affected this Anabaptist deeply. Partly because Canadian troops liberated The Netherlands and partly because the Dutch are intrinsically friendly, I was treated exceptionally well in this region. I also toured part of Belgium.

After Harvey returned we took a cruise on the Rhine River where a German group sang lustily as we passed the Lorelei. We toured the new German parliament building in Bonn. I then hitch-hiked back to Heidelberg for some classes.

We made one more two-day trip. We toured Stuttgart, where its historic inner city was almost totally destroyed by Allied bombs. We were informed that the city had endured 83 bombing raids. The city lay in ruins. After the war ended, the rubble was trucked outside the city and piled high. Today that mountain of rubble is called Rubble Mountain. It dominates the city. As I stood at the top, where a large Christian cross had been erected, I thought of the massive casualties and the almost unbelievable carnage in this one city. I again committed myself to support agencies such as the Mennonite Central Committee, which promote peace. If anyone is inclined to glorify war, he should visit Stuttgart and hike to the top of Rubble Mountain.

The university weeks passed quickly. On July 23, Harvey drove down from Hamburg. The next day, having said emotional goodbyes to all my dear Heidelberg friends, and especially my roommate Hermann Krieg, Harvey and I set out on our last DKW trip together. He was to sell the motorcycle after I left. I was to fly from Paris on July 27. We decided that it would be wise to spend a few days in and around Paris before I needed to embark. Those were exciting days. We visited the truly majestic Versailles Palace and saw the table where the 1919 Versailles Peace Treaty was signed. We visited the Eiffel Tower, the Arch of Triumph, Notre Dame and much more. I then parted from Harvey and our dear DKW which had faithfully carried us on three continents for a total of more than 20,000 kilometres. Thank you, DKW. Thank you, God.

On the evening of July 27 I boarded an El Al Israeli Airlines Constellation and finally began the trip back to the sweetheart who had most graciously agreed to postpone our wedding for a year so that I could have this incredible experience abroad. I have always remained deeply indebted to her. I might note here, if my memory is correct, that I sent her a letter or card for every day I was away except the last few. Doris also wrote very faithfully. I think I received at least 80 letters and some greatly valued care parcels.

The luxurious but rather slow propeller-driven plane landed at London, Shannon in Ireland, Gander in Newfoundland, and finally New York on July 28. After a bus trip to Montreal and a short rail-ride to Ottawa to visit Doris's brother Ruben and his wife Mavis, the CPR, for whom I had served as third cook for several summers, kindly let me ride free of charge to Mission City, BC.

In the early morning, on August 3, I arrived in Mission City and was welcomed by loved ones, especially my Loved One. Months of eager anticipation became a very emotional, love-filled reality.

The home church of John and Doris:
Abbotsford Mennonite Brethren Church (McCallum Road) now called Central Heights.

CHAPTER 9

ROMANCE AND MARRIAGE

The Nikkel family, December 30, 1941.
Back Row L to R: Ruben, Evangeline, Ed.
Front Row L to R: Marie, Miriam, Doris, Henry.

Doris Eileen Nikkel was born in Waldheim, Saskatchewan, on August 12, 1934. Her father was a teacher and a preacher. In the summer of 1944 the Nikkels moved from northern Saskatchewan to a five-acre farm on the northeast corner of King and Jackson Roads in Abbotsford, BC.

It was probably when I was in my early teens that I took note of a very attractive blonde girl attending the MEI. That was Doris, the daughter of the Lead Pastor at South Abbotsford Church, Rev. Henry H. Nikkel.

Doris and I got to know each other in the youth group and in the church choir. As I got to know her better, I soon realized what a very fine person she was. We had our first date, actually a group event, at Easter, 1949.

Doris

We both realized that we were rather young for a serious relationship; I was 16, Doris was 14. In my own mind I soon realized that I truly loved Doris and that she would make a wonderful life's partner. I think it is accurate to say that before too long we both realized, without actually discussing any long-term possibilities, that our relationship might well develop into something permanent.

On January 1, 1950, our two families were part of the group that left South Abbotsford to form the McCallum Road Church. Since we both lived on King Road, less than a mile apart, a more personal relationship developed easily, especially during the times when I walked her home after choir practice. I needed to pass by her home en route to my home almost a mile further west on King Road. Sometimes, when dad let me use our family car, I would have the pleasure of driving her home.

I should add here that Doris was very active in the McCallum Road Church. She was one of the church pianists and also sang in the girls' trio which served the church on many occasions and which also sang in other venues, including the hospital. She and Violet and Frieda, daughters in the Jake Nickel family, were known as The Nickel Trio. Doris also taught a Sunday School class.

All along, I expressed my desire to get an education in preparation for a career. At the time, I had not settled on any particular profession but I had decided to attend the University of British Columbia, then the only university in BC.

In retrospect I can say that my gradually deepening relationship with this loving and very lovable girl was a stabilizing influence in my life during those sometimes difficult years. Without ever saying as much to Doris, in my mind and heart it was clear that in my studies I was preparing not only for some sort of fulfilling and God-serving career, I was also preparing for a life together with the girl I loved deeply.

Although funds were never plentiful, we had many personal and group dates

Doris and John, about 1954.

and events. In retrospect, it seems unusual, I suppose, that even as our relationship deepened and we regularly visited in each other's parental homes, we did not discuss marriage. The main reason probably lay with me. I did not want to begin making such plans before I would be able to assume the appropriate financial responsibility.

That all changed in the spring of 1954. I would be completing my Bachelor of Arts degree in the summer and taking the graduate teacher training course the next winter. By the end of April 1955, I should be a certified teacher.

One of our favourite drives was along Riverside Road between Abbotsford Village and the US border. It had several secluded parking places. May 17, 1954, was one of those spring days when the Fraser Valley is at its best. I had asked Doris if she would be available for a drive that evening. She was. As we drove along Riverside I selected our favourite parking place, under some trees. Grinning a little, I asked Doris for her ring size. She smiled and readily gave it to me. She probably expected the question. As I recall, I wrote it down. One must not forget important information. Nothing more need be said.

Then, a little later, I turned to Doris and said, "Will you marry me?" She was taken aback. She responded with a truly surprised tone of voice: "Is this the real thing?" I assured her it was as real as it would get.

Her lips then spoke what her eyes had already conveyed. "Yes."

I took an engagement ring out of my pocket and slipped it on her finger. Was she ever surprised! Our mutual commitment was sealed! Tears of joy flowed. Asking for the finger size was, of course, only a ruse. I had previously discovered Doris's ring size and had had a very fine ring made for her, the love of my life.

I might add here that I had sold my one cow to buy the ring. Our parents gave a cow to each child when leaving home.

One thing more. In keeping with the practice at that time, I had, as I clearly recall, previously asked her father if I could marry his beautiful youngest daughter. Also, as I remember, both her father and her mother quite readily gave their approval - in confidence, of course. They seemed very supportive.

After an appropriate length of time enjoying the event - one must not rush important relational occasions - we drove to our parents' homes to make the joyful announcement. There was happiness and approval everywhere. I must say that those months of our engagement were truly happy months for me. I had prayed early on that I would find a fine life's partner. As it happened, my prayers were answered rather early.

Although we did not immediately discuss details, we soon agreed that it would be good to get married sometime after I would finish teacher training at the end of April the following year. Soon we began making plans.

Plans were coming along nicely by March 1955 when, as noted earlier, I had the good fortune of winning the top scholarship offered by the *Deutsche Academische Austausch Dienst* (DAAD) at UBC. As described in Chapter 5, Doris very graciously agreed that it would be advantageous in the long-term for me to go to Europe. I thanked her most sincerely and have always remained deeply indebted to her for being so accommodating. That was but one indication of her other-oriented mindset.

Then came my year in Heidelberg. That was the story of Chapter 8.

Although we had done extensive long-distance planning while I was in Europe, primarily by Doris, there was much that still needed to be done after I arrived in Mission City on August 3. Our wedding was set for August 21, 1956, in the McCallum Road Church.

In addition to making preparations for our wedding, I had other matters on my mind. I had no teaching job. I had no car. I had very little money. But that did not prevent me from concentrating on the fact that I was going to be married to a wonderful woman who loved me deeply, as deeply as I loved her. It had been eight years since our first group date at Easter, 1949.

Just before the wedding, we bought a car from our good friend, Abe Warkentin, who owned Gladstone Auto Sales in Vancouver. The two-tone green 1952 Chevrolet served us very well. At this point I do not remember the details but I am quite sure that Abe sold us that Chev almost entirely on credit. He was, after all, the friend who had loaned me $50 while I was in Europe when, as I recall, I needed another $50 to cover my airfare home. It should be remembered that $50 in 1956 was the equivalent of about $600 in 2021.

In the forenoon of our wedding day, Doris and I went to a nursery near Mission and cut gladioli to decorate the church.

Our wedding took place in the evening of Tuesday, August 21. The weather was spectacular. Customs in those days were different from later norms.

August 21, 1956

The beautiful bride

Opening the presents.

Many ladies in the church were busy that day preparing refreshments for the reception in the church basement. We would need several sittings because, given that our fathers were the two pastors in the church, we had invited the entire congregation as well as other relatives and friends. It was a large wedding. The number of guests probably exceeded 300. Both fathers spoke. My father in German, and Doris' father in English. The bride was beautiful. All went well.

For our wedding night, we had rented a very romantic log cabin at the Dogwood Auto Court near Hope.

Our first night together near Hope.

As already noted, I returned from Europe virtually penniless. Somehow I scrounged up enough money to pay for our first-night accommodation and the required gasoline for our driving.

Doris had been working at the Royal Bank in Abbotsford and could pay for our meals. I kidded her then that if I did not behave, I could not eat. I tried to behave all the time! We still chuckle about that.

When we returned from our honeymoon in the Okanagan and at Christina Lake, we rented a motel unit on South Fraser Way, then the Trans-Canada Highway #1, near Abbotsford, across from Frost Auction Market where it existed then, and moved in. The unit, which cost us $65 a month, was furnished. Trying to save funds, we relocated after a few months to what we called the Gosling House where we paid $45 a month.

The Gosling House: $45 per month.

Doris at Mill Lake, Abbotsford, 1957.

A happy couple, 1958.

CHAPTER 10

MY FOUR-YEAR HIGH SCHOOL TEACHING CAREER 1956-1960

Teaching High School

When I returned on August 3, I had no job. I had earlier applied to about four school districts in the Central Fraser Valley but had not been able to land a teaching appointment, probably because I was not available for the customary interview. Almost immediately after I returned, I feverishly applied again. By early August, typically, the hiring has been done. I knew that there were some openings in the north but we preferred staying in the Lower Mainland.

It turned out that for some reason the Langley School District had an opening. When I was informed of this vacancy, the lady on the phone said that I should know that there were already six applicants for that position but the interviews had not yet taken place. She said I could submit an application. I hurriedly did that. I remember the day when seven of us eager young professionals appeared, all hoping to be hired. The interviewers asked many questions. They were greatly interested in my overseas experience. I suppose that I met their expectations because when the results were announced, I was hired.

The situation, however, was not all sweetness and light. Since I was the last teacher hired for Langley Secondary School (LSS), I was given a set of remaining courses. Most of them were fine. I think I had classes in Social Studies, German, English and a Grade 12 Math class. But there was one other course that was problematic. I was assigned a Grade Twelve Girls Physical Education course. I was clueless. I suppose I could have taught them some ping-pong skills. I quickly did some investigation about what was expected. I met the class once. I think they were as surprised as I was. I think I had the girls do some exercises and spelled out some expectations for the rest of the course. It was not an auspicious beginning. Fortunately, a certain experienced English teacher, a lady who had a wide spectrum of skills and experience, took pity on me and offered to switch classes. I think I got an English class for which I was very grateful.

I should note here that after Harvey Dyck and I returned from Europe and our travels in North Africa and the Middle East, we both had numerous opportunities to make verbal and slide presentations, mostly individually but on occasion jointly. Very few people had traveled to Europe, let alone crossed the Sahara on a motorcycle. We were minor celebrities. One major event took place on November 3, 1956, in the MEI auditorium. The large crowd paid good money to hear us: Adults 35 cents; Children 25 cents.

The 1956-57 school year brought with it some other notable realities. Because LSS was vastly overcrowded and the new Aldergrove Secondary School was not yet completed, LSS operated with two shifts. I taught in the afternoon shift which, I think, ran from 1:00 to 5:30 without a recess. This gave me lots of time to prepare a whole set of new courses. For the 1957-1958 school

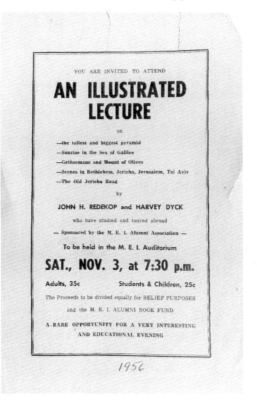

Announcing a Travelogue.

year, with the new Aldergrove school still not completed, the Aldergrove students were organized as a separate Aldergrove shift. This arrangement continued until May 1958, when the Aldergrove students moved into the new Aldergrove Secondary School.

Close to Christmas in 1956 I unexpectedly got a phone call from the BC Education Department in Victoria. The lady wanted to know if I would be interested in teaching English to about 20 professors of the Hungarian Sopron School of Forestry. The entire Forestry Faculty, professors and students, had fled communist Hungary and had come to Canada. They would be housed for a while in the vacant Abbotsford Airport barracks. As I recall, I was to teach them every forenoon for two hours. Somehow this Victoria official knew that my LSS teaching happened only in the afternoon. There was a stipend. Naturally, I accepted. Teaching that group of professors, all much older than I was, turned out to be a delight. That was clearly the smartest class of students I have ever taught. Communication was a challenge. A few of them spoke German so we could get along. Since that was my first year of

John with the Hungarian professors.

teaching, I must have been the least experienced teacher they could have hired. Maybe it was my knowledge of German that got me that job. Be that as it may, the experience was a delightful and treasured one.

I shall interject a sequel here. One Sunday morning, about 50 years later, when I was welcoming newcomers to our Bakerview Church, a couple walked in. I greeted them, and we talked for a bit. The gentleman had an obvious and delightful British accent, but I could not identify the slight accent I detected in the lady's speech. When I inquired about it, she said that she had a Hungarian background. I asked if she had heard of the Sopron Forestry Faculty which had come to British Columbia. She had. It turned out that she was the daughter of one of my professor-students. Michael and Edit Ellis became valued friends.

Many memories come to mind as I think back on those four very interesting and enjoyable years. I shall mention only a few.

Either in my first or second year I organized a Model United Nations session. Many students participated in the large assembly we set up in the gymnasium. They eagerly researched and then emphatically argued their country's perspective on, as I recall, the Suez Canal conflict. The well-attended event was a huge success.

I think that it was during my first full year in Aldergrove that I got myself into trouble. I had a boy in a senior course who did very little work. Try as I might, I could not get him to complete his assignments. When the time came to issue report cards I wrote *Lazy* concerning his work in that course.

Vice-Principal Roger Winter called me in. Apparently the lad's parents were not pleased with my one-word assessment. Vice Principal Winter did not disagree with my evaluation but told me that I should be more diplomatic. I could, for example, have written *Does not apply himself as he should* or *Not working up to his ability*. Somehow I made amends to the student and his parents. I learned an important lesson in educational psychology and teacher tactfulness.

I must also note this experience. One day I emphatically instructed a student to look up a word in the dictionary if he didn't know to spell it. He then calmly replied something like this. "How can I look it up if I don't know how it is spelled?" He was right. I was the one who needed to learn a lesson that day.

After my first year of teaching an important event changed and enhanced our lives. On July 26, 1957, Wendy Marie joined our family.

A happy mother with Wendy.

I was in Summer School at UBC at the time and was delighted to receive the phone call. I regretted that I was not the one to take Doris to the hospital and to be with her at the time, but we had agreed that I should not leave classes and wait at Abbotsford for the event to happen. We were very grateful for the kindness of Doris' parents who took her to the hospital. I made it back to Abbotsford to get her and Wendy from the hospital.

After that Doris and Wendy joined me in Vancouver where, together with Neil and Sophie Toews and Abe Wieler, we had rented a house for the summer. Both Neil and Abe were also taking summer courses.

It was probably in my third year, 1958-1959, that I was elected president of the Langley Teachers Association. This involved a fair bit of work which I

Wendy, a happy little girl.

thoroughly enjoyed. One of my tasks was to chair the teachers' team in salary and benefits negotiations. That, too, was quite enjoyable. At that time the teachers had not yet formed a union which meant that negotiations were informal and rather congenial. I might note here that salaries were rather low in those years. For my first year's teaching, I earned $3,000.

For the last of my four years I earned $6,000. We must remember, of course, that all prices and costs were low. A new Volkswagen Beetle cost about $1,600. A gallon, not a litre, of gas cost about 29 cents. We saved enough money in those years to pay off my small student debt, probably $250, to pay for our car and to help us build a duplex. The lot on Parkview Street in Clearbrook cost us $700. We lived in one half of the duplex and had renters live in the other half. The total cost of the duplex, lot included, was about $8,000. In 1960, when we left, we sold it for $9,000. Those were very good years. During those years, we also built a fine three-bedroom bungalow in the northeast part of the village of Abbotsford. It cost us $10,000, including the large lot. We planned to move into that home until plans changed and I decided to undertake further studies. In 1960 we sold that house for $12,000.

During the 1959-60 school year we decided that I should take at least one year off to earn a master's degree which would put me into the top category of teacher certification in BC. I therefore asked Principal Don Hansen if I could have a year's leave, after which I would return to Aldergrove High School. Soon I was contacted by him and, as I recall, District Superintendent Mr. Stafford. I was rather surprised when, in response to my request, these officials told me that they thought that if I left, I would not come back. I vigorously asserted that I definitely planned to return. They were not convinced by my assertion. Instead, they offered me a major promotion.

After only four years of teaching, I could become an administrator as the

Director of Night School for the Langley School District. This would mean a major increase in salary. That was a very generous and appealing offer but I definitely wanted to earn a master's degree and therefore did not accept the exceptional offer. I did not get an official leave but I was given to understand that if I did return, which they insisted would not happen, they would, as I understood it, be pleased to have me return to the District.

As it turned out, the District officials were right and I was wrong. After I completed my master's degree I did not ask to come back to high school teaching in Langley School District.

It was probably in early 1959 that I asked editor Frank Epp if he would be interested in publishing a special issue of *The Canadian Mennonite* describing the rapidly growing, mostly Mennonite, Clearbrook urban area. He was delighted with my suggestion.

The result of my efforts was a special edition of *The Canadian Mennonite* on June 26, 1959.

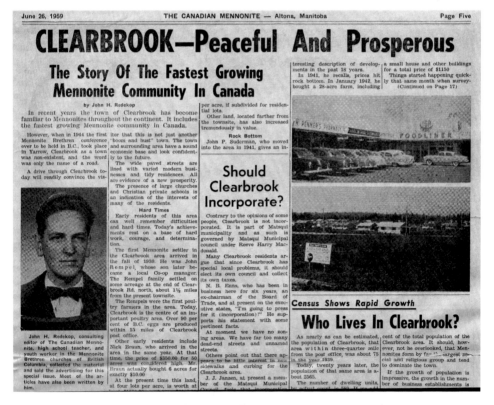

A special issue of *The Canadian Mennonite*, June 26, 1959.

This issue also, of course, included much of the usual content. Since there was no budget and no staff, I had to do the groundwork myself. Checking my sample copy today, I see that I managed to solicit advertising from 56 businesses. I wrote eighteen stories about various aspects of the growing Mennonite presence in this part of the Fraser Valley and included 34 pictures, mostly taken by me. Reading those stories now is interesting. One of the concerns at that time, was whether Clearbrook should incorporate as a separate town or remain part of the Municipality of Matsqui. One story notes that in 1939 the number of people living within a three-quarter mile distance from the intersection of Clearbrook Road and the Trans-Canada Highway, now South Fraser Way, was estimated to be 75.

My unofficial census in 1959 indicated that in that same area the population had reached 2,565.

I truly enjoyed my interaction with the high-energy, extremely talented, and always visioning Frank Epp. He taught me much, including gratitude for heritage and traditional values that had stood the test of time, a responsibility to nurture what is best in the Anabaptist-Mennonite theology, the Christian's responsibility to address issues of the day, the centrality of accuracy as well as integrity in writing and speaking, the impact of media on people's thinking and values, and some writing skills..

While teaching high school I also began writing for other agencies and periodicals. Perhaps the most significant item was *A Study Outline of Christian Nonresistance* written for the BCMB Conference as part of a study program for young people and young adults to increase awareness of the MB peace teaching. I presented it at the June 7, 1958, BCMB convention. This 1958 printing had a five-page bibliography. I greatly enjoyed researching and writing this study paper.

Those were happy years for my parents. My mother continued with her crafts and my father with his teaching and preaching, both of which he enjoyed immensely.

Church Life; My Spiritual Pilgrimage; The Death of My Father

These were important years for me in terms of church life and spiritual involvement. About 1956 the Abbotsford M.B. Church, also known as McCallum Road Church, now Central Heights Church, designated three or four young men to assist in the church's preaching. I was one of them. Every few months or so, we were asked to preach a Sunday morning sermon. As I recall, at that time, there were often two sermons. Unfortunately, I did not keep the notes for those sermons except for one: *"The Faith of Our Fathers"* (likely 1957).

My formal involvement with the Mennonite Brethren Conference began on November 24, 1956 when, only a few months after my return from Europe, I was asked to serve as the first English-language recording secretary at the BC Mennonite Brethren convention. On June 9, 1957, I became a delegate from the McCallum Road Church to the semi-annual convention of BC MB Churches. On November 11, 1957, I again served as the English-language secretary. I greatly enjoyed such involvement. On June 7, 1958, I was elected to serve as the English-language secretary in an ongoing position. At that time the BCMB Conference of Churches was facing important challenges dealing with rapid growth and fundamental redefinition of itself as socioeconomic realities changed and as the younger generation began pressing for the use of English in church services. They also wanted to move beyond a mainly ethno-religious church experience. Religious acculturation proved very challenging. At times there were generational tensions.

During Summer 1958, the Brunk evangelistic tent campaign, headquartered in Virginia, USA, conducted a tent crusade in Abbotsford. As I recall, the huge tent at the northeast corner of Marshall and Ware roads was filled to overflowing every night. I served on the Publicity Team and was pleased to see the large attendance. Obviously, many people got their spiritual lives straightened out. My father, Rev. Jacob F. Redekop, was very actively involved as a member of the Executive Committee.

One evening remains very vividly etched in my memory. Illustrating the importance of making things right with people in our lives and also expressing thanks to those we love, Rev. George Brunk reported the following personal experience. Many years previously, it had become a very powerful thought to him that he needed to have a talk with his father. As I recall, he needed to apologize for something and he also needed to express his sincere thanks to his father for all that he had done for him.

One night this need to act became so strong in his mind that he got up from his bed, drove over to his father's house, woke him, and said what he needed to say. He then said that very soon after that night, his father died; maybe it was the next day. As Rev. Brunk spoke, my father was seated on the platform near him. I looked at my dad and decided that I also should thank my father for all that he had done for me. I decided to do that soon. Unfortunately, I procrastinated.

It was probably in early 1957 that I was asked to become our church's youth leader. I accepted. McCallum Road Church had a very fine youth group of about 35 energetic people and it was a privilege to help the young people organize activities and participate in church services. We had many activities, both inspirational and social. It was during one of our many recreational activities that a major event happened.

On May 23, 1959 the church youth group was having a Saturday evening softball game at the Abbotsford Fairgrounds located near where Abbotsford Police Headquarters is now situated. Suddenly I noticed a van slowly coming from the south and driving right across the playing field. This signalled something serious. I walked up to it and saw our friend, Jake Hooge, at the wheel with his lip quivering. I knew instantly that he was the bearer of bad news. I remember asking, "Who is it?" He responded with "Your Dad." I left my assistant, Neil Klassen, in charge of the youth group and quickly drove home, only a few blocks away. We arranged for Wendy to stay with friends and Doris and I rushed over to our parents' residence on Peardonville Road, less than a half-mile away. There we saw two physicians, Dr. I. M. Fast, our family physician, and his assistant, Dr. John Woods. A neighbour across the street had seen my father drop while he was washing the car.

Rev. Jacob F. Redekop, preacher and teacher.

The physicians had arrived and declared my father deceased. My father, Rev. Jacob Frank Redekop, was only 63 and still teaching at what is now Columbia Bible College, an institution that he had led for ten crucial years and taught at for four more. Mother was in shock. We stayed with her that night. I vividly remember that first breakfast. Nobody felt like eating. Nobody did much talking. The silence spoke loudly.

For mother, in particular, life was instantly turned upside down. My father's funeral was held on May 27 with a packed crowd in the spacious MEI auditorium.

The pallbearers were six preacher friends: Rev. Herman Voth, Rev. John Harder, Rev. C. D. Toews, Rev. John Reimer, Rev. Herman Lenzmann, and Rev. John Stobbe. The two preachers were Rev. C. C. Peters and Doris's father and my dad's pastoral colleague, Rev. Henry H. Nikkel.

As stated above, after hearing George Brunk's report I had definitely planned to carry out my special visit to my father - I waited too long! I could express my sincere gratitude only to his unresponsive, cold, dead body.

Aside from the loss of her spouse, my mother had other concerns. As was common for older women at that time, she did not drive a car. More importantly, there had been no household income other than dad's earnings. What would she live on? Further, who would pay the funeral and burial costs? Fortunately, the church where father had served faithfully as an unpaid assistant pastor for nine years helped with some costs. We, as a family, then stepped forward. Although mother felt bad about it, at least initially, under my brother Paul's capable leadership we developed a monthly budget and arranged that the five siblings who had the means to participate would all contribute a share of the needed funds to Paul, who would deliver the money monthly to mother.

Mom was a gifted gardener.

We pointed out to her that during very difficult years in Saskatchewan, during the Great Depression, she had sacrificed much and worked incredibly hard for her family. Now the time had come for her family to stand by her. She understood what we were saying. I doubt if she ever felt good about it but I have always considered assisting her financially at that time as both a duty but mostly as a privilege. The Bible, of course, teaches that children and grand-children shall provide for their parents as needed. "[B]ut if any widow has children or grand-children, these should learn first of all to put their religion into practice by caring for their own family and so repaying their parents and grandparents, for this is pleasing to God." (*I Timothy 5: 4*) This arrangement continued until mother qualified for other income.

In early 1958 I was elected to the BCMB Youth Committee. In those days, that committee had major responsibilities not only to assist local church youth groups but also to organize various conference-wide activities. That strong committee consisted of Jack Block, John Neumann, Henry Unger, John Isaak, John Wittenberg, Abe Klassen, Henry Regehr (UBC chaplain), and me. We set ourselves some lofty goals. One was to organize a major Youth Rally, at the Clayburn Pentecostal Campgrounds in the foothills northeast of the Abbotsford town-site. We also talked about establishing a camp. There was vibrancy, energy and enthusiasm in the air. We organized the major rally for 1958, during late June, as I recall. With more than 1,800 people attending it was a great success. I served as treasurer and also had the responsibility to barbecue a calf donated by Walter and Rosella Schmidt. I read up on how to do this, and we dug a deep pit. That was a novel and challenging experience but it turned out well. We fed all the people and raised a lot of money for the Kingdom ministry. For all this activity there was no paid staff,

That same year this Youth Committee organized its first children's camp at that Clayburn site. It, too, was a great success. Jack Block was the director, Rev. Abe Wieler served as camp dean and Rosella Schmidt served as crafts director. That 1958 pioneering effort was repeated in 1959 at a site near Cultus Lake and continued operating as Columbia Bible Camp until 2000 when it was renamed Stillwood Camp and Conference Centre.

These years were important in my own spiritual pilgrimage. My year in Europe, especially visiting the historic Mennonite and Anabaptist sites and studying that era seriously, had given me a new appreciation for my Anabaptist heritage. Not surprisingly, for our first Christmas together I asked Doris to give me *The Complete Writings of Menno Simons.* She did. I still have that greatly valued volume. I also purchased numerous other books on Anabaptist theology and Christian apologetics. I found it fulfilling and enjoyable to serve in church as a Sunday School teacher, as the youth leader, singing in the choir, helping to set up a church library, preaching occasionally, and serving in other ways.

The late 1950s and 1960s were very important years for Mennonite Brethren churches and the MB denomination in Canada. Important changes were happening rapidly. The first major development was that churches, partly because they were generally becoming more integrated into Canadian society, demanded or at least desired that their pastors be educated. In the church in which I grew up in Saskatchewan, we had four gifted and effective preachers but none of them, to the best of my knowledge, had acquired formal education beyond the Bible School level, which at that time was not considered to be fully post-secondary education. Such improvement in education was, of course, commendable, but it brought with it another important development.

The second development was that pastors began being salaried. In itself, that too was commendable. All too vividly I remember times when my preacher father would serve in various churches and would receive no financial compensation, often not even funds to cover his gasoline expenses. For all services rendered by preachers in their home congregation there was, typically, very little or no compensation.

We think that Rev. H. H. Nikkel never received a salary, although he may have received a very small stipend during his last few years at the McCallum Road Church.

Within a few years pastors' salaries generally rose to what was called "professional levels." If a teacher or a social worker had a bachelor's or master's degree and was paid accordingly, the same principle should apply to pastors. While this enlightened policy brought fairness and propriety to a truly lamentable situation, it also created some very important new problems, especially because they were not anticipated or even recognized and often not factored into the changing church scene.

These were the major problems as I saw them developing. First, being fully salaried, more than a few pastors began seeing themselves as employees and not primarily as shepherds of the flock accountable to God in a primary sense. Naturally and logically, employees seek to please their employers. Second, as I observed matters, it seemed to me that employee-pastors became increasingly reluctant to speak about matters in a way that might displease the board that employed them. This, of course, varied greatly in the churches. The third problem was that because pastors were hired to serve the church, they now rarely spoke in other congregations and they were also much less available to serve the larger peoplehood. Whereas at one time our strongest pastors were heard in many churches, that practice virtually disappeared.

A fourth problem was that after pastors saw themselves as employees, it became increasingly difficult for guest speakers, missionaries or heads of Christian agencies to address a Sunday congregation. This very unfortunate trend was exacerbated by two other trends - the rather rapid dropping of Wednesday night meetings and then also of Sunday evening services except for special occasions.

A major fifth additional consequence of these developments was that no longer did the congregations become generally aware of the depth and diversity of Christian ministries, including their own conference's activities.

Two further general trends developed in those years. One was that gradually volunteer ministry declined; volunteers were replaced by paid staff. Second, congregations became increasingly individualistic and defined themselves less as a local assembly within one denominational church and more as an almost autonomous congregation. This shift became all too obvious when some church bulletins or worship folders, another fine initiative of those years, began describing that church not as a member of a conference but as a church "Affiliated with" a conference.

When church historians assess what happened to the Canadian Mennonite Brethren Conference in the late 1950s and the 1960s, they may conclude that not only did church services and church operations change drastically but also that much of the distinctive Anabaptist theology of the church was becoming weaker in both preaching content and church polity.

The Jacob F. Redekop Clan, summer, 1957.

Four Generations, summer, 1957.
Henry Nikkel, Marie Nikkel, Heinrich Nikkel (Father of Henry),
Doris with Wendy, John, Agnes Redekop, Jacob F. Redekop.

Enjoying summer holidays, 1959.

CHAPTER 11

POST-SECONDARY EDUCATION PART II 1960-1964

Having decided to pursue a master's degree I needed to determine in what discipline and at which university. In due course I decided that it would be in history rather than in education. Either option would give me the top teacher certification. I applied to the University of California, Berkeley. That university had an outstanding reputation. Berkeley was also advantageous in that the Bay Area would be a fine place to live.

Clearly, costs were a factor to be considered. Fortunately, we had saved some funds. As the planning for 1960-61 progressed, the financial situation turned out well. In the spring of 1960 I was awarded the Christie Scholarship, an award carrying with it a $300 grant. In 2021 funds that would be worth about $4,000. This award was given by the BC Teachers Federation to the most promising teacher "planning to further his qualifications." The presentation in the Hotel Vancouver Ballroom on April 18, 1960, was a memorable event for Doris and me. Fortunately, I also received a $2,500 Fellowship from the Canada Council. The Council stated that in accepting the award, I affirmed that I intended to return to Canada. At the time there was much concern about "the brain drain" to the US. I agreed to that commitment. While this was not a legal obligation, it was for me, an important moral commitment. Later on I discovered that some recipients of Canada Council awards reneged on such a commitment. I decided not to do that and after eight years living in the US, this was a major consideration, but not the only one, in our decision to return to Canada.

Our financial situation was further enhanced when the University of California, Berkeley waived almost all of the M.A. tuition fees. While our living costs were significant, especially during the first semester for which we rented a house in Richmond, our costs were much reduced for the second semester when we were able to move into subsidized student housing.

As a result of the awards, the almost total waiving of tuition fees, and the subsidized housing after Christmas, we were able to complete that academic year with some money in the bank.

University of California, Berkeley 1960 - 1961

Early on, I decided that I would try to complete the requirements for the Master of Arts degree in two semesters. Because about 12,000 of that university's roughly 20,000 students were graduate students, we were given the most attention by the professors. I completed the requirements and was awarded a Master of Arts in History on June 9, 1961.

Master of Arts, Berkeley, CA, June 9, 1961.

We had some interesting church-related experiences while living first in the suburb of Richmond and then in student housing in Berkeley. I must stress that this situation existed in 1960-61. Clearly, values have changed since then. We attended a nearby and very welcoming Nazarene church. Although Pastor Irving and I had some interesting conversations about what it meant to be "saved and sanctified," that Nazarene emphasis was not a problem for us in enjoying excellent preaching and fellowship.

The issue, rather, involved that church's racial policies. That church had an excellent Sunday School program and a very effective plan to bring community children to the classes. But there was a problem. That entire urban area was racially mixed. All children were welcomed into the Sunday School classes - I think until their 13th birthday.

If my memory serves me right, no Black children were allowed to attend that church's Sunday School after their 13th birthday. They were, instead, offered the option of being taken by bus to a neighbouring Black church. The intent, of course, was to prevent a mixed-race romance and marriage. It took me some time to discover this policy. If we had stayed in that area longer than one year, we would have transitioned to a more inclusive church.

M.A. graduation ceremony, Berkeley, California, June 9, 1961.

The Berkeley year was enjoyable for various reasons. Living in the Bay Area enabled us to enjoy many fine parks and other sites in San Francisco and the larger region. The climate was delightful. We were also close enough to the Mennonite areas in the San Joaquin Valley for us to connect with friends and relatives in Fresno and other centres. In fact, I was able to take off sufficient days so that we could attend a North American Mennonite Brethren convention in the large Reedley MB Church which was then, as I recall, the largest MB church in the world.

With the warm climate, lush green growth everywhere, lots of citrus fruits, and many fine times at the local Nazarene Church and other venues, it was an enjoyable and beneficial year for us.

During my studies at Berkeley I realized that my main academic interest was more in the area of political studies, including political ideologies and the interaction of religion and politics, than in researching and writing about the various eras of history. Also, sometime during the second semester Doris and I had serious conversations about whether I should pursue doctoral studies. I increasingly wanted to do that but we knew that this would involve considerable further sacrifice on Doris' part and a full three years of further studies for me if I switched from history to political science, plus writing a dissertation.

In June I stopped in at the University of Washington (UW) in Seattle to inquire about the Ph.D. program in political science. The professors there were definitely interested in me applying and also stated that there would likely be a teaching assistant position for me. Such an appointment would be very advantageous to us financially. This university, rather than Berkeley, also appealed to me because its Ph.D. program in political science was more in line with my interests, housing was cheaper and more readily available, and it was closer to Abbotsford and our families. There was also the fact that because I was abroad as a student we were still entitled to benefit from the much lower medical and hospital costs in BC. Proximity to BC could be very advantageous. We made the decision. I applied to study at the University of Washington for a Ph.D. in political science. I was accepted.

The Langley School District officials were proven right. I would not be returning to high school teaching in Langley. Those District officials knew me better than I knew myself.

During the summer of 1961 we lived in the basement of the house where Doris' parents lived on Holland Drive in Abbotsford. It was a very fine arrangement. Knowing that I needed to pass exams in both German and French at the University of Washington, I spent much of the summer teaching myself basic French grammar and vocabulary. Later I was fortunate to pass the French translation exam the first time I took it. The German exam, of course, was easy for me.

Two important events happened that summer. On July 11, 1961, Gary John joined our family. It was very advantageous financially that he was born in BC because hospital and medical costs in California, even then, were very much greater than in Abbotsford. Gary was a healthy and happy child, and it was a delight to have him join our family.

Gary joins our family.

Gary, a future professor at the University of British Columbia.

The other important event took place a few weeks later. Ever since we moved to Abbotsford I had thought about climbing majestic, 10,700-foot, Mt. Baker. In the summer of 1961 it seemed that this was a good time to do that. A group of four of us decided we would climb. We read up on what the climb would require and acquired the needed equipment.

On Sunday afternoon, July 24, four of us - Don DeFehr, Art Martens, John B. Nickel and I - started our climb. By evening we reached Kulshan Cabin, a mountain-climbers staging point near the snowline. At dawn, on July 25, about 4:30 we were up and with goggles on, sun lotion applied, cleats on our boots, and roped together about 20 feet apart, we set out.

After evading some dangerous crevasses, climbing some almost 45-degree slopes, and crossing some ice-covered areas, we reached the peak by 1:00 PM. The views from that height are spectacular. Not only could we see Vancouver Island, the Fraser Valley, and Vancouver, but looking south, we could also see a series of high volcanic peaks. Looking north we could also see many mountains. Then we spotted some smoke in the north. When we arrived home later that day, we heard that a forest fire was burning near Kamloops.

Resting while climbing Mt. Baker.

Crossing Mt. Baker crevasse.

Four climbers reach Mt. Baker summit.
L to R: John, Don DeFehr, Art Martens, John B. Nickel.

Leaving a Canadian flag at the summit.
(the pre-1965 Red Ensign)

The University of Washington 1961 - 1964

My three years of coursework at the U of W were very enjoyable. I also greatly enjoyed my work as a teaching assistant. My TA income, together with some scholarship funding, including another Canada Council award of $2,000 in 1963, and some additional teaching income enabled us to complete those three years without any student debt.

Every Ph.D. student needs to find a dissertation supervisor fairly early in the program of studies. I was very much drawn to one of my professors, Linden Mander. I was very fortunate to be appointed his teaching assistant. Of him it can be said that although he was probably not a committed Christian, he was a true gentleman with outstanding character. A brilliant scholar and popular professor, he practiced the highest ethics. The good professor agreed to be my dissertation supervisor.

As professor Mander's teaching assistant, I worked closely with him in marking undergraduate exams and essays. He taught me much. I observed how tactfully he dealt with students who had not done well. He would always find something positive to saabout an exam or essay. About an essay he might say, *"You identified some good research sources. Your introduction was impressive. Unfortunately, your analysis and your conclusion were not as good. If they had been as good, you would have passed."*

I observed that his students who failed actually accepted their failure in an exam or essay because they believed that they had the potential to do much better and had been encouraged to do that. While working for this fine professor I determined to follow his example. I think I can with accuracy say that during all my teaching years I always wrote or said something positive about every essay, exam, book report, verbal presentation, or any other student project that I marked. Thanks, professor Mander.

It was also about this time, keeping professor Mander's wisdom in mind, that I formulated for myself a related working adage that I have tried to follow ever since. It goes like this: *"Affirm when you can so that you can with credibility criticize when you must."* It has been very helpful for me in many political, academic, church-related, and other situations. I believe, in fact I know, that putting my adage into practice was appreciated by students.

I am not sure exactly when it was, but probably just before the January 1963 winter quarter began, that one evening, I think it was on a Friday, I got a phone call from professor Hugh Bone, the chairman of the Political Science Department. He informed me that professor Mander had had a serious heart attack and would not be able to continue teaching full-time. He asked if I would be willing to take over professor Mander's teaching of the course for which I was the teaching assistant. He said that I would be given a teaching assistant to help me with the marking for the large class. There would, of course, be an appropriate faculty stipend.

Naturally, I readily accepted this opportunity. I thus became both a student and faculty member. By the next lecture day, likely the following Monday, I was presented to the class as their new instructor for that third-year course. I taught that course again in the summer quarter, 1963, and in the winter quarter, 1964. I have that winter quarter course syllabus before me, *Political Science 328, The United Nations and Specialized Agencies*. I truly enjoyed that teaching experience. Fortunately, the students responded very positively to my lectures. This surprising appointment was, of course, a significant benefit to us financially.

The summer of 1963 was important for us for another reason. On July 29, 1963, Heather Lynn joined our family. Because of the lower medical costs in BC, Doris had gone to Abbotsford for the birth of our third child while I stayed in Seattle to teach the Summer School course. All went well. Heather was a healthy, happy child.

Heather joins our family.

Young Heather in contemplation.

Early in 1964, with professor Mander as the chair of my Supervisory Committee, I began working very seriously on my Ph.D. dissertation while also preparing for the five major exams that I would be writing. At the end of the spring term, I wrote the exams. They varied from three to five hours in length. I was assigned to a small office and was allowed to leave with the understanding that I would not be consulting anyone or searching out any information. I was also allowed to put carbon under all that I wrote so that I still have copies of my written exam answers. Those five days were rather demanding. Fortunately, all went well.

The research for my dissertation and the required revisions took somewhat longer than expected. I completed it during my first term as a faculty member at Fresno Pacific College. The topic of my dissertation was: "Billy James Hargis. A Case Study of the American Far Right." At that time Rev. Hargis' Christian Anti-Communism Crusade was a national organization with broadcasts over hundreds of radio stations, a large printing division, and a major headquarters in Tulsa, Oklahoma. The organization also conducted rallies across the USA, which attracted large crowds, including many evangelical Christians.

Jumping ahead for the moment I can say that at the end of November 1965, Doris and I traveled to Seattle for the defense of my 435-page dissertation. I felt very confident about my knowledge of the American Far Right. As expected, my entire dissertation committee and a totally unfamiliar outside professor grilled me about it for perhaps an hour. I suppose they were satisfied with my responses because suddenly, the conversation changed. This group of academics then began questioning me about the separatist movement in Quebec and Canadian politics generally. Fortunately, I had studied the separatist phenomenon and could answer their questions. In fact, towards the end of my "defense," I actually lectured for some time on Quebec separatism. I actually had fun informing this committee. At some point, they decided that the session would end. I then inquired if I could ask an unusual question. They nodded, as I recall. I then asked if I could take a picture of this group of examiners. They smiled and said I could. I did.

John's Ph.D. Defense Committee.
Department Chairman Dr. Hugh Bone, second from left.
Professor Mander is seated.

At this point in my narrative I ask the reader's indulgence if I reflect on a very personal matter. Every serious student strives to do his or her best. For me, this was especially important during my years at the University of Washington because I had a growing family for whose well-being I was responsible. I could not let them down. Doris, in particular, was sacrificing much so that I could spend years studying. I needed to succeed. I also needed to do well to get a professor's appointment. I worked hard and prayed hard that my studies would be successful. I am pleased to say that in all of my courses and seminars as well as in my doctoral exams and my dissertation, I was able to maintain a straight 4.0 academic record.

I should perhaps explain that at the UW the numbers stood for the following: 4 = A; 3 = B; 2 = C; 1 = D, and 0 = failure. A doctoral student was expected to maintain at least a 3.0 average.

Ph.D. December 16, 1965.
University of Washington.

One other significant experience should be recounted. Some time before we left Seattle, professor Mander asked to see me. I had no idea what his agenda would be. He then told me that when he had been a student someone had told him that he deserved something special and had given him some money to celebrate. He said that he had long ago decided to do the same thing some day, and that now he wanted to do a similar act of kindness.

He then handed me $50, equivalent to more than $600 in 2021 funds, and instructed me, as I recall, to hire a babysitter and take Doris up the Space Needle for a fancy dinner.

A celebrating couple.

Seattle Space Needle

I thanked him most sincerely. You can imagine Doris' surprise. We did as the good professor had directed. The weather was absolutely perfect as we enjoyed a fabulous dinner while the dining level of the Space Needle made a complete circle.

That was a memorable, unforgettable evening - and we had substantial funds left over.

Church and Spiritual Matters 1960 - 1964

In Seattle we very quickly connected with a small Mennonite Brethren church, the Shoreline MB Church, which was in the throes of a modest building program. We were privileged to be part of the excitement as we moved into the new building which seated about 160 people. Our pastor, Rev. Nick Rempel, was both a strong people person and a very effective preacher. The church was dynamic and growing. Both Doris and I greatly enjoyed our involvement in that small congregation.

For me, the graduate years of studying were spiritually good years. My studies often forced me to rethink my commitment and values. While some ethical and lifestyle stances were modified, my faith commitment did not waver; if anything, it deepened. I also tried to define and practice my growing fatherhood responsibilities along Christian lines.

As it happened, we also maintained important church and conference connections in BC. In July 1963 I attended sessions of the Canadian MB Conference in Abbotsford, in the auditorium of my old alma mater, the MEI. One day I heard a report by *Dass Kommittee für die deutsche Sprache*. (The Committee for the German Language) I still vividly remember hearing its chairman make his report. After that session three of us, who happened to chat about the German Language report, were uncomfortable about what had been said. We decided that we would all respond. We made plans. By the next morning, the other two excused themselves. One said that because he was candidating for a pastor's position in Ontario, he was unwilling to speak; he could not jeopardize his future. The second gentleman also had an excuse, which I do not remember. I was thus designated to present our case by myself. I agreed to do that.

As carefully, logically, and as theologically correct as I could be, I developed two lines of reasoning. First, I argued that if we wanted to be effective in spreading the Good News in Canada, we should focus on using the language of our country, not on the language we, as the heirs of an immigrant group, had retained. I stressed that when we sent missionaries abroad, we expected them to spend time mastering the language of the society where they intended to serve; we should be willing to do the same. That argument hit the mark for some delegates.

My second line of reasoning was that although German should be used in ministries for some people, especially some older folk and immigrants for whom German was their heart language, we, and I stressed that I was speaking for a group, did not believe that the church should invest money and energy trying to perpetuate the retention of a language. Here I had an advantage. I could say that I had a great appreciation for the German language and culture, having recently spent almost a year at a German university. I greatly valued German and would like to see it nurtured, but that such nurturing should be done by secular agencies or by Christians outside of Christian ministries. I argued that it was not part of the Great Commission given to the church. My notes written after that event state that I challenged the delegates not to be taken up "with language and cultural matters." I argued that the church's mission "was to bridge cultural barriers, not reinforce them." As I observed the large assembly of delegates, I thought that this also hit the mark for some of them.

Not surprisingly, there was some immediate and emotional opposition. I was accused of being divisive, unappreciative, and antagonistic. A few delegates accused me of being "unspiritual." That low blow hurt. I heard considerable anger against this young upstart who was challenging senior leaders and established norms. There was, fortunately, also considerable support, much of it, unfortunately, expressed privately later on. Many perceptive people, it seems, develop courage and boldness to speak only privately after public discourse has ended. I experienced that again many times in later years.

That language dust-up had two significant consequences. To the best of my knowledge that was the last conference report given by *Dass Kommittee für die Deutsche Sprache.* I think it limped along for another year or two and then was quietly disbanded. The other consequence was that first Rudy Wiebe, and then Peter Klassen had me writing material for the new *Mennonite Brethren Herald.* These negotiations resulted in the launching of my *Personal Opinion* column. I became a regular columnist on January 1, 1964, and continued in that role, with what one might call a sabbatical break, for the next 39 years. Here are some titles of my *Personal Opinion* column for the first year. "On Constructive Criticism," (January 3, 1964) [my first column]; "Mennonites and Bi-culturalism," (March 20, 1964); "Watch your language," (April 10, 1964), "Is it wrong to doubt?" (May 29, 1964); and "Concerning the Beatles," (October 23, 1964).

I had actually already submitted several longer articles to the *Herald* before I became a columnist. "Which Political Party Should I Support With My Vote*?"* (June 8, 1962) and "The April 8th Canadian Election." (March 29, 1963).

Relevant Political and Public Affairs 1960 - 1964

In Canada the early sixties were exceptionally important. Perhaps the greatest change happened in Quebec. Beginning in 1960, Premier Jean Lesage and his government launched what has come to be called *The Quiet Revolution*. Mainly this meant a rapid disestablishment of the Roman Catholic Church and a huge simultaneous decline in attendance. Attendance for Catholics in Quebec dropped from nearly 80 percent in 1959 to about 8 percent in 1980. Declining attendance also affected Protestant churches across Canada. This massive change was accompanied by a huge shift in public thinking about adultery, marriage, having children, and other issues.

There were other major developments. In October 1962, the world came very close to being plunged into a nuclear war with incalculable consequences. On October 22, President John F. Kennedy, in an historic and dramatic televised speech, announced that the Soviet Union had built missile sites in Cuba, only 90 miles from the US, and that Soviet ships were headed to Cuba with missiles. That country, indeed the entire Western world, was shocked.

President Kennedy demanded that the Soviet ships turn around. To Soviet Premier Nikita Khrushchev, Kennedy wrote: "I have not assumed that you or any other sane person would, in this nuclear age, deliberately plunge the world into war...." On October 24 Premier Khrushchev sent President Kennedy this message: "You are no longer appealing to reason, but wish to intimidate us."

That day, October 24, 1962, we teaching assistants had a very somber meeting. We all agreed that President Kennedy would not allow the Soviet ships, now much closer to Cuba, to dock in that country. We believed that unless Premier Khrushchev ordered the arms ships to turn around, there would be major US action. I remember leaving that afternoon meeting, looking at my teaching associates, wondering if I would see them again. Seattle's Boeing factory would be a likely target. I did not tell Doris about our meeting or impress upon her the imminent threat of war.

In the morning of October 25 the world's news media reported that Premier Khrushchev had ordered the Soviet arms ships to turn back. That ended the 13-day showdown.

On November 22, 1963, I was in our rented home in Seattle, already studying for the eventual Ph.D. written and oral examinations. I remember being rather relaxed, slouching in an easy chair or on the couch, indifferent to the program on the TV. Suddenly the renowned news anchor, Walter Cronkite, appeared on the TV screen. His countenance had a stunned look. Slowly and deliberately, he spoke the words, "President Kennedy has been shot." A few minutes later he announced, if I recall his words correctly: "President Kennedy is dead!" The nation and the world mourned the loss of a charismatic, youthful statesman who, while he had his own serious moral failures, had also inspired a world of young people by telling them, "Ask not what your country can do for you; ask what you can do for your country."

With President Lyndon Johnson instantly in office, the US entered a new era. Here we can only note two historic achievements: passage of the 1964 Civil Rights Act and the 1965 Voting Rights Act. These two major laws achieved two results: they corrected some very unfair laws and practices and set in motion pressures and movements to achieve societal racial equality, which is still underway in American politics and American society.

Wendy, 1961

CHAPTER 12

LIVING IN FRESNO 1964-1968

Living in Fresno; Pacific College

In early 1964 I was in discussions with Pacific College (PC) about teaching there. In part, that college's desire to have me lecture there was surprising because I had previously upset some American Mennonite Brethren. While still a doctoral student, I wrote an article for *The Christian Leader,* the US MB monthly, entitled "Comments on the Anti-Communist Movement" (May 29, 1962). As the first article challenging the strong inroads of the anti-communist movement into the evangelical church, I warned against making this the key mission of the church. Negative reaction was swift. Here is part of one reader's published letter.

"I read with dismay the article 'Comments on the Anti-Communist Movement' in the Leader. I am a member of the John Birch Society, and I find that my respect for my compatriots is considerably greater than any I can muster for most of the apathetic members of the church. Don't send me this magazine any more. I have suddenly lost interest in anything it has to say." (July 10, 1962)

Apparently, the Pacific College administration, although heavily dependent on constituency donations, was willing to take its chances with a young academic who challenged majority views when he believed that such challenging was warranted. PC offered me an appointment which I accepted.

At the end of summer 1964, I think it was in late August, after some months of work on my dissertation, we traveled to Fresno. We moved into a rented house at 2016 East Rialto Street. That house served us well, but I immediately began looking around for something that we might be able to buy. We had saved a little money even during my student days and thought that with my new salary, we should be able to buy a house.

One day, while driving along various streets, I saw a For Sale sign on a property with an attractive bungalow at 4612 East Princeton.

I stopped and checked it out. It seemed to be exactly what we were hoping to find. Prices were very reasonable in Fresno at that time. This home was priced at $12,000.

The Armenian owner, Aram Bedrosian, seemed quite eager to sell. My hunch was that at his asking price, this very fine home would sell quickly. I told the gentleman that we would be interested in buying it but that I would have to bring my wife to see it. I indicated that it would be good if he could hold it for us. He could not promise to hold it.

I then said that I didn't have much money with me but added, rather hesitantly, that I could make a down payment of $20. When Mr. Bedrosian discovered that I was a new professor at Pacific College he stated that those were very good people and that a $20 down payment would be fine. We signed the paper, and we proceeded to buy the house on a very generous payment plan. This is the $20 receipt. I doubt if any home has ever been sold with a smaller down payment. So it happened that we moved into our new home on December 15, 1964.

A $20 house purchase receipt.

Teaching a whole set of new courses and getting involved in many faculty activities was demanding but also very enjoyable. At that time PC was growing rapidly. It was also going through full accreditation. There was construction and expansion all over the campus. Almost all of the faculty members were young and eager to make the college a truly first-rate school. President Arthur Wiebe provided excellent and inspiring leadership. Those were exciting times.

When I was hired, I informed the college leaders that for the first term I wanted to teach only a half load because I needed to complete my doctoral dissertation. They accepted that request. Thus, for the first academic year, I had three-fourths of a full teaching load. I was paid $5,000. I realized that a small Christian college would not be able to pay a regular salary and was prepared to accept that sum even though it was $1,000 less than I had earned during my last year as a high school teacher without an M.A or Ph. D. four years earlier. At that time the US and Canadian dollars were basically at par.

At this point I must interject an important development. Probably in October 1964 my brother Paul phoned us from Abbotsford, BC to say that my mother had been diagnosed with cancer, advanced multiple myeloma and that she would not have long to live.

That Christmas holiday we spent much time with her. She was failing but still very alert and as always, as hospitable as she could be.

Mother's last Christmas with her six children, 1964.
Back Row L to R: John, Ernest, Sophie, Paul.
Front Row L to R: Frieda, Mother, Clara.

When I met with her physician I was told that she might have another two months to live. He was right. My dear mother passed away on February 25, 1965. A good and godly woman had finished her earthly pilgrimage and entered her eternal home. Doris and I, assisted by a friend and PC student Jake Janzen and his wife Jean, drove through the night to get to Abbotsford as soon as possible. After the March 1 funeral in the Clearbrook MB Church, we drove home because I needed to get back to my teaching assignment.

Shortly after I was hired, I inquired about a faculty medical plan. Smiles. I was told that the PC medical plan was as follows. If you need a prescription filled, then go to Butler Drugs and tell the owner that you teach at Pacific College. You won't pay much. If you need to see a physician, see either Dr. Louis Janzen or Dr. Irvine Wall. They will either charge very little or nothing.

We soon discovered that these statements were true, although it was somewhat embarrassing to ask for such charity.

For my second year, as agreed, I was assigned a full load for both semesters. When payday came, I was a little surprised that my salary for full-time lecturing was the same as it had been in the previous year when I had lectured only half-time the first term. One of my friends on faculty was professor Dietrich Friesen who taught music and directed the chorale. He had been on staff for many years. One day I explained my situation to him and requested his comment. He smiled and after a pause, said that his salary was lower than $5,000 - he did not have a doctorate - and that I had been given a relatively high salary because of my pending doctorate and that although I taught only three-quarter time in my first year I had been paid a full salary. My question was answered. Soon the faculty salary grid was improved markedly.

It was probably in 1965 that I was asked to travel by car with, as I recall, four Pacific College students to attend a convention of the North American Conference of MB Churches in Oklahoma City, OK. It was a fine trip for the students and also for me except for one experience. As was customary in those days, someone had arranged for us to stay in Mennonite homes for each night during our trip. I was booked to stay in an MB home in Oklahoma. The hosting family was gracious and very hospitable. As we sat down for a late-night snack, the father began describing the town which I will not name here. He described various features and then said almost these exact words: "We have never allowed a Negro to sleep in this town overnight." I was stunned. In fact, I was so taken aback that I did not do what I should have done. I should have challenged him. To my shame, I said nothing, and that has bothered me ever since.

In 1965 I was invited to be part of a 10-person Mennonite delegation from the US to participate in a Peace Conference in Prague, Czechoslovakia. With John Howard Yoder as our main resource theologian and some six other scholars and a few pastors in the group, we were well resourced for the event. In West Germany we rented a large VW van and headed east through communist East Germany to Prague. It had been arranged that en route we would stay in private homes. One night in Czechoslovakia, I stayed in the home of a radiologist. He informed me that after some years working as a medical doctor, he had finally saved enough money to buy a bicycle. Another night in that country I stayed in the home of a single mother with two sons. I remember her telling me that she had voted in the recent national election. Knowing how communist elections are typically run, I inquired if there had been real choice in the voting. Oh no, she said, but she voted so that the authorities were very much aware that she had voted. Maybe her two sons would get permission to attend university. Voting in the one-party election should help!

All went well until we arrived in Prague. When our group went to meet our hosts at the prescribed time and place, these dear people who had worked very hard to arrange this important East-West symposium had to inform us that their government had suddenly cancelled the event. We were all dejected. We would, however, be allowed to walk in the park, relax there and discuss issues. We did that. We would also be allowed to attend Sunday church services in the area. We also did that. We made the best of a very disappointing situation.

I should mention two other interesting items. Firstly, shortly after we entered communist East Germany on our way to Prague, a very knowledgeable, friendly and supposedly Christian East German who traveled with us part of the time mentioned to me that since we were in communist East Germany I should be very careful about what I said. He clearly implied that if I had questions, I should ask him. After we left East Germany, I was informed that this apparent confidant was himself the one spying on us and informing his communist bosses about what we said and did.

The second incident went as follows. On our return travels from Prague we decided to spend some time in East Berlin. We wanted to view the Berlin Wall from the communist side. Our East German guide approved of us doing that and of having our pictures taken while standing near the ominous *Mauer*. As I recall, it was a pleasant day and we all had our pictures taken, generally on our own cameras, with the grey monster as background. Suddenly the police arrived. We were thoroughly scolded in German, which most of us understood. Had we not realized that the *Mauer* was a *Militaeranlage*, a military installation, and must not be photographed? Our youthful East German guide was then taken into custody. We never saw him again and were assigned a replacement guide. As for the rest of us, we were marched down the street to the police station with an armed vehicle behind us. Understandably, we did as we were told. At the police headquarters. we were interrogated individually and each of us had his camera taken. After the interrogations were completed, we were again severely warned but told that no charges would be laid against us foreigners. We then got our cameras back. As far as I know, mine was the only one in which the supposedly offending film had not been removed. I still value that picture of me with the Berlin Wall ominously behind me.

As I recall, it was shortly after that trip to Czechoslovakia that I got myself and Pacific College into trouble. I had been invited to give a presentation on a local radio station. On September 16, 1965, I spoke on "Behind the Iron Curtain" on that major station.

I described my experience in Czechoslovakia and East Germany, identifying many problems but also noting that illiteracy had been virtually eliminated and some other social progress had happened. These few positive statements were accurate, but they infuriated some Christian listeners who complained to the college president.

I was called in to see him, not knowing why. President Arthur Wiebe, bless his memory, was very diplomatic. He informed me that there was considerable criticism about what I had said. People did not want to hear anything positive about a communist government. He did not disagree with me but he had been informed that some people would withdraw their financial support. I readily agreed to try to make amends, which I did, but I believe that for some of the college supporters I remained a dangerous left-winger.

I should mention here that with Dr. Peter Klassen leaving Pacific College and accepting an appointment as dean at Fresno State College, later Fresno State University, I was given the opportunity to do some teaching at that institution which I found very satisfying. I taught American History.

After three years at Pacific College we decided that after another year we would be moving back to Canada. I had not forgotten my commitment to the Canada Council. Since the real estate market at the time was very slow, we wanted to make sure that we would not be stuck with an unsold house. We therefore put our home on the market. After installing a surface pool in the back yard and making some other improvements, we sold the property for $14,000 with occupancy some time later.

We now needed to find a rental home for the coming year. At that time, the PC student body and faculty walked one block from the campus for assemblies in the Butler Avenue MB Church. One day, while walking with a group to the assembly, I suddenly experienced a strange feeling. Next to the church grounds was a fine home. I did not know who owned it. I suddenly had a strong conviction that this was the home we should be renting. I inquired about the property and discovered that the owner lived out of town. I contacted the dear lady, Katherine Schladewitz. She informed me that the current renters would be moving out and that she planned to move into the home. Despite what she told me, I contacted some people I knew and made tentative arrangements for moving about the end of August.

Repeatedly I contacted Mrs. Schladewitz. There were many changes in her stance. It soon developed that she had difficulty selling her other home and might not move. Then she said that she would not move, but she would also not rent. Then she said that she might rent the place but not to anyone with children. I finally convinced her that she should meet our children and that she would find them very well-behaved. At the same time, I coached the children on their best possible behaviour. She finally agreed to meet them at a place of my choosing. I chose the campus prayer chapel, thinking that the ambiance would be calmative for our three lively children.

Perhaps a day or two before the scheduled meeting the lady told me that she had had a change of heart and that it would not be necessary to see the children. I thanked her most sincerely. I then confirmed the tentative arrangement I had made with movers and on September 1, 1967, we moved into a lovely large bungalow at 4867 East Townsend Ave, Fresno, right next to the Butler Avenue Church. My early prayer-based conviction had become reality. Shortly after we left Fresno, that home became the US headquarters for Mennonite Brethren Missions and Services International, which it still is today. Maybe the Good Lord needed us as transitional renters."

During my years at PC, I was not yet heavily involved in speaking engagements. There were, however, some invitations to preach or teach in churches and schools, generally representing PC. There were also some other engagements.

Here are some examples. Probably because an officer's son or daughter was my student at PC, I was invited to speak to an assembly of US Naval Officers in Fresno on November 19, 1964. I delivered a policy lecture entitled, "Rationality and Soviet Foreign Policy." On July 23, 1965 I addressed the East Fresno Kiwanis on the topic, "A Trip to Czechoslovakia." On January 4, 1966 I addressed a General Conference of Mennonite Churches convention in Upland, CA. "The Minister of Christ: The Message He Declares."

During my fourth year at Pacific College I began checking out possible positions in a Canadian university. As I had indicated to the Canada Council, I was committed to return to Canada not many years after having completed my doctoral studies. I applied to several universities and received some positive responses. The university that appealed most to me and our family, was the University of Victoria on Vancouver Island. I contacted that university and was invited to visit the campus. Upon arrival, I was interviewed and asked to give a guest lecture. I was pleased to do that with a row of political science professors and perhaps others sitting in the back. Apparently, that went well. I was then taken to have lunch with the officials. They then stated that they were pleased with me and offered me a position. I tentatively accepted, wanting to discuss matters with Doris first.

During the discussion someone raised the matter of immigration procedures for me to move to Canada. I promptly replied that I was a Canadian and that there would be no problem. Suddenly the climate in the room changed. I was told that they would be corresponding with me. Soon I received word that the position for which I had candidated was no longer available. I was surprised.

Eventually, the truth came out. It happened that almost all, perhaps even all, of the political science professors at the University of Victoria were Americans and they did not want to hire a Canadian, only another American.

While I was wondering with which university I should connect next I got a surprise phone call from Dr. Frank C. Peters, then Academic Dean but also president-designate at Waterloo Lutheran University, Waterloo, Ontario. We had met several times. He was in Fresno and wanted to see me. I accepted his invitation and we met in the Fresno Air Terminal. He had followed my writings in various periodicals. I think he had also heard me speak somewhere, perhaps a few times. He then offered me an associate professorship in the Department of Political Science at WLU. At Pacific College at the time, I was earning $9,000. He offered me a salary of $12,000 and full coverage of moving costs. The two currencies were almost equivalent at that time. WLU also offered excellent benefits, including fine medical and pension plans. Dr. Peters also told me that he had not checked with the WLU Department of Political Science but was offering me this position on his own initiative and that the political science professors would surely be pleased. I asked for some time to think this over.

Doris and I had planned to settle in Western Canada. Now we faced a different but very attractive offer. Since Doris had never been to Ontario, she was not very excited about moving that far away from our families and friends in BC. In this situation, as also in others, Doris was, however, again fully supportive of whatever path forward would work best for us.

Rather hesitatingly, I then informed Dr. Peters that I would accept his invitation but with one major proviso, namely, if after one year we felt we should leave, then that would be acceptable to him. He accepted this response. I suppose that he believed, as history would prove him right, that we would decide to stay in Waterloo. As it turned out, we stayed there for 26 very fine years.

Two pleasant developments happened towards the end of our stay in Fresno. First, the editorial board of the Pacific College yearbook, PORTAL, decided to honor me in the 1968 issue:

> *"It is with both pride and gratitude that we honor Dr. John Redekop by dedicating PORTAL 1968 to the cause of world peace. For his efforts to alert the student body to the necessity of peaceful and constructive relations between the peoples of the world, we are grateful. Of the progress we have made as a college community and as individuals toward the realization of these ends, we are proud. The contributions of Dr. Redekop to this cause will long be remembered and by the students of Pacific College."*

Naturally, I was humbled and grateful for this surprise development.

Doris, 1968, before leaving Fresno.

The second pleasant development was the publication of my first book.

Scholarly Research and Writing; My First Book   1964 - 1968

My first book was published in the spring of 1968. A somewhat shortened version of my doctoral dissertation, it was entitled, **The American Far Right - A Case Study of Billy James Hargis and Christian Crusade.** It was published by the well-known *Eerdmans Publishing Company*.

The publishers had managed to get US Senator Mark Hatfield to write a very fine *Foreword*. I was greatly pleased to read his statement that "Professor Redekop's very scholarly study of the American Far Right should do a great deal to increase understanding of this movement."

Reviews of the book appeared in many religious and secular periodicals. A few were critical, most were affirming and complimentary. An important one appeared in the *San Francisco Chronicle* written by book critic Lester Kinsolving. For a beginning author it was certainly encouraging.

*"**The American Far Right** is both a monumentally documented and compellingly achievement of political science - which may well be the definitive study of this steadily growing American movement. Professor Redekop is sufficiently objective to mention what he believes to be the sincerity of Hargis - as the revival of what he contends is a part of Americana. At the same time he provides a devastating scrutiny of the inconsistencies and often ludicrous excesses of a vast storehouse of Hargis sayings or writings. In the counteracting of this movement which continues to grow in American ('True believers are not easily discouraged'), this book would appear to be compulsory reading."*

Other fine reviews included Harold Bienvenu's in the *Los Angeles Times*. He described the book as "massively documented" and "certainly objective and for that reason far more impressive and disturbing." He also wrote, "The book flows, it moves, it has style."

During these years I continued writing the *Personal Opinion* column. Here are some titles of those years: "Formalism in the Church Service," (April 3, 1964); "Race and the Gospel of Love," (April 2, 1965); "Needed - More Discontent," (July 8, 1966); "Women - Second Class Christians," (June 24, 1966); "Fathers of our Faith," (September 16, 1966); "Sellabrating Christmas," (December 23, 1966); "Chorus or Cantata," (May 19, 1967); and "Saved by a Black Heart," (January 26, 1968).

Every writer is interested in whether his or her writings are read and what readers' reactions might be. Reader surveys provide information. In May, 1968 the publishers of the *Mennonite Brethren Herald* undertook a reader survey. I was, of course, pleased to read that my *Personal Opinion* column was the most read, with readers reporting that they read it *Usually* (75.5%) or *Occasionally* (21%). The next highest, with an almost identical combined total, was *Editorials* being read *Usually (53.5 %)* and *Occasionally (43.5 %)*.

Church Life and Christian Ministries   1964 - 1968

For the first three years in Fresno, we attended the College Community Church, a Mennonite Brethren congregation then consisting mostly of fairly young Pacific College faculty members and other mostly young professionals and their families. We were seen as a rather radical and questioning congregation. We had many highly profitable and vigorous discussions and fine worship services. Pastor Werner Kroeker provided strong leadership for the College Community Church.

For the last year of our stay, we transferred to the Butler Avenue MB Church which was located next door to our rented home. This, too, was a fine church home, although we felt a little uncomfortable with the significant amount of Christian-Americanism taught in the children's clubs. While I don't hold the church leaders responsible for everything promoted in the church, I was disappointed to see a fairly large poster in that church promoting the film, *God's Country*, "This production is a patriotic presentation of our great American Christian heritage, plus the star-spangled message of eternal faith and freedom found only in Jesus Christ." The poster was soon removed.

During the first months of 1968, the Board of Reference and Counsel of the North American General Conference of MB Churches asked me to prepare a study paper on *The Christian and Labour.* My 13-page report was presented at a conference in May 1968 in Winnipeg. It was then printed as a separate publication and distributed throughout the Canadian and US MB constituencies.

Relevant Political and Public Affairs 1964 - 1968

By the mid-1960s the socioeconomic situation for Canadian Mennonites had progressed to the point that most were now firmly in the middle class. Some had actually become wealthy through manufacturing, real estate development, and agriculture and could rightly be described as in the upper class of society. With this economic advancement came a shift of political loyalties from the immigration-sponsoring Liberals to the more traditional, more religiously oriented, and more business-supportive Conservatives.

With this new middle and even upper-class identification came a widespread shift to political activism. While there had been a few attempts by Mennonite Brethren and other Mennonites to run as candidates in the 1950s, mostly as Liberal, by the 1960s and thereafter there were many Mennonite Brethren and other Mennonite candidates for provincial and national office. In fact, between 1960 and 1969, there were 64, mostly Conservative and Social Credit (also conservative) Mennonite candidates for provincial offices across Canada. Of these 17, were successful. During these same years 37 Mennonites ran for seats in the national Parliament of whom 5 were elected as Conservatives and two as Liberals. Interestingly, three of the five Conservative Members of Parliament were Mennonite Brethren.

Canadian polity and society also changed markedly in that the Canadian government created the national Canada Pension Plan (CPP) in 1965 and a national Medical Insurance Plan in 1966. It was noteworthy at the time that although most Mennonites, along with other religiously conservative groups, were traditionally not supportive of socialism, they quite readily welcomed the introduction of a social pension system and socialized health care.

In the US, Mennonites also experienced political shifts. Without analyzing the reasons why let it simply be said that in the 1960s many US Mennonites became very patriotic and most Mennonite Brethren expressed this sentiment by placing the US flag in their churches. Also, a significant cohort identified strongly with not only the conservative Republican Party but also with the various far-right movements.

During the 1960s there were widespread political discussions among US Mennonite Brethren, sometimes becoming quite emotional, about the growing Mennonite political activism. In those years I submitted three articles on church-state issues to the US Mennonite Brethren publication, *The Christian Leader*. "Religious Observance in Public Schools," (February 5, 1963); "Is the United States a Christian Country?" (October 15, 1963); and "Church and State; A Fresh Look," (April 12, 1966). These were the first articles in that denominational periodical which dealt with contemporary political issues. All three challenged widely affirmed Mennonite Brethren views. There was considerable feedback, some of it negative but most of it positive.

On April 4, 1968, Dr. Martin Luther King, Jr. was assassinated in Memphis, Tennessee. I believe that Dr. King's amazing teaching and modelling of Christian response to injustice, similar to traditional Mennonite teaching, played a key role in motivating Christians to address pressing racism and other social problems. Following his death, civil disobedience and other political activism mushroomed, also among younger Mennonites.

A Sunday in Fresno, 1968.

Heather, John, Gary, Doris, Wendy.

CHAPTER 13

LIVING IN WATERLOO
PART I 1968-1980

Moving to Waterloo, Ontario, 1968

On July 31, 1968, a Mayflower van with our belongings left Fresno, headed for Waterloo, Ontario. On that same day our family left our Townsend Avenue home in Fresno, headed for some interim activity in BC before motoring to Waterloo.

Heather, Doris, Wendy, Bonnie, John, Gary.

Before leaving Fresno I had received an invitation from Rev. Hargis's Christian Crusade organization to visit its headquarters and participate in a major debate. Since I had researched this organization extensively for my doctoral dissertation, I was quite prepared for such an undertaking. In fact, I relished having such a debate. It was agreed that I would fly from Portland, Oregon to Tulsa, likely on July 31. We drove to Portland where Doris and the children stayed at the home of my sister Clara Hoff while I flew to Tulsa.

In a sense I was surprised that the Hargis movement asked me to be a guest at their headquarters. I had, after all, been severely critical of the man and his organization. During my two-day visit I was treated extremely well. The organization leaders stated that although I had been very critical, I had also made positive comments where I considered them warranted. I suppose they were also pleased by the fact that my recently released book would give the organization added publicity and perhaps more credibility.

On August 3, 1968, as part of the organization's Annual Convention, a large assembly listened to the debate I had with David Noebel, Executive Assistant to Rev. Hargis, on the topic: "Can Christians Support the Philosophy and Anti-Communist Activity of Christian Crusade?" I took a qualified negative stance. The lively debate, if my memory serves me right, lasted more than two hours. I still have the entire event on tape. Although our disagreements were deep and consequential, we were very respectful of one another. In fact, concerning my treatment by Rev. Hargis and his entire organization in their very impressive, large Tulsa headquarters, I must say that it was altogether first class.

Upon returning to Portland, I was immediately informed that Doris' ailing mother had passed away on August 2. We then drove to Abbotsford to be with her father, Rev. Henry H. Nikkel, to be supportive and to attend the memorial service. A very fine, godly, supportive, and much-loved saint had completed her earthly life. After the funeral on August 9 we visited in the area before setting out on a leisurely cross-Canada trip to Waterloo.

Living in Waterloo 1968 - 1980

We had had very little connection with Waterloo or Ontario in general. Doris had never been to Ontario. I had visited there briefly on my way to Europe in 1955. It happened that when I delivered a lecture at a conference in Winnipeg in the spring of 1968, one of the attendees was a Victor Hiebert who lived in Waterloo. He had heard that we would be relocating there.

Our Willowdale Ave. home, Waterloo, ON.

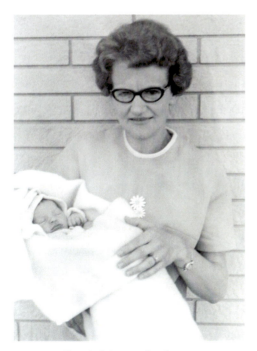

Bonnie joins our family.

A smiling Bonnie.

Four fine children: Gary, Wendy holding Bonnie, Heather.

Although he was a total stranger, he invited our family to stay with him, Alyce, and their three children for some days until we found a place to live. I happily accepted his very generous and amazing offer of Christian hospitality. That was the beginning of a life-long friendship.

Grandpa Nikkel with Gary, Wendy holding Bonnie, Heather.

On Sunday evening, August 18, 1968, we arrived at the Hiebert's. Vic and Alyce and their children, Cheryl, Phil, and Cynthia, gave new meaning to the concept of being gracious hosts. For ten days our family of five lived with their family of five. This arrangement worked out very well.

Within three days we had found a suitable place. The owners were asking $29,500 for their attractive split-level three-bedroom house at 208 Willowdale Avenue and asked for one month before occupancy. Given our clearly short-term accommodation with the Hiebert's, we could not wait that long. We countered with an offer of $28,500 with occupancy within a week. By late evening that day our offer was accepted. We greatly enjoyed our new home.

Our fourth child, Bonnie Eileen, was born on September 27, 1969. We were delighted to welcome our third daughter into the family. With this addition we were in a different situation than with the other three children. Now we had an available babysitter - our oldest daughter. Wendy had turned 12 in July and aided by brother Gary and sister Heather was a big help.

Although he was getting on in years, Doris's father, Rev. Henry H. Nikkel, maintained relatively good health and regularly traveled from Abbotsford to visit us in Ontario. He was the only grandparent our children had, and his visits were always a highlight for our family.

Our Ferndale Place home, Waterloo.

By the early 1970s we decided that we needed a larger home, a place suitable for six people. We prayed and hoped for something we could afford. In 1972 I was teaching a Saturday course to a mostly adult class. During a coffee break I happened to mention that we were looking for a larger home. One of my students, a successful businessman named Robert Schaub, said that he and his wife were planning to relocate from Waterloo to a rural residence. When he gave me the address, 298 Ferndale Place, I realized that this was a high-end location, only a few blocks from our current home.

In ascending order: John, Gary, Heather and Bonnie.

We visited the Schaubs and promptly liked the place. A much larger four-bedroom two-story home with a full but unfinished basement, situated on a large, treed lot, and with a double garage, it was exactly what we needed. The asking price was $49,500. We countered with an offer of $48,500. They accepted it. We rejoiced. We closed the deal. Real estate prices had hardly changed over four years. We eventually sold our Willowdale home for $29,000 to Christian acquaintances.

We moved into our new home - 298 Ferndale Place - on September 30, 1972. Our family greatly enjoyed living in that home. We finished the basement and added a large deck built around a tree. This fine home served us well until we moved to the Fraser Valley in May 1994.

During those thirteen years Doris and I became increasingly active in Christian ministries. Our home church was Waterloo Mennonite Brethren (WMB). Initially, the congregation of about 60 members consisted mostly of some 15 or so young families. Our very fine pastor was Al Enns, who at first served us half-time while also ministering to campus students. By 1973 our church had left Brighton School and built a fine new building on Lexington Street on land bought for us by the mother congregation, Kitchener MB Church.

Both Doris and I sang in the choir and served in Sunday School. Doris sang in the church trio which frequently ministered in WMB and also at other places. I soon became the leader of the College and Career Class which grew over the years to become approximately one-third of the congregation. The group was organized into committees with various responsibilities. A few times, this class presented the entire Sunday forenoon worship service.

Many a time we had some of them at our home for a variety of events or simply to relax and have fellowship. For some years I was privileged to lead the WMB congregation as moderator.

Soon there were invitations to preach, not only in our home church but also elsewhere. During these thirteen years, according to my records, I preached in my home church, Waterloo Mennonite Brethren, about five times a year and in other churches about three times a year

Doris and I both served on the Inter-Varsity Christian Fellowship Committee for the two universities in Waterloo. This was both stimulating and challenging. There were events to organize and considerable fundraising to undertake. It was always rewarding to see the students' deep concern to be effective Christians in their university settings.

In 1979 we were privileged to have an unusual experience. From May 17 until June 2, we had a family of five Vietnamese "boat people" live in our home. I clearly recall the Huynhs walking up to our house. They were inadequately clothed for the very cool weather we had that day. They were also still in shock. They had fled Vietnam in a small boat. They had been attacked by pirates who had robbed them of the personal belongings they had managed to take with them. About the same time, as I recall, the grandmother had died at sea. They came with virtually nothing. They did not speak English. They knew "Coke" and "Thank you."

Our Vietnamese "Boat People" guests.

Although Hunghua, the father, had been a successful merchant, he readily began his working life in Canada as a restaurant dishwasher. I think it took only a few years until he was head chef. They wondered why we, with fellow church members, would have sponsored them. We explained. Although they were Buddhist, as I recall, they observed us and others carefully and soon became regular worshippers in the Waterloo Mennonite Brethren Church. It was both intriguing and affirming to hear the parents say that in the large Pidong refugee camp, I think in Thailand, where people could sign up for countries to which they desired to go, almost no one signed up for any Muslim or communist countries. Almost all wanted to go to countries where Christianity was dominant.

Wilfrid Laurier University 1968 - 1980

My first year at WLU - Waterloo Lutheran University until 1973 - brought with it many new experiences. I shall recount a few. Shortly after the university year began, President Frank Peters asked to see me. He stated that our moving costs had been higher than the maximum that WLU allowed for moving costs but that university would, instead, be willing to add $1,000 to my initial $12,000 salary. Would that be acceptable to me? I could hardly believe my ears. Naturally, I agreed. I suppressed my elation. Not only did I receive that $1,000 each of the 26 years that I taught there but with the increase in salaries during those 26 years, I estimate that WLU paid me at least $130,000 over 26 years instead of the original $1,000.

My introduction to the political science professors was unusual. I came as a tenured associate professor without the department knowing anything about me. Fortunately, the departmental professors and I blended well. In fact, all of my colleagues in the department became personal friends. Since I was the last professor hired for 1968-69, I was the last to be assigned courses. As it happened, I had 8:00 AM classes, Monday to Friday. As an insomniac, that was not the best for me, but I made the best of it. I arranged for a more satisfactory schedule for the next year.

In any university teaching situation the professor gets to know many fine students. Some of my students had problems and challenges - financial, emotional, marriage and assorted other types - which some shared with me. I tried to help them resolve their problems. In some instances I referred them to other individuals or agencies.

I must mention one unusual experience. I think it was during my first year at WLU that American Government was one of my 8:00 AM courses. There were perhaps 30 students in the class. After a few weeks I noticed that a certain girl had stopped attending but had not officially dropped the course. In those days a professor could make inquiries about such a situation. I was able to contact the girl. She told me that the reason for her absence was that she was pregnant and had morning sickness. I then offered to teach her the course personally in the afternoon until her morning sickness ended. She very gratefully accepted and soon was back in class. She and I had some important conversations. She knew that her parents would be very angry if they found out, so she kept the matter secret. She decided not to have an abortion but to give the baby up for adoption.

I believe it was on November 30, 1971, while I was lecturing, that there was a knock on the door. Such interruption is unusual. I opened the door and there stood the smiling university president, Dr. Frank C. Peters. He handed me a letter. It was dated November 29 and came from the WLU Board of Governors. It stated that I had been "promoted to the rank of Full Professor." I thanked him most sincerely for this unexpected early promotion.

During the first years I taught Canadian Politics, American Politics, Introduction to Political Science, and Political Thought. Later on I also taught Research Methods, Canadian-American Relations, Comparative Politics. Political Parties, and specialized topic courses such as *The Meech Lake Accord.*

When I accepted the appointment at Waterloo Lutheran University I decided that I would make myself available to serve the university in whatever way I could. Opportunities developed rather quickly. I served as Chair of the Department of Political Science 1972 - 1975 and again 1977 - 1980 and on numerous departmental and university committees, ranging from chairing the Faculty Appeals Committee to chairing the Canadian Studies Committee and from chairing the WLU Telecollege Committee to serving as the Secretary of the Board of Governors Presidential Search Committee. From 1971 - 1981 I served on the University Senate, and from 1973 - 1976 on the University Board of Governors.

One of the most interesting offices for me was my term as president of the WLU Faculty Association, 1971 - 1972. One of my tasks in that office was to lead in negotiating salaries and benefits. As it turned out, for part of the time I found myself negotiating with the university president, Dr. Peters. I am sure that neither of us anticipated two Mennonite Brethren in a university negotiating faculty contracts. We both took our roles very seriously, keeping in mind that we shared the same ethic. We had only amiable negotiations. Let me add that President Peters did his best to provide well for the faculty members. It was a privilege to negotiate with him.

An autobiography should not deal only with what was positive. With that in mind, I shall relate two negative experiences I brought on myself.

First, at the beginning of each course, I told the students that if I ever did not show up within 10 minutes of starting time, they should assume that something had gone wrong and leave. One day I was so engrossed in some project that something did go wrong. I forgot to go to a large lecture hall to lecture. My embarrassment was great.

The second embarrassment was, for me, even more consequential. Although I did not verbalize my faith unduly, after the first years I began all courses by noting that I was a Christian, and though I would always try to be objective, the students should be aware of my life-view. I did this partly because some Marxist colleagues announced their Marxist commitments.

Clearly, my colleagues, students, and many staff members knew of my Christian faith. One day in our large departmental office, several of us professors were standing around for some reason. As it happened, one of my colleagues related a really funny but very crude joke. Along with the others I laughed. Our head secretary turned to me and slowly said, "I would not have thought that of you." Her honest statement taught me a hurtful and powerful lesson, namely, that while my testimony had been heard, in this situation my judgment was sub-Christian. I also discovered that I was being observed and assessed more closely than I had thought.

Scholarly Research and Writing; Books   1968 - 1980

Part of being a university professor involves doing research and getting one's writings published. During these thirteen years I managed to get three articles published in refereed academic journals, five chapters written for books edited by others, and three books produced by me. The first book was **The Star-Spangled Beaver: Twenty-Four Canadians Look South** (Toronto: Peter Martin Associates, 1971). 253 pp. This book, of which I was the editor and a contributor, was selected as a Book-of-the-Month by the Readers Club of Canada in 1972. I was deeply honoured when one of Canada's foremost political scientists, Dr. Paul Fox, reviewed this book in the December 25, 1971 issue of *The Globe and Mail*. He wrote as follows.

"Editor John Redekop has done an excellent job in skillfully and unobtrusively blending together many different authors on a number of different aspects of the problem of Canada's relationships with the United States. As a result, he succeeds in producing a tasty yet nourishing mix of fact, mood, humour, earnestness, detailed academic argument, poetry, and some blobs of pomposity and bombast."

The second book was **Labour Problems in Christian Perspective** (Grand Rapids, MI: Eerdmans, 1972), 364 pp.

Here, again, I was editor and contributor. The third book of which I was again editor and contributor was the textbook, **Approaches to Canadian Politics** (Scarborough, ON: Prentice-Hall, 1978), 377 pp. It was adopted as a text quite widely by professors of political science across Canada.

As stated, during these years five academic colleagues invited me to contribute chapters in books edited by them. Such an assignment is always an exciting opportunity as one tries to fit one's own contribution into a larger project. The five chapters I researched and wrote in these years for books edited by others included "The State and the Free Church" (1976) and "Church and State in Canada: Co-operation and Confrontation" (1979).

The three articles in refereed academic journals included "A Re-interpretation of Canadian-American Relations" (1976), "Civil Religion in Canada" (1976), and "Authors and Publishers: An Analysis of Textbook Selection in Canadian Departments of Political Science and Sociology" (1976).

A university professor is also expected to present research papers at scholarly conferences. During these thirteen years, I presented research papers at academic conferences at McGill University in Montreal and the University of Alberta in Edmonton. Another very important event took place at Queen's University on March 18, 1972, a University Symposium on Foreign Ownership. I presented an invited research paper on the topic, "Foreign Ownership - a Dilemma for Rational Nationalists."

Writing for the Christian Community 1968 - 1980

During these years I wrote articles for a variety of reading audiences. The editors of **Baker's Dictionary of Christian Ethics** (1973) invited me to contribute five articles which I was pleased to do: They were entitled "Arbitration," "Boycott," "Guaranteed Income," "Labour Relations," and "Strikes." The Mennonite Central Committee asked me to write a chapter on "Christians in a World of International Confrontation," for a book entitled **Citizens and Disciples: Christian Essays on Nationalism** (1973).

As already noted, I was writing my *Personal Opinion* columns weekly from 1964 until 1972 and then biweekly in the *Mennonite Brethren Herald*. Here are some titles for these years. "Cla$$ War," (May 16, 1969); "Class and Brotherhood," (April 21, 1972); "Delinquent Delegates," (June 14, 1974); "The New Conscientious Objectors," (March 21, 1975); "Evangelical Salt," (April 2, 1976); "Who is a Mennonite?" (August 20, 1976); "Prince of Peace and Pacifism," (November 26, 1976); "Is Guilt a Myth?" (April 15, 1977);

"How many banquets?" (December 9, 1977); and "Nuclear Madness," (October 12, 1979). I thank Harold Jantz for being an excellent editor.

As a columnist I received many letters from readers. I have not done a count but the total must be many hundreds. One dear brother living in Winnipeg wrote that he needed to tell me that he knew I was trying to be "the first Mennonite pope." I never quite understood his reasoning. One Mennonite wrote me several letters from his prison cell wanting me to intercede for him with the relevant authorities. An NDP Member of Parliament wrote to say that I was insufficiently supportive of NDP humanitarian policies given that they were in line with the Christian ethic. More than a few readers, however, complained to me that I was too supportive of NDP policies.

One letter, in particular, really put me in a state of embarrassment. My November 1, 1968 column was entitled "A Letter From Asia." The whole thing was a fictional letter from a refugee in a refugee camp. The writer referred to numerous Ottawa policies which no Asian refugee would have known. I thought that because of this fact and other words I used, readers would realize that the letter was fictitious. I had him sign off as *Soo Long,* which I thought was an obvious pun on a greeting. I made what I thought was a logical plea to the Canadian government to help these refugees.

I felt good about the column until I got a very nice letter from a lady in Yarrow, BC, who included a substantial cheque for Soo Long. What should I do? I could not tell her that she should have realized the letter was fictitious. There was nothing else I could do except eat humble pie, admit my unintended deception, apologize to her, and tell her that I had forwarded the cheque to the MCC for refugee relief. That is what I did. I fear that this dear lady probably never again believed anything I wrote.

Between 1968 and 1980 I also wrote about fifty articles, other than columns, which were published in various Christian periodicals. Some were requested, some I just submitted. The list includes the following. "Church and State, A Fresh Look," *Mennonite Brethren Herald* (January 21, 1966); "Americanism and Christianity: An NAE Convention," *Mennonite Brethren Herald* (April 14, 1967); "CLAC and Success," *The Guide* (January 1970); "Will Faith Survive College?" *Eternity* (June, 1970); "Wanted: Committed People; A Word to Graduating Students," *Mennonite Brethren Herald* (April 30, 1971); "Christianity and Political Ideology," *Sunday Digest* (September 5, 1971); and "Canadian and U.S. Elections; Campaigns Change Roles." *The Mennonite* (October 17, 1972).

Additional titles included "Faith and Work," *Mennonite Brethren Herald* (May 3, 1974); "Christians in a world of international confrontation," *The Mennonite* (July 9, 1974); "Another Way for Christian Workmen," *Mennonite*

Brethren Herald (March 5, 1976); "Unions and the Christian's Witness," *MIBA Newsletter (* April 29, 1977); "Have we a future as a believers' church?" *Mennonite Brethren Herald* (July 21, 1978); "Unemployment - Coping with the Unthinkable," *Life of Faith,* (February 1979); "A Christian look at the '79 election," *Mennonite Brethren Herald* (April 27, 1979); "Discipleship in Business," *Mennonite Industry and Business Associates Newsletter* (March 1979); and "A brotherhood in convention," *Mennonite Brethren Herald* (June 6, 1980).

It was likely in late 1971 that I received an invitation to deliver the annual S. F. Coffman Peace Lecture in the United States. This presentation comes with an award of $500, which was a large sum at that time, equivalent to about $5,000 in 2021 dollars. It also brings with it the publication of the lecture. The hosting and reception were truly first-class. My lecture, delivered to a large audience in Minneapolis, MN was entitled *Making Political Decisions; A Christian Perspective.* My manuscript was then published as a 46-page booklet in a series as *Focal Pamphlet No. 23.* It was for me a very humbling experience to see my presentation included in a series which listed booklets by outstanding Anabaptist scholars and authors whom I had for years held in very high esteem, saintly leaders whose writings had shaped my thinking. They included Mennonites Harold S. Bender, John Howard Yoder, and J. Lawrence Burkholder, as well as the nationally-known evangelical scholar Vernon C. Grounds.

Addressing Christian Audiences 1968 -1980

It was, of course, also my personal desire, if requested, to serve the local and larger community as a Christian professor, writer, and speaker. During these years I accepted quite a few speaking engagements from Christian groups, averaging about twenty each year. These events included banquets, Christian college assemblies, fundraising dinners, and assorted other occasions. Here are some examples: "Questions a Servant Must Answer," Goshen College, Goshen, IN (May 10, 1969); "Down the Wrong Road," Christian Businessmen's Committee, Saskatoon, SK (November 21, 1969); "Learning from Solomon," Ebenfeld MB Church, Hillsboro, KS (January 11, 1970); "How Should Christians Respond to Big Government?" Ontario Teachers Christian Fellowship and Ontario Nurses Christian Fellowship Fall Conference, Toronto (October 25, 1975); and "The Christian Response to the Military as an Institution; Practical Interpretations," Tabor College, Hillsboro, KS (October 30, 1976).

Of special significance for me were invitations to address the large public assemblies of the Canadian Mennonite Brethren Church annual conventions. In 1973 I spoke on the topic "Christian Non-Resistance: Another Perspective - Limitless Love." In 1978 I spoke on "The Mennonite Brethren as a Believers Church: Past, Present and Future." Given that I had not studied Anabaptist history or theology in depth at any college or seminary, I had to undertake considerable research and study. I enjoyed doing that.

In 1977 Dr. John A. Toews, a stalwart in the Canadian and North American MB Conferences and at that time chairman of the North American Board of Reference and Counsel, asked me to prepare a study paper on the topic "Involvement in the Political Order." He pointed out that MBs, especially in Canada, were becoming active in political parties, standing as party candidates, and serving in various political offices, both elected and non-elected.

Many church members were raising serious questions about this growing reality. Dr. Toews asked me to review biblical teaching and develop biblical guidelines. I accepted his request. The result, which I submitted to the board, was a five-page report including ten guiding principles. The report was published in conference papers with a lengthy introduction by Dr. Toews. He included these sentences. "At meetings in Winnipeg earlier this year, the board studied this paper and found itself in basic agreement with Redekop's position....The board is also preparing a resolution, based on this paper, which will be presented at General Conference sessions in 1978." My statement was published as "Involvement in the Political Order," *The Christian Leader,* (September 27, 1977). I was both delighted and humbled when, in 1978, the stance and principles I recommended were adopted as our Mennonite Brethren stance.

Ministries In Mennonite Brethren Conferences 1968 - 1980

The reference to conferences needs to be explained. The North American Mennonite Brethren churches have organized themselves into various conferences. The six major Canadian provinces each have a conference structure. The US churches are organized into four regional conferences. Canada and the US each have a national conference. In addition, until 2001, there was a North American General Conference.

My first major involvement with the North American or General Conference of the Mennonite Brethren Churches, which actually happened before our move to Ontario, was an invitation to address a North American Faith and Life Consultation in Winnipeg, in early May 1968 on the topic *"The Christian and Labour Unions."* This presentation was then published and distributed to all MB churches in Canada and the United States.

My first invitation to serve the Canadian MB Conference also came in 1968. I was invited to address an issue which, because of the anti-war peace reaction to the Vietnam War, had become a major concern for churches and especially younger folk, namely, what were the appropriate and the inappropriate means of expressing traditional Anabaptist peace teaching. Before we left Fresno I traveled to Abbotsford, BC, to speak at a national Faith and Life Conference on July 8, 1968, on "The Expression of our Peace Witness."

My first involvement with the Ontario MB Conference was to address the Annual Students Conference on October 19, 1968, in Hamilton, where I delivered three lectures: "Christians on Campus — Areas of Tension," "Student Power - Good or Bad," and "The Cult of Intellectualism."

In 1976 I wrote a 40-page report for the Canadian Conference of MB Churches in which I summarized and analyzed the influential 1975 book by Howard Kauffman and Leland Harder, **Anabaptists Four Centuries Later.** This report was widely distributed.

From 1969 until 1977, I served as vice-chair of the Canadian MB Board of Higher Education, which had as its main mandate the operation of Mennonite Brethren Bible College in Winnipeg. My friend Henry H. Dueck served as chair. When those eight years ended I was elected in 1977 as a member of the Canadian MB Board of Spiritual and Social Concerns, later renamed the Board of Faith and Life. Beginning in 1973, I served on the board of our North American Mennonite Brethren Biblical Seminary in Fresno, for about four years as chairperson. My board membership continued until 1987.

In connection with my service on the seminary board, I must recount an unusual experience. In 1973 the Canadian MB convention was held on the campus of Prairie Bible Institute in Three Hills, Alberta. A main item on the agenda was whether the Canadian MB Conference would become a partner with the US Conference in the operation of the MB Seminary in Fresno, CA. When that was approved, the next big question was whether the Canadian Conference would pay its share of the total subsidy in Canadian or US dollars. As a newly-elected board member I spoke strongly against the Board of Management's recommendation that it be paid in Canadian dollars and made that an amendment to the motion. I argued that since the budget was done in US currency, the Canadian contribution should be paid in that currency or the equivalent in Canadian dollars. Also, relative currency values changed, which would affect the percentage of the Canadian subsidy. My amendment was supported by the delegates. The Board of Management recommendation was thus defeated.

As we left that large hall on the Prairie Bible Institute grounds, four members of the Board of Management, I suppose out of frustration, grabbed my arms and legs and began carrying me. As it happened, I was wearing a leisure suit made of rather smooth, almost slippery, fabric. Suddenly they dropped me on the concrete surface. I was out cold and stayed that way for some time. I believe I had a concussion. I was taken to the college infirmary. I received some medical attention.

By the supper hour I felt well enough to go for some dinner in the dining hall. Never before or since have so many members of a committee watched me closely to see how well I was managing to eat and drink! It can be said that winning that argument for the seminary in Three Hills, Alberta, in 1973 was, for me, a real headache.

For the Canadian Conference of Mennonite Brethren Churches these were very fine years. A new conference structure had been created in 1968. It reflected our Anabaptist theology and our denominational emphasis on the priesthood of all believers as well as an emphasis on collective decision-making and accountability to the membership. We had six elected boards, with eleven members each, which all had clearly delineated responsibilities. The three-person executive also had its tasks spelled out. Generally, the 69-member Council of Boards, the six boards and the three-person Executive, met in January and immediately preceding the summer convention. Each board reported what had been done and presented resolutions. These reports were discussed, and the proposals were evaluated and, on occasion, even rejected. That was healthy group discernment at its best. Each board learned what the other boards were doing. The various boards then presented their reports and their recommendations to the assembled delegates at the annual or bi-annual convention.

The conventions were well-attended. At times we had more than 500 voting delegates. Almost every member church sent delegates. We also welcomed and heard reports from a spectrum of fraternal delegates such as the MCC and the Evangelical Fellowship of Canada. The delegates not only heard board and executive reports and recommendations but, very importantly, they also critiqued the recommendations and made decisions. Perhaps most importantly, we had financial management by a board of qualified people. This process differs markedly from later convention practices in which delegates rarely vote on theological, ethical, financial, or other proposals other than to approve reports and decisions presented in final form by conference leaders for approval.

It was a privilege and a delight for me to serve from 1969 until 1977 on the Board of Higher Education and then on the Board of Spiritual and Social Concerns from 1977 until I was elected assistant moderator of the Canadian MB Conference in July 1980, and then as a moderator in July, 1983.

Throughout those years, I was a regular attender at Canadian MB conventions. I must recount an unusual incident that happened in July 1980, when Doris and I were returning to Waterloo from a Winnipeg convention. That summer, our daughter Wendy was completing a two-year MCC assignment in Winnipeg. Since she was moving back to Waterloo, she asked us to take a large trunk of her possessions in our car. We, of course, did so gladly. We left Canada and traveled through the US to Sarnia, ON. Some hours before we approached the border to leave Michigan to re-enter Canada at Sarnia, Ontario, we discovered that Wendy's trunk was locked and we did not have a key. We also did not have a list of the trunk's contents. We could not contact Wendy. We did not know what to do. As we approached the border with its approximately 12 border kiosks, I prayed that God would direct us to an understanding customs official. I selected one of the kiosks and prepared my little speech. As I drove up to speak to the official, she called out, "Hello Professor Redekop," or words to that effect. The smiling countenance belonged to one of my very fine students in the past year. We had no difficulty proceeding through customs and into Ontario. I am reminded of an insightful saying I heard some time ago: "Coincidences happen when we pray." This was one of many experiences which illustrate the truth of that saying.

Other Christian Ministries 1968 - 1980

In these years, two significant undertakings involved evaluating Christian agencies. In 1978 the Mennonite Central Committee (Canada) asked me to evaluate the effectiveness of its Ottawa Office which operated under the direction of Bill Janzen. This involved interviewing politicians, civil servants, clients and reading many documents. My findings were that the Ottawa Office was carrying on a very effective information and even lobbying ministry. The delivery of information consisted of informing the large Mennonite and Brethren in Christ constituencies about relevant political developments and also informing bureaucrats, politicians, government agencies and departments, and even the cabinet itself about MCC perspectives, concerns, and proposals.

I found that Bill Janzen, the Director of the MCC Ottawa Office, was consistently held in very high regard and that the reports and submissions he wrote and submitted to bureaucrats and agencies such as CIDA and to politicians and political bodies were given high credibility. I submitted my report in November 1978.

In 1980 I was asked to chair a Task Force appointed by the Canadian MB Conference Board of Spiritual and Social Concerns. Our assignment was to assess the mandate and evaluate the effectiveness of the Mennonite Central

Committee as an arm of the church. After extensive reading and many interviews by me and also others, I submitted the 44-page report in July 1980.

Our conclusion was that

"Though we may not all agree on the specifics of all of the ministries, there is very little disagreement about the vast majority. There is much for everyone to endorse and support wholeheartedly. MCC (Canada) remains an excellent agency of Christian service."

Although my more substantial involvement developed later, I should note here that my service with the Evangelical Fellowship of Canada, founded in 1964, began in 1968 when I was elected as the first chairperson of the Social Action Commission and continued in this role for about four years. This put me on the General Council on which I served for 27 years until 1995.

Writing for the General Public 1968 - 1980

As a contribution to strengthening what was called gown-town relationships, WLU in 1974 launched a news service called *WLU Newsfeature Service*. The intent was that faculty members would write fairly brief articles for daily and weekly newspapers in Ontario. The *Newsfeatures* office would then distribute these to about 40 newspapers free of charge. By the end of 1980 I had written about 15 such articles, mainly dealing with political topics; more were written later. Note that the dates for each item varied considerably depending on when a given newspaper carried the article. My early titles included "Trudeau careless with his words," (December 12, 1975); "Westerners upset with the East and for lots of reasons," (March 15, 1976); "Why the Republicans will lose the next election," (November 2, 1976) [They did]; "The economics of Quebec's separatism," (August 17, 1977); and "Abandoning Taiwan a gross example of opportunism," (January 2, 1979). Although not all newspapers carried every *Newsfeature*, they had a wide readership. By 1993 I had written 66 *Newsfeatures*.

During these thirteen years I also had various other articles published in major newspapers. The 10 or so in this category included "Canada needs generosity, not animosity to face future," *Toronto Star* (August 17, 1971); "12 duties make the US president's job an impossible one," *Kitchener-Waterloo Record* (October 18, 1974); "The New Conscientious Objectors," *Regina Leader Post* (May 31, 1975); "Nuclear stockpiling is madness," *Toronto Star* (November 10, 1979); and "New policies needed to tame inflation," *Kitchener-Waterloo Record* (November 24, 1979).

For all categories of writing, it was a delight to read the many readers' responses to my analyses and opinions.

General Speaking Engagements 1968 - 1980

WLU had a policy that faculty members should try to serve the regional community and the larger society as much as possible. In fact, we needed to report each year what we had done in this respect.

Having checked my files for those years I note that I had about twenty of what I call secular speaking engagements per year. The audiences included service clubs - notably Kiwanis and Rotary - annual general meetings, conventions, high school assemblies, and a variety of other venues. Here are a few examples: "Where Do We Stand? Christians and Politics," at the Election '74 Rally held in the Pacific National Exhibition Agrodome, Vancouver (June 26, 1974); "Separatism in Quebec; What Lies Ahead for Canada?" Waterloo County Board of Education" (February 11, 1977); and "Canadian Citizenship," Citizenship Court Ceremony, Kitchener-Waterloo," ON (April 24, 1980).

A particularly important occasion was a policy presentation, "Limits of Radical Action In a Democratic Society," a lecture given to senior RCMP officers in the Security Division, Ottawa (June 28, 1973). All of the approximately 250 presentations during these 13 years were interesting assignments. I never tired of sharing ideas in this vast array of situations.

One additional area of involvement developed. in these years. I became a regular commentator on elections and other political events for the Kitchener CTV station, CKCO-TV. That, too, was very enjoyable.

Church Matters and My Spiritual Pilgrimage 1968 - 1980

For our local MB congregation in Waterloo these years saw amazing growth. Under strong pastoral leadership by Alvin Enns during the early years and later Marvin Warkentin, we developed various programs for the church community and also the surrounding area.

It is always a challenge to describe one's spiritual pilgrimage. It is typically complex and blurred around the edges. One can, of course, recount some aspects. Already at the beginning of this period I had to remind myself, a person who enjoys being involved in various projects, that when God evaluates a person's life, he does not focus primarily on what that person did but on who that person is. For a person with a Type-A personality such a reminder is always timely.

During these years I also made progress in processing the place of doubt in a Christian's life. Somewhere in my growing-up years I acquired the notion that having doubts was a truly negative, if not actually sinful, experience.

I came to realize that having doubts alongside faith is normal and that processing doubts honestly is part of spiritual maturing. By processing doubts, we learn more truth.

As I recall, it was also in the late 1960s that I heard a very important account, one that greatly impacted me, of what had happened to some of my older relatives. Some historical background and context is needed. As described earlier, my father passed away on May 23, 1959. A younger brother, Peter Redekop, had died on December 8, 1948. His oldest brother, Frank, had passed away on November 23, 1960. It happened that in July 1962 Frank Redekop's widow, Katherine, became very ill. Death seemed imminent. On August 14, 1962, Henry Redekop, the youngest of my father's brothers, died of a massive heart attack and was found dead near his tractor out on a field. Because Katherine was considered to be near death, she was not told that her brother-in-law, Henry, had passed away. On August 24, 1962, Katherine Redekop was at the end of her life. Several close relatives were with her. Just before she took her last breath, she said in German, and these words are very close to verbatim: "*Ich sehe Franz, ich sehe Peter, ich sehe Jacob, aber was macht der Heinrich da?*" and with that, she passed into her next life. Her words in English are "I see Frank. I see Peter. I see Jacob. But what is Henry doing there?" With that she died. This historical reality is for me compelling evidence that there is, indeed, life beyond this earthly pilgrimage.

Another branch of thought I had in those years, perhaps even earlier, was the realization that for some of the truly foundational questions one has, there are no answers. For example, I cannot reconcile the obvious disparity between the Genesis account of creation and the compelling geological evidence for an incredibly longer existence of the earth and the universe. I am, however, at peace about that fact. It is not always necessary to find answers. There will come a time when the now unknowable will become known.

Winter in Waterloo

John with Bonnie.

Gary, Bonnie, Heather.

Relevant Religious Developments in the Larger Arenas, 1968 - 1980

These thirteen years witnessed major changes in the religious scene in Canada. I shall identify four general developments and two phenomena relating particularly to the Mennonite Brethren people. My comments are based on research provided by sociologist Reginald Bibby, findings of the Pew Foundation, and my own observations, research, and experience.

The first reality is the national decline of both church membership and church attendance. The peak in church attendance in Canada occurred in 1968. In Quebec the decline, an intrinsic part of the Quiet Revolution initiated by Premier Jean Lesage already in 1960, fundamentally altered the religious landscape in Canada. A side benefit, if one could call it that, was that a freer Quebec enabled Canadian MBs and others to initiate evangelism and church planting in that province. While Mennonite Brethren did not themselves experience any decline, the gradual weakening of a pro-Christian climate affected education, the media, political agendas, and much else in Canada.

The second reality was urbanization. This shift affected all churches, including Mennonite Brethren. As late as 1960 the clear majority of Mennonite Brethren in Canada lived in rural areas and generally pursued farming or associated skills and trades. By 1980 most MB churches were urban. The traditional ethno-religious, agrarian community which had under-girded and reinforced the local church community, was largely gone. For better or worse, the ethnic glue was weakening. In addition, the emerging big city congregations had begun to deal with a new set of ethical, social, economic, and marital challenges.

The third major development was the emergence and maturing of the Evangelical Fellowship of Canada (EFC). Founded in 1964, the EFC was hardly visible and barely viable until the late 1970s. Compared to the mainline Canadian Council of Churches, founded in 1944, the EFC was at first almost inconsequential. Fortunately, with an increase in membership, funding, and office strength, that situation gradually improved. By 1980 it had become the significant voice of evangelicals in Canada. The Mennonite Brethren Conference had become a strong supporter.

The fourth major reality was the emergence of new faith groups, some of which drew significant numbers of MB young people and also impacted MB churches. These included the Jesus People and, perhaps most significantly, the Vineyard Church. The point is that by 1980, in contrast to earlier times, a significant percentage of MB young people were no longer identifying with the church of their parents. This meant, among other consequences, that the fairly rapid biological growth of the MB Conference in Canada was not to be assumed. At best, biological growth stalled.

Two developments related more narrowly to the Mennonite Brethren Conference. The first was the shift from German to English in almost all of the MB churches across Canada. A few made the change earlier and a few later, but by 1980, the Mennonite Brethren were no longer an immigrant group speaking a foreign language. This shift brought with it many advantages but also the loss of what could be called a cohesive glue and the decline of some rich hymnody and ethnocultural values. A general commonality of church members was ending. Many new names appeared on MB church membership rosters.

The second reality for Mennonite Brethren, already evident and noted previously, was gaining momentum. I speak of the gradual professionalization of the clergy. Whereas until the 1960s MB churches were generally staffed by volunteer preachers, by 1980 almost all Canadian MB churches were staffed by what were actually hired employees. This change made much sense. Preachers, like all others, deserve to be compensated. As noted previously, the negative consequences were major. As also noted previously, there were at least three negative pressures. First, there were pressures tending to limit what the paid employees could say. Second, in many cases, the denomination's top preachers were no longer as available to serve the larger MB constituency as guest preachers. Third, with the clergy paid to serve a congregation, it became much more difficult for other MB preachers, MB schools and other agencies, and even Conference leaders to have pulpit access on Sunday morning. This last situation became increasingly problematic as churches, beginning with the urban congregations, discontinued Sunday evening services.

Relevant Political and Public Affairs 1968 - 1980

Several developments in Mennonite Brethren communities in both Canada and the US deserve comment. In Canada the large-scale secularization of Quebec society which began about 1960, basically transformed that society from being largely Roman Catholic to being largely secular. This became very significant politically because it gave rise to several strong separatist movements. The dominant one was the FLQ which in October 1970, resorted to violence, kidnapping British diplomat James Cross and killing Quebec Deputy Premier Pierre Laporte on October 17, 1970. Major rallies were held on both sides. Prime Minister Pierre Trudeau invoked the War Measures Act. The country was tense. Eventually, matters calmed down but Quebec was permanently changed. Would Christians in Canada have to face a dismembered country?

I believe it is generally correct to say that if most people in a jurisdiction abandon one unifying cause, as the French in Quebec largely abandoned Catholicism in these years, they then need another cause larger than individualism to give meaning to life. I believe we all, especially thoughtful people, need a cause larger than ourselves to which to give ourselves.

In any event, in Quebec traditional Catholicism was replaced by a new and assertive secular Quebec nationalism. A pro-separatist Parti Quebecois, led by the charismatic Rene Levesque, won a provincial election in 1976 and carried out its first separatist referendum in 1980. The people of Quebec rejected separation by 59.6 percent. National unity was then preserved but certainly not guaranteed in the long term. Mennonites, like other Canadians, wondered what would happen next.

A major development for Mennonites in Canada was a surge in partisan activities. These have been documented in two major research publications, which I wrote in the next era. "Mennonites and Politics in Canada and the United States," 1983, and "Decades of Transition: North American Mennonite Brethren in Politics," 1995. Although there had been some Mennonite electoral candidacies and a few victories in earlier years, a major surge of partisan political involvement developed after 1960. Consider the following Canadian data. Between 1960 and 1980, 77 Mennonite candidates stood for the national Parliament involving about 45 people. Of the 77 candidacies, 20 were victorious. These victories were won by seven Mennonite men.

At the provincial level between 1960 and 1980, there were 141 Mennonite candidacies involving about 105 different men. Of the 141 candidacies, 38 were successful involving 21 persons. Most Mennonite candidates ran in areas where the Mennonite voter base was substantial. Note the following data. In three Manitoba elections - December 14, 1962, June 28, 1973, October 11, 1977 - all the candidates in the Rhineland constituency were Mennonites. Similarly, in Saskatchewan all the candidates were Mennonite in the Rosthern constituency in April 4, 1964, and June 23, 1971. For Mennonites in Canada who had largely become middle class and upper-middle-class, this era marked a major shift to conservatism and to involvement.

The situation in the US was different. Very few Mennonites were candidates at the state level. For the decades in question, two were elected to the Kansas state legislature. Significantly, in the 1970s, Mennonite Harvey Wollman was elected first as Democratic Lieutenant Governor and then as Governor of South Dakota. It seems that no Mennonites ran for national office.

It is probably noteworthy to mention a significant social-political event here. The famous Woodstock Festival in August 1969 in New York state was not only a massive demonstration against the Vietnam War and a loud rejection of traditional sexual norms; it was also a statement about new musical expressions and was one of the factors weakening traditional hymnody.

In the US, the Nixon Watergate Scandal dominated events for several years. It reached its apex in 1974 when the House of Representatives passed three articles of impeachment with bipartisan support. President Richard Nixon then resigned before the Senate could try him. Vice- President Gerald Ford became president. The many American Mennonite homes which had the wall plaque, *This is a Nixon Home,* needed to do some serious rethinking.

Another major political reality of this era was the escalation of the Vietnam War. An important American myth is that the US does not lose wars, partly because of its might and partly because it is on the side of right and has God's blessing. The American self-image had already taken a serious hit when the costly Korean War ended in a stalemate and a second one when President Kennedy's April 1961 Bay of Pigs invasion in Cuba ended in disaster.

The Vietnam War was, of course, a major phenomenon. With significant US involvement beginning in 1965, the undertaking escalated rapidly. This was to be the war that stopped "the domino effect," the expansion of communism in Asia. It soon became evident to the US government and population that despite its huge and very costly effort, it was not winning the war. In the end, the US leaders watched with humiliation as the last escapees were lifted by helicopter from Saigon rooftops.

The Vietnam War undercut America's self-image and cost it dearly. Given 58,148 deaths and 75,000 veterans disabled, 23,000 permanently, the human cost was staggering. The financial cost was also immense. Although the Vietcong and North Vietnamese won the war, the Vietnamese' loss was huge. The best estimates are that more than 365,000 Vietnamese civilians died during the war and more than 225,000 Vietnamese military personnel died, almost equally divided between North and South.

While the war carried on, a major anti-war or peace movement sprang up in the US with the slogan "Make love, not war." One of the spin-offs of the Vietnam War debates was a sharp division in society, churches, and families. Divisions in Mennonite communities and Mennonite families also ran deep. When, on April 30, 1975, the US finally accepted its loss in Vietnam and signed a cease-fire agreement with the communist victors, the US as a country had to face the fact that it had suffered its first major military defeat. That's a difficult reality to acknowledge for a country widely claiming moral superiority, divine blessing, and historical exceptionalism. The realities of history can be disillusioning and cruel.

CHAPTER 14

LIVING IN WATERLOO
PART II 1981-1994

Living in Waterloo

For our family these were very good years. We greatly enjoyed our fine home and, as our guest book indicates, had the benefit of many visitors. With good health, a good income, many friends, a very fine church community, and many service opportunities, we were an abundantly blessed family.

The year 1981 marked our 25th wedding anniversary which brought some major celebrations. As a family, we had an excellent celebration with friends at the Stone Crock in St. Jacobs, Ontario. The event was largely organized and orchestrated by our children, which was much appreciated.

Wendy speaking at our 25th anniversary dinner.
St. Jacobs, ON, September 12, 1981.

Doris and I also undertook a tourist trip to Europe together with friends Corny and Irene Braun. to celebrate our 25th anniversary. This was Doris's first trip to Europe. Together we greatly enjoyed our travels through The Netherlands, Germany, Switzerland, Austria, and Italy.

Music at our 25th anniversary celebration.
Gary, Heather, Bonnie and Wendy.

Celebrating our 25th anniversary at our home.

In March 1982, with the older children launching their own careers, it was time for one last family holiday. We spent a week in March at a fine resort in Acapulco, Mexico. Although most of the family had to spend some time battling a tropical ailment, I was spared and could help as needed. We had a truly fine holiday. One of the remarkable aspects was that all six of us went parasailing out over the ocean.

Enjoying Acapulco.

Doris getting ready for parasailing, Acapulco, Mexico, March, 1982.

Doris parasailing in Acapulco.

By this time Wendy had become a social worker, having completed both a B.A. and a Master of Social Work degree at Wilfrid Laurier University. We were greatly pleased to see her serving others effectively in this important profession. After our Acapulco family holiday she left for her first posting in Alberta.

In July and August of 1985 we heard from family members in the Fraser Valley that dad's health was declining. We were informed about his condition but were told that there were no signs of imminent death. When we described dad's health problems to our family physician and friend, Dr. Helmut Mathies, who had gotten to know dad from his visits, he stated that the situation looked very serious to him. In fact, he advised Doris to rush to Abbotsford as soon as possible if she wanted to see her father once more. Doris then left as soon as she could. When her plane landed in Vancouver, she was informed that her 89-year-old father had already passed away. He died on August 29. Our good friend, Dr. Mathies, making a long-distance diagnosis, was more discerning than dad's Abbotsford physicians.

I then also flew out to be with the relatives as we celebrated his long and significant pilgrimage and buried dear dad. Given that my own father had passed away in 1959 when I was only 26, I had treated my father-in-law as my own father, which I considered a privilege. He was a real man of God, a fine teacher and preacher, a true Christian gentleman with a stellar reputation.

Other transitions were more pleasant. On May 16, 1987, our son Gary married Lee Ann Wills, a fellow medical student at the University of Western Ontario in London. In fact, they had both very recently graduated with their M.D. degrees.

Gary Redekop M.D., May, 1987.

Lee Ann Wills M.D., May, 1987.

Wendy Redekop MSW, 1982.

We attended their graduation ceremony and were greatly pleased to see them win numerous awards. They continued living in London where Lee Ann completed a two-year residency to be a family physician and Gary undertook a five-year residency to become a neurosurgeon.

During these fourteen years Doris and I continued to be involved in the ministry of Waterloo Mennonite Brethren Church, increasingly known as WMB. Doris continued with her music ministry with the Ladies Trio. This trio - Doris, Alyce Hiebert, Esther Regehr - sang together for about 20 years. They ministered not only in their home church but also regularly in Pineview Nursing Home and in other locations. We still enjoy the fine cassette they produced.

For many years Doris and I served as care group leaders and for a term as deacons. Both of us were heavily involved in the leadership of our large College and Career Group. When I was asked to take on the leadership of that class, about 1975, it consisted of about 10 members. The February 10, 1991 class list consists of 158 names. It was a delight to guide this group in its Sunday classes and other activities and often to have large numbers of these fine young people in our home.

Meanwhile, I continued to serve on Church Council for some years and also as church moderator. During the years in this era I served as a lay preacher, speaking on average about eight times a year in my home church, WMB.

Another important local activity involved chairing the WMB Building Committee, beginning in 1988. The medium-sized WMB congregation, numbering about 280, realized that our existing building was too small for the growing congregation. The church members voted that we should build. As the building committee we engaged an architect and then submitted a plan. The projected cost was to be about $1.9 million. With booming construction at the time, the submitted bids totalled closer to $2.5 million. We therefore dropped plans for the gym. With the help of a team of outside experts, we raised almost $1 million and the construction began.

At this point I shall recount an interesting event. In 1988 and 1989 the WMB Building Committee, which I chaired, had many meetings. On one occasion, two days before a crucial meeting, I became ill and was hospitalized. I was treated and was recuperating when the day came for a crucial meeting. I felt that I was strong enough to chair it and contacted my physician and friend, Dr. Helmut Mathies, who had put me in the hospital.

I asked whether I could leave my hospital bed for the evening meeting and then return for further recuperation. A member of WMB, he was as interested as I was in the progress of the building project. With less than total enthusiasm, he said I could go. I would be away about two and a half hours. I arranged for a car to pick me up and drive me to the church. At the right time, I dressed and walked out of the hospital to a waiting car. I acted as if I was a departing visitor.

We had a very important meeting. About 9:15, as I recall, I stated that I would be closing the meeting as I would need to return to the hospital. I think there was laughter. I rolled up my sleeve and showed the group my hospital shunt and patient's band. There was no laughter. I silently left, stepped into the waiting car. I walked briskly to my hospital bed, quickly changed and put on my hospital gown, crawled into bed, and lay there relaxed when the nurse checked on me a little later. She seemed pleased with my progress. I was resting nicely. I believe this nurse was not aware of my evening excursion. All was well.

The impressive new church building was dedicated on September 17, 1989, with a large assembly in attendance. I am sure that I was not the only member of the Building Committee whose eyes filled with tears as our excellent choir, led by Robert Shuh, filled the acoustically-designed sanctuary with *Bless This House.*

In 1990 I had the privilege of leading a tour group of 18 to the United Kingdom. This group included many of our Waterloo and Kitchener friends. As it happened, shortly after we arrived, London experienced its hottest day of the century. The heat with considerable humidity was oppressive. I suddenly found myself with two tourists who wanted to be taken to the airport to fly

Waterloo Mennonite Brethren Church, 1989.

home. Something had to be done. We needed to find some relief from the heat! Dr. Helmut Mathies and I scouted around and found a McDonald's that had air conditioning and which could handle our group. That was probably the longest visit I have ever made to a McDonald's. Soon the grumblers changed their tune. Subsequently, the group had excellent times seeing the sights of London, taking in a fantastic military tattoo in Edinburgh, watching British warships sail out of Scotland's Firth of Forth to take part in the Gulf War, and taking in the many storied and historic sights and the scenic beauty of England, Scotland, and Wales.

Another important milestone deserves mention. On June 1, 1991, Doris graduated with a B.A degree from Wilfrid Laurier University. She had taken some university-level courses many years earlier in Fresno, CA, but with family responsibilities and other involvements, she had not pursued further studies at that time. After our 1984 tour to the Soviet Union, she decided she wanted to study Russian history. For several years she was a part-time student completing all requirements for the degree.

Doris Redekop, B.A., June 1, 1991.

At the convocation, at which I was privileged and delighted to hood the love of my life, Doris was honoured and given a medal for having the highest academic standing of all part-time students. Our whole family took immense pride in her commitment as an older student and her outstanding academic achievement.

To celebrate Doris's impressive achievement I decided we should go on a trip. Actually, because it would make sense to go to a warm spot in winter, I decided that we should take a holiday during the university's Reading Week even before Doris had completed her studies.

I informed Doris that on a certain day, which I had cleared with her, we would be leaving for a week of holiday in a warm area and that she should pack accordingly. I did not tell her where we would be going. In the Toronto Airport waiting room, when the announcer made a boarding call for the flight to the Dominican Republic, I got up and only then did Doris find out where we would be going. We had an excellent holiday.

During our early years in our Ferndale home, we had contractors enlarge the kitchen and add a sunroom. I also built a 24-foot deck and a heavy-duty dining set to be used on it as well as a small barn for garden storage. The younger children enjoyed the hayloft and the split doors. Some of the building skills which I had learned from my brother-in-law, Abe Wieler stood me in good stead.

Enjoyable in summer; beautiful in winter.

Two other important achievements must be mentioned here. Heather, who had earlier graduated from WLU with a B.A, graduated with her M.S.W degree in 1987 and promptly began her career in that profession. In 1994 our youngest daughter, Bonnie, graduated with a B.A. degree from WLU. In 1997 she graduated with a LL.B. degree from Osgoode Hall. Fortunately, when any of our children and when Doris graduated from WLU, it was my great privilege to hood each one of them.

Heather Redekop MSW, 1987.

Bonnie Redekop LL.B., 1997.

During these years, we undertook various travels. Ever since 1962, if I remember the year correctly, our Redekop Clan, the six siblings with their spouses and their descendants, met every three years at some members' cabins and cottages on Little Shuswap Lake near Chase, BC.

I believe we held the last one in 2002. During the intervening years, the trip to those reunions, later at times with only some of our children, was a much-anticipated event.

Redekop clan gathering at Little Shuswap Lake, BC.
Couples L to R: Paul and Rosella Redekop, Frieda and Abe Wieler, Neil and Sophie Toews, John and Doris Redekop, Wes and Clara Hoff, Ernest and Jean Redekop.

Redekop clan reunion at Little Shuswap Lake, BC.

On August 21, 1991, Doris and I reached another important milestone. On the day of our 35th wedding anniversary Gary and Lee Ann presented us with our first grandchild, a fine baby boy named David.

Grandson David Redekop

About a year later, we had another very welcome addition to our family. On September 12, 1992, we welcomed the birth of our second grandchild, Danielle Marie, daughter of our daughter Heather and husband Phil Charbonneau.

Granddaughter Danielle Charbonneau

By 1993 we had decided that I would take early retirement and we would return to British Columbia. It was hard to think of leaving our many Ontario friends whom we had come to value and love for 26 years, but we had decided that there were important reasons for us to move back to the Fraser Valley. A major reason was that I felt that I should accept the request to lecture at Trinity Western University.

Well before our departure we sold our lovely home on Ferndale Place for $234,000. I must add a note of thanks here. As it happened, on February 22, 1994, I had laparoscopic hernia surgery. After a few days I was back at work. Then, on May 10, I had laparoscopic bladder surgery. This kept me weak and not able to do heavy lifting until we moved. Fortunately, we had many friends who pitched in to help us finish packing and especially with loading the moving van. These folk demonstrated true friendship and I thanked them most sincerely.

I should add here that when in 1993 we decided to relocate to the Fraser Valley in British Columbia, three of our children were pursuing careers in Ontario and one in Alberta. By the time we moved in mid-1994, Gary and Lee Ann had already moved to West Vancouver. Wendy and Craig Carmichael moved to Abbotsford in late 1996. Bonnie moved to BC's Lower Mainland in 2004. Heather moved to Abbotsford in 2011.

Wilfrid Laurier University 1981 - 1994

Not surprisingly, my last 14 years as a professor at WLU were both the most demanding and perhaps the most successful. It is expected that faculty members who have been promoted to be, as is said, full professors should make significant contributions in teaching, research, publications, and service to the community, locally and also further afield. I sought to fulfill such expectations.

My teaching did not change greatly, although I became heavily involved in our new Master of Arts program in Political Science. While my service in various university committees and offices took considerable time, that too was not a main focus. Rather, I became heavily involved in research, publication of papers, writing chapters in books, editing or authoring books, and lecturing elsewhere. I was fortunate that in these 14 years I received 12 research and publication grants which enabled me to engage assistants as needed and also to get research results published.

Scholarship, Research and Writing; Books 1981 - 1994

My textbook, **Approaches to Canadian Politics**, was published in a second edition in 1983. In 1989 a Japanese translation of this book was published by *Ochanimizu Press* in Tokyo. Sometime later, I was informed that it had received an award for being the most significant book translated into Japanese that year. There was a financial gift accompanying this award. Unfortunately, the fine print in my author's contract with the Canadian publishers, Prentice-Hall, stipulated that such funds would go to the publisher. They did.

During those years, I also produced the book **Two Sides: The Best of Personal Opinion, 1964 - 1984.** As stated, this was a collection of selected columns I wrote for the *Mennonite Brethren Herald* over a twenty-year period. Reviewers made very kind comments. WLU President, Dr. Frank C. Peters, wrote:

"Dr. John H. Redekop has the gift of discernment and is able to focus his rich background of training and experience on current issues....The author's clear biblical point of view and evangelical commitment are evident in his articles. He has done his brotherhood a great service."

Dr. Carl Armerding, Principal of Regent College at the University of BC, kindly wrote this statement:

"John Redekop's pithy wit and practical wisdom deserve a wide hearing. Cutting through the fog of pomposity and super-spirituality that frequently blinds Christians to biblical truth, Professor Redekop calls all of us - Anabaptists or otherwise - back to Christian action that is rooted in Scripture, relevant to the times, and unafraid to be as authentic as that of its Lord. Many of these small essays are tracts for our own times; we can be thankful that they are available in a fresh format."

The volume, **A People Apart: Ethnicity and the Mennonite Brethren**, was published in 1986. This project was assigned to me by the Canadian Mennonite Brethren Board of Spiritual and Social Concerns (BSSC, later renamed the Board of Faith and Life). The reason for this assignment was that the BSSC was concerned by the fact that many Mennonite Brethren churches were dropping the name Mennonite Brethren. The associated and more important concern was that simultaneously they would also marginalize the distinctive Mennonite Brethren doctrinal beliefs. This project involved extensive research. Although this book had a very specific religious theme, it was also reviewed as an academic publication.

When the book came out, I made a mistake, one of many in my life. When some people write about their life, they say that as they reflect on their past, they would change nothing. That has always puzzled me.

I like to think that I have learned from the mistakes I have made. In this case, I allowed various media people to interview me and report on the book. I should, of course, have arranged for the management of the book's release to be done by the BSSC. My failure to do that created unnecessary complications.

As expected, this book generated substantial controversy and debate. There was much healthy discussion but also some emotional accusation. The book became important. In fact, the Center for Mennonite Brethren Studies in Fresno, CA, organized a weekend symposium on the book, November 19-21, 1987. The ten presentations delivered at that symposium were then published in the Spring 1988 issue of the academic quarterly, *Direction*.

During these years I was able to have ten of my academic research articles published in refereed journals. These ranged from "Civil Religion in Canada," (1976) and "Mennonites in Politics in Canada and the United States," (1983) to "Dilemmas of Nationalism and National Unity in Canada since 1945," (1985) and "The Christian in Politics: Some Basic Problems," (1985). A somewhat controversial article entitled, "Ethnicity and the Mennonite Brethren," was published in the Spring, 1988 issue of *Direction*.

I also wrote nine other academic articles published in smaller publications. These included "Christians in a World of International Confrontation," (1974); and "Religious Pressure Groups in the Canadian Political System," (1984).

From 1981 to 1994 I was invited to research and write ten chapters in books edited by others. These included "*Reinhold Niebuhr, Christian Idealism and Political Realism*" (1981). Some of these are described more fully in Appendix B. Considerable introspection and self-analysis went into my 1988 12-page article "More than Ethnic: Redefining Mennonite Identity" in **Why I Am A Mennonite,** edited by Dr. Harry Loewen.

In 1990 I was truly excited when I became the professor who edited and improved the second edition of a dominant North American textbook, **People, Politics and Government,** by James J. Guy (Collier Macmillan, 1990). I was doubly grateful when the publishers asked me to write the Introduction. For this product of a crowded one-room school in totally obscure Main Centre, SK, this was something I could never have imagined.

In 1991 the **Mennonite Encyclopedia** released its final volume, Volume 5. It included three articles I was asked to write: They were entitled "Government," "Politics," and "Labor Unions."

A university professor is expected to present papers at academic conferences and colloquia. During these fourteen years I delivered papers at nine such assemblies. These took me to many locations. "Uniqueness in Canadian-American Relations; Trends, Problems, Consequences," New York City (September 5, 1981); "Dilemmas of Nationalism and National Unity,

1945-1985," Edinburgh Scotland (April 11, 1985); "Canadian Politics: A Systems Analysis," Cork-Kinsale, Ireland (April 13, 1985); "A reassessment of Church-State Analysis," Elkhart, Indiana (June 21, 1985); "Focus for a Non-Discipline: Contents for an Introductory Course in Canadian Studies," Winnipeg (June 1, 1986); "Student Perceptions of Canadian-American Relations; A Canadian-American Sample," Southampton, United Kingdom (March 25, 1988); "Canadian Evangelical Thought and the Social Gospel," Simon Fraser University in Burnaby, BC (April 22, 1988); and "Canadian Mennonites and the Challenge of Nationalism," Winnipeg (May 6-8, 1993).

On June 13, 1982 I spoke at the three-day symposium on "Mennonite Studies in North America: State of the Art." This symposium at the University of Toronto was organized by Dr. Harry Loewen, Chair in Mennonite Studies at the University of Winnipeg. All presentations were later published in *The Journal of Mennonite Studies*.

During these years I was privileged to deliver 35 guest lectures at post-secondary schools. Included are the 16 lectures I gave at Central Baptist Seminary in Toronto, January 7-10, 1991 and the following. "The American Far Right: Its Causes, Content, and Consequences," Simon Fraser University (January 11, 1985); "The American Far Right," University of British Columbia (January 15, 1985); "Capital Punishment," Conrad Grebel College (May 28, 1987); "Ideologies as Contrasting Life Views," Trinity Western University, Langley, BC (February 5, 1988); "The Case for Canadian Neutrality," Associated Mennonite Biblical Seminary, Elkhart, IN (April 29, 1988); "Sociopolitical Consequences of Canadian Evangelical Thought," University of Waterloo (November 4, 1988); "A Comparative Perspective on the Impact of Religion and Politics: Canada and the United States," Fresno Pacific University (October 1, 1992); and "What Makes a College Christian?" Redeemer College, Hamilton, ON (May 28, 1994).

Living in Waterloo

Heather helping

Bonnie and a night-time visitor

Writing for the Christian Community 1981 - 1994

These fourteen years were probably my most productive years writing articles and columns. By and large, I really enjoyed such writing although it became somewhat less enjoyable when an assignment kept me away from some meeting I wanted to attend or kept me up late. But I reminded myself that none of us is busier than we allow ourselves to become.

In 1984 Dr. Frank C. Peters and I produced a 53-page manual entitled **Leadership Handbook** as a guide for the Canadian MB Conference of Churches and the provincial conferences.

It was probably in 1985 that I wrote a six-page document entitled *"The Religion of Marxism."* This depiction of Marxism and communism as a religion has not been published but has been widely circulated and has generated considerable interest.

Beginning in 1993 I became involved in the writing of guideline pamphlets for the Canadian MB Conference. The first one was entitled **Anabaptism: The basic Beliefs.** It was reprinted many times and also translated into French, German, Portuguese, Spanish, Lithuanian, Mandarin and Telegu. Sometime later, I co-authored **Christians and War: A Call to a Biblical Counter-Culture** with Henry Huebert.

It was a special privilege for me to be asked to write the anti-capital punishment half of a publication in which my friend and distinguished scholar, Dr. Elmer Martens, president of our denominational seminary, argued for capital punishment. **On Capital Punishment**, 31 pp., was published in 1987. We smiled about the fact that we had been together in elementary school in Lobetal, SK, and now we were debating in print. This publication was translated into French. It had a wide distribution.

The Canadian MB Board of Faith and Life requested that I research and write a statement on civil disobedience. I did. It was published under the title, *"The Christian and Civil Disobedience."* 1990, 42 pp. This booklet was also published in French.

In 1987 I was invited by editor Harold Jantz to become a columnist in the newly launched *ChristianWeek*. Dr. Paul Marshall and I and occasionally a third writer took turns providing a weekly column. It was a privilege to work with this pioneering and outstanding Christian editor in the new publication. Between 1987 and 1999, I contributed a total of 142 columns; about half were written during this fourteen-year period. Titles in these first 14 years included the following. "Capital punishment, let's ask the right questions" (May 5, 1987); "The providing state," (May 19, 1987); "Character poverty causes crime," (April 14, 1998); "Preparing a Christian political agenda." (September 22, 1987); "Two questions - An Open Letter to Prime Minister Mulroney," (February 21, 1989); "Jake Epp - A Christian Statesman," (April 14, 1998); "Some answers to questions about abortion," (February 23, 1988); "Jim Bakker and the church," (January 10, 1989); "Praying for a government you don't support," (May 2, 1989); "Communism, the 'God that failed'," (September 12, 1989); "Right Christians are not blindly rightist," (February 20, 1990); "Christ's cross - history's most hopeful statement," (March 19, 1991); "Sometimes silence is sinful," (August 6, 1991); and "Seven basic myths about public sector strikes," (October 22, 1991).

Throughout these fourteen years, I continued writing *Personal Opinion* columns for the *Mennonite Brethren Herald*. Here are a few of the titles. "Three kinds of Mennonites," (February 12, 1982); "Righting Past Wrongs," (May 7, 1982); "What should governments expect from us?" (November 19, 1982); "Are majorities always right?" (September 9, 1983); "God and the Republicans," (September 21, 1984); "The Influence of Affluence," (June 14, 1985); "The Islamic Ethos," (July 25, 1986); "Immoral winds of change," (April 3, 1987); "Mennonite Members of Parliament," (October 14, 1988); "3,500 lives per year – tobacco." (December 7, 1990); "The peace witness in peacetime," (November 22, 1992); "Women in Leadership," (August 6, 1993); and "A response to critics of the Air Show," (August 26, 1994).

In addition to my *Personal Opinion* columns I also wrote some longer articles for the *Mennonite Brethren Herald* during these years. Here are five titles. "A Response to 'Evangelicals in Vancouver'," (January 27, 1984); "A Denomination under Lordship," (October 6, 1984); "Leadership; One body - biblical and functional unity," (May 18, 1984); "Anabaptist ecumenicity," (November 1, 1985); "The Case Against Capital Punishment," (April 17, 1987); and "Citizens in this world," (June 29, 1993).

Beyond my writing for the *Mennonite Brethren Herald,* both columns and other articles, during these years about 100 of my articles appeared in other so-called popular Christian periodicals. Some were adaptations or even reprints from my earlier writing, but many were original. The list includes the following titles. "The Charter of Rights: What's at stake?" *Mennonite Reporter* (November 8, 1981); "Overtime," *Gospel Herald* (August 14, 1984); "Relief or Prevention," *Earthkeeping* (April 1985); "Glimpses of life in today's Soviet Union," *The Christian Leader* (April 30, 1985); "The future of our Canadian Conference," *Evangelism Canada* (June 1987); "Capital Punishment - No," *Faith Today* (July/August, 1986). The "Yes" side was argued in the same issue by Professor Clark Pinnock. Also "The unrecognized double standard," *Christian News* (April 24, 1988); "Who controls the church?" *The Christian Leader* (July 19, 1988); and "The most needed ministry," *Gospel Herald* (August 8, 1989).

Additional titles in other religious periodicals included "Canadian Labour - a place for Christians?" *Faith Today* (September/October 1989); "The 80s: A Decade of Shifting Ideologies," Resource, *Church Ministries Leadership Magazine* (November-December, 1989); "Yes, There is a Better Way," *The Guide* (May 1990); "Canadian justice - is it just?," *Faith Today* (November/December 1990); "National Unity - A Guest Editorial," *The Messenger* (November 8, 1991); "Can I stay open on Sunday?" *The Marketplace* (July-August, 1992); and "Church and State: the Boundaries Blur," *MCC Peace Section Newsletter* (September/October, 1993). Perhaps my most significant article was `"Anabaptism: Reviving the Vision," *The Christian Leader* (August 15, 1989).

The Mennonitische Rundschau carried several of my articles. "Das heutige Russland," (May 15, 1985); "Das Heutige Russland - #2," (June 12, 1985); "Denominations-Ethik - zu Gottes Ehre leben," (August 7, 1985); "Kanadier die als Christen bekannt sind," (January 15, 1992); and "Christen als Bürger" (June 30, 1993). "Anabaptism: The Basic Beliefs," was published in Chinese in the March, 1994 issue of the *Chinese MB Herald*.

At times it was a bit of a challenge to get the various columns and other articles done on time, but I was motivated by the knowledge that at least some of my columns were widely read and some even by elected politicians.

Addressing Christian Audiences   1981 - 1994

Addressing Christian audiences was one of the most enjoyable and rewarding activities during these 14 years. My records indicate that the average for these years was about 18 such presentations each year.

Some orations were presented at conventions or similar venues. These included the following. "Church and State, An Anabaptist View," at the Lutheran Church in America Church-State Seminar, Chateauguay, Quebec (November 6, 1981); "Brotherhood and the Believers Church," Ontario MB Youth Conference, Guelph Bible Conference Grounds, Guelph, ON (November 19, 1982); "Continuity and Change. An analysis of the Mennonite Experience with the Political Order; A Canadian Perspective," Laurelville Church Centre, PA (March 8, 1985); "Understanding Canadian Evangelicals," EFC Conference, Ottawa (March 28, 1985); "Health Care Workers in Canada and the United States; A Contrasting Analysis," Mennonite Health Care Workers National Convention, Denver, CO (March 4, 1986); "The Christian Book Business; Some Guidelines," Christian Booksellers Suppliers Association Convention, Scarborough, ON (April 6, 1987); "Servant Leadership," Convocation

Address, Trinity Western University (September 10, 1987); "Facing Today's Crisis," Christian Writers Conference, Toronto (November 13, 1987); and "Ethnicity and the Mennonite Brethren: Issues and Responses," Mennonite Brethren Centre, Fresno, CA (November 19, 1987).

Other convention presentations included "Christian Involvement in Social Policy," National Convention of the Christian Legal Fellowship, Muskoka Baptist Conference Centre, ON (April 1, 1988); "Accountable Stewardship," National Convention of the Mennonite Foundation of Canada, Kitchener, ON (April 9, 1989); "How Can We Have Influence?" Convention of the Reformed Christian Business and Professional Organization, Niagara Falls, ON (April 4, 1990); "Developing a Healthy Skepticism," Canadian Church Press Convention, Waterloo, ON (April 26, 1991); and "Faith, Farming and Public Policy," Annual Convention, Christian Farmers Federation of Ontario, Guelph, ON (December 2, 1993).

Other presentations in this category during those years, not involving conventions, included the following. "Service as Vocation," Aylmer Bible School Graduation Service, Aylmer, ON (April 12, 1987); "Religion in School - Bane or Blessing?" Bramalea Baptist Church, Bramalea, ON (November 18, 1989); "The Potential Effects of Canada's Political, Educational, and Social Conditions on the Gideons in the '90s," Gideons Canadian Headquarters, Guelph, ON (December 10, 1990); "Called to Affirm," Commencement Address, Mennonite Brethren Biblical Seminary, Fresno, CA (May 19, 1991); "The way we were," MEI 40th Graduation Anniversary, Abbotsford, BC (June 29, 1991); "Three Key Questions for the Columbia Bible College Community," CBC Annual Meeting, Abbotsford, BC (October 17, 1992); "God Gives the Increase," Columbia Bible College Building Dedication and Convocation, Abbotsford, BC (October 18, 1992); "What Makes Canadians Canadian?" Eighteenth Annual Community Prayer Breakfast, Waterloo, ON (May 3, 1993); "Canadian Mennonites and the Challenge of Nationalism," Concord College, Winnipeg (May 6, 1993); and "What Makes a Business Christian?" Christian Businessmen's Committee, Chilliwack, BC (June 21, 1994).

Of special significance for me was the opportunity to preach the main sermon at the 40th anniversary of Central Heights Church in Abbotsford. I sang in that church's choir during the church's first service on January 1, 1950. Now, 40 years later, I could celebrate with what had been my home church for more than a decade. "Becoming the Church God wants us to be" (June 24, 1990).

Ministries in Mennonite Brethren Conferences   1981 - 1994

These were important years for me in denominational ministries. At the provincial level, from 1977-1986 I served on the Ontario Board of Spiritual and Social Concerns which dealt with a broad spectrum of theological, organizational, relational, and church polity questions and concerns. For part of that time I served as chairman. It was a privilege to work with a group of mature and wise sisters and brothers in the faith.

In July 1980 I was elected as assistant moderator of the Canadian MB Conference. Interestingly, that was a position my father, Jacob F. Redekop, held from 1941 until 1943.

In July 1983 I was elected moderator of the Canadian Conference of Mennonite Brethren Churches.

For me this was a humbling affirmation. I had observed over the decades how influential the moderator was in shaping the direction of the conference. I knew my limitations and hoped and prayed that I would be able to serve well in this role. As I told the assembled delegates, my aim was to be a servant-leader. Fortunately, two strong associates were also elected at that St. Catharines, ON convention. Pastor Herb Neufeld was elected as assistant moderator and Robert Friesen as secretary. Notably, we three were the first Canadian-born Conference executive committee. I shall always remain deeply indebted to these two outstanding associates.

One of the important duties of the Canadian Conference moderator was to deliver the annual moderator's message. It may be of interest to note the titles on which I preached: "A Denomination Under Lordship," (1984); "Denominational Ethics: Living for God's Glory," (1985); "Jesus Christ the same: yesterday, today, and forever," (1986); and "Running God's Race." (1987).

These four years of conference leadership brought with them many challenges and also memorable occasions. I shall briefly describe two historic events. The first took place on July 8, 1984, in the large Sevenoaks Alliance Church in Abbotsford, BC. During that 73rd Annual Convention of the Canadian Mennonite Brethren Conference, the delegates welcomed the Quebec Association of Mennonite Brethren Churches as a member conference. Assistant moderator Herb Neufeld, secretary Robert Friesen and I, as moderator, officially signed the documents and welcomed the Quebec leaders, Jean-Marc Nantel, Andre Bourque, and Claude Leclerc and embraced them as fellow leaders in the Canadian Conference. An audience of about 2,000 people, delegates and others, welcomed and affirmed them. There was excitement in the air. When the entire Quebec delegation sang the French version of *Onward Christian Soldiers,* the warm feelings were palpable. There were tears of joy.

L to R: Robert Friesen, Herb Neufeld and John Redekop.

The second major event took place on July 5, 1986. Some background information is needed. Not long after I became Canadian Conference moderator, Rev. Isaac Tiessen, an esteemed veteran MB pastor retired near London, Ontario, came to see me to share a great burden. It turned out that he felt that an apology should be made to what was then called the Mennonite General Conference, a sister conference, for the fact that in the era between 1935 and 1960, some MB churches had excommunicated members for marrying someone from a Mennonite General Conference church. The reason was that those "other Mennonites" had not been immersed; that conference practiced a different form of believers' baptism. Rev. Tiessen had been part of such action. Now it bothered him immensely. Research revealed that while it was never an MB Conference position that such action should be taken, some MB churches had acted on their own to carry out such excommunication. In fact, some of the couples affected were still living.

After consultation with other Canadian MB Conference leaders it was decided that such an apology should be made. As it happened, I believe providentially, the two national conventions: MB and General Conference were taking place in Waterloo, Ontario at the same time in 1986. An appropriate statement was drafted and approved.

After requesting permission to address the General Conference delegates but not stating why, on July 5, 1986, I led an MB delegation including Rev. Isaac Tiessen and Conference Minister Henry Brucks. I vividly recall the three of us marching into the hall of assembled GC delegates with many eyes on us, delegates not knowing why we had come.

The Apology Delegation.
L to R: Mrs. Tiessen, Isaac Tiessen, John Redekop,
welcoming host Jake Franz and Henry Brucks.

John Redekop and Jake Franz embrace in Christian reconciliation.

With an emotion-filled voice, I read out the statement of apology. I looked up. More than a few people, including myself, shed tears of authenticity, remorse, and repentance. The emotion-filled GC platform leaders readily accepted our request for forgiveness. We embraced. There was complete reconciliation. As I recall, we marched back out to thunderous applause. This was for me, the highlight of my four years as conference moderator.

There was a sequel. A reciprocal visit was requested. As moderator I readily gave my approval. The next day a delegation of those who had been sinned against, led by GC Moderator Jake Franz, came and addressed the MB assembly, requesting forgiveness for negative attitudes towards the MBs that they had had. Forgiveness was immediately granted by me on behalf of the assembled delegates. There was more embracing. There were more tears. There was a second round of authentic reconciliation. A sad chapter in MB history had been rightly concluded. As historian Conrad Stoesz wrote in an April 29, 2005 article in the *Mennonite Brethren Herald:* "The convictions of one person can change a church, even a church conference." My second two-year term as moderator ended in July 1987.

After I completed my four years as Conference Moderator, I was again elected to the renamed Board of Faith and Life and served until 1994.

In 1985 the Canadian MB Conference appointed a Task Force to investigate and study the state of MB higher education in Canada. It consisted of Herb Kopp, chair, Arthur Block, and me. Having visited all the schools and done the research, we reported our findings to the convention in 1987. We were then given a new mandate, namely, to recommend the best way forward. In 1988 we recommended that a federation of MB post-secondary schools in Canada be created under a national board. We spelled out some working principles. The national convention approved this plan subject to approval by the provincial conferences which operated some of the schools. If fully approved, the plan would be implemented at the 1989 convention. Not all provincial conferences approved the proposal, so it died.

Mennonite Central Committee Canada

Another very interesting area of ministry for me was serving on the board of Mennonite Central Committee Canada (MCCC), also known simply as MCC, which is the acronym I shall use. Although I served previously as an alternate member, I was a regular member on the Canadian MCC board from 1983 until 1994. There were many highlights; I shall recall three.

On one occasion, probably in 1979, an MCC delegation, led by Dr. Frank Epp, asked to see the Minister of Indian Affairs and Northern Development, the Hon. Warren Almand. We were assigned a half-hour on a Sunday evening in his Ottawa office. The minister had been informed that a Christian delegation had asked to see him.

After we were ushered into his private office, the minister asked if we were there to oppose capital punishment or to ask something for ourselves. He mentioned the first issue because, as Canada's Solicitor General, he had abolished the death penalty in 1976. After that action, he had had many Christians complaining to him about that. Apparently, the good minister could not envision a Christian delegation wanting to see him about something other than these two items. When Frank told him that we were not coming for either of the two reasons mentioned but, rather, we wanted to discuss with him ways in which the MCC could help him deal with problems relating to the Native community, as they were then called. I clearly recall the minister being totally surprised. Then he said that since we had come to help, he had the whole evening for us. That evening of candid and forthright discussion with a Canadian cabinet minister was perhaps the most significant political conversation I have ever experienced. We, who had done significant preparation, were able to help the Canadian government shape policy.

A second issue arose. For many years before I became a board member at MCC I had been bothered by the following reality. I remembered that in my high school days at the MEI, some fellow students talked about living on a "Jap farm." A little research a few years later had revealed that quite a few Mennonite farmers and others in the Abbotsford-Aldergrove-Langley area had purchased farms owned by Japanese-Canadians before they were evicted in 1942. These farms had been bought at very low prices. These people of Japanese ancestry, many native-born Canadians, had been evicted because of the racist hysteria which set in promptly after the Pearl Harbour attack on December 7, 1941. I did some additional research. The facts could not be denied. I therefore asked to do a presentation to the MCC board. On September 29, 1984, I read my background statement and presented a draft motion. The members were surprised and also impressed. My motion was amended and passed.

The Statement of Apology was read at a news conference in Winnipeg in October 1984. Now it was representatives of the Japanese-Canadian community who were surprised. They could hardly believe that more than 40 years after the unwarranted expropriation of their homes and farms with only a pittance - apparently less than 15% of the compensation paid to them, a group of Mennonites would be prepared to acknowledge guilt and request forgiveness.

Money was not the issue. The agenda was making things right! There was forgiveness and reconciliation. As an effort to make the apology tangible, the MCC also announced the establishment of a perpetual Japanese-Canadian Peace Scholarship. After some days Mr. Art Miki, President of the Association of Japanese Canadians, issued a statement of thanks. In part, it read as follows:

"The National Association of Japanese wishes to accept the expression of regret and apology extended to 46,000 Canadians of Japanese ancestry by the Mennonite Central Committee of Canada for the mistreatment and exploitation to which Japanese-Canadians were subjected during and after World War II. Your organization should be commended for taking this position and publicly recognizing these past injustices."

This event got extensive media coverage. It was widely reported that I had instigated this apology. I received many affirming responses but also a few very angry letters from some Canadians. Those letters of criticism are, for me, a badge of honour. That initiative remains one of the highlights of my life.

A third issue needs to be told. Some time later, while still on the MCC board, I raised the matter of apologizing to the native community, the First Nations peoples who were the initial inhabitants in this land. I believed that Canadians generally should apologize and somehow make amends for wrongs committed against them in earlier times. Some colleagues took up this cause with me. Again, an apology which I helped draft was adopted and presented. Space constraints prevent me from chronicling this story. Again there was widespread agreement but also substantial criticisms. Again I wear those criticisms as a badge of honour. Although the overall situation is incredibly complicated, there was certainly enough wrongdoing to warrant trying, in a small way, to help make things right.

Another MCC-related development deserves mention. Since 1968 the MCC Canada senior staff members had arranged for the national moderators and secretaries of participating MCC conferences to meet for consultation a day in advance of the annual MCC meetings. MCC hosted the meeting and set the agenda. After I was elected moderator in 1983, I attended several of these very helpful sessions. It then occurred to me that the conference leaders should form their own group. After testing this idea with some key people and with MCC officials, it was decided to proceed in that direction. I invited all conference leaders to attend what would be a founding meeting. The response was uniformly positive. Thus it happened that on January 22, 1987, we established the Canadian Council of Mennonite and Brethren in Christ Moderators. At that first meeting, we elected Dr. Arden Thiessen of the Evangelical Mennonite Conference as chairman. I became vice-chairman.

Evangelical Fellowship of Canada

During these years, I also became more involved in another organization very dear to me, the Evangelical Fellowship of Canada. In 1968 I was one of a group of denominational leaders committed to keep the struggling organization alive, indeed, to have it grow. I served as the chairman of the Social Action Commission. Gradually the EFC achieved financial viability. A major step forward was taken when the EFC hired Brian Stiller in 1983 as the first full-time executive director. He gave the EFC what it needed - bold, courageous, skilled and visionary leadership. After that appointment, the organization flourished. Brian is the architect of the present impressive organization. Its publications, seminars, committee undertakings, parliamentary and judicial briefs, new commissions, and Brian's media appearances soon gave the EFC credibility as the voice of evangelicals in Canada. His leadership in launching the magazine *Faith Alive,* soon renamed *Faith Today,* was a major milestone in giving the EFC national credibility and national impact. Brian served the EFC with great distinction until 1997.

In April 1985, I was elected vice-president of the EFC. On April 3, 1991, I was elected president of the Evangelical Fellowship of Canada. This office brought with it significant new responsibilities. I served in this role for four years. As president I had the opportunity to represent the EFC in many settings, including political venues in Ottawa. These were real highlights for me.

On March 28, 1985, I addressed a large assembly in the Ottawa Skyline Hotel on the topic, "Understanding Canadian Evangelicals." Some elected politicians were present. Doubtless, there were shortcomings in my analysis, but perhaps I helped all hearers to understand the breadth, essence, and significance of the growing and increasingly significant Canadian evangelical community.

Additional Involvements

In 1993 I accepted an appointment to the founding board of *The Centre for Renewal in Public Policy.* This conservative political think tank publishes a journal, sponsors seminars, undertakes and publishes research and generally seeks to promote conservative Christian values. I served for about four years.

There were other involvements, including substantial Christian media activities. The most important one, by far, was serving as a panelist on *The Stiller Report,* later renamed *Crosscurrents,* from 1989 until 1995. With Brian Stiller as moderator, he and three other panelists interviewed guests.

This weekly half-hour program on VISION TV gained a large national audience. As I recall, we once received a pollster's report stating that occasionally we had a larger audience than the CBC Evening News. As I recall, the number was about 600,000. That was another exciting experience.

The Stiller Report. Brian Stiller is on the right.

Writing for the General Public   1981 - 1994

Universities strongly encourage faculty members to write for newspapers and magazines. Ever since the 1950s, I have enjoyed writing articles and columns for what is called "the popular press" in contrast to academic publications. Among the approximately 25 in this category published in mostly large daily newspapers during these 14 years were the following, with some published in several papers. "Does Canada need a new political party?" *St. Thomas Times Journal* (January 2, 1982); "Exporting illness and death to the Third World," *Kitchener-Waterloo Record* (November 13, 1985); "The doctrine that failed; Soviet Communism," *Kitchener-Waterloo Record* (December 11, 1989); "Canadians must accept Quebec's 'idiosyncrasies'," *The Calgary Herald* (August 2, 1991); "Canada needs generosity not animosity to face the future," *Toronto Star* (August 17, 1991); "Banning tobacco ads; as with opium, a ban will surely come," *The Globe and Mail,* Toronto (August 19, 1991); "Postal workers have no right to break the law," *Kitchener-Waterloo Record* (September 12, 1991); "Should Canada maintain its universal social welfare system?," *The Moncton Times-Transcript* (October 5, 1991); "Clash of tendencies; individual and community rights must be balanced," *Kitchener-Waterloo Record* (June 4, 1992); "Let's get involved in peace movement," *Toronto Star* (September 5, 1992); and "Drawing the line between charity and tax evasion," *Toronto Star* (October 30, 1993).

As noted above, in 1974, WLU launched its *WLU Newsfeature Service*. I continued as one of the professors who regularly submitted articles for distribution to about 40 Ontario newspapers. Between 1981 and 1994, when I left WLU, I wrote 66 Newsfeatures for distribution across Ontario. Later topics included the following: "Quebec's separatism express; too much zeal caused a derailment," "A sad story - Some dark clouds on Mulroney's horizon," "Quebec erects new iron curtain," "Canadians and Americans; what's the difference, eh?" "Should Canada Keep the Monarchy?" "A Citizen's Salute," "Sad realities of public sector strikes," and "Paying for health; only graduated user fees can save our medical system." It was a delight to receive reader responses forwarded by the professional News Clipping Service. Readers' reactions were both informative about public opinion and encouraging. A few were critical. Unfortunately, we professors did not have time to reply to the many readers and editors who responded to our columns.

General Speaking Engagements 1981 - 1994

In 1982 I received a surprise invitation to address a large audience. The CTV television network decided to telecast a series of short university courses. I was invited to do the first one on Canadian politics and was requested to develop the course. I was given almost total freedom in developing the title and the lectures. I chose the title *Interpretations of Canadian Politics*. The course, recorded in the studios of CKCO- TV in Kitchener, Ontario, was aired in September and October. The producers encouraged me to use a variety of props and it was a delight to select those and then to teach the lessons to a national audience without a formal script.

Universities strongly encourage professors to undertake speaking engagements as part of the "Town and Gown" engagement. During these fourteen years I had many opportunities to speak to secular groups; service clubs, seniors groups, political groups, and others. Presentations to conventions or conferences included the following. "Is Sanctioning the Best Method of Dealing with South Africa?," World Affairs Conference, Upper Canada College, Toronto (February 20, 1990); "Meech Lake and the Canadian Crisis," Up With People Conference, Kitchener, ON (February 20, 1990); and "The Clark-Mulroney Constitutional Proposal," National Credit and Financial Executives Forum, Toronto (November 13, 1991).

Presentations to smaller groups or assemblies included the following. "The Politics of Confrontation," Kitchener Public Library Lecture Series (September 26, 1983); "Hammer, Sickle, Cross; A trip to the USSR," Adult Recreation Centre Lecture, Waterloo, ON (May 10, 1985); "The Love-Hate Relationship Between Canada and the United States," Listowel Rotary Club, Listowel, ON (March 5, 1987); "Why Canadians Won't Vote Socialist," Rockway-Kitchener Kiwanis (September 1, 1988); "Televangelists," Kitchener Public Library Lecture (March 19, 1990); and "Industrial Relations in the New Canada," Cara Community Club of Cambridge (May 23, 1992).

During these 14 years, I averaged about six to ten such presentations a year to larger and smaller groups, about 110 in total.

I also did numerous interviews on CBC Radio and on local stations in Seattle, Toronto, Guelph, Calgary, Kelowna, Victoria, and Vancouver. For two years, 1981 - 1983, I was a frequent participant in WLU's own television program IN TOUCH WITH U. It was also my privilege to appear quite a few times as the guest on the Tom Cherrington Report on CHCH-TV in Hamilton. Perhaps my most interesting television interview happened on October 16, 1993, when Lloyd Robertson interviewed me in his National News on the topic "The upcoming election and the mood of voters in the Kitchener-Waterloo area."

The Debates - Marxism versus Christianity 1986 - 1988

It was probably in early December 1985 that I received an unusual phone call. A leader of the InterVarsity Christian Fellowship at Carleton University in Ottawa phoned to report a major concern and to extend a request. He stated that recently there had been a debate between a Marxist professor and a spokesperson for Christianity. It had not gone well for the Christian. He reported that the Marxist professor was willing to have a second debate if the IVCF could find another person to debate him. The caller wondered if I would be willing to be that person.

Such a challenge immediately interested me. After a few days to think and pray about it and consult with others, I accepted. Soon the date was set. I would be debating Dr. Marvin Glass, Professor and Head of the Philosophy Department at Carleton University, on January 13, 1986.

As I recall, Dr. Glass was at that time also the Leader of the Communist Party of Canada. The debate topic was: "***Marxism versus Christianity - Which is More Valid?***" It is no exaggeration to say that I spent as much time as I could in preparing, in immersing myself in both Marxist and anti-Marxist writings and in the essence of Christian theology. IVCF groups in Ottawa and also at WLU, as well as many people in my home church, Waterloo MB, were praying diligently for me. I needed such support.

On the evening of January 13 my Ottawa host took me to the Carleton campus early. As my host was guiding us to Southam Hall, we were obstructed by a crowd of students which we had to circumnavigate.

I asked my host what this might be. He turned and said that they were lined up for the debate. I was taken aback. I did not assume that so many students would be interested.

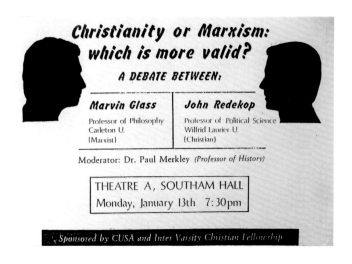

Dr. John Redekop of Laurier, left, and Dr. Marvin Glass of Carleton University, right, debated the virtues of Christianity and Marxism before a crowd of more than 1,000.

The debate and the debaters.

The large lecture hall was packed. The debate began. I think it was scheduled to go for one hour and thirty minutes. It soon became obvious that although there were some Christians present, probably most attendees did not support me and probably anticipated that Dr. Glass would again score an unquestioned supremacy.

As the debate progressed with hard-hitting arguments from both sides, I felt an unusual sense of freedom and enablement. One must be careful not to make too much of any such sensation, but I felt myself articulating arguments more effectively than I would normally do.

We each had the opportunity to make two rebuttals. I think we both had strong first round rebuttals. Dr. Glass pressed me hard on the problems of pain and evil under a loving God. I felt that in my second rebuttal and final statement, God gave me the ability to counter all the main assertions and accusations Dr. Glass had just made. I pressed him hard on many issues, especially the failure of communism to produce the "new socialist man." I sat down. The debate moderator then called on Dr. Glass for his final rebuttal and closing statement. To my surprise he stated that he would not be making a second rebuttal. After a few seconds of stunned silence the large audience burst into applause. I went to Dr. Glass and we shook hands. I congratulated him on his strong performance.

After the session I met with the IVCF leaders. They were, as the saying goes, "All smiles." We celebrated what they considered an excellent event for the cause of Christ on campus. Allow me to say that I felt like Moses of old. God had given me clarity of thought and words to speak beyond those which I had prepared. Sometime later I received a letter from a Carleton University administrator, William Harrison, obviously a Christian, in which he wrote: "Your clear and cogent presentation of the Christian viewpoint was all that could have been desired." I thank God for the effectual prayers of a lot of his saints.

The large Ottawa event was, however, not the end of the story. In my interaction with Dr. Glass, I sensed that he was inclined for another debate with me. For various reasons it took a very long time for another event to be scheduled. The eventual result was that on March 11, 1987, Dr. Glass and I met for a second debate in the large gymnasium at Wilfrid Laurier University. The debate topic was again: "Marxism versus Christianity - Which is More Valid?"

Again many IVCF students and church people prayed diligently for me. The event was widely advertised. Media reporters and a CTV crew came to cover it. Approximately 1,300 people, including many of my own students, attended. We had both learned what our opponent would likely say and had prepared accordingly. We had another vigorous debate.

This time Professor Glass had fewer supporters in the audience, but it was generally agreed that both debaters were treated with respect and appreciation. I felt that we both had clear concluding rebuttals. Professor Glass and I again shook hands. Actually, in the intervening months, we had had significant exchanges and were on friendly terms. After the event, the local IVCF leaders expressed total satisfaction with how the debate went. Again there were many smiles. Again I thank the many prayer supporters and God for allowing me to speak for the Christian faith. God had used a very earthen and flawed vessel.

There was a third installment in this saga. Dr. Glass and I had had some important conversations about our life views. At one point, I told him that I would read any communist literature he wanted me to read if he would read the New Testament. He had, after all, almost boasted about his open-mindedness. As I recall, he agreed. I do not recall exactly what I was supposed to read, but that created no problem for me. I think that Dr. Glass said that he had read to the end of Matthew. It is not stretching the truth to say that with the passage of time we had become academic colleagues and friends. At some point I asked Marvin whether he would be open to have a third debate. I was actually not surprised when he readily agreed.

On February 6, 1988, Dr. Glass and I met in the large gymnasium at Trinity Western University for a third round on the same topic. The crowd was large. I remember hearing comments about it being at least 1,200. This time, as Professor Glass and I both knew, the crowd would be overwhelmingly Christian. I assured Marvin that he had nothing to fear. He would be respected and would be treated very well. Indeed he was and expressed gratitude for his very gracious reception at TWU.

These debates were never structured to have anyone declared a winner. The intent, rather, was to present convictions to the best of the debaters' ability and let the listeners sort out issues for themselves. After this debate, as also after the other two, the Christian organizers were greatly pleased with the event. Again I thank the many saints who prayed for me.

After this third debate we received an invitation to have a fourth debate, in the People's Church in Toronto. Dr. Glass and I discussed this matter. I said that I would be pleased to accept. After some time Dr. Glass informed me that he would not debate in a Christian church. I chided him about who now was really open-minded. In fact, I said that if he wanted to arrange a debate in any communist setting anywhere in Canada, I would be pleased to participate. I could not get him to change his mind about speaking in a church. Nor did he ever invite me to a fourth debate. Thus a very interesting three-act drama in my life came to an end.

Activity in the Political Arena

In February 1988 I was asked by the Ontario Ministry of Colleges and Universities to be part of a three-person Government Task Force to assess the degree-granting qualifications of "Private Bible Colleges and Seminaries" in Ontario. I was pleased to accept. Our Task Force visited many campuses. It was encouraging to see the academic strengths of many of them but also disappointing to see some very weak enterprises. In due course, we made our recommendation about each school. I understand that several soon lost their provincial charter.

During the 1980s and early 1990s I became involved in advising various politicians and writing political statements. As it happened, some of my columns in *ChristianWeek* and the *Mennonite Brethren Herald,* as well as some articles published in several large dailies were circulated and discussed by some politicians, apparently even some cabinet members, in Ottawa. This generated some interesting reactions. I was even quoted once in *Hansard*, the House of Commons record of proceedings, as an expert commentator. That was humbling. Both dad and mom would have liked that.

I clearly recall that on one later occasion, February 25, 2000, when I was addressing a large assembly in an auditorium in the Parliament Buildings with a good number of MPs present, I said that I believed that political leaders were accountable not only to the people in the land but ultimately also to God. At that point one MP stood up and publicly contradicted me. I didn't mind. I let him have the last word. I think that our little interaction got people to think.

The 1984 Trip to the Soviet Union

Ever since I began studying the Soviet Union in the early 1960s, I hoped that someday I could visit that land, a country which, in its territory until 1991, included Ukraine, the land of my parents and grandparents, both paternally and maternally. When travel restrictions eased, and a few tourists began reporting on their visits to that intriguing country, I decided it was time to start planning.

On July 29, 1984, I was privileged to lead a group of 18 on a seventeen-day trip to the USSR. The group included my sister Sophie and her husband, Neil Toews, and Doris' sister Evangeline and her husband, Gordon Dancer. Here I can only describe a few highlights. I should say that for Soviet purposes, the group was known as the **Peace Choir** with Neil the very capable conductor and Doris as the fine pianist. I was the speaker.

When we arrived in Leningrad, later renamed St. Petersburg, from Helsinki, we naturally had to go through customs. I had been asked to bring in the first set of the newly printed Russian translation of **Barclay's Commentary on the Bible**. I had distributed the volumes among our group. The customs official checked only a few suitcases, including mine. In mine he found quite a few English and Russian religious books and a few Barclay volumes. He asked me why I was bringing these books to the USSR. I said they were gifts for people we would visit. That did not satisfy him. He then lifted each book separately and asked if I could read it. I was allowed to retain each book I could read; he took the rest. I was devastated but there was nothing I could do about it. All the Russian books were lost. Later, when I visited the Moscow headquarters of the All-Union Council of Evangelical Christians-Baptists (AUCECB), I reluctantly reported what had happened. Rev. Alexie Bichkov, the General Secretary, and his associates smiled. Then they said that they would be offered those books for money very soon. At one level, I was greatly relieved. I think that an under-the-table deal was carried out some days later.

Our time in Leningrad was memorable for various reasons. I shall summarize four. First, I believe it was during our first supper in Leningrad that I was paged in perfect English to report to the front desk. I, of course, immediately responded. You do that in the USSR. On the phone, a gentleman, speaking perfect English, said that the ruble exchange rate we were getting at the hotel for our dollars was poor. He could give us a much better rate. I informed him we were satisfied with the official rate. I had been warned of such a KGB trap.

Second, early in our Leningrad stay, Doris and I and our guide, Lyuba Czerkova, were walking across a plaza when Lyuba pointed out a store. She called it a Beriozka, a store where you can buy all sorts of imported and high-end Russian goods with Western credit cards and hard currency. Russian rubles are considered a soft currency. Russians could enter it only as guests of foreigners. I noticed there were fine shelves in the window with absolutely nothing on them. I asked Lyuba about that. She said that if the store staff put items on display, then people would come in to buy them and the staff would have to restock the window shelves. If you don't display your wares, you don't have so much work. Marketing obviously has different meanings in Western and Soviet economies.

Third, one day our group visited a Beriozka. Our clerk/cashier spoke English. I asked when the store closed and was told at 4:00 o'clock. About twenty minutes to 4 this lady came to me and said that we must leave. I reminded her that she had said 4 o'clock. She smiled and said that the staff leaves when the store closes, therefore we needed to leave early. We rushed our purchasing.

Doris in front of a Beriozka.

Fourth, one day, during the supper hour, Lyuba came to me and said that our group would be going on a night tour to see the lights of Leningrad and especially the raised bridges allowing boats and small ships to pass. She reminded me that Leningrad is called "Venice of the North." I thanked her and said that we preferred not to take that night tour. She then said rather sternly that the authorities had said the Canadian Group would go on the night tour and we had no choice. She instructed me to tell the others.

In the Soviet Union, one does not ignore what authorities say.

While our group was still enjoying a late supper, perhaps it was close to 9, I told them about the night tour. I instructed them to have the luggage at their doors by 1:00 AM, as I recall, and that we would be leaving the hotel about 1:30. After the night tour, the bus would take us directly to the airport. I had 17 unhappy fellow travellers.

We were in the Soviet Union, and we did as we were told. Some members in our group got a little sleep, but most of us, as I recall, got none. As we left the hotel we encountered about 20 East German tourists entering the hotel. Much later it occurred to me that the hotel would likely be booking those tourists into the same rooms we had just vacated. As I recall, when later I asked Lyuba about my idea, she said that this was likely the case. The hotel management had figured out how to increase hotel revenue. I discovered a new meaning for "double booking."

There was an epilogue to this night-tour saga. After drearily seeing what is actually a beautiful sight, Leningrad at night, the bus took us to the airport about 4:00 AM, as I recall. There was no place to buy anything to eat or drink. We slouched around in what was apparently a large KGB interview room with many small side rooms. Around 7:30 or so, very tired and groggy, we were taken to our plane to fly to Moscow. The pilot could not get the engines going. We were then taken to another plane where the propellers were going and the plane seemed ready to leave. At that point a ramp was set against the door of the readied plane. Eighteen people were removed from that plane, after which we walked up the ramp to take their places. We felt very bad about what was happening. That morning on the plane there were 18 very sleepy passengers who left behind 18 very angry displaced persons.

We spent the first Sunday at Hotel Ukraine in Moscow. I had arranged for our group to attend the officially sanctioned Moscow Baptist Church. Because it served diplomats and foreign business people, it was not closed by Stalin. Our group was to come by bus in time for the 10 o'clock service. Because I was to preach, I left much earlier by taxi. I showed the taxi driver the written church address. He nodded and we drove off. He soon dropped me off near a large building. I paid him; he drove off. I quickly realized that this was not the church. He had tricked me. This was a building of the Communist Party of the Soviet Union (CPSU). He probably had a long laugh about my misadventure. I managed to flag down another taxi and got to the church just on time to be ushered to the platform. Seating had been reserved for "the Canadian delegation," but the bus never came to the hotel. Taking taxis, the others arrived a bit late. Because they had not arrived on time, their reserved seats had been filled. No problem. The usher required the right number of people to leave the service, and our group was seated. That bothered our group but the ushers insisted on doing that.

The Moscow Baptist Church seats about 800 but had a membership of about 5,000. I preached at two of the three Sunday services that Sunday. People stood crowded in the aisle and sat on all the steps. Our fire marshals would have had a fit! During the service, some people standing traded places with some people seated. To see that, was for me, an incredible experience. Preaching in Moscow in the largest Baptist Church during the communist era remains one of the high points of my life. I imagined how my late father would have felt about it.

Before the service began, I was told that as part of the service, there would be a wedding. Separate Christian weddings were not permitted. During one of the sermons, which was of course translated for me, the preacher began talking about Biblical verses dealing with a wedding.

John preaching in the Moscow Baptist Church.

Soon the bride appeared from somewhere. Then the groom appeared from somewhere else. Then a bouquet of flowers was passed forward over the heads of the worshipers. Then the preacher walked down and urged some of us to follow. He kept preaching about the biblical teaching about marriage and then married Petrovich and Tanya Mitzkievitch. I shook hands with the newlyweds. Without missing a beat, the preacher kept on preaching as he walked back to the pulpit and carried on. The preacher had illustrated his sermon. The Soviet spies in the congregation could not really object to that. The bridal couple then disappeared from whence they had come. Doubtless they rendezvoused later for their honeymoon.

During the tour I preached in six churches, and our Peace Choir sang in five. Our guide, Lyuba, was an excellent translator. We had many conversations. Raised an atheist, she became very interested in Christianity. One day she told one of the ladies in our group that one thing about our group greatly impressed her. When asked what it was, she said it was how the husbands treated their wives.

One day I discovered a rather embarrassing problem. Before the trip I had been cautioned by certain experts that I must be sure never to say anything about politics, economics, or East-West problems in my sermons. I therefore decided that for several preaching assignments, I would preach on a Psalm. I selected the 112th. I think it was after my third sermon on that Psalm that I discovered that in the Russian Bible the Psalms are numbered slightly different. Our 112th is the Russian 111th. On three occasions, I preached on a Psalm other than the one being read in Russian by Lyuba. The crowded congregations listened intently. I never did find out what the Russian-speaking congregations thought of that. All I could tell myself is that there is some similarity between the two Psalms. Hopefully, those dear folk were blessed despite my mistake.

The 1986 Trip to the Soviet Union

In early 1986 I was contacted about being part of a small group being organized by the Mennonite World Conference and the All-Union Council of Evangelical Christians-Baptists to go to the Soviet Union to try to gain greater freedom for evangelical Christians. I was humbled and delighted to accept and began diligent preparation. Keston College in England, then as now probably the top centre for the study of religion in communist countries, provided excellent material. The four of us - two Canadians, one American, and one German - left Frankfurt, Germany, on September 30.

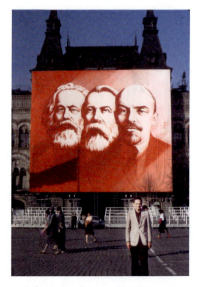

John in Red Square in Moscow.

Soviet heroes.

The 12-day trip, September 30 to October 10, was filled with amazing and exciting experiences of which I shall briefly describe five.

The delegation of four Western church leaders.
L to R: Paul Kraybill, Abram Enns, Jake Peters, John H. Redekop.

On the evening of October 6, we attended a service in a large Baptist/Mennonite church in Donskoye, near Orenburg, pastored by Rev. Daniel Janzen. The low-ceiling and rather unimpressive church was packed with perhaps 500 people. We arrived just as the Thanksgiving Service was about to begin. Pastor Daniel, who spoke German, then told us that we were scheduled to sing at least one quartet song. I was stunned. I said that we had no book and had not practiced and had no pianist. He handed me a book with German words which at least one member of our group could not read and said that there would be a pianist. We had no time to rehearse. We found a familiar tune and hummed a little as rehearsal,- two basses and two baritones, none with a good voice. When we were called up we took the book and, as I recall, sang in German, *O Mein Jesu Du Bists Wert* (O My Jesus Thou Art Worthy). The musical quality was pure mediocrity but we sang very loudly, and when we could we smiled a lot. The congregation graciously smiled broadly. Perhaps they understood our challenging situation.

The second experience involved a visit to the city of Orenburg on October 8. We were not told why. We had learned not to ask too many questions. A convoy of about six cars, mostly rather road-beaten Ladas, escorted us.

In the city we made our way to a large building. I knew enough Russian letters and the symbol of the Communist Party of the Soviet Union (CPSU) to realize that this was a party building. Nothing was said. The Mennonite pastor of the Baptist Church led the way.

One large door after another was opened for us. Eventually we entered a large office about 20 feet by 25 feet. At one end was a large desk with a gentleman sitting behind it. A woman adjutant was, as I recall, standing next to him. I was encouraged to take the lead and go to meet this gentleman. Imagine my surprise when he greeted me in perfect Low German; *"Eck sie Heinrich Abramavich Unger"* (I am Henry Abraham Unger), and he shook hands with me. It seemed to me that this Communist Party official must have known that one of the four church leaders was also a political scholar. Given that my conversational Low German is passable, we had a very interesting conversation.

Later I discovered that this ethnic Mennonite was indeed a high-ranking CPSU regional official who had played a role in major persecution and banishment of Christians. Now, however, with Glasnost and Perestroika underway and a bit more religious freedom granted, the situation had improved. Amazingly, these deeply pious Baptist/Mennonite folk had decided that they would show Christian forgiveness and love towards their former persecutor and still foe. That they did. The pastor told me that Comrade Unger's mother attended his church and that she had recently died. The church people were surprised when Comrade Unger came to his mother's funeral in the church. I think the pastor said he had slipped in and sat at the back.

Some years later this Pastor Daniel Janzen and his wife visited us in Waterloo, Ontario. I inquired what had happened to Comrade Unger. The pastor told me that after the collapse of communism, Comrade Unger had suddenly again become a member of the German-speaking Mennonites. He had identified with the *Aussiedler* (emigrants) who left Russia and were accepted by the

Comrade Heinrich Abramovich Unger and John.

German government as returnees. As I recall, the pastor told us that Unger was living in Germany, profoundly tormented by his guilt but somehow not able to accept Christian forgiveness.

The Western delegation, Comrade Unger and associates.

The third experience also happened in that region. It is actually a very interesting area because there was no wartime destruction in that part of central Russia. On October 8, we attended an evening service in the large Susanova Church. As I recall, all four of us had to preach briefly. Typically, all preachers present are asked to preach, even if only briefly. In the front row sat four people, I think all men, in white coats. I inquired about them and was told that they were KGB "observers" who, if my memory is correct, regularly attended services when foreigners were present. Interestingly, the church provided translators for them. Since I was seated on the platform right in front of them, I managed to photograph these unusual church attendees.

The four were actually very attentive and even participated. When the speaker asked the congregation to stand for prayer, they heard the translation a few seconds after the others and then also stood to their feet. There they stood, four avowed and dogmatic atheists identifying at least outwardly with the Christians whom they were harassing. Never before or since have I preached with my message being translated for "Secret Police." For the first time in my life, I had the privilege of expressing Christian greetings to communists. I could convey the message of Good News directly to four avowed communists sitting perhaps 20 feet in front of me. They paid close attention to what I said, to what all of us said. I think both my father and grandfather would have found my reporting of that reality hard to believe. For me, this was also an almost unbelievable opportunity and experience.

After the service ended, about 10:30, the four of us were invited to Pastor Daniel Janzen's home for what is called "the second supper." I was surprised to see one of the four KGB agents also coming to the pastor's house. He had simply invited himself. In the Soviet Union one does not uninvite a Soviet official who decides to drop in! We sat at the table until after midnight. For more than an hour we had an animated, but guarded, conversation about Canada, religion, world affairs, freedom and much else. Eventually, the KGB "guest" left.

In an instant the intellectual and conversational climate was transformed. Pastor Janzen joyfully announced that now we could talk freely. We did. He bombarded us with questions - theological, political, and ethical. I remember him saying that his theological library consisted of three books. He wanted us to help him as much as possible. I was slated to spend the night at his home. As I recall, we talked until very late, probably 2:00 AM or later.

On another occasion, the fourth of these memorable experiences, we were again having a late second supper, this time in the basement after another exciting and very long church service. We were treated royally and given amazing gifts. I wanted to thank the lady in charge, probably 40 years of age, who spoke German. I politely asked her, *"Wie heisen Sie?"* (What is your name?) She answered, *"Mein Mann ist noch nicht hier."* (My husband has not yet arrived.) I discovered later that he had to work late but would come when he could. He arrived some time after my questioning. Then he brought his wife to me and gave me her name. Clearly, at that time and in that place, the Women's Liberation Movement still had a considerable distance to go.

The fifth experience I shall recount involves the event which was the main purpose for the trip we, four church and conference leaders, were making. On the appointed day we were brought to Red Square in Moscow, and after security checks, this four-man delegation of Christian leaders from the West was taken behind the high wall into the heart of the Kremlin. That was an awesome and almost unbelievable reality. Here I was, seated in a conference room in the Kremlin, the heart of communist rule. We had, of course, brought our own translator. It is customary, especially in such high-level, sensitive and consequential negotiations, not to rely on only one translator. Most of the time, only one translator is speaking while the other listens closely and, of course, checks for correctness. Occasionally they will help one another with a word or phrase.

After a short wait, the Commissar for Religious Affairs entered the room. I think he had one or two officials with him. We were introduced as church leaders. I was then Moderator of the Canadian Conference of Mennonite Brethren Churches and Vice-President of the Evangelical Fellowship of Canada. The other three were similarly introduced. The Commissar seemed to know what our religious designations meant. He was probably briefed on who we were. What the Commissar probably did not know was that I was also a political scientist who had studied communism and the Soviet Union.

After some pleasantries and our expression of gratitude for being given this audience with the Commissar, he asked us what we wanted. By prior arrangement, one of the other members in our group stated that while we were grateful for significant improvement in recent years, we had come to ask for greater freedom for religious groups in the USSR. While we represented the Christian faith, our concern extended to people of all faiths. The Commissar was fully knowledgeable about the religious situation in the USSR and for some time described how some faith groups were functioning as registered groups and as registered congregations. We acknowledged this reality but reminded the Commissar that there were still large numbers of religious believers who were not allowed to operate even with only adults attending. The Commissar did not dispute that reality.

Soon, as had been arranged by us, it was my turn to speak. I should say here that Keston College had provided me with some highly relevant documents. I had the key one with me. I slowly and deliberately then stated that I had with me a document issued by the leaders of the USSR which said that if the Soviet Union was to reach the goals of its current Five-Year Plan, it should appoint more Christians to various positions and to the workforce generally because these people are honest, work hard, and don't come to work drunk. I vividly remember leaning forward to be about four feet from the Commissar, I believe his name was Konstantin Kharchev, but I am not sure of that. Speaking rather deliberately, I made my case.

Our translator, Tatyana Orlov, also spoke deliberately and also forcefully. I cannot provide a verbatim script, but the following statement is very close to verbatim. Looking the Commissar straight in the eye, I said,

> "Commissar, why do you harass evangelical Christians? According to your Government's own statement, they are good people. They are not enemies of the state. Your own economic planners have said that if you want to reach the goals of your Five-Year Plan, you need to appoint more such people to economic positions because they are honest, they work hard, and they don't come to work drunk. It is in your own interest to treat these people better, to give them religious freedom and to let them live freely. Why don't you let them have religious freedom?"

I think it is not an exaggeration to say that I caught the Commissar off-guard. After a short silence the Commissar said, "What do you want?" or words to that effect. We had discussed this matter with Rev. Alexie Bichkov in the Moscow office of the All-Union Council of Evangelical Christians-Baptists (AUCECB) and were ready to relay his requests. I do not recall which one of us spoke, but this is almost verbatim what we said. "The AUCECB, representing the large number of evangelical Christians in the USSR, has four requests." At this point the Commissar was listening very closely. Again, I do not have the verbatim statement, but I have a record of the content. Our response was very close to the following:

"Commissar, we thank you for your response. We have discussed this matter with the All-Union Council of Evangelical Christians-Baptists headquarters staff here in Moscow. This group has four main requests. They want freedom to have more religious services. They want the right to bring children to religious services. They want permission to print Christian literature, and they want permission to practise Christian charity."

There was silence. After a little while, the Commissar said that he had heard what we had said. My notes of that meeting record that the Commissar said he "could not guarantee" that our requests would be granted but his tone seemed to be positive. I got the distinct impression that he had been favourably impressed by us and appreciated the fact that we came prepared. He thanked us for coming to this session which had lasted about 30 minutes. We sincerely thanked the Commissar for receiving and hearing us.

We then had a press conference. Interestingly, the Commissar stayed for that session. Given that in the Soviet Union there were only a few news agencies, actually only two major ones, we had only two "journalists" present. That was the preferred term in the Soviet Union. The press conference lasted more than an hour and a half. The Commissar and we were asked many questions. It turned out that the Commissar was not only quite knowledgeable about religious affairs, he even had some knowledge about the Mennonites in the USSR. Amazingly, as the Commissar left the press conference, he sent greetings to "the brothers and sisters." We were not exactly sure what he meant by that but his good wishes were much appreciated.

Never before or since have I been part of a press conference with a leading communist official. This experience was certainly unique. It was a highlight of my life.

Our group then got up and left the hall. As we were ushered out of the Kremlin compound. I remember having a sense of unreality about what had just happened. Had I actually been in the heart of the Kremlin negotiating with the Commissar for Religious Affairs? Had a top communist official listened to me? My emotions were welling up within me. Such a Christian ministry had never crossed my mind until I received the invitation. Now, this amazing experience was part of my life's work. It was now history.

A press conference following Kremlin negotiations.

For the four of us this was an historic session. We had spent time in the seat of Soviet power. We then had a debriefing. We believed that our session had gone well. We, of course, had no way of knowing whether we had changed any opinions, let alone Soviet government policies.

In retrospect we can say the following. Within not many months after our Kremlin session with the Commissar, all four of the requests we relayed were granted. We realized then, as now, that at the time Glasnost and Perestroika as initiated by Soviet leader Mikhail Gorbachev, were gradually loosening governmental controls, easing Soviet oppression of evangelical Christians. Perhaps the granting of significantly more religious freedom in the USSR would have happened without our formal petition. We will never know. Be that as it may, maybe God did use us, four ordinary churchmen from the West, as agents to help in a small way to bring about much greater freedom of religion in the USSR. I wish that I could have reported this to my dad. I think it would have made him feel good about me.

The 1987 Trip to the Soviet Union

In 1987 it was again my privilege to lead a group of 20 people, from April 17 to May 4, on a tour of the Soviet Union. My associate was Menno Martens, an eminent retired education administrator from Swift Current, Saskatchewan, who also served as our very able choir conductor. Doris again served as our reliable and competent pianist. Again I did the preaching. Also, with this group we had many exciting times. Because of space constraints, I will describe only two events.

We had had services in five churches and were scheduled to have another one in Karaganda. That evening, as we approached the large, white church building, we saw something I had not seen before. A window was open, and bench after bench was being handed out to some men waiting outside to stack them. I inquired of our guide what was going on. She explained that in order to make more standing room for people eager to get in, the benches were being taken out. Sure enough, when we entered the large church, almost all the people were standing, shoulder to shoulder. There was seating only for some older folk and our group.

As I prepared myself mentally to preach that evening to the large assembly of standing believers, I was filled with respect and admiration for these faithful Christians. Many had suffered severely for their faith. I also reflected on the fact that back in Canada virtually all churches have cancelled midweek and Sunday evening services and that at times there are many empty seats on Sunday morning.

The second event also happened in Karaganda. I shall describe it as accurately as I can. One day our group had several hours to spend in the downtown area where there were major stores around a large plaza. After wandering around a while in this fascinating place, Menno, his wife Annabelle, Doris and I were sauntering across the square. I noticed a large crowd standing around a man on what seemed to be a flatbed truck apparently selling what I took to be nylons. This was a colourful scene and I took a picture. We had been assured that taking pictures, other than of military significance or related to security, was permitted. We were even allowed to photograph Soviet soldiers in uniform.

Almost immediately I saw a man in uniform, likely an army officer, walking directly towards me. My camera was loaded with many USSR pictures, which I did not want to lose. We were not far from an entrance to a large department store. I started walking towards it with Doris, not too quickly, trying not to arouse further concerns. The man was walking faster. Wise Menno realized what was happening and managed to slow the officer down with an urgent question. Then the officer also walked to the store.

Once we were in the store we ducked down and hurried through it. There seemed to be various exits. I had noticed that on one side there was a large parking lot with many vehicles. Ducking low, we ran out of that store and far into that lot and hid behind vehicles. As far as I could tell, no one came to that area looking for me or us. I remained very much alert and a little frightened. I had arranged to have the tour members meet the bus at a certain time where it was parked next to the plaza. I then took the film out of my camera and, deeming it safe to do so, had Doris go to the bus with it. I waited in hiding.

At the appointed time I made my way to the plaza. I looked around and could see no danger. Getting close, I made a quick dash to the bus.

When we got to the hotel, the only major hotel catering to Intourist groups, I hurried to our room and changed clothes. Shortly after that we went down to the dining hall for our next meal. I did not wear the maroon-coloured cap I had worn during the day. There, at the door, stood a man who I think was the officer who had been walking towards me rather quickly in the plaza. Mingling with others, I walked by him. He did not recognize me. Thank you, God.

Awards and Affirmation 1981 - 1994

At this point, I should mention an interesting development but first some background information. In the early 1980s the Evangelical Fellowship of Canada had set up a parallel organization to train Christian writers. This committee organized an annual writing school called **God Uses Ink.** One of the key people in this venture was Leslie Tarr, a truly eminent Christian writer. When he retired, I think it was in 1987, the committee established an annual award in his honour: *The Leslie K. Tarr Award in recognition of outstanding contribution to the field of Christian writing.* In 1989 I again attended the **God Uses Ink** conference where I had for several years given writing workshops or a plenary address. Each year the three-day event ended with an elegant banquet. This year Doris said she wanted to attend the banquet with me. I don't think she had ever before indicated she wanted to attend but since the event was held at a nearby Conference Centre near Guelph, that would work out well. I was pleased to see her interest.

At the banquet, the time came to announce the winner of the Leslie Tarr Award. Imagine my total amazement when my name was called. I looked at Doris. She smiled. She had known. To this day as I think of the tremendous influence Les Tarr had, despite his severe physical handicap, I remain deeply humbled to have received this honour. The mounted award certificate on our study wall is treasured.

In May 1990 the *Canadian Church Press* organization totally surprised me by awarding me the top award in the general category of columnist. This award was not given for any one column but for all my columns over time.

The award read:

Canadian Church Press Award of Excellence
Best Column, All Divisions
Mennonite Brethren Herald
"Personal Opinion" **by John Redekop**

I had not been aware that my long-running column was being evaluated and was really thrilled to have it ranked first among the many columnists writing for the large number of Christian publications in Canada.

One result of my increased political but non-partisan activity was that in 1992 I was awarded a *Commemorative Medal for the 125th Anniversary of the Confederation of Canada.*

The citation read:

"In recognition of significant contribution to compatriots, community and to Canada."

I was doubly honoured when two local Members of Parliament, John Reimer and Walter MacLean, arranged for the ceremony and made the presentation.

The Canada Award. L to R: John Reimer MP, RCMP officer, John, Walter Maclean MP.

During my last few years of full-time university work I received several awards. At its Spring Convocation in 1992, Wilfrid Laurier University awarded me **The WLU Outstanding Teacher Award.** I was, of course, delighted but also humbled by this action by my university colleagues and the WLU Board of Governors.

In 1993 the Ontario Confederation of University Faculty Associations (OCUFA) gave me its **OCUFA Teaching Award** for "Outstanding Contribution to University Teaching." Again I was very grateful but also humbled by this designation. Here are excerpts of the recommendation by the WLU Department of Political Science, of which of course I knew nothing at the time, to the Selection Committee deciding who would be Ontario's distinguished professor or professors for 1993.

> *"His teaching evaluations show, in terms simply of numerically-compiled data, the excelent quality of Dr. Redekop's record as a teacher, for time and again he receives the top ratings possible in categories such as "overall effectiveness as a teacher." Dr. Toivo Miljan notes that Laurier has perhaps the finest system of teaching introductory students in Canada, not just because of Dr. Redekop's approach to first-year students but also because of his willingness to provide exceptional direction in teaching the tutors as well as the students. Department Chair Dr. Barry Kay writes that Dr. Redekop's overall evaluations of "excellent" year-by-year from close to 90% of the students are regularly the best in our department."*

Words failed me then and still fail me in expressing my sincere thanks not only to my Political Science colleagues but to the many other professors and students who, I was informed, had written letters of support.

When I became a university professor, I made a firm commitment to do my very best in my chosen profession. I prayed that God would help me to do that. I am deeply grateful to God that he enabled me to do whatever I have managed to do.

In early 1994 I received a big surprise when I was informed by Trinity Western University that if I was in agreement, I would be receiving an honorary doctorate, a Doctor of Humanities (*honoris causa*) at TWU's Spring Convocation on May 1. What a surprise that was! It did not take me long to be "in agreement." Fortunately, all of our children and spouses and all of my siblings could attend the ceremony in the large Sevenoaks Alliance Church in Abbotsford. That May Day is one I shall never forget. I was sorry only for the fact that my parents were no longer with us to be present.

I owe very much to them. The advance press release read as follows:

"Trinity Western University is pleased to announce that at its forthcoming graduation exercises on May 1, 1994, it will award Professor John Redekop of Wilfrid Laurier University, a Doctor of Humanities honoris causa degree. Professor Redekop is being given this honour in recognition of his contribution to higher education and society through his excellence in teaching, his widely recognized scholarship, his outstanding service to the faith communities of Canada and beyond, and his leadership in presenting a Christian worldview on issues facing contemporary Canadian society."
[The full citation which was read at the event is given in Appendix 4.]

Naturally, this event ranks as one of the highlights of my life. I make no claim to have deserved such recognition. I only did my best and, if with God's enablement, that effort was successful, I give glory and thanks to God.

In early 1994 I announced to the Political Science Department and to the WLU officials that I would be taking early retirement at the end of May of that year. Shortly after my announcement, the president of WLU, Dr. Lorna Marsden, wrote a letter to the Department of Political Science and to me. I was simultaneously very thankful and also deeply humbled by several of her statements in that letter.

"Dr. Redekop is probably the single individual who is associated with Laurier in the minds of the world. In meeting alumni – which I do all the time – Dr. Redekop is the person who they believe influenced their careers. For example, Susan Brown started off in quite a different program when Dr. Redekop convinced her to take Political Science.
She is now an officer with CIDA working all over the world. Marian Shull is working with me on the National Task Force on Social Security Reform. She too recalls Dr. Redekop changing her life....Dr. Redekop has also added to the University. He has incorporated the depth and riches of Waterloo County, the Mennonite and Lutheran base of our community, with the insights of Political Science. He has brought the world to Laurier and Laurier to the world..."

I thank my departed parents, my teachers who encouraged me to write correctly and how to speak in public and how to organize my thoughts logically, my professors who corrected my mistakes and sometimes my ideas, my many university colleagues who aided me and encouraged me, my thousands of students who helped me do my best, but most of all my God who has given me some ability to instruct and influence others, hopefully always for the good of others and ultimately for his glory.

The six of us at my Honorary Doctorate ceremony.
L to Right: Paul, Sophie, Frieda, John, Clara, Ernest.

Relevant Political and Public Affairs 1981 - 1994

In 1982 Canada finally adopted its own official constitution. In this connection we should note that for the first time Canada had a constitutional Charter of Rights and Freedoms. Whether this move actually strengthened Canada's strong tradition of upholding human rights is still being disputed. One thing is certain, this step has unleashed a torrent of judicial decisions reducing the place and influence of Christianity.

Gradually the courts have redefined rights and freedoms to legitimize recreational drug consumption, to legitimize euthanasia, to legitimize same-sex marriage, and to challenge other Christian norms.

For example, in 1988, Canada's Supreme Court ruled that Canada's abortion law, as written, was unconstitutional. The Court's recommendation was that Parliament should legislate a new one. Unfortunately, there has been only bickering in Parliament about that issue. The result is that Canada is the only democracy in the world that has no abortion law, no regulation of what is legal or illegal.

The Quebec provincial government organized a second separation referendum for October 12, 1995. The proposal to separate Quebec from the rest of Canada came extremely close to being approved: 50.67% rejected it, but 49.33% approved it. Nobody knows what might have happened if the referendum had passed. One fact is certain; all faith groups would have faced a crisis.

For the US this era is noted for the explosion of the Challenger spacecraft (1986) and the development of a new and generally popular conservative ideology spelled out by President Ronald Reagan.

In the United States and elsewhere, this was also the era that saw the emergence of a new disease, AIDS, and of the computer as an instrument for public use. The eventual impact of computers on all of us, and certainly on church life and the Great Commission itself has become immeasurably great.

My Spiritual Pilgrimage 1981 - 1994

During these years of extensive involvement in various arenas, including religious offices, I had to remind myself frequently that for a Christian, the most important reality is not what one does, nor what one knows, but who one is. It is not the spectrum of what we do but our personal relationship with God that will determine our eternal destiny. For an active Type A person such as I am, I need this constant reminder.

One hesitates to describe personal challenges in detail but let me say the following. Perhaps the area of Christian commitment in which I have had the most significant mental challenges, if I am not spiritually careful, is the matter of assurance. Maybe it's because of persistent inadequacies in my Christian life, or maybe that is an area in which I am being tempted, but whatever the reason, I find it necessary to remind myself with Scripture that God's promise of forgiveness and eternal life applies to all who believe the Gospel and personally to me. Another challenge I encounter frequently is to make sure that prayer, especially unspoken prayer, does not transition into mere thinking. Thinking about God and thinking about issues is not the same as praying to God.

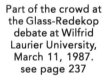

Part of the crowd at the Glass-Redekop debate at Wilfrid Laurier University, March 11, 1987. see page 237

CHAPTER 15

LIVING IN ABBOTSFORD 1994 - 2010

Returning to a burgeoning city

When our family first arrived in Abbotsford in 1944, the combined population of Sumas, Matsqui and the Village of Abbotsford was about 17,000. In 1972 the Village of Abbotsford amalgamated with the District of Sumas to form the new city of Abbotsford. On January 1, 1995, Abbotsford amalgamated with Matsqui to form the new City of Abbotsford. At that time, the population of the new city was about 118,000. Now, in 2021, it has reached 162,000.

As at all other times, we again greatly enjoyed our car trip across Canada. What a bounteous and fascinating land we are privileged to inhabit. We arrived in Abbotsford, June 1, 1994. We rented an apartment while our Mountain Drive house was being completed. We moved in on September 7, 1994. Our new home had lots of space, excellent accommodation for guests, an indoor hot tub, and an incredible view of Sumas Prairie, the nearby mountains, and Mt. Baker. We never tired of the view. On the six terraces behind the house we grew lots of flowers as well as vegetables, strawberries, raspberries, and several varieties of grapes.

The view from our Mountain Drive home.

I greatly enjoy gardening. That's when a human being works in partnership with God to produce amazing results, both delicious and beautiful.

On February 17, 1994, we were delighted to welcome our third grandchild, Michelle Renee, daughter of Gary and Lee Ann. Every grandchild brings us special joy.

Granddaughter Michelle Redekop

As planned, I regularly lectured at Trinity Western, mostly one course a term, from January 1995 until 2011. Some months into either my first or second term I was asked why I was not attending faculty meetings. I said that I was not aware of any meetings and had no record of being invited to attend. My answer baffled my colleagues. Eventually I figured out what had happened. Since I was volunteering my services and thus was not on the university payroll, the computer did not have me listed as a professor. With the mystery resolved, I began receiving notices and attended faculty meetings. Also, after the first year, I was paid a modest stipend.

For the first two years at TWU I was the Scholar in Residence. After that I served as adjunct professor on a part-time basis. Later, when a professor was on sabbatical leave in the fall of 2016, I again taught the American Government course. That term we had a vigorous and publicized student debate about candidate Donald Trump with an American student staunchly defending the unorthodox candidate. On December 16, 2016, I administered my final university exam. At that time it had been 61 years since I began teaching in Narcosli School. Although I obviously did not teach all of those years and in the last years only part-time, I estimate that if calculated as full-time teaching, including when I was a teaching assistant, that I taught the equivalent of about 44 years.

I should perhaps insert here that I was invited to teach two courses at Columbia Bible College. In the Fall Term of 1996, I taught "Christians in the Political System," and in the Winter Term of 1997, I taught "Issues in Mennonite Theology and Practice."

Although we greatly enjoyed hosting guests, children and grandchildren in our large Mountain Drive home, by 2004, it became evident that the time had come to move into a smaller residence. Real estate values had hardly changed over the past decade, and we sold our lovely home with its incredible view in late 2003 for about $411,000, less than $10,000 more than we had invested in it more than nine years earlier.

We were pleased to buy a townhouse, and on January 21, 2004, we moved into a townhouse by a lake, #31 - 31450 Spur Avenue. Again our prayers were answered. We acquired a very fine and suitable home.

In late 2002 I accepted appointment to the Abbotsford Symphony Orchestra (ASO) board of directors. For the year 2004-2005, I served as co-president with Joanne Field. It was rewarding to see between 450 and 700 people attend the very fine concerts in Central Heights Church with much larger crowds at Christmas. A highlight for several years was the formal **A Night of Splendour** celebration in the Ramada Plaza Ballroom. We featured amazing local talent, including the very popular Bowker brothers, Mel and Holden. I clearly recall how the large audience gasped in amazement when these two skilled performers and comedians, each turned from his own piano, reached across and played the other brother's instrument. That has to be seen to be believed. I completed my ASO service in 2006.

On October 6, 2003, I had an unusual experience. We had driven to Portland, Oregon, to attend the funeral of Don Anderson, the second husband of my sister Clara. (Clara's first husband, Wesley Hoff, had passed away some years earlier.) For some reason, prior to the service in Hinson Memorial Baptist Church, we had carpooled to go to the cemetery where the burial took place. Some of us relatives were then assigned to ride with others to the church. Doris and I were directed to a certain car. As we traveled, I discovered that our driver was the church pastor, Rev. Wayne Frank. I introduced myself as Clara's brother. He then casually commented that he had heard of me and that I would be speaking at the church. As Clara later, in embarrassment, admitted, she had forgotten to ask or tell me. The drive to the church took about 20 minutes; we had about 15 minutes left.

Fortunately, Doris had her New Testament and Palms with her. I had one small piece of paper. I have it in front of me now – about 4 inches by 6 inches and a pen. I quickly focussed on II Corinthians 5: 1-9, where St. Paul speaks of us living in a tent, that will be destroyed. Don had been an outdoors person who died in the woods. I jotted down a few ideas. We had arrived at the church. There was no time for further preparation. I was soon called on to speak. I had prayed that God would help me do reasonably well. I drew on whatever ability I had for the impromptu speech. My UBC training again stood me in good stead. Although every speaker has a sense of how well he or she has communicated, one cannot be sure. Believe me, I was greatly relieved when at the reception, one lady inquired whether I was a pastor.

What could I have done if we had traveled to the church in a different car? I credit divine providence.

During these years, my flexible teaching assignment allowed us to do considerable travelling. We greatly enjoyed an Alaska Cruise, several trips to Hawaii, two short vacations in Arizona, and several holidays in Mexico.

One of our other trips warrants description. We had invited our dear Waterloo friends, Dr. Helmut and Nell Mathies, to join us for a car trip down the US West Coast to take in many fine sights. In preparation I had our 98 Oldsmobile serviced, including a lube job, and checked over. All was good. The Mathies arrived and on April 19, 2000 we set out. We had a fine time until we got into Oregon. The car balked in a manner unknown to me. We limped along to a garage. It took the mechanic about 1 minute to discover that the oil plug had not been tightened and that almost all of the motor oil had leaked out. The motor was wrecked. We rented a car and continued on our trip. The giant redwoods, the Easter Pageant at the Crystal Cathedral, Salt Lake City, and the breathtaking Bryce Canyon were major highlights. As it turned out, our car was hauled back to Abbotsford on a truck. We received funds for a replacement.

From June 4 until June 19, 2000, I had the privilege of leading another tour group to Europe. This was an excellent group of enthusiastic and congenial people from various parts of Canada who thoroughly enjoyed many of the great sights and sites of Germany and Switzerland. The highlight was spending one day, June 8, taking in the truly amazing and altogether inspiring Oberammergau Passion Play.

On August 19, 2006, Doris and I had the great privilege of celebrating our 50th wedding anniversary. We had selected Stillwood as the venue and had invited about 140 relatives and friends. We had a fabulous time remembering what had happened since August 21, 1956, and all the blessings that had come to us.

We also had a second celebration. On October 12, 2006, Doris and I undertook *The Grouse Grind*. It took us considerably longer than the average of 1.5 to 2.25 hours to hike up the south slope of Grouse Mountain in North Vancouver. The trail consists of some steps but mostly a steep, cleared, zig-zag lane in the woods. It feels like constantly climbing stairs, although mostly there are no man-made steps. The 2.9-kilometre Grind has "an average Grade of about 30 degrees." The climb begins at 300 metres above sea level and takes climbers to 1,100 metres above sea level. As stated in other terms, the climb involves ascending a little more than 2,800 feet. At the top we enjoyed a delicious lunch at the summit restaurant and then took the Grouse Gondola down. Trekking down the Grouse Grind is not permitted.

In 2007, from November 2 to 16, Doris and I were on a trip to mainland China. Various friends, including Harry and Gail Edwards, Al and Sue Enns, and John and Viola Eckert, were also in our group. There is much one can say about even such a short trip but I shall limit myself to four observations or experiences.

First, the significance of this vast country comes into focus when one is told that in China, more than 300 cities have a population exceeding 1 million.

Second, the extent of the smog in every city was startling. No wonder that masses of people often wear a mask.

Third, the contrast between the big cities and the rural population is striking. In their appearance and operation, large cities such as Beijing, Shanghai, and Hangchou differ only marginally from large Western cities but when one drives through the countryside, one sees large numbers of people working in the fields using very traditional, if not inefficient and primitive, methods. Doubtless, in some regions agricultural pursuits are more modern.

The fourth item requires some context. Before we left Canada, I had managed to get addresses of registered churches in some cities we were scheduled to see. On Saturday, November 10, in Hangchou, I asked our guide, Peter Lee, if it would be possible to attend a church service on Sunday forenoon. I had an address for a church in Hangchou. Peter said that there was not much to that church and it would not be worth going there. He was very dismissive. It was clear that he would not be of any help. When we returned to our hotel I showed the desk clerk the church address. She replied that the church was located in that same part of the city. My booklet showed that the service began at 8:30. I asked her to get us a taxi for a little before 8, as I recall.

Ron and Josie Martens, from Ontario, joined us on the taxi ride. We soon came to the officially registered Si Cheng Protestant Church. The building was impressive. We were given front-row seats and an interpreter. The place was crowded. I estimate the attendance was between 300 and 350, maybe much more given that the service was apparently shown on screens in adjacent rooms. We were also told that there had been an earlier service at 6:30 AM. I saw no other foreigners in the service. After the service we met some of the leaders. When I mentioned that I had been president of the Evangelical Fellowship of Canada, I was invited to speak briefly in the evening service.

The evening service was again crowded. As part of my presentation I was expected to introduce myself. That is what I did, very carefully. Suddenly, for no reason that I could understand, the huge audience burst into loud applause. I wondered if I had broken some local or communist government protocol.

John speaking in SiCheng Church, Hangchou, China.

After the service I asked Lilly, our translator, why the people had suddenly burst into very loud applause. Here is her response. For generations the people in Red China have been told that Christianity is only something for old people and people of weak minds. No intelligent people and certainly no university professor still believes in those religious tales.

Doris and John in Tiananmen Square, Beijing, China.

Doris and John on the Great Wall, China.

When I said that I was a university professor they finally saw someone who contradicted what the communist leaders had proclaimed. I was the first Christian professor they had heard of, let alone seen. The communist authorities had been proven wrong. These Christians had been vindicated. I was humbled to think that my fairly brief testimony and other comments in that evening service in Hangchou, China, could have such a positive impact.

On March 13, 2008, while having some tests done in a lab, Doris was told that given her heart condition she must go to the hospital immediately. She was not allowed to drive herself there. An ambulance was called. I was shocked when I got the phone call. On March 17, 2008, Doris received her first pacemaker. She now has a second one. They have served her very well.

Early in 2008, we decided to make a cross-Canada car trip. We left on August 1. The many sights and visits were truly memorable. From the island of Newfoundland, we took the ferry north and drove into Labrador to the end of the pavement. Near that spot we enjoyed a delicious Labrador lunch. On the wall of that restaurant hung a large picture of a huge fish with the caption **In Cod We Trust.** Sadly, because of massive and reckless over-fishing, the cod fishery had fallen on hard times.

We returned on September 3. Such a trip makes one truly grateful for the splendid country in which we live.

In the fall of 2008, perhaps a week after our return home, I had an unusual health challenge. During our trip east, I had helped some friends move to a new home in Waterloo. During that activity a car trunk lid came down hard on my head. I had a bad headache and before long, a half golf-ball-size swelling grew on the side of my head. Soon both disappeared. I thought nothing more of it. A few weeks later, while I was attending committee meetings at a campsite east of Williams Lake, BC, I could not think straight. I wandered around the campgrounds trying to find the building in which we had met the previous evening. I had developed a subdural hematoma. Blood between my skull and brain was pressing in on and draining the brain. On September 20 I was rushed into surgery in Vancouver General Hospital. The fluid was drained. I recovered. After surgery I asked the surgeon how long I would have lived without surgery being done. He said, "A few days." Then he popped back into the doorway and said, "Not that long."

Then, about four weeks later the symptoms reappeared. This time the symptoms were even worse. At times I could not speak. On October 24, I underwent a second brain surgery. I was told that in about 15 percent of the cases, there is a reoccurrence. This time the liquid had congealed, and part of the skull was removed. I now have titanium screws in my head. After ten days in the hospital and some additional weeks of taking it easy, I recovered fully.

A far as I am concerned, God performed a miracle through the skill of my physician. I was also very grateful that after I was admitted to the hospital, Doris drove to Vancouver General Hospital every day to visit me and got me on the last day.

During blood work relating to my surgery it was discovered, on September 29, that I had Type 2 Diabetes. Fortunately, it was detected before I had any symptoms, before the disease could cause damage. With watching my diet and minor medications, this disease has been manageable thus far.

We both thank God for the measure of health and strength he has given us even in these later years. I am increasingly reminded of these blessings now that the obituary section is often the first one I check in the newspapers. I may not always read about someone familiar, but I note that most of the life pilgrimages reported are shorter than mine.

Bakerview Church 1994 - 2010

It was not easy for us to decide which church to join. Central Heights Church had been our home church. Both of our fathers had been pastors there. We were married there and had served in various roles there in the 1950s. After some months we joined the Bakerview Church. It offered excellent traditional music as well as strong preaching by Pastor Harry Heidebrecht and his associates.

It was also a friendly and warm congregation with a vision for its future. Also, we already had quite a few friends in that congregation. Doris soon joined the Chancel Choir and for some years sang in it as well as in the Seniors' Fellowship Choir. Both choirs not only served very effectively in worship services but also on other occasions. The Fellowship Choir toured various areas of the province, putting on fine concerts. Both Doris and I served on various committees. I had the privilege of serving for six years on the Church Council and as church moderator from 1996 until 1999.

One day it occurred to me that with its array of musical talent, Bakerview should produce a cassette and CD which would include various groups. I then put myself to work to make this happen. Fortunately, the various musical groups were very cooperative. I also found church members willing to advance the needed funds. There was much to be done concerning copyrights, finding a sound engineer, finding a recording venue, getting the jackets and labels designed and printed, getting the cassettes and CDs mass-produced, planning the release event and organizing the marketing. The result was the 1998 production of ***Bakerview Sings!*** in both cassette and CD versions.

This production features the Vespers Ensemble, the Chancel Choir directed by Rudy Baerg, the Three Tenors (Wilmer Neufeld, John Thiessen, Ray Harris, pianist Helen Nickel), the Male Quartet (Ray Harris, John Thiessen, Paul Heidebrecht, Dave Spenst, pianist Heather Shantz) and violinist Calvin Dyck with pianist Heather Dyck. As executive producer, it gave me much delight to see the very positive reception this production received. Even today, in 2021, it is still played on several radio stations and on at least one religious television channel.

Bakerview Sings!

One area of involvement at Bakerview consisted of doing presentations in the large adult class called **Current Issues.** Between my first presentation on Sunday, August 14, 1994, and the last pre-pandemic one on Sunday, September 29, 2019, I was privileged to deliver 89 presentations in the **Current Issues** class in the Bakerview MB Church. For about 70 of those instances I prepared a 4 to 6-page handout for the class numbering anywhere between 110 and 180, somewhat fewer in later years. As also for others who taught in this class, each lesson required considerable research and preparation and often included overheads and, in later years, PowerPoint enrichment. I happily thank my always helpful friend, David Giesbrecht, for the many PowerPoint enhancements he created for me.

I should mention that around the turn of the century, Bakerview Church while retaining the original Traditional Service, established first a distinctly Contemporary Worship Service and then a distinctly Liturgical Worship Service. They were all well organized, and soon each developed its own congregation.

I was moderator when the Contemporary Service was established. For various reasons I did not support such sharp diversification but a majority voted for it. I believed that over time such sharp diversification would create disunity. What this unique arrangement may mean for the future unity of Bakerview, after Covid-19, remains to be seen. Will it be seen as an experiment that was successful or will it be seen as an experiment that failed?

Scholarly Research and Writing; Books 1994 - 2010

When I retired from full-time teaching at Wilfrid Laurier University, I planned to do considerable writing, both articles and one or more books. The result became something more than I anticipated. I became involved in several writing projects.

In its 1994 Fall issue, the quarterly *Direction* carried my article, "The Politics of the Mennonite Central Committee." My critical evaluation of a BC government policy was published as "An Assessment of the Citizens Assembly on Electoral Reform," in the Autumn 2005 issue of *BC Studies, The British Columbia Quarterly.*

In 1996 the *Journal of Mennonite Studies* published my article "The Roots of Nazi Support Among Canadian Mennonites, 1930-1939. a Case Study Based on a Major Mennonite Paper." This analysis was based largely on Dr. Frank Epp's unpublished doctoral dissertation.

In 1997 Herb Brandt and I wrote **Finding Fulfillment In Retiring** for the Canadian MB Conference pamphlet series.

In 2004 my chapter entitled, "Urbanization, religious dispersion and secularization: Personal Reflections on Mennonites in the Fraser Valley, 1940s and 1950s," appeared in **First Nations and First Settlers in the Fraser Valley (1890-1960).** In this chapter, I sought to describe what happened to Mennonites in the Fraser Valley in those years. That challenging project required me to do considerable research and much rethinking.

My article, "Group Representation in Parliament Would be Dysfunctional for Canada," was published in the textbook **Contemporary Political Issues** in 2006 and also in a second edition in 2009. That text was edited by Professor Paul Barker and my former teaching colleague at Trinity Western University, Professor Mark Charlton.

My book, **Politics Under God,** was published in 2007. Written especially for pastors, for students in high school and post-secondary schools studying Evangelical Anabaptist beliefs and experiences, but also for all others interested in this topic, this 223-page book describes my basic understanding of church-state and Christian-government relationships. It holds closely to what I consider relevant biblical teaching. Interestingly, the publisher, Herald Press, received the following endorsement from Chuck Colson which appears on the back cover.

> "***Politics Under God*** *is a thoughtful review of the Christian's relationship to government that draws conclusions that will surprise readers who expected an Anabaptist perspective. A good addition to the bookshelves of Christians who wrestle with the ethics of the two kingdoms."*

Also in 2007 this book was translated into French and published by *Editions Mukanda* as **Politique soumise a Dieu** for rather large-scale distribution in French-speaking African countries. In 2010 a Spanish edition, **Poliyica de la mano de Dios,** was published by *Instituto Biblico Asuncion, Universidad Evangelica del Paraguay* for readers in Spanish-speaking lands.

A totally different book was published in 2008. Entitled **Stillwood - The First 50 Years; 1958-2008,** it was published by Stillwood Camp and Conference Centre. As editor, main writer, and main photographer for recent years, and also as layout person, I sought to present the Stillwood story in as interesting, enjoyable, and highly readable form as possible. In this challenging task I was very ably assisted by Associate Editor Peter Enns, a former camp Executive Director, and others listed in the book

Funding was needed for the project, so I raised about $36,000 to cover all costs, which enabled us to sell the book for $10 with all sales income given to Stillwood ministries. This book recounts the amazing vision, work, sacrifice, and. miracles which made Stillwood a reality. It tells how God miraculously guided every board member, individually, to suggest the same spot for

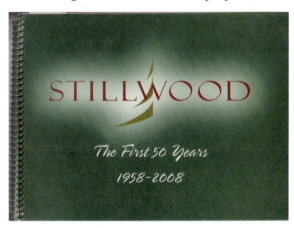

Stillwood - The First 50 Years

water well-drilling, which was successful. It tells how two adjacent hobby farms were bought even though neither was for sale. It tells of a camp and retreat centre where thousands of children, young people, and adults have found a divine purpose for their life. With hundreds of pictures, this book describes a place where many thousands have experienced spiritual purpose, renewal, relaxation, restoration, and revitalization. Stillwood has become many things but perhaps, most importantly, a Christian oasis.

The Stillwood book was welcomed by many. We received numerous statements of thanks. As editor, I received only one complaint. One book buyer wanted his money back because his picture was not in the book.

For me, perhaps the most significant article I wrote during these years was "A Reflection on a Spiritual Pilgrimage, or What UBC did to me and for me," *Direction* (Spring, 2008).

During these years, I had various opportunities to deliver lectures at colleges and universities. Here are some titles. "Continentalism: the Key to Canadian Politics," College of the Cariboo, Kamloops, BC (October 6, 1995); "Mennonite and Community; Origins and Significance," University College of the Fraser Valley (May 23, 1997); "Does God Prescribe Different Ethics for Christians and Politicians?" UBC Graduate Students and Faculty (March 11, 1999); "A Theological/Biblical Rationale for Christian Participation in Politics," ACTS - MB Seminary, Trinity Western University (November 8, 2000); "A Perspective on the Iraq Crisis," MCC Arts and Peace Festival, University of the Fraser Valley (March 7, 2003); "How Should Christians Respond to Growing Political Pressures?" MB Biblical Seminary, Fresno, CA (February 14, 2007); "Political Reality Today: Challenge or Opportunity for the Church?" Fresno Pacific University (February 15, 2007); and "Can Civil Government Function According to Christian Ethics?" Trinity Western University Laurentian Centre, Ottawa (March 3, 2009).

A particularly significant opportunity for me was to deliver an academic lecture to a large audience at the place where I first began full-time university-level teaching. "*Church and State or Christians and Politics, a Revised Anabaptist Perspective,*" Council of Senior Professionals, Fresno, CA (February 13, 2007).

Writing for the Christian Community 1994 - 2010

During these years, I continued writing *Personal Opinion* columns for the *Mennonite Brethren Herald,* although less frequently in the later years because the magazine had become a monthly publication. Some titles for these years included the following. "Why Remain MB?" (July 2, 1995); "The urgent homosexual agenda," (June 14, 1996); "Democracy versus Morality" (March 20, 1998); "Can Christmas be Secularized?" (December 4, 1998); "Does pacifism apply to government?" (May 28, 1999); "Suppression in the name of freedom," (June 9, 2000); "Revisiting the alcohol question," (May 11, 2001); "Perspectives on Islam," (January 11, 2002); and "Dealing with wealth," (July 12, 2002).

My final column appeared on February 28, 2003: "The Iraq War." That column was the last of the 870 Personal Opinion columns that were published in the *Mennonite Brethren Herald*. It might be useful to recall that the first one, printed in the January 3, 1964, Herald was entitled, "On Constructive Criticism." Throughout all those years, I tried to write in line with that guideline.

Why did the column end? At that time, I had become aware that the Canadian MB Conference leadership was re-evaluating all programs and since I was unsure of plans for the *Herald,* I did not submit any column after February, 2003. Since I was then not contacted about continuing to write the column, I took that as a signal that the new Conference leaders wanted it discontinued. I thus concluded almost 39 years of writing *Personal Opinion* columns with one sabbatical interlude.

I greatly enjoyed that long run and while I managed to respond to many, but not all, of the good folk who wrote me, I thank them all, including the many whose letters of agreement or disagreement appeared in the *Herald.*

It is not necessary to analyze the hundreds of letters I received, but one situation will interest readers. In 1985 I began getting strange letters, almost all mailed from either Eugene, Oregon or Salinas, California. All had the same handwriting. Unfortunately, I could not read anything this person wrote. Nor have I been able to identify the language used. Nor have I found anyone else who can read the contents or even identify the language. The letters were written edge to edge in very small handwriting and often also on the backside. They continued coming into 1986. What amazes me is that they reached me, given the written address. I'm sure it was the postal code that got these letters to me. 298 Ferndale Place never looked so strange. I still have 112 of those letters. As I recall, I gave some away as souvenirs.

I reproduce one to show what they were like. Since I could not make any sense of the return address, I could not respond.

In addition to writing columns for the *Mennonite Brethren Herald,* I also wrote some longer articles for it such as "Contemporary challenges in missions," (December 15, 2000) and "After one year, a report card on the Harper Conservatives," (March, 2007).

Submitting columns for *ChristianWeek* was another of my writing pursuits during these years. Typically my column was carried every two or three weeks. Column titles included the following. "Reweaving the social welfare net," (February 28, 1995); "Why capital punishment is not the answer," (October 3, 1995); "Pre-emptive murder not the answer," (February 18, 1997); "Character poverty causes crime," (April 14, 1998); "A more responsible press, please," (May 14, 1998); and " 'Decency deficit' a natural effect," (July 13, 1999).

One of the 112 almost Illegible envelopes.

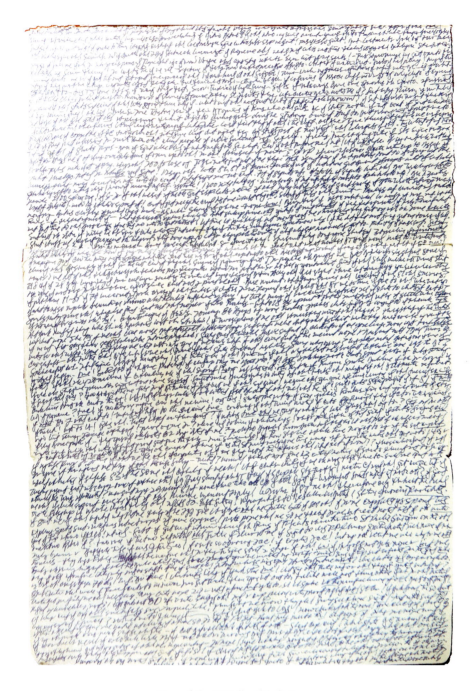

One of the 112 Illegible letters.

During these 16 years, I wrote numerous articles for the regional Christian monthly, *BC Christian News*. I have 17 on file. Here are some titles. "Political, religious conservatism not the same," (February 1996); "Key Christians who shaped Canada," (August 1998); "UN Sanctions are destroying Iraq," (February 2001); "Christians, socialism and the B.C. election," (March 2001); "Advice for a frustrated Christian electorate," (May 2001); "A Christian response to B.C.'s political theatre," (March 2002); "Why are Christians so indifferent to gambling?" (June 2005); "Guidelines for Christian citizenship at election time," (October 2008); and "Moral issues to consider in the voting booth," (May 2009).

Before I move to the next section, I must note a truly unusual happening. In its April 2007 issue, *BC Christian News* carried this headline: "***Two political experts tackle each other's work***." On page 16, Lloyd Mackey reviewed my book, **Politics Under God**, and I reviewed his book, **The Pilgrimage of Stephen Harper.** I am not aware of any other instance in which two authors reviewed each other's books, let alone on the same page in a magazine. Lloyd and I are friends and, for me, it was a delight and privilege to share this page with him.

It was my privilege to have about five to ten articles a year published in other Christian periodicals. Here are some examples. "Responding to Evil-Doers in the Kingdom," *Pentecostal Assemblies, Resource* (November/December 1995); "Consequences of the Quebec Referendum," *Focus on the Family Citizen* (November 25, 1995); "Religious Morality and Public Policy," *Centre Point, Centre for Renewal in Public Policy* (Spring 1996); "Does the Bible offer a verdict?" *The Christian Leader* (January 1998); "Saints in Caesar's Realm," *Faith Today* (March-April, 1999); "Politics & the Christian," *The Christian Leader* (October 1999); "God is not in the camp of any country or government," *Christian Courier* (March 31, 2003); "Christians and Government," *The Christian Leader* (November 2004); "Expectations of a Candidate," *The Messenger* (November 15, 2000); "Reflections on Congolese politics and faith," *The Christian Leader* (November 2004); "The great promise of Christian camping," *Mennonite Brethren Herald* (April 8, 2005); and "Christians and the Ongoing Crisis in the Middle East," *Christian Week* (August 18, 2006).

Sometimes articles were translated into other languages. Here is one in French. "Les grandes questions de la mission d'aujourd'hui," *Le Lien* (December, 2000).

Addressing Christian Audiences 1994 - 2010

As already noted, during these 16 years I delivered presentations to the large Current Issues Class in the Bakerview MB Church in Abbotsford, generally between three and five a year, including the summer months. Titles ranged widely. "The Cross and the Nations at War," (April 16, 1995); "Constructive Social Criticism," (May 31, 1997); "Report on My Trip to Russia, Kazakhstan, Kirghizstan," (October 11, 1997); "Is the Church the Conscience of Society?" (November 2, 1997); "Books that have Changed the World," (May 3, 1998); "Living and Working in a Post-Christian Canada," (July 5, 1998); "Should God be in the Constitution?" (July 18, 1999); "Canada's Changing Religious Profile: Christianity and Pluralism," (January 30, 2000); "Government and the Military; A Peace Church Perspective," (November 26, 2000); "Worsening Global Persecution; The Growing Oppression of Christians," (May 20, 2001); "The Church in Caesar's Realm; An Analysis of Biblical Teaching," (July 6, 2003); "God loves the world even when it persecutes his people," (August 8, 2004); "The Mennonite Brethren as a Believers Church," (August 19, 2007); "Comments on the Koran," (May, 2008); "What's Right and What's Objectionable about John Howard Yoder's Classic Analysis of Church-State Relations?" (July 26, 2009); "Harassment and Oppression of Christians in North America," (August 16, 2009); "Selected Major Political and Economic Developments in 2009 and their Significance for Christians," (January 3, 2010); and "*The Armageddon Factor* and the Canadian Far Right," (October 24, 2010).

Let me mention an unusual experience. For January 20, 2002, a guest speaker was to address the Current Issues class on "A Christian Response to Islam." For some reason, still unknown to me, he did not appear. A large class had assembled. The presiding official did not know what to do. I then offered that I would give a presentation on the same topic.

He happily accepted. I got up and gave about a 40-minute presentation followed by a question period. This was one time I did not need to check my notes – I had none. God gave enablement. The session went well.

During these 16 years I typically addressed other Christian groups about 10 times each year. Some presentations took me far afield, others kept me near home. Here are some representative topics and occasions. "Mennonites and Governments; Some Comments," Health Care/Seniors Care MCC Seminar, Langley, BC (January 14, 1995); "Christ for Today's Businessman," Christian Businessmen's Committee, Trail, BC (March 4, 1995); "The Way of Peace," Kingwood Bible Church, Salem, OR (May 21, 1995); "The Challenge of Growth," Christian Labour Association Convention, Surrey, BC (April 13, 1996).

Additional examples include these. "Can Mennonites be Proud of their Heritage?" Mennonite Historical Society of British Columbia, Abbotsford, BC (October 18, 1997); "Christianity and Pluralism," Theological Graduates Forum, Shamshabad, India (January 8, 1999); "Canada and Quebec; 'Two Jilted Valentines`," Faith Church, Richmond, BC (February 11, 1999); "Some Reflections on Evangelical Anabaptist Christianity," Assembly of MB Leaders, Osaka, Japan (January 19, 1999); "A Historical Perspective of the First Decade; The Central Heights Church in the 1950s," Central Heights Church 50th Anniversary Celebration, Abbotsford, BC (May 21, 2000); "Honoring the Past: Learning from Mennonite Experiences in Health Care," Conference of the Canadian Mennonite Health Assembly," Richmond, BC (October 23, 2000); "The Changing Mennonite Church in Canada," and two other hour-long lectures at the Steinbach Bible College Leadership Conference (March 15-16, 2002); "What Does It Mean to be The People Of God?" Main Centre MB Church Reunion, Main Centre, SK (August 18, 2002); and "The Challenge: Fundraising for Columbia Bible College," Willingdon Church (October 2, 2003).

Additional occasions included the following. "Godly Women; Key Servants in Building God's Kingdom," Batela Mennonite Brethren Church, Kinshasa, Democratic Republic of Congo (June 13, 2004); "Serving God in Politics," Mennonite World Conference, Asuncion, Paraguay (July 17, 2009); "Biblical Standards for Governments," Mennonite World Conference, Asuncion, Paraguay (July 18, 2009); "Realities and Trends in Mennonite Faith and Life in Russia, 1789 - 1914," Kelowna Mennonite Church at Camp Squeah, BC (September 15, 2009); "Realities and Trends in Mennonite Faith and Life in North America in the 20th Century," Kelowna Mennonite Church at Camp Squeah, BC (September 16, 2009).

A particularly interesting and for me stimulating event occurred on March 3, 2009, when I had the privilege of speaking at a Parliamentary MPs Prayer Breakfast in the Parliament Building in Ottawa. My presentation, "Can Civil Governments Function According to Christian Ethics?" was followed by a lively discussion.

During these years I had the opportunity to speak on many special occasions. Perhaps the most significant for me happened when I was invited to give the keynote address at the 100th Anniversary Celebration of my childhood church, the Main Centre, Saskatchewan Mennonite Brethren Church. When this church was founded in 1904 my grandfather, Rev. Johann P. Wiebe, on whose birthday I was born and for whom I was named, had been a founding preacher. Now, 100 years later, I followed him on the same platform. What a great privilege that was for me.

Presentations at post-secondary institutions included the following. "Will we still be a peace church in the next century?" Columbia Bible College (April 13, 1996); "The Modern University and Christian Assumptions," Trinity Western University (October 4, 1996); "What is ethnic? What is Biblical?" Trinity Western University (October 20, 1996); "The Modern University and Christian Assumptions," Graduate and Faculty Christian Forum, University of British Columbia (October 29, 1996); "Convocation Address," Trinity Western University," (September 10, 1997); "Some Reflections on Evangelical Anabaptist Christianity," Seminary students and faculty seminar, Osaka, Japan (January 19, 1999).

Additional campus presentations included the following. "The Christian University in a world of many gods," Patrons Reception, Canadian Mennonite University (April 26, 2003); "Where in a university is God?" Graduation Address, Canadian Mennonite University (April 27, 2003); "Political Reality Today: Challenge or Opportunity for the Church," Fresno Pacific University (February 15, 2007); "What does God Expect of Governments?" TWU Laurentian Leadership Centre, Ottawa (March 4, 2009); and "What does God Expect of Citizens?" TWU Laurentian Leadership Centre (March 5, 2009).

Ministries in Mennonite Brethren Conferences 1994 - 2010

In 1995 I was requested to write a major research paper dealing with the future of the Mennonite Brethren churches in North America. My 22-page report entitled, *"Vision and Revision: Some Preliminary Comments on the Future of the Mennonite Brethren Church,"* was presented to the North American MB Executive Council in March 1995. It was revised slightly in April 1996.

In 2007 I began four years of membership in the BCMB Conference Executive Committee. I found this service both interesting and rewarding. Clearly, there was significant dynamism in many conference churches and their main ministries: Columbia Bible College, church planting, and the five camps and conference centres. I served in this capacity until 2011, the last two years as secretary of the Committee.

An important involvement began in 1994 when I was elected to the North American Mennonite Brethren Historical Commission. This body funds and also undertakes extensive research and publication of articles, shorter items, and books relevant to Mennonite Brethren history and present life. I served on this commission until 2002.

Given that I was deeply concerned about what was happening in the Canadian MB Conference, I wrote several documents about that situation. Several other concerned former and present church and conference leaders critiqued drafts before the articles were posted online. The main statement, "*Conference Restructuring - some Concerns and Suggestions*," was posted October, 22, 2004.

Mennonite Brethren Missions and Services International

From January 1, 1996, until July 1999 I had the privilege of being a member of the board of Mennonite Brethren Missions and Services International (MBMSI). For the last part of the term, I was also the board secretary. During this ministry I undertook two major tours of mission locations.

My first trip, together with Franz Rathmaier, the MBMSI Secretary for Europe and the Former Soviet Union, from September 15 to 29, 1997, took us to Russia, Kazakhstan, and Kyrgyzstan. It is always helpful to see missionaries at work. One gets a whole new understanding of the challenges, the successes and, yes, even the problems when ministries are not developing well. We had crucial sessions evaluating the Moscow Mennonite Centre, the very successful church-planting efforts in the Vologda region some 500 kms, north of Moscow, and the pioneering work in Almati, Kazakhstan.

For me, the highlight was to observe the incredible ministry of Heinrich Voth and his Ray of Hope ministry in Bishkek, Kyrgyzstan. I consider it a great honour to have met and observed this giant saint. Small challenges for me were when all the students and we ate out of the same big porridge bowl, amount to nothing when compared to the fact that brother Voth eschewed migrating to Germany with its freedom and prosperity and chose, instead, together with his equally self-giving and amazing wife, to give himself unreservedly to his pioneering and incredibly successful ministry among the Muslims in Kyrgyzstan.

Before I describe the second trip I should report the following. During this trip we had a Russian driver. To my surprise, I discovered he was a fellow Christian, who was absolutely the worst driver I have ever had. In addition to driving much too fast, he would speed up when, because of oncoming traffic, it seemed there might not be enough time to pass a vehicle. Several times I thought that my life would end then and there in a fiery crash. I asked him to be more cautious but that made only a temporary difference. I asked him what he thought would happen if there was not enough driving space to complete passing another vehicle? He smiled and said that he expected the other driver to slow down and make room for us. I hoped and prayed that drivers of oncoming traffic would not be as nonchalant, to put it diplomatically, as this heavy-footed Slav. I vowed never again to travel with him.

My second trip, December 29, 1998, to January 21, 1999, took me to Indonesia, India, Pakistan, and Japan. Accompanying me were MBMSI senior staff members David Dyck and Russell Schmidt. I shall highlight only a few items from each country visited.

In Indonesia we saw evidence of Muslim attacks on Christian churches. In some regions the persecution had become severe. We heard that in the previous eight months, 68 churches had been partly or totally destroyed - 520 since 1967. Some congregations had begun to meet in a church without walls - outside! Despite the persecution and prosecution, the Muria Synod, with its fundamental Anabaptist teachings, was growing rapidly.

We learned that after September 1, 1999, the Muria Synod would be called the Mennonite Synod. This large group of churches really likes the Evangelical-Anabaptist emphasis on trust in the Bible, believers baptism, a church of believers, mutual aid, discipleship, the peace teaching, and respectful evangelism. As I reflect on those exciting days with strong leaders, inspiring men and women in the churches, and wonderful hosts, I still recall how I resisted at first to be moved from one location to another by a rickshaw pulled by a young man. I would rather have done the pulling or ridden a bus.

India is surely the most diverse country in the world no matter what aspect one considers: economics, religion, culture, languages, politics, and society generally. All of society is, of course. overlaid with the outlawed but still pervasive and debilitating caste system. One finds this evil even in the churches. The reality is so complex that, at times, it becomes blurred. As is widely known, there has for years been a deep controversy between two leadership factions. We tried to address this as best we could.

Here are five memorable experiences and observations concerning India.

First, The Indian Conference of Mennonite Brethren Churches is growing rapidly and already in 1998 was much larger than the combined Canadian and US parent conferences. The Indian Conference is now largely self-sufficient.

Second, while being driven to the Chadcherla MB Medical Centre, the Hindu physician with whom I shared the back seat, told me emphatically that we North American Mennonites must not leave India. In particular, we must not withdraw from medical services. As he put it, before the Christian missionaries came, (Mennonite and others,) the low-caste Dalit people of India were largely ignored concerning medical care. Only the Christians seriously helped these people.

He candidly acknowledged and asserted that the Hindu ethic does not include helping the Dalits and certainly had not provided largely free medical care for them. This Hindu physician pled with me, as MBMSI board member, "Please stay!" Most of the medical work in India is, of course, done by nationals. MBMSI provides some funding and some expertise when needed.

My third major memory is that during one long day, January 7, 1999, we Westerners from MBMSI heard 74 Mennonite Brethren bicycle evangelists report to a large assembly in the Bethany MB Church in Shamshabad, Andhra Pradesh. Each itinerant bicycle evangelist had been given a bicycle, and each received the very modest stipend of about US $50 a month. They each had 5 to 10 minutes to report. Some spoke in English, some reported through a translator. We heard of one bicycle evangelist being beaten twice by Hindu attackers, of assorted harassment and even persecution, but mainly of impressive success and urgent needs.

It was for me heart-rending to hear them plead for funds to buy prescriptions for very ill or dying family members. Some help could be given. I may never forget one bicycle evangelist pleading for a few extra dollars a month so that at least one of his children could go to school. The evangelists' passion was compelling. I was also particularly touched by the report of evangelist Elijah. He was impressive. He was also illiterate but he knew his Bible. In his report he would cite Scripture texts and then a literate associate would read them.

The fourth vivid memory is that because of the generosity of my home church, Bakerview MB in Abbotsford, I had arranged for the delivery of 27 badly needed new bicycles for MB itinerant evangelists whose bicycles were giving out (wearing out). What a great surprise that turned out to be for these dear brothers and what a marvelous celebration we had. All 27 men were profoundly grateful.

My fifth vivid memory was learning how to eat curried chicken with rice by hand - for good reason, always the right hand. I carefully watched the large number of other delegates at a convention do this with great dexterity and soon learned the trick.

One more thing. One Sunday, I was preaching in a fairly small rural MB church with attendees squatting on the dirt floor. Just as I was saying the closing benediction, someone, I think it was the mother, placed a baby in my arms. As I recall, I was to name the child and also pray for its healing or at least well-being. The translation was not always specific. As I recall, I quickly adjusted my thinking and complied with a 10-second naming process.

Spending some days in Pakistan brought a profoundly different set of experiences. The Muslim suppression is severe. I was sternly warned not to use any Christian words or expressions on the streets or I might disappear. A small but effective Christian radio station manages to survive by broadcasting from a hidden and, I understood, frequently changed location. I had to ask myself the following question. "Given that very impressive results are being achieved with MBMSI's limited resources in other lands, how much time, effort, and resources should be expended in this largely closed society?" Much better minds than mine and missiologists with insights and experiences need to answer this question.

What a delight it was to visit Japan for the second time. It quickly becomes evident that the Japanese Mennonite Brethren Conference has excellent leaders, healthy churches, impressive training programs, adequate financial resources, and praise-worthy policies and programs. We have much to learn from Japan. For several reasons, however, the entire conference finds it challenging to impact society.

First, Buddhism is very deeply entrenched in the Japanese family relationship and the overall way of life. For a person to abandon Buddhism for Christianity is much more than a change of religion. It can mean a break with family and much of society. One does not want to overstate the case, but the reality is fully evident.

The second barrier Christianity must overcome in Japan is that it is an imported western religion. While there is widespread Japanese respect for Western achievements, desiring this western faith system is not included in that stance.

Third, Japan is a highly industrialized, highly educated, and prosperous society. There are some poor people, obviously, but not a struggling underclass. There are no Dalits. It is hard to convince people that you have answers when they think, at least apparently think, they have no questions, no spiritual problems needing resolution.

As I reflect on these mission trips, and also my Congo trip described below, many impressions come to mind. One must be stressed. In all of these wonderful countries we have much to learn from the people who live there.

In July 1994, I completed my second round as chairman of the Canadian MB Conference Board of Faith and Life. My final board report was published in the May 27, 1994 issue of the *Mennonite Brethren Herald*. That completed a time, 25 years, of continuous board membership or leadership from 1969 until 1994 in the Canadian MB Conference of Churches. I thank God and the Canadian MB Conference for that opportunity.

Mennonite Brethren Biblical Seminary 1994 - 2010

In 1985, with the intent of enhancing its service to its Canadian constituency, the denominational seminary in Fresno, CA opened a BC Seminary Centre at Abbotsford, BC. The occasional course was taught in Abbotsford by a faculty member of the Mennonite Brethren Biblical Seminary in Fresno. Some courses were taught by local MB leaders. Canadian students could also take approved courses at Regent College and Trinity Western University. For the term January to April 1997, I was appointed Adjunct Professor at Mennonite Brethren Biblical Seminary and taught a course entitled *"Anabaptist Beginnings and the Mennonite Brethren Church."* It was taught in the Central Heights Church in Abbotsford. For the term January 1 until June 30, 1999, I served as Interim Director of the Mennonite Brethren Biblical Seminary BC Centre in Abbotsford.

In early 1998 Dr. Henry Schmidt, president of Mennonite Brethren Biblical Seminary in Fresno, asked me to serve as a consultant in helping that school determine how it should serve the Canadian MB constituency. I accepted. This became an almost two-year part-time engagement and also a very vague one. The plan was to establish a major teaching centre in British Columbia, but there was no clarity concerning where it should be located and with which other institutions, if any, it should be affiliated. President Schmidt gave me virtually no guidelines. He asked me to investigate possibilities and come up with one or two basic recommendations. It soon dawned on me that I had been given an historic assignment. I was to recommend the location and general direction of seminary training for the entire Canadian MB Conference.

Initially, I investigated four options: affiliation with Columbia Bible College, affiliation with what is now the University of the Fraser Valley, affiliation with the Associated Canadian Theological Schools (ACTS) at Trinity Western University, or establishing a new campus. I fairly quickly set aside affiliation with UFV because of insufficient commonality of interest, curriculum, faculty expertise, and institutional values. After investigating costs, I also soon set aside establishing a new campus. That left two options: affiliation with Columbia Bible College or with ACTS at TWU.

For almost six months I researched the two options thoroughly. Extensive consultation, data collection, interviews, and analysis covered many areas: location and accessibility, parking, housing, curriculum, specific course offerings, faculty expertise, institutional compatibility, library resources, teaching facilities, campus life, support services, governance, constituency preference and support, buy-in costs, and very importantly operational costs.

Another key factor was consultation with BCMB conference leaders, pastors, business people, and various academics. I submitted my lengthy report to President Schmidt on June 20, 1998. The main thrust of my detailed report was to compare the CBC and ACTS options.

President Schmidt and I, with the approval of the MBBS board, then decided to hold a major consultation with pastors, conference leaders, businesspeople, professional and academic leaders on July 14, 1998, at the Northview Church in Abbotsford. For that historic session, I prepared a 51-page binder for each participant, about 60, comparing the advantages and disadvantages of the two affiliation options. After several hours of questioning, discussion, and prayer, the assembly voted by a large majority to pursue the ACTS-TWU option.

At that point I thought that my assignment was completed., but that was not to be. President Schmidt and the MBBS Board of Directors then asked me to negotiate matters with ACTS and TWU. I agreed. This turned out to be an even more demanding but very interesting task. The chief negotiator for ACTS was Dr. Guy Saffold. He is knowledgeable and highly skilled in negotiation; the kind of tough protagonist any negotiator wants on his or her team. A few times we seemed to be at an impasse, but eventually all issues were settled. President Schmidt then asked me to organize a suitable signing celebration.

On Sunday, September 26, 1999, we had an exciting event held in the Central Heights Church in Abbotsford. I had recommended that on this occasion MBBS should award an honorary doctorate degree to one of our truly distinguished theologians and Bible scholars, Dr. David Ewert. The MBBS board accepted my recommendation. Although that entire Sunday afternoon celebration remains a highlight of my life, the high point for me was when seminary dean Dr. James Pankratz and I jointly recommended Dr. Ewert for the degree of Doctor of Divinity. We then hooded him. How could I ever have guessed that someday I would participate in thus honouring my esteemed hero and mentor? I was also greatly pleased that we publicly honoured Lena Ewert. Christians, I think, are uniquely delinquent in acknowledging and affirming leaders and their spouses.

A Missions Trip to Congo (Kinshasa) 2004

I should perhaps explain here that Africa has two Congos. The Democratic Republic of Congo has Kinshasa as its capital city. The adjacent Republic of the Congo has Brazzaville as its capital city.

In 2004 I received an invitation from Dr. Nzash Lumeya, a scholar, evangelist, and a leader of the Congolese Mennonite Brethren Conference, although now living in California, to help the MB churches in Congo deal with their government. He identified two main areas of concern. First, there were challenges growing out of some government policies. Second, some Mennonite Brethren church members, including Nzash's own brother, Maleghi, had become active in party politics. This was a request I could not decline.

John visits an orphanage in Kinshasa, Congo.

After extensive planning and preparation I left for the Democratic Republic of Congo (DRC), the Kinshasa Congo, on June 9, 2004. A rather full schedule awaited me. I arrived, via Ethiopia, on June 12. When I left on June 23, I had completed 25 presentations.

As I interacted with pastors and church leaders I developed very great respect for what they were doing with limited resources and often without adequate facilities. I was particularly impressed to see, at a large assembly in Kikwit, that these dear people, who were generally poor financially, urged one another to contribute funds to give to the truly desperate and very needy people in the war zone in eastern Congo. They had little, but they wanted to give and they gave.

There were many surprises. I remember once when I was walking down a street in Kinshasa, I saw a large vacant lot with a light bulb dangling off centre. As I recall, there were perhaps four chairs to one side. When I returned to my guest suite in a Christian compound, I inquired what this meant. I was informed that this was where a good-sized church met on Sundays and at other times. This church had no walls, no windows to open, no doors to lock, no nursery to furnish, no library to stock with books and CDs, no choir pews, no sound system, no acoustic problems to be remedied by sound engineers, no custodial and janitorial expenses, no insurance premiums, no heating system that required maintenance, no steeple, and no signage. This "church without walls" did not need to discuss the colour of the carpet or the design of new furniture for pastors. That congregation unintentionally shamed me as it should most North American and European Christians by what they did not require to be a healthy, growing church.

On Sunday, June 13, I was privileged to preach in the Batela MB Church in Kinshasa. This congregation taught me a lesson in the joy of giving. The first surprise was that there were two offering times, one for the men and one for the women. They were in competition. When the results were announced, the winning side, the women, danced in the aisles and sang. They were a happy and generous congregation.

Several other events should be mentioned. On Thursday, June 17, I was scheduled to fly to Kikwit. Upon boarding the fairly small plane I noticed that about half of the seats, perhaps 20, had been removed from the front part of the cabin and luggage was stacked there, kept in place by strong netting. Then I observed Congolese resourcefulness and ingenuity at work. All the seats were taken but several more people wanted to board. No problem. In short order several lawn chairs were brought in and set in front of the fixed seats. They were quickly filled, and we took off. All went well. Since the fixed seats had no seat belts, that did not create a seat-belt problem for the portable seats.

On Saturday, June 19, 2004, I was assigned a one-and-a-half-hour session to speak to some members of the national parliament. I was introduced by Maleghi Leonard Lumeya, a Deputy in the National Assembly. Dr. Nzash Lumeya, his brother, again served as an exceptionally competent translator. Given that I had been told about some of the problems in the parliament, namely hyper-partisanship and corruption, not uncommon in many lands, I delineated the basic biblical principles which God expects rulers to follow, whether they are Christians or not. As at many other times, I tried to be respectful but candid.

All went well until, at one point, a certain politician, who I discovered later was a Muslim, severely criticized me. I could get that much but nothing else out of what he said in French. Later on, Nzash told me that the Muslim's criticism of me as a Christian spelling out Christian principles was so bad and severe that he had not translated it accurately for me. I assume that all of the French-speaking politicians in the hall realized what Nzash was doing to spare me serious embarrassment because no one challenged his faulty translation.

John and members of Congo's national parliament.

Dr. Lumeya had arranged for me to meet the President of the DRC. Unfortunately, he was suddenly required to fly to South Africa so the Vice-President, Zahedi Ngoma, substituted for him. After being escorted through numerous security checks I was ushered into the Vice President's private office. For some reason I did not have a translator with me that evening so I had to rely on the one provided by the Vice-President. It is always good to have two translators in such situations to ensure accuracy.

The session went well. The impressive Vice-President had many questions and I, in turn, also queried him tactfully but directly.

He acknowledged the problems I was describing, especially the bribing and other corruption, which is widely seen as partly a consequence of severe poverty. He assured me that progress was being made. Although I do not speak French, I took note of his excellent French. When the scheduled time had passed, and I got up to leave, I thanked him most sincerely. He then also got up and, with a broad smile on his face, addressed me in perfect English.

John with
Zahedi Ngoma,
Congo Vice-President.

That session with the Vice-President was followed by a high-voltage joint press conference. Both Vice-President Ngoma and I answered questions, sometimes both responded to a question. That was exciting.

Unemployment was a huge problem. I was informed that in most areas it hovers between 50% and 70%. Let me quote a few sentences from my official trip report to the MBMSI board.

"In one church, I was told that of all the men I saw sitting in the benches, 90% were unemployed. I marveled that they could be so dynamic and happy and spiritually committed while experiencing such severe economic hardships. It was a good thing that they, and the masses of financially poor people, are not sitting in the back pews of our churches or in our denominational conventions when we hear again and again that we have no money for missions, that our giving is "maxed out." On the other hand, maybe it would be a good thing for them to be present. Maybe their presence, and especially their reports, would help us refocus our Christian vision and rearrange our collective priorities."

My 11-day schedule with 25 lectures, sermons, and other presentations was challenging but also very rewarding.

On-site missionaries Dr. Murray and Faith Nickel were very helpful in many ways. I am indebted to them. As I reflected on what the faithful Congolese, both men and women, were achieving with very limited resources but with great faith, fixed courage, unshakable determination, amazing optimism, and a deep trust in God, I was simultaneously humbled and inspired.

Columbia Bible College 2002 - 2011

In 2002 I was approached by President Paul Wartman to ask if I would help raise funds for the planned Student Building-Dining Hall. I agreed to contact some potential donors, which I did. One couple came through with almost $250,000 to fund the modern kitchen. By the grace of God, I raised a total of about $320,000 to help fund the cost of the excellent building.

For several years, approximately 1998 to 2002, Rudy Baerg, the widely acclaimed and long-time Columbia Bible College (CBC) music professor and chorale conductor had presented community concerts featuring students from a specific decade. After the last one it occurred to me that the earlier decades had been overlooked. Surely there were still many students around from the 1940s and 1950s who could be assembled and would be delighted to prepare a concert. As I pondered the possibilities, it occurred to me that two other realities could and should be included in any such gathering. In the first place, there should be a recognition of all of the British Columbia Mennonite Brethren Bible Schools, which had closed and more or less been absorbed, sometimes unofficially, by CBC. I knew of at least four.

The second reality I had in mind was that CBC needed to establish an Alumni Association which could prove very beneficial for student recruitment, financial support, and general promotion. I therefore approached President Wartman. He was very supportive, encouraged me, and said that CBC staff would be available to assist me.

I invited the following former CBC students to serve on the planning committee: Ernie and Elfrieda Block, Abe J. and Betty Klassen, Len Doerksen, Betty Kampen, Rudie and Louise Willms, and Doris Redekop. They all accepted my invitation. Merv Boschman served as *ex officio* CBC rep. I served as chairperson.

We had our first meeting on August 29, 2002. Rather quickly, our mandate expanded. Eventually, we set eight goals for ourselves:
1. We would plan a major alumni reunion for CBC students from the 1940s and 1950s. (It should be stated here that in 1970 Mennonite Brethren Bible Institute and Bethel Bible Institute, operated by (GC) Mennonite Church BC, joined to form Columbia Bible College.)
2. We would extend invitations not only to CBC students from those years but also from the other Mennonite Brethren Bible Schools in BC that had officially or unofficially been assimilated into CBC. (This was soon changed to include a non-MB Mennonite school, aside from Bethel Bible Institute, that had closed.)

3. We would create a list, as complete as possible, of students from all of the schools, who attended in the 1940s and 1950s.
4. We would organize a major weekend reunion for February 14, 15, and 16, 2003.
5. On Sunday afternoon, at the main celebration in Central Heights Church, we would arrange for all 1940s and 1950s students from the other schools to be accepted as alumni of CBC.
6. We wanted to establish funding for a 1940s and 1950s annual scholarship and an annual bursary.
7. We would try to set in motion the formation of a Columbia Bible College Alumni Association.
8. We hoped to help create a policy of annual homecomings for alumni, according to years and perhaps according to founding schools.

With determination, hard work, and God's blessing, we achieved the first five goals and partially succeeded in the sixth. Unfortunately, the last two were not achieved. Using any and all available sources of information ranging from old yearbooks - for some years, there were none - to contacting relatives, friends and acquaintances and by any other means, we developed a list of 1,885 names of students who attended one of the schools in the '40s and '50s. We found addresses for about 1,445. Registered attendance at the reunion was about 550.

From September to December 2002, I spent about 25 percent of my time on this project. After that, until the event itself in mid-February, about half of my time. While all committee members worked hard and achieved much, certain tasks fell to me. I did the fundraising, prepared agendas for the various programs, wrote the scripts for the Sunday afternoon decade skits, managed the budget, arranged for event participants, and much else.

Fortunately, I had some CBC secretarial assistance in Carol Boschman and Ruthanne Wartman. CBC official Merv Boschman also provided valued assistance.

Our extensive research involving all schools turned up fascinating findings. I shall describe three. We discovered that the Elim Bible School in Yarrow had actually held its first classes in the fall of 1930. To our amazement, we then discovered that three girls who were part of that first class in Yarrow were still alive and doing well. Seventy-three years after they were students at Elim Bible School, these three ladies all attended the Sunday afternoon celebration at Central Heights Church, where they were publicly honoured. The three were Katie (Dahl) Hooge; Nettie (Esau) Wiebe; and Sarah (Enns) Martens.

Our second surprising discovery was that when the Coghlan Bible School, which later became Bethel adjacent to the West Abbotsford Mennonite Church, opened in 1939, the times were so difficult financially that the students paid no tuition and the teachers received no salary. Presumably, the teachers all had some other vocation.

The third discovery was that on January 7, 1941, as recorded at the time by student Sylvester Dirks, a three-member delegation from the Department of Education visited Elim Bible School in Yarrow to investigate the curriculum. They had been informed that some classes were taught in German. On January 7, 1942, exactly one year later, a local policeman came to Elim for the same reason. What the police constable had to do with the language of instruction is not explained. Apparently, suspicions lingered. On February 6, 1942, another RCMP officer came to Elim and "engaged Principal [C.C.] Peters in a lengthy interview." This interview was complicated by the fact that Principal Peters' first language was German, and his English was weak. Apparently, however, his skill in communicating what was being taught satisfied the authorities. There were no more police visits.

Friday evening, February 14, we had an amazing Welcome Celebration in Columbia Place gymnasium. Saturday forenoon attendees came back to Columbia Place to view outstanding displays for all the schools. I am still amazed that we located the many hundreds of excellent pictures, artifacts, and curios. Fortunately, we later had all pictures photographed. Saturday afternoon we had tours, workshops, videos, and choir rehearsal led by the highly skilled Ernie Block, as well as more time for viewing the extensive displays. Saturday evening we were guests at a CBC international basketball game in Columbia Place. Thank you, Fred and Ella Strumpski, for funding this outstanding facility. Lunch and *faspa* for about 500 guests were served in nearby Garden Park Tower. Sunday afternoon we had the **Celebration of Worship and Praise.** Students from the forerunner five schools were officially welcomed as CBC alumni. The 100-voice choir directed by Ernie Block was marvellous. The local paper reported that 1,000 people had attended the event. The afternoon celebration was followed by a light supper at Bakerview Church for about 500 ticketed guests. That was followed by an amazing musical evening put on by CBC in the Bakerview Church gym. That historic Sunday was indeed a day to remember. For me it was another amazing highlight.

For me this entire CBC alumni undertaking was perhaps the most demanding but also the most rewarding of my volunteer ventures other than my lengthy Stillwood ministry.

Some time later I wrote an 18-page report which I submitted to President Wartman. It included a set of 19 recommendations for the future. Some of our recommendations were accepted, others not. Unfortunately, although our committee offered to be the first alumni board, our main recommendation, namely, that CBC should build on this weekend and establish an alumni association was not taken up. Also, we thought we had raised enough investment money to award both a scholarship and a bursary. The bursary did not materialize. Perhaps we should have done more fundraising.

In September 2009 I accepted a request from CBC President Ron Penner to serve on a Residence Planning Team. The College was planning to build a men's residence. While fundraising was our main challenge, many related items needed to be discussed and recommendations made to the College board and administrators. The challenge was substantial. The college had on hand about $500,000 for the project but another $2.8 million was needed. We developed various strategies.

While we were making some progress in fundraising, a very delightful and gainful development happened. Two members on the Planning Team, John Redekop and his son Randy, announced that they would be providing most of the needed funding. What an answer to prayer that was. The excellent building was named Redekop Hall. It must be stated here that while the Redekop family provided most of the funding, a significant number of other Christian business people also made major donations, either financially or by providing services and materials.

The Planning Team held its last meeting on December 12. 2011. Our main agenda item, fortunately, was planning the Residence Dedication Celebration and Donor Recognition on January 15, 2012. Thanks to the generosity of many people, this undertaking had a very successful conclusion.

Mennonite Faith and Learning Society

Beginning about the year 2004 I began wondering whether it would be wise and timely to establish a Centre for Mennonite Studies at the University of the Fraser Valley (UFV), generally similar to the Chair in Mennonite Studies operating very successfully at the University of Winnipeg. At a UFV function on August 5, 2006, I found myself standing next to Dr. Skip Basford, President of the University of the Fraser Valley. I mentioned my idea to him. He was very supportive. After discussing the idea with certain friends, a meeting of Mennonite community leaders was called for July 23, 2007; I presented my idea to them. The result was the formation of the Mennonite Faith and Learning Society which, after numerous additional meetings, was incorporated as a society in British Columbia on May 6, 2009.

Discussions and negotiations with UFV had begun already in 2008. An agreement was drawn up between the MFLS and the UFV to establish a Chair in Mennonite Studies at UFV. As president of the MFLS I was delighted to sign the agreement with UFV at a major signing celebration held on June 24, 2009, on the UFV campus. The attendance was impressive. Ethnic Mennonite refreshments were served. There was excitement in the air. Eventually the emphasis shifted somewhat to Peace Studies but the undertaking continues to grow.

After further consideration, it was decided to work towards establishing a second university centre, a more theologically oriented one, at Trinity Western University. Again the university was very supportive. The signing of the agreement between MFLS and TWU took place at a major celebration on February 14, 2011. As president of the MFLS I was again delighted to sign for our organization. Sometime later, Dr. Myron Penner, a professor at TWU, was appointed as Director for what would be called the Anabaptist-Mennonite Centre for Faith and Learning at Trinity Western University. Under his leadership this centre is offering various courses and events to achieve the society's goals.

Stillwood Camp and Conference Centre 1996 - 2010

It should be mentioned here that Stillwood was known as Columbia Bible Camp until July 2, 2000.

When we moved back to the Fraser Valley in 1994 I had no intention of reconnecting with what was then Columbia Bible Camp. In 1958 I had been part of the group that established the camp and even served as secretary of the initial organizational meeting on October 3, 1958, in the Fraserview MB Church in Vancouver, but I had not maintained contact with that undertaking. My general plan was to teach at Trinity Western University on a part-time basis and to continue with various writing interests. I intended to heed the advice of my good friend and excellent physician, Dr. Helmut Mathies, who several times cautioned me about undertaking too many tasks.

My almost 21 years of volunteering for the Stillwood ministry took me well beyond 2010. The later developments, both successes and disappointments, will be described in the next chapter.

In March 1996 Henry and Elizabeth Esau, long-time friends and ministry colleagues in Waterloo but recently relocated to Chilliwack, invited Doris and me to join them for a holiday in Honolulu. We happily accepted. One day Henry, then the Executive Director at Columbia Bible Camp, urged me strongly to help him in achieving major redevelopment and expansion at Columbia. Little did I know what awaited me when I agreed to my good friend's request. I immediately began working as a member of the Development Commission. On May 4, 1996, I was elected at the BC Mennonite Brethren AGM as a regular Camp Board member.

Initially I agreed to raise about $20,000 for one cabin. This one would serve as a model to assist with the rest of the fundraising plan. My predecessor in charge of fundraising had developed a complex undertaking he called the Andrew Plan which would involve the participation of many church representatives.

When my first contact, the one I thought most likely to rise to the challenge, turned me down very firmly, I almost quit. I decided, however, that I would make one more attempt. This time I contacted another long-time friend and a successful businessman, Abe Warkentin, and his wife, Tina. I knew that he was a camp supporter because he had taken me to the campsite not long ago and had expressed strong support for such a ministry.

I still recall clearly, how I hesitated to leave the car and go to his apartment building. Finally, I went. I was warmly welcomed by Abe and Tina. Once again, I presented my case as clearly and convincingly as I could, complete with plans and drawings. I looked up to see that Abe was almost overcome with emotion. He said that he had been waiting a long time for this to happen. With a strong voice he said that he and Tina would be happy to contribute the full amount. Emotion overcame all three of us. It is correct to say that Warkentins' strong support launched me to undertake further fundraising. Since no one was willing to do the extensive contacting, training, and supervision that the Andrew Project required, nothing more came of it. When I informed the board that I was willing to do my best to collect funds, not having any idea how many cabins and other buildings would be needed, they unanimously urged me to proceed. At about this time, because of cost efficiency, the planned cabins became duplexes.

For the next 20 years camp concerns became a major preoccupation for me. For most of those years I was board chair as well as chair of the Development Committee and a member of the Finance Committee. As I became knowledgeable about what was happening at Columbia and what the potential could be, I gave myself fully to the cause. I decided I would do what I could to bring about what obviously needed to happen. I knew that all of the existing buildings were not up to code and that conditional occupancy had been granted. Major changes and replacements were needed. Henry had, in fact, already achieved major improvements. It was actually he who laid the foundation for the next phase of development.

Early on I realized that the needed funds were present in the community and that the challenge was to make people willing to make donations. For me it was clear; given that there was no other similar centre south of the Fraser River between the coast and Hope, and given the growing regional population, and also considering the increased affluence of most people, the need for a truly fine camp and conference centre was urgent, both for the Christian community with its many congregations and also for the larger community.

In March 1997, Harry Edwards was hired as Henry's successor as Executive Director. He and Gail who, within a few months became the director of food service, were indeed wonderful ministry colleagues. I shall allow myself to state here that because of the financial challenges at Columbia, Gail took no salary for many months and then for several years only a partial salary. Harry, too, for many years was paid much less than warranted. Neither Harry nor Gail ever complained. As already stated, on July 2, 2000, Columbia Bible Camp and Conference Centre was renamed Stillwood Camp and Conference Centre which is the name I shall use from here on.

It is clearly not possible to describe the many interesting, puzzling, unusual, rewarding, encouraging, and also frustrating experiences in fundraising during two decades, but I shall report several experiences. In my first round of fund solicitations my goal was to find 20 donors who would each contribute $20,000 for a cabin which became half a duplex which we called a cottage. One of the potential donor couples I contacted was John and Elizabeth Enns, friends of ours since the 1950s. I knew that John had been a camp supporter from the beginning and also that he had been a successful contractor. I made an appointment to visit them. The couple welcomed me warmly. I completed the presentation. Apparently John had forgotten a different commitment when he suddenly said that he would have to leave for about half an hour, as I recall. After he left, Elizabeth candidly informed me that they had given funds to charity and no longer would be able to fund a cottage. I thanked her for her candour and got up to leave. She insisted that I stay until John returned. I did. We had another short visit. It was always inspiring to visit the Ennses.

A few days later John Enns phoned to say that I should drop by to pick up the cheque. I was truly surprised but one does not pry into a donor's finances. I was profoundly happy, drove to the Enns's and thanked them very sincerely. Sometime later I discovered that this dear saint, already in his 80s, had gone to the bank, borrowed the money, and then called me. I was humbled!

On one occasion I made an arrangement to contact a Vancouver developer whom I barely knew. As is my practice, I try to schedule meetings in homes or, if necessary, at a quiet alternative location with both spouses present.

Harry and Gail Edwards

I try to avoid restaurants and coffee shops. They are too noisy and too many friends drop by and almost derail my undertaking.

This man, named Peter, suggested that I meet him, as I recall, at 8:30 in the dining area of his church, right after a men's group would have had a prayer breakfast.

I arrived a little early and waited in an adjacent room. When the men's meeting ended, I assumed that Peter would ask to see me privately. Instead, he invited me to make my presentation to the entire group of about ten men, mostly successful businessmen. I think he wanted them also to be challenged. Great idea! I would do my very best. Little did he know what this might mean for him.

The group knew that my appointment had been to see Peter but welcomed me warmly. After I had finished my presentation Peter needed to respond. He said something about my presentation being good and the camp cause excellent but at this time he would not be participating. Then his pals rose to the occasion. They were going to have some fun! As I recall, one began by saying, "You buy each grandchild a new car when they graduate from high school, you can easily do this, Peter." Another said something to the effect that "Your business has been very good, Peter. You can easily do this." There was laughter. I smiled happily and hopefully.

Very soon Peter had heard enough. His friends had put him on the spot. He turned to me and said that I could have the full amount shortly. Then the tables turned. Peter had been outwitted - now he turned his wit on his pals. Never before or since have I watched anything quite like it. Now Peter, with enthusiasm, reminded his friends that they, too, could fund a cabin. He made some of them squirm. I smiled some more, again happily and hopefully. As I recall, I got two or three more commitments from that group. Thank God for Killarney Park Men's Group.

Another potential contributor was my friend Fred Strumpski. I knew that he was a successful businessman and a generous supporter of many charities. We met in a coffee shop. Again I carefully explained my cause. After I finished he said that he would be pleased to be one of the 20 donors I needed. Then he said that he had two brothers and a brother-in-law whom I should also see. I did not know any of them. He gave me their names and phone numbers. I thanked him most sincerely. He then said that when I met each of the three couples I should say that Fred had said that he wanted that couple to join him in funding a cottage. I did as Fred told me. All three couples became donors. I wish Fred and Ella had more wealthy brothers and brothers-in-law.

My main fundraising activity for Stillwood, at least for the main site renewal phase, was completed by 2008. Information and pictures are provided in Appendix C. Later there were two more phases. By 2008, according to my records, I had, by God's grace and with his enablement, raised close to $11 million. While most donations were fairly modest, some were large. I thank all donors. It is quite possible that some who gave rather modest amounts - the smallest capital campaign donation was $20 - may have sacrificed the most. Expressing thanks is important. It is Biblical. In the 17th chapter of Luke we read that Jesus healed ten lepers but when only one came back to thank him, Jesus said, "Were there not ten cleansed? Where are the other nine?" Expressing thanks is always right.

I deem it right to acknowledge that four donors or households gave exceptionally large amounts. I am publicly thanking them again. Without their generosity Stillwood would not be what it is today. David and Hilda Froese, John and Edith Dyck with daughter Carol, Henry Schroeder, and Ken Dyck. These all modelled very generous support which, in turn, greatly helped me when I invited other people of means to become major donors.

With David Froese's permission I shall recount part of my soliciting relationship with him. Some context is needed. We had received notice that the two hobby farms immediately west of our campsite had been zoned by the Agricultural Land Commission as suitable for hog-raising - "Intensive swine operation" - and poultry farming. We greatly feared what might happen.

Given the prevailing westerly winds, we knew that if such development should take place, it would be almost impossible to maintain our present ministry. We faced two huge problems. First, both properties were not for sale. Second, we had no funds to buy those farms. We prayed and planned.

One day, unexpectedly, I got a phone call from my friend David Froese to ask if we could have coffee together at the A & W. I naturally agreed. I did not know the purpose of his call. When we sat down, he told me that he had recently had a very serious heart attack in Hawaii. In fact, he had almost died. He asked whether we still needed a large donation for the Red Barn, about which I had contacted him some months earlier. He had then kindly heard me out and made a significant but for him not stretching donation. I said, "Dave, now we have a different, very urgent need." I told him about the two adjacent hobby farms and that if they became large hog or poultry operations, they could almost destroy Stillwood's ministry. David is astute. He also has a farming background and knew exactly what was at issue.

After a pause David asked how much the adjacent 10-acre farm would cost. I was surprised. I said it was not listed but I had arranged to have it appraised by a realtor friend, Leona Janzen, and that her estimate was $300,000. He said that he would provide the funds. I could hardly believe my ears. I had come for a cup of coffee! He then asked about the second farm, the 30-acre property also with a house.

I said that the realtor, Leona, had given me the estimated figure of $500,000. After a pause David said that he would also provide those funds. Now it was even harder for me to believe my ears. I happened to have a pen with me but no paper. I grabbed an A & W napkin and wrote up the commitment. David signed it. Praise God. Thank you, David! I was so excited, my eyes filled with tears of gratitude. I think Dave's also. I was so elated that I could hardly drive home.

Now the needed funding was in place, but the target properties were not for sale. What to do next? It occurred to me that we should pray over those two hobby farms and claim them for God. I therefore arranged for some Stillwood Board members, David and Hilda Froese, camp executive director Harry Edwards, and a few other key camp supporters to meet in a circle, half on one farm and half on the other. We met in that circle. We prayed fervently, claiming those properties for the Stillwood ministry.

I then again contacted the owners who both again stated they were not interested in selling. I was not about to give up. At times I can have a stubborn streak, especially for a good or a just cause. God answers prayers but we have to do our part. I asked Bob Eades, the owner of the 10-acre place, the adjacent one, if he would come to his cottage so I could meet him.

He was a busy lawyer in Vancouver. I was almost surprised when he agreed. We set a time. Harry Edwards and I then went to his lovely cottage to see him.

The Prayer Circle "claiming" two adjacent properties for Stillwood.

I knew that the lawyer's first wife had passed away and that he had recently remarried. I expected that he would be there by himself. I did not know what to expect. Realism and doubt made me hesitant; idealism and faith made me hopeful. When we were invited in, I was surprised to see the lawyer's wife there as well. I immediately assessed this reality as a good omen.

After some pleasantries we quickly got to the main agenda. The gentleman said that he would like to accommodate us and the camp work which he affirmed, but the place was definitely not for sale. He wanted to keep this place, with its outstanding vista, including Cultus Lake, for family vacations. Then his wife chimed in. She said that because the first wife's ashes were spread around this house, she did not want to come there. Bob Eades seemed as surprised as we were. The two had obviously not had sufficient prior conversation.

With that God-given bombshell - I believe it was divine intervention - the tone of our meeting changed markedly. Bob Eades was not interested in much additional conversation. Inwardly I rejoiced in anticipation but tried not to show anything. Not much more was said at that meeting. I believe I said something about contacting with Bob later. I imagine that during the drive back to Vancouver, there was some unusual conversation in the Eades' vehicle.

Prayer Circle Members

Back Row: Lorraine Dyck, Bill Friesen, Donna Sawatzky, Gerry Sawatzky, David Froese, Hilda Froese, Betty Letkemann, John Letkemann, Arthur Loewen.
Front Row: Harry Edwards, Gail Edwards, Anne Friesen, Doris Redekop.
Missing: John H. Redekop (photographer).

After some major additional conversations in the next weeks we closed the deal for a sum modestly higher than what Leona Janzen had estimated. The sales contract stipulated that if Stillwood would be asked early in spring, then we would set aside a Stillwood cottage for the Eades' sons for two weeks of free use every summer. Both Harry and I considered that to be a small disadvantage in the scheme to acquire the property. As it turned out, the Eades' sons never applied to use a cottage. I thank God for Leona! I thank God for Mrs. Eades! I thank God for Bob Eades!

Now for the other property, the 30-acre farm on which the owner Borge Olsen, a widower, lived in retirement and kept some prize horses. Harry and I visited the dear Dane. He certainly supported Stillwood's activities but he wouldn't budge. His wife had recently passed away and he was lonely. He insisted that he would remain in the home that they had shared. His place wasn't for sale.

In the following days I prayed and tried to think of something that might move him. I then consulted my lawyer friend, Ed Fast. He suggested we might try a proposal in which Olsen would be paid now. We would allow him to live in that property as long as he wished. We would fence off a few acres for his two or three horses. Stillwood would have use of the rest of the acreage. Ed drew up a draft agreement.

Harry and I then visited Borge Olsen again. I vividly recall sitting in his living room and telling him that it surely would be advantageous for him to accept our proposal. He could live in his home as long as he wished.

His beloved horses, which Harry and I knew were getting well on in years, would have the needed pasture. He could have the funds now, perhaps years before he would otherwise get them. He could invest his funds as soon as the sale was finalized. I tried to sound as persuasive as I could without overdoing it. Surely this would be advantageous for him. We convinced the tall Dane. I then introduced him to David, so he knew who was providing the funds. With this arrangement we knew there would be no hog or poultry operation which, given the prevailing west winds, would cripple Stillwood. As it turned out, Borge's beloved horses soon went to horse heaven. Dear Borge lived in his home until 2014 or 2015. He then relocated to a nursing home in Chilliwack. Borge passed away on October 9, 2017.

Today Stillwood's executive director David Seeley lives in the lovely house that lawyer Bob Eades' second wife did not want to inhabit and the Olson home is used for Stillwood ministry.

Dave Froese, Hilda Froese, John H. Redekop, Borge Olsen.

Other Christian Ministries 1994 - 2010

A truly unusual ministry opportunity developed in 1996 and came to fruition in May 1997. The World Evangelical Fellowship convention was scheduled to take place in Abbotsford. An ad hoc assembly of local church leaders elected Dr. Vern Heidebrecht as chair of the Host Committee and me as vice-chair. We were challenged with many problems ranging from setting up the hosting organization to finding venues and from trying to get permission for delegates to come from closed countries to coping with the crowds. Fortunately, we had several strong committees assisting us. Interacting with Christian leaders from around the globe turned out to be an incredible experience.

Another area of ministry involved **NOW TV,** a Lower Mainland television station which was launched, as I recall, probably early in 2000. Doug Kooy, one of the station's anchor hosts, hosted an hour-long program called *On Line.* Typically he had a guest with whom he discussed major issues of the day, often based on current network television coverage. My appointment calendars indicate that I was a frequent guest on his program from 2002 until 2005. During the last year or so I functioned a few times as the host. The highlight for me happened on June 6, 2002, when for one hour Doug interviewed me on terrorism. That was an exciting interview and the entire involvement was a stimulating ministry. This well-watched program ended when, for financial reasons, the station was sold and became a totally different channel with new station call letters.

During 2000 and 2001 I served as chairperson for the Pacific Mennonite Children's Choir "Legacy 2000" initiative. This involved raising funds for the production of a CD, organizing special concerts, and assisting in other ways. It was a delight to work with Nancy Dyck and other skilled leaders and the enthusiastic children.

Soon after I completed my term as president of the Evangelical Fellowship of Canada in 1993, I was appointed to its Religious Liberty Commission. This assignment involved commission strategy sessions, research, and writing. We developed some important guidelines and principles for both democratic and non-democratic countries. Because of the distance in travelling from the Fraser Valley to Ottawa or Toronto for consultations, I terminated my membership in February 2002.

Because of encouragement from my friend, Dr. John D. Friesen, beginning about 2002, I participated in the attempt to revive the Mennonite Brethren student ministry at the University of British Columbia. Over the next decade we were involved in various committees, initiatives, planning sessions, etc. A major consultation took place on April 30, 2006, in our home when 21 invited leaders met to think, pray, and plan. I had prepared a binder for each person with an assortment of relevant material. It was a very stimulating session. Although, in the end, this initiative did not produce tangible results, it stimulated broader discussion. For a few years, there was interest on the part of some BCMB Conference leaders, especially Conference Minister Steve Berg, but there was insufficient conference support for any substantial ministry.

In 2004 I was asked to serve as a development consultant and fundraiser for *The Mark Centre,* a Christian retreat and training mission in Abbotsford. It was a privilege to work with Dan Ratzlaff, the Advisory Council Chair, who modelled generosity, and Steve Klassen, the gifted and effective director.

Activity in Political Arenas 1994 - 2010

In 1997 I received an unusual request. Apparently, there had been some very serious disagreement in the Reform Party Caucus in Ottawa about whether the party platform aligned with biblical teaching. I was asked if I would do a thorough study of the Reform Party platform and policies and then report concerning the extent to which they aligned with biblical teaching. After giving the matter careful thought I accepted the contract offer knowing that troubled waters lay ahead. I carried out extensive research and identified considerable overlap in ethics. That was only part of my response.

As I had anticipated, on the main issue, whether populism aligns with Christian teaching, I had to report as tactfully as I could that I had not found any extensive overlap. Populism holds that the best moral guidance comes from the grassroots, the mass of ordinary folk, and elected politicians should always try to follow the views of the grassroots. This is the right thing to do because the common people know what is best and make the best judgments. I had to report that the New Testament teaches that the majority among the masses tend not to choose what is right, virtuous, and God-pleasing. Also, speaking as a political scientist, I had to say that they tend not to be particularly well-informed and further, many think more of their own benefit and advantage rather than the national common good. I quoted data and experts. I think I made a very strong case for my conclusions on about ten key issues.

Before long I received a reply. The gist of it was that while the Caucus members, or at least some of them, did not fundamentally disagree with my analysis, it would be appreciated if I would soften my conclusion. I did the best I could. My hunch is that some Reform MPs felt reassured in their beliefs while some others were very upset with this Christian professor who had let them down.

On November 20, 1999, I was elected to a three-year term on the Abbotsford City Council. The population of Abbotsford at that time was about 128,000. This position came with a modest stipend of about $1,800 a month. It was assumed that being a city councillor required the equivalent of one day of work each week. I soon discovered that if one took all assignments seriously and read all the background papers for the council and committee meetings as well as the public hearings, that being a councillor required at least two days a week.

I thoroughly enjoyed serving the residents of Abbotsford to the best of my ability. At times all of us came under major cross-pressures. For example, the large Indo-Canadian community in Abbotsford made a very logical and compelling case for the construction of a very large Sikh Gurdwara temple in the north-western part of the city. Scores of non-Sikh residents living in the area strongly opposed the project. They stressed that they were not prejudicial against the Indo-Canadians but they believed that if the gurdwara was built, the resulting noise and heavy traffic would reduce the value of their property. The council unanimously voted for the construction to proceed. We did the right thing.

During my time on City Council I held several concurrent positions. One of these was to serve as a member of the Fraser Valley Treaty Advisory Committee. We became quite involved with treaty negotiations with First Nations in this region. We held many meetings in Chilliwack to address issues. For me, two realities became dominant. First, without a doubt, the coming of Caucasian settlers had a huge and unsettling impact on the First Nations' way of life, both for good and for bad. The second foundational reality is that the treaty negotiations have become so complex and far-reaching that success becomes almost impossible. With experts to assist us, we discussed schools, school buses, hunting rights, hunting out of season, fishing rights, fishing out of season, fire protection, police protection, hospital care on reserves, ambulance service, compensation for lost use of land, public use of reserve roads, the applicability of municipal taxes for certain purposes, and an array of other concerns. I soon concluded that it is not surprising that very few treaties are ever signed.

The City of Abbotsford has a Japanese Twin City, Fukagawa, located on the northern island of Hokkaido. To promote goodwill, expand educational exchanges, increase economic relations, and encourage tourism, it was decided that Abbotsford should send a delegation to our Twin City. On May 8, 2002, our delegation of 14 people, including representatives from the school board, the University of the Fraser Valley, and the business community, flew to Japan. Some of us paid for spouses to travel with us.

As one would expect, we were treated royally. Doubtless, the costs were warranted. Abbotsford and British Columbia gained extensive and positive publicity.

One of the events scheduled for us was participation in a rice planting operation. Rice, as we know, is planted in standing water. We were given rubber boots, some rice shoots, and basic instruction. We waded into the water. We soon discovered that under the water was a deep layer of mud. Our boots sank into that muck. At one point my wife, Doris, found that her booted feet had sunk so far into the mud that she could not move them. Immediately a sturdy Japanese fellow stepped into the rice paddy to help her. The helpful gentleman pulled hard, and then he and Doris both fell into the water and mud. There was much laughter. Doris was a good sport and graciously accepted the partial mud-bath. Eventually both were "rescued," totally covered in mud. It was soon time for our group of dignitaries to get onto a bus and return to our accommodation. I don't recall what happened to the Good Samaritan but I found a garden hose and washed Doris down on all sides. Totally drenched, she was wrapped in a large towel which appeared from somewhere. We boarded the bus.

After several weeks of doing goodwill in Fukagawa the rest of the group flew back to BC while Doris and I flew to Osaka on the southern island of Honshu to meet our friend, pastor Sumako Furubayashi, and the good people in the Osaka Bible Church. It had been my privilege to visit and preach there previously. Also, Sumako had brought ESL students to Abbotsford several times. We had been involved in that project. Here, too, we were hosted graciously. The Japanese excel in the art of hosting. During this and my other visits to Japan I have, however, been struck by the following reality. Either most Japanese are not aware of the terrible atrocities inflicted by Imperial Japan on captured soldiers and even civilians, or they do not want to talk about it. Also, the December 7, 1941, devastating attack on Pearl Harbour is certainly viewed differently in North America and Japan. Nationalistic blinkers can have a distorting effect on all of us.

During my time on City Council a major energy crisis developed. In 1999 the Sumas Energy Company was planning to build a large second co-generational energy plant, the SE2 plant, in Sumas, Washington, just across the border from Abbotsford. It would be fueled by Canadian gas. The project had already been approved by the Washington State government. When I was on council, we were informed that if the huge plant were built, Abbotsford would experience serious effects from pollutants. Canada's National Energy Board (NEB) decided to hold hearings in Abbotsford. It could veto the use of Canadian gas which would mean the plant would not be built. I was privileged to be one of the spokespersons approved to present a brief.

On July 8, 2003, I had the opportunity to testify before the National Energy Board, which was conducting hearings in Abbotsford. I enjoyed describing the negative consequences of the proposed gas plant. Fortunately, in 2004 the Canadian NEB ruled against the SE2 project.

From January 5, 2000, to January 5, 2002, I served as a member of the Fraser Valley District Patrol Citizens Advisory CommitteeAt the local prison. Our main task was to review files and documents describing a prisoner and then recommend either parole or not. Sometimes we specified conditions. This assignment was very interesting but also very revealing as we repeatedly dealt with recidivism and frequently with convicts who had experienced serious mistreatment in their early years. It was a constant challenge to balance compassion with reality.

In 2003 I was surprised to receive an invitation from the House of Commons Standing Committee on Justice and Human Rights to present a brief to the Committee on my views on "*Marriage and Legal Recognition of Same-sex Unions.*" The Committee would be holding hearings in Vancouver as well as at other locations. I readily accepted what I considered to be an historic opportunity. I worked hard in developing my brief.

I addressed the Parliamentary Committee in Vancouver on the afternoon of April 1, 2003. My 11-page brief was entitled "*Pragmatic and Practical Reasons for Defining Marriage as only Heterosexual.*" I felt that it was probably the clearest and strongest brief I had ever written. As it happened, the other main presenter that afternoon was a Simon Fraser University professor who also presented a compelling case for retaining the traditional definition of marriage. As I watched the members of the Committee, it seemed to me that most of them were favourably impressed. That conclusion was then borne out by the questions asked and the statements made. It appeared that we had convinced two wavering Liberal members not to support same-sex marriage. After the session ended several of the Committee members spoke to me. I was especially pleased when the leading Liberal member, Vancouver Centre MP Dr. Judy Fry, told me that we had made a compelling case. When the SFU professor and I debriefed we were quite sure that the majority report of the Committee to the House of Commons would be that in Canada we should retain the traditional definition of marriage.

Newspaper reports of the hearing and of committee members' views indicated that our assessment of the hearings was correct. Unfortunately, before the Committee could submit its report to the House of Commons, Prime Minister Jean Chretien removed the two formerly wavering Liberal members from the Standing Committee, the two who had become supportive of retaining the traditional definition of marriage, and appointed two replacements who had not attended these hearings and who were already fully committed to same-sex marriage. Prime Minister Chretien's actions were duplicitous and reprehensible. It was surely very unfair to replace the informed committee members with others who had not attended the hearings. Thus our cause was lost.

In 2003 the British Columbia government, appointed a Citizens Assembly to recommend a new electoral system for the province. On May 25, 2004, I had the privilege of addressing members of the Citizens Assembly. I presented my eight-page brief entitled, "*A Blended Electoral System: Plurality Single Member Districts with Regional Proportional Representation.*" It was well-received.

Writing for the General Public 1994 - 2010

During these years, I was fortunate to have quite a few articles published in major newspapers. Here are a few of the numerous items. "Democracy and fairness were casualties in the Quebec referendum," *Kitchener-Waterloo Record* (December 5, 1995); "Can Christians be socialists?," *The London Free Press* (January 4, 1997); and "STV in practice falls far from the theory," *The Vancouver Sun* (March 30, 2005).

The perhaps less consequential ones included "The Components of Successful Teaching," *Laurier Campus News* (January 24, 1995); "A National Referendum on Quebec Separatism Might Embarrass Ottawa," *Laurier Campus News* (Spring, 1997); "The great promise of Christian camping," *Mennonite Brethren Herald* (April 8, 2005); and "Stillwood Camp and Conference Centre," *GAMEO online* (March 2010).

In these years, our local paper, *The Abbotsford News*, generally had two pages of editorials, letters and opinion articles. *The News* published about 15 of my submissions. The many response letters in my own community made this a stimulating and delightful exercise. My list of articles appearing on those pages includes the following. "Democracy a casualty in Quebec," (December 11, 1995); "Canadian leadership was expressed in building Arrow," (August 28, 1997); "Strong evidence supports Christianity as roots of democracy," (July 22, 1999); "A math review is in order," (October 8, 1999); "Councilor points out 'flaws' in argument," (March 9, 2000); "Electoral system needs element of proportionality," (June 8, 2004); "Our political system is not a farce," (October 22, 2004); "Notwithstanding clause should be perfectly acceptable option," (February 3, 2005); and "Questions and answers about Gaza conflict," (January 8, 2009).

General Speaking Engagements 1994 - 2010

Among my varied speaking engagements during these years were the times, typically two to three a year, when I addressed an Abbotsford seniors organization, Learning Plus. Each event consisted of two one-hour periods with time for discussion and questions in the second hour. Here are some topics presented. "Terrorism and its Consequences," (November 7, 2001); "Crisis in the Middle East," (November 12, 2003); "Is Canada a Colony of the US?" (February 10, 2005); "A Third World Country in Crisis – Congo," (February 15, 2005); "Politics Under God; What are the Issues?" (November 22, 2007); and "Understanding the American Election, 2008," (October 15, 2008).

My non-Learning Plus presentations included the following. "The Sumas Energy 2 Plant," Langley Rotary Club (October 11, 2000); "The Death Penalty," Arts and Peace Festival, University College of the Fraser Valley (February 26, 2001); "What can City Government do in the Development of Abbotsford?" Abbotsford-Sumas Rotary Club (August 7, 2002); "Urbanization, Secularization and Religious Dispersion," University College of the Fraser Valley (June 7, 2003); and "Can Chinese in Greater Vancouver Work in Solidarity for Good Will and Peace?" Overseas Chinese Association, Vancouver (October 9, 2005).

During these years, I was privileged to do numerous interviews for radio audiences. Here are some examples. "Socialism in BC Politics," with Terry O'Neil, radio 1050 (August 11, 1999); "Civil disobedience," interview with Manny Bazunis, CFUN, Vancouver (May 21, 2001); "Broadcast News," interview with Link Byfield on various topics, Edmonton (June 6, 2001); "The SE2 Power Plant Controversy," CBC Radio (May 24, 2002); Interview with Michael Smith on the political scene, CKNW and the Corus Radio Network (May 16, 2005); Interview with Sean Lesley on "The World Today" CKNW radio (December 30, 2005); General Interview CBC Radio The Early Edition (August 27, 2009); and CKWX Radio 11:30 interview about Stephen Harper, Jack Layton, and Michael Ignatieff (September 13, 2009).

Awards and Affirmation 1994 - 2010

Some months after my early retirement from Wilfrid Laurier University I was informed that the WLU Board of Governors had awarded me the title Professor Emeritus for my 26 years of professorial work at and for the university. I was and remain deeply grateful for this designation.

Early in the morning, August 25, 2000, I got a phone call from our son, Dr. Gary Redekop, a neurosurgeon living in West Vancouver. I knew he was an early riser but he had not previously phoned me that early. He asked if I had already read the *Vancouver Sun*. I said I had not. As I recall, he made no further comment. I went out to get our copy. I did not know for what I was looking. I noticed the two front-page headlines: "Who are B.C.'s biggest thinkers? Meet the top 50" and "Missing teen was beating victim." I looked further. Then I began reading the top story. It continued on two more pages. Then I suddenly saw it. I could not believe my eyes, but there it was. **23. JOHN REDEKOP, TWU** *This dogged political scientist at the Christian private school, Trinity Western University, articulately advocates responsibly injecting more religious values into the public sphere.* It is not an exaggeration to say I was stunned. At that time I had no idea that *Sun* columnist Douglas Todd had been reading my writings for some years. Naturally, as the ranking and the publicity sank in, I was both humbled and grateful. I read all three pages. When I read that I ranked eight spots higher than Dr. Martha Piper, President of UBC, I smiled but not too much; that would be unseemly. Later I got to know Douglas Todd. I discovered that while he does not identify with evangelicals he has great respect for us, especially evangelical Anabaptists, for our theology and our impact on society. I shall always remain deeply grateful to Douglas Todd.

At this point, I shall recount another major and unexpected development. A typical Stillwood Board meeting was scheduled for the evening of January 23, 2001. For me, this was somewhat problematic because the next morning Doris and I were leaving for a week's holiday in Hawaii. At that time John Letkemann was the board chairman. For the previous three and a half years I had had the joy of reporting major donations for our site renewal and expansion project. As I recall, about $7 million had been received by that time. When Chairman Letkemann handed out the agenda I noticed a Special Item on the agenda. Hopefully, this would not take too long because I wanted to get away as early as possible. When we got to that agenda item the chairman began reading the following document.

Stillwood Fundraiser Fund

"These funds are earmarked for the private use of the fundraiser for the purpose of pleasure, relaxation, rejuvenation, recharging, stimulation, exhilaration, revitalization, similar big words that may apply as defined by the fundraiser designated in this....[The fund will cover] one all-expense paid trip for two to Hawaii.
(At this point, the truth suddenly dawned on me!) [It] includes airfare, lodging, food, snorkel rental, transportation, recreational activities, video rentals, hula lessons and various and sundry expenses but not including tobacco.
Conditions and Limits: Upon successful return, the fundraiser must prove that the funds were appropriately used by the demonstration of the hula dance at the next board meeting."

What an incredible surprise for me. Doris had been informed in advance. Doris and I had a wonderful holiday in Honolulu from January 24 to 31.

Enjoying Hawaii

It is always a delight when others find your speaking or writing helpful and especially when what one does is affirmed. During these years, **The Word Guild,** a national association of writers, publishers, and a variety of other folk, saw fit to grant me a total of seven writing awards, one in 2008, three in 2009, and three in 2010. I will mention three. "Is all punishment bad?" *Mennonite Brethren Herald* (2009); `Stillwood, the first 50 years," *Beacon Magazine* (2009); and "Moral issues to consider in the voting booth," *B C Christian News* (2010).

As I recall, it was in early 2009 that Harold Jantz, an esteemed writer and one of Canada's top Christian editors, contacted me to say that he was preparing a book about key men and women who had shaped the Canadian Mennonite Brethren Conference and that I would soon be contacted by another established writer, James Toews, pastor of a church in Nanaimo, BC. Soon James set up an interview. In 2010, the book **Canadian Mennonite Brethren 1910 - 2010; Leaders who Shaped Us,** edited by Harold Jantz, was published by Kindred Productions. The volume consists of 25 short biographies about ten pages in length. I am deeply indebted to James and to Harold for the kind and affirming words about me that appear in this book. Here are some excerpts.

> *"John became, arguably, the most well-known Canadian MB and at times the most trusted voice of the conference.... This sense of responsibility to his parents and the that they had passed on to him would be an impulse that would carry him through the challenges he would face as a change agent within the church....[He became] the most prolific, visible and longest-running voice of the Mennonite Brethren in the second half of the 20th century,...*
>
> *In the end, however, it may well be his 40 years as the writer of the Personal Opinion column by which he is best remembered. It is here that he was able to bring the insights of a scholar onto the ground on which Mennonite Brethren actually lived. For an Anabaptist scholar, that is, after all, the ultimate test of credibility, to scratch where it itches. On that score, John's place as noteworthy figure in the MB world is unambiguously established."*

Thank you, James. Thank you, Harold.

Relevant Religious Developments in the Larger Arenas 1994 - 2010

The Canadian religious landscape was changing markedly in these years. Here are some numbers provided by the Pew Research Centre. Between 1971 and 2011 the category *Religiously Unaffiliated* increased in Canada from 4% to 24%. In that same period the percentage of Canadians who described themselves as *Protestant* declined from 41% to 27%. Church attendance also dropped sharply. In 1986 reasonably regular church attendance in Canada was 42%; by 2012 it had declined to 27%. The US situation, while also disappointing, was significantly better. Between 1986 and 2012 total church attendance in the US declined from 54% to 46%.

Not surprisingly, during these years specifically, Christian programming, including the popular *Hymn Sing,* virtually disappeared from the CBC radio and television networks. Aside from paid broadcasts, they also gradually disappeared from the other networks.

Denominationally these were very difficult years for Canadian Mennonite Brethren. What follows are personal observations and experiences. Some context is needed. By various metrics, the Canadian MB Conference structure adopted in 1968, with several revisions, served its constituency well. Not surprisingly, some members and some leaders pressed for basic change. When Jascha Boge, a highly respected churchman and also a very successful Winnipeg businessman, became Canadian Moderator in 2000, he and the Executive Board began initiating major changes. Most importantly, key national boards with demonstrated competence in their area of responsibility were eliminated. This trend reached its apex at the 2004 Toronto national convention when, under moderator Boge's leadership, all boards were eliminated except the Board of Faith and Life which was kept in an advisory role and, of course, the Executive Board itself. A new position was created, the office of the national Chief Executive Officer, the CEO. I was disappointed by these developments and thought they would turn out to be dysfunctional for the Canadian MB Conference.

The new CEO was to be given immense authority and power. The 26-page job description and rationale basically assigned to him all of the responsibilities formerly assigned to the national boards. The national boards consisting of both elected and appointed members with expertise in that field were gone. The CEO position included an array of roles from financial manager to conference minister.

At this point my reporting becomes personal. At the 2004 Toronto convention I publicly opposed this proposed transition. As an experienced conference leader, I could not support a major proposal which I considered to be very seriously flawed. I had prepared a statement explaining why I thought that this shift was theologically flawed and organizationally unwise. When it was my turn to speak I carefully read my statement. I argued that the results would be negative and detrimental. After I had finished my speech a fairly young delegate spoke. He said that for me to question the executive board's recommendation was "like slapping God in the face." There was stunned silence. Importantly, neither Moderator Boge nor any Executive Board member rose to set the young delegate straight and to remind him that open debate had been invited and was appropriate. All of the leaders let this inappropriate condemnation stand. I have attended at least 35 national conventions but never before or since have I seen national leaders allow such an insulting and misguided statement to go uncorrected.

I had warned that abolishing the Board of Publications, the Board of Management, and the Board of Evangelism would lead to problems. So what happened? Not surprisingly, it took some years before the policies and practices of the earlier organization were lost and the new reality took full effect. Subsequent history has validated my concerns and warning. One crucial example is that the conference's financial situation gradually deteriorated very seriously. The reserves fell from $17.7 million to $2.9 million. Apparently, many millions of dollars were mismanaged and misappropriated. Reliable estimates put the mismanaged total at more than $20 million. The problems did not involve illegality, as far as I know, but bad decisions. In a candid report of failure, issued on October 23, 2019, Canadian Moderator Bruce Enns stated that "We were reluctant to hold individuals and MB family entities accountable." "We spent too much money while engaged with other things." Reflecting on the situation, an earlier national moderator, Harold Froese, wrote that "The financial statement is devastating...the numbers are staggering." I firmly believe that had we kept the Board of Management in place, then this financial fiasco would not have happened.

The *Mennonite Brethren Herald,* with all of its sometimes controversial but widely-read columnists removed and all timely and interesting controversy avoided, lost much of its reader interest. It soon consisted mainly of conference reports, fine Biblical studies, and mission reports. All of these segments are commendable but they are weak in holding readers' interest. Instead of revitalizing this key conference flagship periodical, the Conference leaders then shut down the *Mennonite Brethren Herald.*

With no program boards reporting, with virtually no issues presented for discussion and decision, and with the locale shifted to big downtown hotels, delegate interest flagged and almost disappeared. During the past year or two, the historically vital conventions have been replaced by meetings of provincial and national leadership boards. Direct accountability to delegates has ended. With no periodical and no conventions, it is hard to see how member interest and financial support will be sustained. Social networks and websites may not be up to the task. It has become abundantly evident that not all change is necessarily commendable.

There is a minor sequel to the 2004 convention. A few weeks after that historic Toronto session, two highly-regarded members of the Executive Board asked to meet with me. Because of my respect for them, I shall not name them. They wanted me to withdraw my objection to the fundamental changes made in Toronto. They stressed that I should support what had been decided. They wanted me "to end well," not in opposition. I calmly stated that I could not withdraw my objection because I believed it was valid. We parted on friendly terms but without resolution.

Relevant Political and Public Affairs 1994 - 2010

The second Sovereignty Referendum held in Quebec on October 30, 1995, almost broke up the country; 49.4% of Quebec voters supported separation while 50.6% were opposed. With a turnout of 93%, that was an ominous outcome. How MBs or Christians in the rest of Canada would or should react to a dismemberment of Canada was discussed widely. Good answers remained and remain elusive.

On July 25, 2005 the Liberal government led by Prime Minister Paul Martin legalized same-sex marriage. It is true that some court decisions had pushed the Ottawa government in this direction but the Liberal government made no serious effort to uphold the traditional, and the traditional Liberal, definition of marriage. Significantly, Catholic Prime Minister Martin once told a reporter that he left his Catholic ethics at the door when he entered the House of Commons.

On January 23, 2006, with a Conservative electoral win, Stephen Harper, apparently a member of a Christian and Missionary Alliance Church, became Prime Minister. Many Christians hoped that he would uphold certain evangelical and long-standing Canadian views on abortion and other issues, but they were disappointed. Prime Minister Harper believed, perhaps rightly, that to achieve electoral success, there must be no restriction of abortion. This policy left Canada as the only developed country that has no abortion law. In the 2006 election campaign Prime Minister Harper again pledged not to place any limitation on abortion.

He and the Conservatives won a second minority victory. On May 2, 2011, the Conservatives finally won a majority victory with the same promise. Prime Minister Harper held firm to his views on abortion policy.

Another noteworthy development was that Bradley Wall, a long-time member of the Bridgeway Mennonite Brethren Church in Swift Current, Saskatchewan, became Premier of Saskatchewan on November 21, 2007. He served in this office until February 2, 2018. All along, he retained high voter support. Many Christians and obviously many Mennonite Brethren were surprised and disappointed when he resigned. More than a few pundits had considered him to be a possible future prime minister.

Concerning the US in these years, three developments deserve special mention. President Bill Clinton's impeachment and Senate trial in 1998-1999 shook many Americans' respect for the office of president. In the US Senate sixty-seven YES votes were required to convict the president. Fifty senators voted for conviction and fifty against. This result was widely seen not as a vote on the merits of the case but as a politically partisan decision.

The second item is the "9-11" tragedy. On September 11, 2001, nineteen Muslim terrorists, fifteen of whom had roots in Saudi Arabia, hijacked four planes. They flew two into the World Trade Center Twin Towers in New York, which created massive destruction and huge loss of life. They crashed the third into the Pentagon. In the fourth plane, the terrorists were challenged by passengers and crashed in Pennsylvania. The two key consequences were a deep antagonism towards Muslims and the embarrassing realization by Americans that the continental USA no longer enjoyed security against terrorist attacks. Many US Christians became even more passionate patriots. Sadly, some took up anti-Muslim stances with fervour.

The third item was the election on November 4, 2008, of Barak Obama as the first African-American president. Many Christians affirmed this result even when disagreeing with some of the 44th president's policies.

My Spiritual Pilgrimage 1994 - 2010

I believe that every person's spiritual pilgrimage is a complex blend of thoughts, convictions, commitments, and actions. It is therefore difficult to present a complete picture. What one can do is convey some important elements.

I do not recall a time when I did not believe the basic teachings about Jesus and God's dealings with humanity. I frequently had to remind myself, however, that mere knowledge is insufficient in God's purview. After all, we know that Satan and his minions fully believe the facts of God's dealings with people. Such knowledge is necessary but insufficient. Given my numerous roles and offices and consequent extensive activities, I needed to remind myself that God is much more interested in our being than our doing. Doing is never a substitute for being. God's first desire is to have disciples who have a strong relationship with him. Activities, while important, are always secondary. Christian ministry and accomplishments should not be minimized or judged as unimportant but should be viewed in line with Matthew 5: 16: "Let your light shine before men, that they may see your good deeds and praise your Father in heaven."

A related challenge for me was to set the right priorities. My goal was to set my relationship to God first, my family second, and then my many activities third. The temptation for me was to reverse the order. I believe that many busy Christians are tempted to settle for the better while missing the best. I remind myself frequently that Christianity is not a performance industry. My Saviour and Lord is much more interested in who I am than in what I do.

John building a garden bridge, 2003. Woodwork was a secondary hobby.

Stillwood Memories

Stillwood's theme building: "Be still and know that I am God."

Stillwood supporters. L to R: Doris, John, Verna Wiens, John Wiens, Abe Kroeker, Kroekers' son, Anne Kroeker, Peter Dueck, Lena Dueck.

Left: Henry Schroeder cutting the celebration cake.
Right: Henry Schroeder and John at the dedication of the Mary Schroeder Pool.

CHAPTER 16

LIVING IN ABBOTSFORD 2011 - 2021

Living in Abbotsford

Although we greatly enjoyed living in our townhouse on Spur Avenue in Abbotsford, we gradually realized that the time had come to move into a residence without stairs. We therefore sold our home and on November 22, 2013, moved into a fine condo unit, #1002, in Garden Park Tower on Clearbrook Road. I have missed even the limited outside gardening I could do at the townhouse but I have not missed shovelling snow from the driveway. Given that we knew many residents in the tower, that many of our friends lived in the region, and that many of our activities at home and elsewhere did not change, this relocation did not require significant adjustments. Our daily and weekly routines generally continued as before, only with more free time. I should add that we greatly enjoyed the views from our tenth-floor condo and we also very much enjoyed dining in the Rose Room Coffee Shop and in the Magnolia Room Restaurant in our building. We also enjoyed being able to buy fresh and frozen meals on site.

Less than two years later we faced another decision. Much as we enjoyed our tenth-floor condo we missed being able to see the mountains to the east and especially the majestic, snow-covered slopes of Mt. Baker. In late spring 2015 we were informed that if we were willing to relocate, we could purchase the lend-lease agreement to move into a 16th-floor condo unit facing east and south. We decided to make the move. We had no difficulty in selling the lend-lease ownership of our tenth-floor unit and on July 11, 2015, we moved into #1607 on the 16th floor. From here we have an amazing panoramic view of more than 160 degrees, including an incredible view of Mt. Baker. Fortunately, the almost 1,600 square feet of space in our corner unit still enables us to host many visitors, including groups. We greatly enjoy living in this condo, almost surely our last private home.

During these years, our three grandchildren continued to bring much joy into our lives.

Three grandchildren: Michelle, Danielle, David.

Like all of God's people we have had many opportunities to help others, some local and some farther, even much farther, afield. One of our projects for about ten years has been to provide between 40 and 60 jars of jam, generally not small jars, to a family in Vancouver which deserved such support. Generally, I picked most of the fruit and Doris did the bulk of the work required for canning. We are pleased that we are able to continue this ministry in 2021, although for the first time on a reduced scale.

Doris and jam jars, 2020.

Jam jar production in an earlier year.

During these years we have been able to take various holiday trips, typically a week-long stay in Mexico or Hawaii or some other warm location, and also to Canadian and American destinations. Our friends Carl and Mary Durksen accompanied us on most of the longer trips. Although times spent in Honolulu, Mazatlán, Los Cabos, Jamaica, Cuba, New York, Mesa and other tourist areas were all very enjoyable, one trip had a very strong impact on me.

Holidays with Carl and Mary Durksen.

On the Mexican coast with Carl and Mary Durksen.

In July 2018 the Durksens and we drove to Drumheller, Alberta, to see the Passion Play in the Badlands. We have seen other excellent Passion Play productions including the elaborate one in Puyallup, Washington and, of course, the famous one in Oberammergau, Germany, but for me the one in Drumheller was the most realistic and nspiring. I might add that we also greatly enjoyed touring the Badlands and museum and seeing the dinosaur skeletons. That part of the trip once again raised a lot of theological, geological and creation questions in my mind.

John and Doris with their Bakerview Church Care Group in Stillwood Chapel.
L to R: John, Doris, Keith Hostetler, Luella Unger, Nora Kroeker, Helmut and Gerda Fandrich, Carl Durksen, Lena Block , Mary Durksen, Laura Unger, Dorothy and Diet Rempel.

Doris and John in Mexico.

On August 21, 2016, Doris and I would celebrate our 60th wedding anniversary. We decided to celebrate this important milestone by offering our children and grandchildren an expense-paid holiday at Whistler, BC. All of our children and spouses and one of our three grandchildren could come. We had a fabulous time, August 5 to 7, in this justifiably renowned mountain retreat.

Our 60th wedding anniversary dinner.
L to R: Wendy Carmichael, Craig Carmichael, Bonnie (also known as Satya), Danielle Charbonneau, John, Doris, Billy Wright, Lee Ann Wills, Heather Harmony, Gary Redekop, Yun Kang (then Heather's husband).
Missing: David and Michelle Redekop.

Aside from our celebration dinner on August 6, for me the highlight was taking the Peak-to-Peak Gondola from one mountain to another. The panoramic views are breathtaking.

Celebrating our 60th anniversary in the Whistler mountains.

On August 23, Doris and I again celebrated our anniversary with a holiday in the delightful town of Leavenworth, WA, where we enjoyed the Sound of Music in the amphitheatre setting in a nearby wooded hillside.

We have greatly enjoyed living in Garden Park Tower for seven and a half years. Apart from the COVID-19 interruption we have continued worshiping and being active in the Bakerview Church and have had many enjoyable and blessed times participating in our care group. I also served as chairperson of the Board of Human Resources and on Church Council for several years until April 2017.

Since we moved to Garden Park Tower in 2013 I served for several years as chair of the Events Committee, and from May 2014 until July 2016, I edited the 20-page monthly *Garden Park Journal*. This magazine was very well-received in both hardcopy and online versions. It closed in July 2016 because of some disagreement about whether the subsidy was worth the result. Since September 2018, I have edited the four-page *Garden Park Newsletter,* which is also well-received in both hardcopy and online.

Stillwood - Later Developments 2014 - 2021

In later years I again did some fundraising for Stillwood. By 2017 I had, by the grace of God and the generosity of several major donors, especially John, Edith and Carol Dyck and Ken Dyck, raised the needed $1.6 million to build the beautiful Stillwood Chapel.

In 2020, when the COVID pandemic closed down Stillwood and a financial emergency was imminent, I was again asked to help. By contacting known supporters I was able to raise about $220,000 in a few weeks to help in this crisis. Some months later I was contacted about another Stillwood project. This time a more modest $20,000 was needed. That, too, could be found.

Giving a Stillwood tour to donors and potential donors.

According to my records, I was able, with God's enablement and empowerment, to raise about $13 million for capital purposes for Stillwood and, over the years, about $300,000 for other purposes ranging from funds for our anniversary book to buying a small truck. I thank all donors and I also express sincere thanks to the many businesses and tradespeople whom I contacted and who, after always congenial negotiations, donated a broad spectrum of services and materials. These ranged from landscaping supplies from several nurseries to a large number of chairs from a condo complex and from a huge amount of delivered concrete by Greystone Concrete - thank you, John (recently deceased), Verna, and Graeme Wiens - to an excellent Kubota tractor with the needed attachments which Ken Dyck helped us get for Stillwood. They also ranged from concrete services by Darrell Rempel, "Captain Concrete," to electrician service over almost two decades by Peter Unger. Many companies not named here donated material or provided it at a reduced cost.

Special guests at the dedication of the Red Barn.
L to R: John and Doris Redekop, Edith and John Dyck, Canada's finest.

They cannot be listed here but God knows who they are. A special thanks must also go to the hundreds of volunteer workers who toiled to help develop the new Stillwood. Harry and I both recruited many.

One special undertaking must not be overlooked. In about 2015, Abe Friesen, an Abbotsford taxidermist of considerable renown, contacted me about seeing his collection. I was impressed. His wife, Mary, had recently passed away and, as he put it, he was also getting older. He then said that he wanted to donate his entire collection to Stillwood. I was surprised. I was then greatly impressed after viewing the collection. Abe's exhibits included every animal native to BC and a few birds. Importantly, he had validation certificates for all of them except for one small bird. It was obviously a very valuable collection. There were some negotiation challenges to overcome. Even the Stillwood board was very hesitant. In fact, Abe passed away before all the negotiations were completed. After his death the last problems were resolved, and I am delighted to say that this amazing collection is now housed at Stillwood.

My various Stillwood tasks took considerable time. In fact, if I take into account all the meetings, the preparation for meetings of the Stillwood board and its committees, computer time, phone time, the preparation for fundraising, related research, correspondence, planning for project dedications, meetings with architects and trades, soliciting donations, recruiting volunteers and arranging for their transportation, travel, tours given to potential and past donors, keeping my files up to date, and many other activities it is safe to say that for the first ten years of my involvement at Stillwood I averaged about two days, 16 hours a week, in Stillwood-related activity. That amounts to 40 percent of the usual work-week. My best estimate is that during the last ten years of my volunteering, the total of Stillwood-related work was considerably less, averaging about 8 hours or one day a week.

Appendix C lists the individual capital projects for which I solicited funds and includes pictures of some of the major projects.

Some people have asked whether I enjoy fundraising. I have to think about that question. The work itself is not enjoyable. For most people, the most sensitive nerve runs to their wallet. It is not enjoyable to touch that nerve. At all times one must be ready for an unceremonious rejection, on occasion even from a friend, although that happened only a few times. Many a time I have driven up to a building for an appointment and then sat a while in the car wiping the dashboard, tapping the steering wheel, praying, checking my materials, or rehearsing my introductory words. Usually, when I got out of the car and walked towards the building my courage returned. I should admit, however, that more than once I secretly hoped that the people had forgotten and were not home.

Maybe I should end my Stillwood story at this point, but that would leave it seriously incomplete.

These later developments have continuing major impact on the BCMB Conference, its member churches, the larger community and, indeed, the whole Lower Mainland. The termination of further site development and the abrupt and totally unexpected termination of my leadership and fundraising were very consequential developments. Also, many people are still asking questions about what happened. Finally, this story was a very large part of my life. For these reasons, I will summarize the rest of my Stillwood-related experiences.

Some historical context is needed. When the private sector Columbia Bible Camp Society handed over Columbia Bible Camp to the BCMB Conference in June 1992, the Conference spelled out two conditions. First, because it very much wanted to have a retreat and conference centre the name must be changed to Columbia Bible Camp and Conference Centre. That was done. Second, because the BCMB Conference did not want to deal with any of its camps directly; an intermediary body encompassing camp leaders and persons elected by the BCMB Conference, the Camp Ministries Committee, should be created. That body was created and with this model, Stillwood and the other camps, eventually five in total, all flourished.

In 1993 Henry Esau, who had a very strong record of leadership and success with Mennonite Brethren camping in Ontario, was hired as Executive Director to improve existing facilities and bring about the establishment of the desired conference centre. In March 1996, as already described, he convinced me to come on board to help him and his board achieve the dual goal: renewal of Columbia and, most importantly, development of the retreat and conference centre. Henry soon made impressive progress. Major improvements were made.

In March 1997, Harry Edwards became the new Executive Director. He assisted in major ways in the site redevelopment and expansion. By 2007 the renewal and major expansion of the original campsite was nearing completion. As a Board, we then began planning seriously for the retreat and conference centre. All along, we had included BCMB leaders in our development, most notably at groundbreaking and project dedications. We received only grateful affirmation. Also, of course, the leaders of the owning Conference had to sign or authorize the signing of all legal documents and thereby approve the projects.

Because of the 2008 recession, major donor development and actual fundraising, other than for the conference-approved Stillwood chapel, was halted for some years. Major donors continued to express caution and were very reluctant about writing large cheques. By late 2014 the situation had improved. Also, as described previously, thanks to a very generous donor, Stillwood had acquired the two hobby farms immediately to the west of the main campsite. During 2014 we discussed various aspects in the development of what we called Phase Two on those 40 acres. The BCMB leadership would also be involved because, as already noted, as officers of the owning Conference they made the final decisions concerning applications for all permits, zoning changes, variances, etc.

Because we were anticipating required funding of at least $20 million, I was concentrating on donor development, focusing on about 30 potential major donors. All donations of whatever size were, of course, always much appreciated, but for this huge project I was in discussion mainly with potential major donors. All along, Stillwood's very capable Executive Director, Harry Edwards, and the Stillwood Board made sure that all planning, as well as all ongoing activities, were fully in compliance with Canada Revenue Agency, regional, and other requirements. Any later complaints that he was not doing this were not based on the facts.

Then lightning struck! In July 2016, the BCMB Executive Board, under the leadership of the Conference Minister and the Conference Moderator, suddenly halted all planning and donor development. They ignored the fact that their decision-making process violated the 1992 transfer agreement and that the reasons given for their action were vague and flawed. The next year, on October 31, 2017, all my Stillwood activity came to an end. Again the decision-making process violated the 1992 transfer agreement. The continuing Conference Minister and three BCMB Conference Moderators in quick succession thus broke the main Conference commitment not to deal directly with any one camp, let alone interfere in a camp's operations. Inexplicably, they also ignored the Conference's strong request in 1992 that a retreat and conference centre should be developed as soon as possible.

The Stillwood Board and, of course, I, as Board chair, were stunned. We asked if we had done something wrong. Had we created any financial, legal, moral, or any other kind of problem for the owning BCMB Conference? At that time the Conference leaders and a senior staff member did not raise any problem about Stillwood's entire operation. Stillwood has nothing on file about any concerns ever raised by the BCMB Conference leaders about Stillwood before my dismissal.

For me, this turn of events, this surprising action, this public humiliation was by far the most painful experience I have ever had. I remember sitting in my chair in our living room for several hours in bewilderment and grief. I tried to make sense out of what made no sense. I had to come to terms with the fact that my more than 20 years of volunteer Stillwood development for the BCMB Conference had been rejected by them. For several weeks, while under medical care, I was sorry that I had ever begun volunteering, let alone working so hard, for the BCMB Conference in developing Stillwood. For a few weeks I thought that doing this demanding ministry was the biggest mistake I had ever made.

During the next two and a half years I tried at various times to meet with the Conference Minister and the Moderator to find out why they had acted as they had, to hear their reasons, to discuss matters, and work toward a resolution. I had no success. They agreed to meet with me but only if my dismissal would not be on the agenda. That did not make much sense to me. Here are a few excerpts from some of our correspondence.

In response to one of my requests for a meeting, the Conference Minister wrote on June 14, 2019, that he and the Moderator were prepared to meet with me, but "The objective in this meeting is pastoral and personal…This meeting is not to arbitrate or mediate disputes." On June 21, I wrote to him saying that "it is important that when there are differences between Christians, they need to be in communication with one another and should try to clear up whatever needs to be cleared up." I then asked if we could at least meet to talk about what should be on the agenda. On July 2, he responded by writing that "This agenda is simple…and remains as it was originally made. I do not believe it is helpful or appropriate for you and me to meet to determine a different agenda…." On July 5, I wrote to both the Conference Minister and the Moderator stating that:

> *"It is right for Christians to settle disputes between them. I hereby ask you, as a Christian leader, together with [the Moderator], are you willing to meet with me to talk things through with me, and a trusted facilitator? This is not a complicated problem. We can resolve it if we want to. That is the outcome for which I hope and pray."*

I specifically hoped to hear from the Moderator. She is, after all, our Conference leader while the Conference Minister is the senior staff person. She did not respond. She repeatedly ignored letters from me and others. The Conference Minister's response had not changed. They were willing to meet with me but only to give me pastoral help in my pain and only if my dismissal would not be on the agenda. I was, however, offered free attendance with my wife at a weekend retreat for failed pastors, as I understood it.

Following my dismissal I received many expressions of support. Also, during these years many Stillwood supporters wrote to the BCMB leaders about my situation. Several sought to achieve resolution. All such efforts were rebuffed. During these years several Stillwood support groups organized themselves informally and tried to help. There were petitions with many signatures. They were all rebuffed; some submissions were not even acknowledged. In January 2020, another such group organized itself as the Reconciliation Advocates. It was determined to bring satisfactory closure to this fatiguing saga. This group hired a highly competent, widely acclaimed, and totally neutral Christian investigator, David Leis, to investigate the situation and report his findings. He had no knowledge about the controversy. He had no significant relationship with any of the people involved and had never even been to Stillwood. He approached his assignment with an open mind and no pre-conception.

After thoroughly investigating the twelve allegations which the Reconciliation Advocates had identified as accusations that the BCMB Conference leaders had eventually made against me – after my dismissal on October 31, 20117 - he reported on December 1, 2020, that "none of the twelve [allegations] as stated have validity." In detail, he documented how each one was false. Importantly, a member of the BCMB Executive Board, present at all meetings of the Executive Board when action against me was discussed, had written after reviewing the twelve allegations before David Leis began his investigation, that "I have no recollection of any other noteworthy accusations being raised [against John] or discussed at our Executive Board meetings." This was obviously a very important statement. It confirmed that the twelve allegations included all substantive accusations made against me.

Significantly, on October 18, 2017 the BCMB Conference Moderator wrote the vice-chair of the Stillwood Board, Colin Reimer, but not to me as chair, that "John's presence on the Stillwood board has been a risk factor for BCMB [Conference]."

I did not see that letter until much later. That concern was never raised with me, let alone discussed with me. Surely such discussion should be normative for Christian leaders as it is in education, business and government employment. Significantly, David Leis investigated that accusation. In his official report he wrote that "based on the information reviewed it is NOT evident that John H. Redekop was indeed a risk. Rather, what is evident from this review is that he was a committed ministry leader who provided both support and incisive critique which, at times, was not welcomed or a risk to the implementation of various conference goals."

During David Leis's investigation, a very important document surfaced. It was written by a BCMB Executive Board member who, as mentioned above, was present at every meeting when the case against me was being developed. Importantly, this person is a highly regarded and ordained clergyman whose word is truth and whose character is impeccable. When I first read this excerpt quoted in the Leis Report, which was sent to all BC MB churches and to many Stillwood supporters, I was profoundly surprised, disillusioned and shocked. I was again stunned and developed serious insomnia. I had never before been dismissed from anything. Why should I, why should anyone, get fired for doing what is good? These words pierced me like a sword to my heart.

The quote is as follows:

"Furthermore, whenever these accusations were mentioned at the Board meetings, it consistently occurred to me that these accusations were based on assumptions without factual, documented evidence. The accusations were based on emotions and misinformation, notions which have been categorically proven to be false. The growing unchristian spirit and anger bordering on hate toward John Redekop around the Board table resulted in the firing of John Redekop, which I could not support....I knew that this action toward our own brother who had served the Stillwood Camp and the BC Conference with honour and distinction was misguided and unjust." (quoted with permission)

The realization that the BCMB Executive Board, which I had served faithfully and successfully as a hard-working volunteer for more than two decades, had strategized against me to a degree "bordering on hate," brought me to a state of stunned disbelief. I was humiliated and deeply hurt. My health and well-being were affected. I could not sleep.

I experienced other health challenges. I again sought medical help. This was a deep and dark valley in my life.

Not surprisingly, the Executive Board member who submitted this statement to David Leis found himself in such deep disagreement with how the Executive Board was treating me that he soon resigned from the Executive Board.

Given that there had been a series of mailings, by both sides, to the BCMB churches, the Reconciliation Advocates quite logically mailed the investigator's report to all BCMB churches. They hoped and assumed this would settle the matter and bring closure.

Unfortunately, the BCMB Conference leaders immediately rejected the neutral expert's detailed report. On February 9, 2021, the Conference Moderator sent her rejection of the investigator's report to all BCMB churches. I found it puzzling and somewhat amusing that in her letter rejecting David Leis's thorough and objective report, she named the investigator, David Leis, only once but continued her relentless opposition to me by referring to me by name no less than 13 times in her three-page letter about David Leis's report.

Fortunately, that was not the end of this very sad saga. In the spring of 2021, Herb Neufeld and Peter Nikkel, two highly esteemed retired pastors and former leaders in our conference, decided on their own that they would try again to bring about resolution and closure. With Christian firmness, determination, and grace, these two brothers achieved what I could not achieve. They convinced the Conference Minister and the Moderator to meet with me to discuss the basic problem. What a breakthrough that was! I was very grateful for this turn of events even though I had to sign a Covenant of Confidentiality which I considered to be unbiblical and inappropriate for such dealings among Christians. I most sincerely thank Herb and Peter.

On May 26, 2021, there was an historic session including the Conference Minister, the Conference Moderator and me, with two pastors present as observers, during which there were apologies and forgiveness was expressed by all. Together with the others present, I rejoiced that official closure had been achieved. That was a positive day for all of us. As stated, I was delighted and relieved to achieve what we did, namely, bring closure to this long, sad saga even if we did not achieve all that I had hoped we would achieve. Long before May 26, 2021, I had stressed that pursuing truth and coming to an agreement on what had happened were prerequisites for complete resolution. Many experts have stressed that the key prerequisite for resolution is to establish truth, and then proceed accordingly. I believe that is the right biblical guideline.

For valid reasons, the important statement all five of us signed was entitled ***A Statement of Closure***. I thank the Moderator and the Conference Minister for going at least that far.

Some readers might think that nothing more should be said about this depressing and absurd episode after forgiveness has been expressed. In response to such thinking it is instructive to recall how biblical writers dealt with failures, antagonisms, and difficult developments of many kinds. They did not gloat over them nor dwell on unnecessary details, but they did describe many of them at considerable length. Accordingly, we are told how and why Abraham lied in Egypt about Sarah; how Jacob deceived Isaac; how Joseph was brutally mistreated by his brothers; how, in 50 verses in Samuel 11 and 12, David committed major moral failings; about the quarrel between Paul and Barnabas; about Peter's three-fold denial of Jesus, and about the tragic deception by Ananias and Sapphira. These misdeeds and many others, many of them forgiven, are recounted by the inspired writers for us as helpful and instructive information. That has been my guideline in describing the major aspects of this multi-year saga.

As we all know, forgiveness, as officially happened on May 26, does not make the past go away. When we do wrong, we need to say, "I'm sorry," as was done on May 26, but that does not cancel the unfortunate consequences of the wrongdoing. Results remain, they cannot be undone. They cannot be blotted out and some have major and long-lasting consequences.

For me, the most important and truly sad consequence of this entirely unwarranted interference and obstruction by the continuing Conference Minister, by the BCMB Executive Board, and by three Conference Moderators is that the planning for and possible construction of a first-class retreat and conference centre was jettisoned. It is unfortunate that Conference leaders vigorously and consistently blocked the establishment of what their predecessors in office and their own supporting churches wanted and approved, a development that would have facilitated many ministries in the coming decades and beyond.

Knowing my cohort of faithful and generous Stillwood supporters and knowing the various stages of donor development, I believe that a $20 to $25 million excellent retreat and conference centre which would also have allowed for major expansion of the summer camp ministry, might now be under construction. The completed project would then be presented to the BCMB Conference without any cost. I speak here of a facility which our research indicated would have filled an urgent need. Our earlier investigation had confirmed that in the entire Lower Mainland of BC, with its more than 1,400 evangelical churches and more than 3.4 million residents, there was no substantial Christian conference and retreat centre. Because of the truly perplexing and short-sighted actions of BCMB Conference leadership, there still is no such centre. Sadly the confluence of factors that were in place and that made such a centre feasible no longer exists.

Let me stress the point. On May 26, 2021, I forgave the Conference Minister, the Conference Moderator, and the Executive Board members, although they were not present, for what they did to Stillwood and to me.

We now turn to some very important remaining questions. Why did the Conference leaders do what they did? Why did they not talk to me before the end of October 2017 about the concerns they later claimed they had? They never discussed them with me. Why did they, without the approval of the member churches, cavalierly reverse the longstanding Conference mandate that Stillwood should develop a retreat and conference centre? Why was the independent and neutral report by an outstanding investigator summarily rejected? I still shake my head in disbelief. When Conference leaders do something that goes against their own ethics and their own self-interest, as in this case, then it is hard to determine motives. When they act in a manner that is clearly not in the best interest of the Conference that they lead, then their decisions are puzzling.

It has been suggested that these Conference leaders got bad legal advice, or that from their perspective the Stillwood camp ministry was getting too large. It has also been suggested that they saw my major fundraising success not as a service for the Conference but as a threat to themselves, the Conference leaders. Sources close to the scene have also suggested that the Conference leaders were jealous of my major fundraising for the Conference or even, to quote one knowledgeable official, that ego and a "power trip" were involved. The truth remains a puzzling mystery.

Why would any charity abruptly terminate the work of its highly successful volunteer fundraiser who for two decades has worked hard to help fulfill the charity's mission, and do so without ever discussing their concerns with him? It is hard to imagine any other charity doing what the BCMB Executive Board and leaders did to a highly successful Stillwood Board and to a successful volunteer fundraiser. Be that as it may, the case is now closed. One fact, however, is clear. During this long, absurd, and sad saga it became very clear that the ethics practiced in a secular university are much higher than the ethics practiced by the BCMB Executive Board, the last three Moderators, and the continuing Conference Minister.

I cannot list all of the scores of people who did their best to achieve resolution. Four key people must, however, be recognized. Henry and Linda Esau deserve my special thanks. I cannot express too strongly my gratitude to them, especially Linda. In the months prior to May 26, the perceptive and wise intervention and major involvement by Herb Neufeld and Peter Nikkel, widely acknowledged as wise elder statesmen in the Conference, was crucial in achieving the meeting, which at least brought closure.

I also thank the hundreds of other supporters who connected with me.

All along, I heard from many people who said they supported me and were praying for me. That sustained me. I thank them all most sincerely.

Now I want to note one other matter. Although this has nothing to do with why my fundraising was terminated on October 31, 2017, it is a fact that while I was in deep grief and humiliation and under medical care, including medication after my dismissal, I did raise the matter of possible legal action and financial compensation. I even raised the possibility of contacting the public press. At the time, my mind was not thinking right. After I had recovered from my mental and emotional valley, I promptly apologized, in writing, to the Conference leaders and the Executive Board for even thinking of such action. Of course, nothing of this type of response was ever undertaken and, as stated, this had nothing to do with the termination of my fundraising activity – this happened later. I also inquired of the Moderator of that day whether there was anything else for which I should apologize. His answer was that there was nothing else.

For the future, I wish our BCMB Conference leaders all the best. Their responsibilities are extensive and their tasks are demanding. I hope and pray that they will be successful in their endeavors.

As I reflect on the vast array of experiences I had during my almost 21 years volunteering for Stillwood, my mind races through a vast spectrum of experiences. I think of the excellent board colleagues, Executive Director Harry Edwards and his wife, Gail, the incredible and always welcoming and genial Director of Food Service, of exceptionally competent Vice-Chair Colin Reimer and the many other amazing folk, both staff members and volunteers, who were part of the team. I think of the awesome expansion of the ministry and the thousands of children and others who decided to make Jesus the Lord of their life. I think of the many thousands of young people and adults for whom Stillwood was and remains a spiritual oasis. I think of the many thousands of community people for whom Stillwood was a wonderful mountain retreat. Of course, I also think of my list of hundreds of donors and the 54 projects they funded.

I also remember various challenges. We had to carry out tough negotiations with BC Parks because, for several important reasons, we wanted to do a land exchange with them. One reason was that BC Parks was planning to construct a road across our upper property. Our ever-alert and always very helpful supporter, Art Loewen, had alerted us about this planned incursion. We also had to deal with some very complex First Nations' claims. Sometime later we also had challenging negotiations with the BC's Agricultural Land Commission. Fortunately, the ALC granted Stillwood indefinite conditional use of the two hobby farms we had acquired.

In the last years, as noted above, I had to come to terms with the altogether unexpected strong opposition from the Conference Minister, one other senior staff member, the BCMB Conference Executive Board, and three Moderators. This was obviously not a happy ending to what I consider the most important Christian ministry of my life. This sad saga, however, does not negate the great joy I have had in contributing in some measure to the development and ministry of Stillwood. May God continue to bless it. May God continue to bless the tens of thousands who each year come to that mountain oasis for renewal of body, mind, spirit and soul.

Scholarly Research and Writing; Books 2011 - 2021

Although retired from full-time university teaching I have continued my research and writing. A caveat is needed. After my dismissal in October, 2017 and again after I became aware of the BCMB Executive Board and Conference leaders' intense animosity towards me, I often had difficulty concentrating on my reading and research. But with prayer and God's enablement I soldiered on as best I could.

In 2013 I wrote a chapter on *"The Mennonite Contribution to Abbotsford,"* for a book entitled **Being the Church in Abbotsford** published in 2013. It was enjoyable to research the contributions that Mennonites have made in an array of pursuits and their contributions during the approximately 80 years since the first Mennonites arrived in this part of the Fraser Valley.

In 2015 I produced a book entitled **The Tory Book**. It consists of two parts. The first part is a one-page or two-page set of mostly political statements and brief readings for each day of the year. The second part is a virtually complete summary of all of Prime Minister Harper's policies, programs, and legislation during his time in office. That detailed information is presented chronologically as well as by topic. The last 22 pages include serious and humorous definitions of major political ideologies, election data, population numbers, and the achievements of all previous Conservative Prime Ministers of Canada. I should explain that this book was published about six months before the October 19, 2015 Canadian election as a contribution to that election campaign.

In his Foreword to the book Preston Manning, the national Leader of the Reform Party in the House of Commons from 1993-2000, and Leader of the Official Opposition from 1997-2000, wrote these words:

> *"One of John's particularly valuable qualities is the ability to innovate, and this book is the latest example. Anyone can have a great idea, but John has put his inspiration into material form in this unique book that combines a compilation for each day of the year with a fascinating and impressive summary of the Conservative record under the leadership of Stephen Harper.... In sum, this book is an excellent resource for anyone interested in the coming election. It provides information not readily available elsewhere. For anyone who wants a quick resource about the Harper years in office, this is the book to get."*

Because of donations from Conservative supporters, copies of this book were made available to all constituencies across Canada. When it became clear that publication of the Harper record itself would be useful, a second book was published entitled, **The Harper Record**. Also published several months before the election, this smaller volume includes the Harper record and all the appendices. It also was made available to Conservative constituency organizations across Canada.

In 2018 a book was published entitled **The Church in Surrey & White Rock: The Untold Story.** I served as one of three editors and chaired the editorial committee. The four of us who worked hard to bring this project to completion - Neil Bramble (chair), Lloyd Mackey, Ross Johnston, and I - attempted, we believe with success, to inform churches, schools, social service agencies, community and political leaders, the media, educators, as well as the general public about what the Christian presence has meant and is meaning today for Surrey and White Rock.

In her back cover endorsement a former mayor of Surrey, Dianne Watts, wrote as follows:

> "***The Church in Surrey & White Rock: The Untold Story*** *is a great resource for people who are looking to understand the extensive impact the faith-based community has on our cities. It provides both an historical account of churches and first-hand experiences that affected change in the community and in people's lives. I am honoured to acknowledge both this book and the contribution our faith-based community has made in shaping our cities."*

The book includes a listing, with denominational and contact data, of all Christian places of worship in these two cities. We identified 336. It also includes data for worship centres of all other faiths. The book also provides listings of all Christian and other faith-based agencies ranging from nursing homes to Christian theater.

I wrote two chapters in this book and co-authored a third. I consider my concluding chapter, *Why Do Churches Do What They Do?* as my best statement on why Christians strive to make the love of Jesus practical in their communities.

In 2018 I submitted a six-page analysis of the various electoral systems to the BC Electoral Reform Commission: "British Columbia's Electoral Reform Referendum, October 14, 2018," (October 10, 2018).

On October 23, 2018 I posted a six-page analysis online: "Understanding and Explaining President Trump." It evoked considerable response, mostly supportive. I also received and welcomed some sharp criticism.

Interesting research and many delightful memories went into writing, "The Hungarians Come to Abbotsford," a chapter published in **Abbotsford, A Diverse Tapestry** (2021) edited by Robert Martens.

At various times I was invited to deliver academic lectures. On October 30, 2015, I presented a research paper entitled "How the Mennonite Experience Informs our Understanding of Religious Freedom," at a Trinity Western University Faculty Seminar. "A Critique of John Howard Yoder's Classic Analysis of Church-State Relations," was presented to the Council of Senior Professionals, Fresno, CA on April 16, 2019. A very interesting assignment for me was to research and write an analysis of President Trump, his policies, and political behaviour. On February 3, 1921 I presented "Trump and Trumpism: Some Reflections," to an online chat group.

At this point I should perhaps note that over the years I have had the privilege of writing a Foreword statement in books for quite a few authors. The list includes Arden Thiessen, Brian Stiller, Robert Thompson, Preston Manning, Walfred Goossen, John Sutherland, Jack Block, and Maria Foth. It is always a delight to read a new manuscript and write such an introductory endorsement.

Writing for the Christian Community 2011 - 2021

As in other years, I continued to write for Christian periodicals and organizations. "A Summary Description of the Organization and Operation of the Bakerview Mennonite Brethren Church," *Bakerview Church Council* (March 24, 2015); "Columbia Celebrates 75 years" *Light Magazine (*October, 2011); "Ministering to Low-German-Speaking Mennonites," *Square One World Media* (February 6, 2016); and "Some Comments on the Canadian Conference of Mennonite Brethren Churches" *On line Mennonite Brethren Herald* (January 30, 2017).

Of particular importance to me was the invitation to write a critical analysis on what was happening to the Canadian MB Conference. It appeared as "Canadian MB Crisis; Former denominational leader describes problems, offers ideas to overcome shortage of funds, loss of loyalty," *Mennonite World Review (*February 27, 2017).

A slightly modified version of this statement is available online as "Canadian Mennonite Brethren Crisis," *Mennonite World Review (February 27, 2017).*

Addressing the Christian Community 2011 - 2021

Among the many enjoyable speaking engagements in this period were my continuing presentations to the large Current Issues Class at the Bakerview Church. "A Critique of John Howard Yoder's Classic Analysis of Church-State Relations," (July, 2011); "Amazing Mennonite Success in Paraguay; a Prison Church," (September 25, 2011); "Key Issues Concerning the Legalization of Marijuana," (November 13, 2011); "What is Stuart Murray Telling US? Part I" (January 12, 2012); "Reflections on a Contemporary Anabaptist Vision - Stuart Murray Part II," (April 1, 2012); "How Should the Great Commission Guide Christians in the Secularization and Islamization of Europe?" (July 15, 2012); "Issues Facing American Voters November 6, 2012" (November 4, 2012); "Secular Humanism and Christian Faith; The Conflict Concerning a Law School at Trinity Western University," (May 26, 2013); "How Should We Live in the Midst of Religious Pluralism?" (August 11, 2013); and "Christianity and Islam; Demographics and Trends," (August 31, 2014).

Additional Current Issues presentations included the following. "Key Political Issues for Christians: Locally, Provincially, Nationally, Globally," (September 28, 2014); "Changes in Being a Senior," (May 24, 2015); "Does Christianity Align with any Political Ideology?" (October 11, 2015); "Assisted Suicide; Fit to Die," (September 11, 2016); "Four Responses to the Erosion of Public Morality," (February 26, 2017); "Islam Today: Threat and Mission Opportunity," (July 9, 2017); "Is God's Kingdom Declining or Expanding?" (April 8, 2018); "The Persecuted Church," (January 13, 2019); "Are Youth and Young Adults Leaving the Church?" (May 2, 2019); "The State of the Church in Canada Today," (July 7, 2019); and "Moral Issues in the Coming Canadian Election," (September 29, 2019).

Non-Bakerview Christian presentations included the following. "Remarks at the Final Concert in honour of Dr. Wes Janzen," Clearbrook Mennonite Brethren Church (March 23, 2014); "Why this Centre?" Launch Event, Anabaptist- Mennonite Centre for Faith and Learning, Trinity Western University (October 24, 2014); "Walking with God in Politics: What does God Expect of Christian Citizens?," Mennonite World Conference, Harrisburg, PA (July 25, 2015); "Mennonite World Conference,"

Retired Ministry Leaders," Abbotsford, BC (September 25, 2016); "How Should a Faithful Church Relate to the State?" Fresno Pacific University (April 16, 2019); "The State of the Church in Canada," Retired Ministry Leaders, Abbotsford, BC (May 30, 2019); and "A Church Within a Prison," Seniors Cafe, Bakerview Church, Abbotsford, BC (January 21, 2020).

Ministries in Mennonite Brethren Conferences 2010 - 2021

For me it was an exercise in conference ministry to research and write about what had happened to weaken the structure of the Canadian MB Conference and how, in my estimation, some of its decisions needed to be reconsidered or even reversed. Investigating this agenda involved interaction with about fifteen other senior MB leaders across Canada. If there is merit in what I wrote, they deserve credit because they contributed and edited along with me. On July 18, 2019, with the consultations completed, I distributed and posted a four-page document entitled "*A statement of Concern with Some Proposals.*" This statement focused mainly on the recent merger of MB Mission with C2C, but it also questioned the wisdom of changing the name from MB Mission to Multiply. This document was circulated to a large number of past and present conference and church leaders. A second document, one which focussed on the problems facing a weakened Canadian MB Conference, was entitled "*Concerning Canadian MB Conference Developments.*" It was released on December 7, 2019, and circulated widely. It, too, generated considerable discussion. The fifteen or so other members of our concerns group also contributed to the content of this document.

In 2011 I completed my four-year term as a member of the BCMB executive committee. For the last two years, I was the council secretary.

A Mission Trip to Paraguay 2011

On May 20, 2011, Doris and I left on a 19-day mission trip to Paraguay. This trip was scheduled to follow soon after the publication of the Spanish translation of **Politics Under God - Politica de la manno de Dios. (2011)** This translation was published by a division of Universidad Evangelica del Paraguay. It was my privilege to address students, academics, pastors, politicians, media folk as well as the general public.

One cannot describe in detail the numerous sessions and meetings we had but several basic impressions should be noted. Perhaps the most important one is that Mennonites in Paraguay are heavily involved in local, state, and

national politics. While we were there, an election campaign was underway for the presidency of the country. One of the two leading candidates was a Mennonite. It was amusing to hear that while many Christians were praying that he would win the election, his mother, so I was told on good authority, was praying diligently that he would lose. Her prayers were answered.

A second major impression is that while the Mennonites are a small percentage of the country's population, they have progressed amazingly from being a poor immigrant sector into becoming a major part of the national economy. We were informed that the Mennonites play a major role in the meat exporting business and apparently dominate the dairy industry. The production facilities we toured gave credibility to such assertions.

My third general impression is that the Mennonite communities, really congregations, have been surprisingly successful in relating to the large Indigenous population, especially in the Chaco. They provide educational opportunities, skills and vocational training, and charitable assistance where needed. I was truly amazed to note, for example, when we visited a Mennonite radio station, that significant blocks of time were allotted to broadcasting in the languages of the Indigenous peoples. It is clear that the government of Paraguay, aided by the Christian sector led by the Mennonites, has had much greater success than Canada in relating to and addressing the needs of Indigenous peoples. We have much to learn from them.

For me, the most startling and impressive example of Mennonite ministry in Paraguay involves a truly unique prison ministry. Here is a brief summary. A few decades ago, an MB church in Asuncion, the capital city, launched a more or less standard prison ministry. The Christians responsible quickly realized that something more was needed. The prison conditions were so deplorable that something more inclusive and more basic was needed. They prayed, dreamt, and planned outside the box, as the saying goes. They approached the prison authorities and asked if they could rebuild part of the large prison, house some of the prisoners there, and then run their own restorative Christian ministry right there in prison. Permission was granted.

What we witnessed and experienced on Sunday, May 29, 2011, was for us almost unbelievable. After going through typical security checkpoints and passing some truly dark and dingy small cells with prisoners lounging in them, we passed through another set of doors where we were suddenly part of a totally contrasting scene. Prisoners were in decent prison garb, walking around in a large open area. In order to qualify for this definitely upscale prison environment, prisoners had to apply and meet certain standards, including abstinence from drugs and alcohol. While not all prisoners in this section were Christians, probably the majority were.

John and Doris with the baptismal candidates in the Liberdad Church.

We sat down among the prisoners to take in a Sunday morning worship service. Our translator kept us informed. The speaker, as I recall, was in prison for murder. The worship leader had committed very serious crimes. At least one participant was a rapist. All the ushers, who also handled the offering, were prisoners. For the prisoners, this was a special Sunday. A significant number of prisoners, I think the number was 15, were going to be baptized. We were invited to have our picture taken with them.

A prison church in prayer.

Whoever wants to see a success story of prison ministry, this is the place to visit. The prisoners are offered education. Many are taught trades with tools and facilities provided for them to work at their trades. The prisoners have a large store where visitors can buy what the prisoners have made.

In a very praiseworthy effort to maintain family bonds for prisoners, they have fine visiting areas and for married couples even private conjugal rooms. Equally impressive for me was the fact that after the truly unique prison church service, some of the prison church leaders, all convicts, told us that they were hoping to build a larger church assembly hall in the prison compound because so many prisoners want to attend the church services.

Another startling comment made by the Mennonite Brethren church leader responsible for this amazing prison ministry is that outside employers come to the prison to try to hire prisoners when released. They want to hire ex-convicts who have been part of the Liberdad program because they know that those men are well-trained, that they are hard-working, and that they are honest.

After seeing how relatively well these privileged prisoners were eating, I inquired why, given the low cost of beef in Paraguay, the other prisoners were not also offered good meals. I was then told that while adequate food supplies, including beef, are delivered to the prison, the various levels of authority take substantial amounts for themselves so that the prisoners get reduced rations, especially very little beef. Perhaps a bit naively, I then asked why this corruption was not reported to the prison warden. My translator smiled and said that the warden was part of the scheme to steal food.

I left Liberdad deep in thought. How can a few hundred deeply committed Mennonite Brethren Christians in a church in Asuncion achieve such incredible success when all our highly-educated and high-priced experts in Canada achieve so much less. As we drove from the prison and passed an evangelical church, I knew the answer.

Music Mission Kiev

In the fall of 2011, Dr. Wes Janzen, musical conductor and general director of Music Mission, Kiev, asked me to organize and chair a Canadian committee to help organize a Canadian tour of the Kiev Symphony Orchestra and Chorus (KSOC). I agreed to do that for this ministry. By late 2011 the Canadian KSOC Committee was off and running. Funds were needed for the mission itself and the Canadian ministry. By the grace of God, I fairly soon raised just under $50,000. One of my other tasks was to assist in booking venues.

These preparatory trips took me to northern Washington, Calgary, Edmonton, the Okanagan Valley, and to many sites in BC's Lower Mainland. Some of these scouting trips were made by Wes and me jointly.

On September 12, 2012, the 2012 Canadian tour group of 90, which included a few non-musician assistants, travelling on two large buses began their amazing Canadian ministry. It continued until September 23 with performances in Alberta, British Columbia and a few cities in northern Washington. I accompanied the tour to 11 concerts - I had to miss a few others - where my task was to present the financial challenge. In thinking and praying about this I got an idea - maybe it was God-given. Between some incredible musical selections I was called on to speak. I went on stage, looked up and began to speak. My words were similar to the following statement.

"Dear Dad, I have something to tell you. When you used to tell us about Ukraine and about the Communist Soviet Union, you lamented the fact that the Christian witness in the land of your birth was being brutally suppressed. You were sad because in the Ukraine the Gospel could not be proclaimed. Now I have something to tell you, Dad, the situation has changed. Yes, Dad, it has really changed. Today there is a large group of singers and instrumentalists preaching the word in song - in Ukraine! They are drawing huge audiences. The people love the Christian music. You, too, would love it. Dad, you would hardly believe what is now happening. People are responding to the Gospel, the love of Christ...."

The audience quickly realized that I was having a one-way conversation with my departed father. As I paused between phrases, I noted that the large audience was totally quiet. When I had finished my monologue, I sat down. The audience loved the excellent music. The offerings were generally large.

I continued leading the Canadian KSOC Committee for a few years and then served as a consultant, assisting in drafting documents and general planning. It was a delight to work with Wes and Kim Janzen and their associates. I doubt if I have ever met more skilled music leaders. I have certainly not heard more celestial music.

The Tabor Home Society

The Tabor Home Society, an association formed by ten regional Mennonite Brethren churches in BC's Lower Mainland, operates Tabor Village, a multi-level Campus of Care in Abbotsford. In the fall of 2017 I was asked to serve as a development consultant and as volunteer fundraiser for a planned major building. I served in these roles until April 2019. It was a privilege to present the Tabor challenge to many potential donors.

It was, however, at times difficult to overcome the assumption that "the government is paying." In fact, the provincial government basically funds much of the operation, but only by special grant are any capital funds provided by the government. There was considerable, positive response. Thanks to a major donor who wishes to remain anonymous but who provided a very large lead gift, I was able, by the grace of God, to raise about $3.6 million for the project.

Writing for the General Public 2011 - 2021

Having articles published in secular publications, sometimes by invitation, continued in these years. Those printed in major papers included the following. "Dealing with Sir John A. and then George Washington," *Hamilton Spectator* (August 17, 2018); "The life and times of two founding fathers," *Waterloo Region Record* (August 18, 2018); "Pro-rep backers wrong to warn of 'dictatorship'," *Vancouver Sun* (September 15, 2018); "Pro-rep a good idea, but not options offered," *Vancouver Sun* (November 5, 2018); "NDP mishandled electoral reform referendum," *The Vancouver Province* (January 18, 2019); "What does the BC Government's SOGI 123 mean for our families?" *The Patrika* (October 23, 2020); "What is the teaching of SOGI 123?' [In Punjabi] *The Patrika* (October 30, 2020).

On October 2, 201,5 I posted the following six-page analysis online: "Thoughts on the Electoral Challenges Facing the Conservative Party in Anticipation of Canada's General Election in October, 2015." Other publications include "Defaming Sir John A. Macdonald," *Abbotsford News* (July 1, 2021).

General Speaking Engagements 2011 - 2021

During these years, I typically addressed an Abbotsford's seniors' organization, *Learning Plus*, two or three times a year. Each session consisted of two one-hour presentations with a question period. Here are some of the topics for these years. "Have Canadian Politics been Transformed?" (November 8, 2011); "Who Will Win the US Presidential Election 2012?" (October 25, 2012); "Issues in the 2016 United States Election - Part One," (October 20, 2016); "The BC Election," (April 13, 2017); "Understanding Trump," (October 25, 2018); "Socialism, Nationalism, and the other Isms," (March 28, 2019); and "The State of Canadian Politics," (November 14, 2019).

There were other speaking engagements in this category. They include the following. "The Muslim Challenge to Freedom," PROBUS CLUB, Abbotsford, BC (February 17, 2014); "How Should I Vote on May 9, 2017?," Clearbrook Golden Age Society, Abbotsford, BC (May 3, 2017); "BC Voting Methods," Primrose Gardens Meeting, Abbotsford, BC (October 16, 2018); "Understanding and Explaining President Trump, Can it be Done?" Abbotsford and Matsqui Rotary Club (November 15, 2018); and "BC Election Issues," Clearbrook Golden Age Society, Abbotsford, BC (October 20, 2020).

As in earlier times, there were numerous media events in these years. Here are some examples. Interview with Mike Lloyd on Premier Christy Clark, NEWS 11:30 CKWX (June 22, 2017); and an Interview with Dr. John Neufeld, Back to the Bible Canada on "Christians and Government," (July 6, 2017).

Awards and Affirmations 2011 - 2021

Probably about a month before April 27, 2014, I was informed by some members of the Stillwood Camp and Conference Centre Board that the board, together with Executive Director Harry Edwards, was arranging for "a special dinner in honour" of my many years of service to Stillwood. That announcement came as a total surprise. The event, held on April 27, 2014, was for me a very humbling but also a very encouraging celebration. I thank God and the many people who all along supported me during my two decades of service for Stillwood. In his "Tribute" board vice-chair, Colin Reimer made some very kind comments. Here are a few excerpts from his four-page statement:

"God has blessed John with several gifts...and John has honoured God by using the gifts he has received to further God's kingdom here at Stillwood and at other ministries as well... John has also been blessed with many friends and connections in the community. One of his strongest gifts is to help people recognize the gifts God has given them and to understand their potential to God's kingdom.....John has Stillwood flowing through his veins for sure, but it isn't just Stillwood he is interested in, it is the ministry of Stillwood, God's ministry at Stillwood....During his time as Stillwood Camp Board Chairman, John has overseen the complete revitalization of the facilities....We here at Stillwood felt it was time to say thank you to a man we all love and appreciate. This evening is not about heaping praise on a great man, although many may agree that he is, this evening is about telling a humble servant of the most high God that we all appreciate his obedience and that he has done for Stillwood, for all of us, and for generations to come."

Near the close of the evening celebration, I was greatly surprised when Harry Edwards announced that the main lane circling through the camp accommodation area had been renamed the Dr. John H. Redekop Way. He showed me a street sign. My parents would have gotten a good chuckle out of that innovative and very kind gesture.

A lane at Stillwood

I shall remain incredibly grateful to my Stillwood Board colleagues and executive director Harry Edwards for arranging this lane designation. It is a timeless affirmation. I am also deeply rewarded every time I attend a Thursday evening assembly at the Stillwood amphitheatre in the summertime and witness the reality that scores of children and young people respond to the invitation to live their lives as Christians. What greater reward could there be?

In 2015 Bakerview MB Church published a 50th anniversary book, **Mosaic of Grace; Bakerview MB Church 1965-2015.** While it was being prepared, I was contacted by Dr. Walter Unger who said that the book would carry something he was writing about me as a writer and therefore he needed to interview me. We had a fine session. I also provided the requested *curriculum vitae* about my life. When the book was published I was humbled by the very kind and affirming statements Dr. Unger had written in his full-page article. Here are a few excerpts:

"*John Redekop is leaving a strong and lasting legacy as a writer, political scientist, evangelical Anabaptist scholar and active churchman.... John is a prolific writer whose inkwell never seems to run dry.... Above all else, John is an ardent evangelical Anabaptist whose church-oriented publications have made an enormous impact.*"

I am indebted to Wally, a former president of Columbia Bible College, and a greatly valued friend for his very kind words.

The Betty Urqhart Community Service Award

On October 10, 2019, the University of the Fraser Valley announced I had been awarded the *Betty Urquhart Community Award* for my community service. At the presentation event on November 19, the award statement, which focused primarily on my more than two decades of volunteer fundraising and other work at Stillwood Camp and Conference Centre, included the following state-ments:

"In his 1,250 days of volunteer time over approximately two decades, John raised $12.5 million along with an additional $400,000 worth of supplies from regional suppliers.... The fact that he led by example and volunteered so much of his time is a major reason why hundreds of people followed his example and became donors or volunteers.... A tired camp was transformed into a world-class, year-round camp and conference centre.... John's commitment to giving back and his ability to motivate others to do the same has significantly benefited children, families and community groups in the Fraser Valley."

With this award came a financial grant for which I needed to designate a recipient. Without any hesitation I, of course, selected Stillwood as the recipient.

Beginning in May 2014, I was asked by the executive of the Clearbrook Golden Age Society, which operates Garden Park Tower as a residence and also offers other services, to establish a monthly magazine for the society. I selected a committee and the monthly magazine was launched. I was truly delighted to hear from *The Writers Guild* that one of my editorials, "*An oppressive ruling*," had won first place in the Editorial Division for 2016.

The Betty Urqhart Award

In 2019 I was delighted to win two additional awards from *The Writers Guild*. My chapter "*Christian Contributions to Political Affairs*," in the Surrey, White Rock book won first place in the category General Article - Long Feature. I also won a first-place award, along with the other two editors, for the book **The Church in Surrey & White Rock - The Untold Story.**

Reviewing my records, I note that since 1990 I have won 11 national writing awards, one from the *Canadian Church Press* and ten from *The Writers Guild*. My goal is always to do the best I can in service to God and others. If my words are affirmed by others, I thank God and the judges.

Developments in the Larger Religious Arenas 2011 - 2021

The most important religious development in Canada during these years is the continuing decline of religion and church attendance. In 2005, 81% of all Canadians said they believed in God. By 2016, only 11 years later, that number had shrunk to 65%. When a later survey asked with which faith the respondent identifies, then the 2021 results for Canada are as follows: Christian 67%; No religion 24%; Muslim 5%; Hindu 1.5%; Sikh 1.4%; Buddhist 1.1%; Jewish 1 %; and other 0.7 %.

Other surveys show that evangelicals, broadly defined and including evangelical Catholics, constitute about 13% of the total population, with the percentage increasing slowly. While church attendance figures vary widely, mainly because the definition of attendance varies greatly, all point to major declines in all mainline denominations. Sadly, research revealed that the most requested model program requested by United Church congregations is now the program for closing a church. I have a copy in my files.

Already on July 28, 2012, a hard-hitting report in the Toronto *Globe and Mail* had this headline: "*The Collapse of the Liberal Church.*" The article described tragedy. It stated that today the United Church "is literally dying"; "all the...liberal churches are collapsing." The United Church lost one-quarter of its members in the preceding decade. "Back in the 1960s," the *Globe* article reported, "the liberal churches bet their future on becoming more open, more inclusive, more egalitarian and more progressive...it was a colossal flop." Between 1960 and 2000, the United Church lost nearly 60% of its members.

For my own denomination, the Mennonite Brethren, I see the Canadian Conference receding in significance for reasons described previously. Concerning the successes and challenges of any organization, leadership deserves much of the credit for successes and must also shoulder responsibility when things do not go well. The same holds true for Canadian Mennonite Brethren in our time. While some online publicity can be found, for many church members, it seems to me, the national conference is disappearing from their radar. No longer do we have national conventions. No longer do we have a denominational periodical. No longer do we have a national college. No longer do we have national conference clergy visiting churches.

Local churches are, of course, partly to blame for the last loss. Already 30 or more years ago, full-time, paid pastors were very reluctant to let any conference personnel or school or mission representatives address Sunday morning congregations. With no periodicals, no conventions, and no clergy personnel to inform the mind and to warm the heart, one wonders what the future will hold for the once strong and healthy Canadian Conference of Mennonite Brethren Churches.

In earlier generations Mennonite Brethren, along with other ethno-religious groups, experienced expanding congregations. The main reasons for substantial increases for the Mennonite Brethren were the fact that most families had numerous children who generally joined their parents' church. Also, most children married within their ethno-religious communities. Further, in earlier times congregations incorporated ethnic values which helped retain members of that ethnic group. In addition, for several generations the immigrant language bonded the group and also for several generations the collective memory of a unique and enriching history reinforced community and church bonds.

Finally, most Mennonite Brethren lived in at least partly homogeneous communities in which the church was central. For better or worse, all those realities are seriously weakened or gone.

Canadian Mennonite Brethren have become a more Canadian and indigenous denomination and now function along with other faith groups in carrying out the Great Commission with decreasing ethnic glue. It is not yet clear whether Canadian Mennonite Brethren will not only survive this multi-faceted transition but thrive and prosper in it. That is the challenge and the opportunity that our leaders face. Will Canadian, indeed North American, Mennonite Brethren be successful in retaining their distinctive theology, in affirming and upholding essentials in honouring their amazing past, and in building on their heritage for the future?

The overall US religious scene is still somewhat healthier, although also experiencing declining numbers. The number of Americans who classify themselves as "religious nones" ["none of the above religions"] has grown by 30 million in the past decade. A decade ago, 77% of Americans classified themselves as Christian. By 2021 that percentage has dropped to 65%. In the 14-million-member Southern Baptist Convention, still the largest Protestant denomination in the US, only 4.4. million of 14 million members classify themselves as "regular attendees." In a recent 12-month period, that Convention lost 288,000 members.

Fortunately, the US Mennonite Brethren numbers are holding and even increasing.

Relevant Political and Public Affairs 2011 - 2021

On October 19, 2015, Justin Trudeau was elected Prime Minister of Canada. Many Christian folk feared that he would weaken the moral fibre of the nation. They had reason to be apprehensive. On June 17, 2016, the Trudeau Liberal government voted for the legalizing of physician-assisted euthanasia. The new policy was called MAID - *Medical Assistance In Dying*. The protection against misuse, it was argued, was the requirement that the person needed to be experiencing "extreme physical suffering." There were other "protections" involving delay, witnesses, etc. On March 17, 2021, this second Trudeau government expanded MAID. No longer would it be required that a person's natural death was "reasonably foreseeable." Also, the eligibility was lowered to 18 years of age, and mental illness was included. One requirement seen by many Christians and others as subject to abuse is the statement that there must be an "advanced state of irreversible decline in capability." What could that mean?

According to the latest available data, 13,946 people had been put to death by MAID in Canada from June 2016 to the end of 2019, with 5,631 killed in 2019.

Many of us see two serious problems with euthanasia and especially with the now weaker requirements. First, it should not be made easier for any human being to have someone else kill him or her. Second, there is fear that for people with a serious disability, or serious chronic health problems, either physical or mental, the opportunity to have one's life ended might become an obligation to have one's life ended.

On November 8, 2016, Donald Trump was elected the 45th president of the United States. He was in office from January 2017 until January 2021. His ascendancy to office and his governing deeply divided the US and also other societies. His election and governance divided many Christian families, many Christian congregations, indeed the entire Christian community. For some people, he was God's man for our time; for others, he was a threat to democracy and perhaps even international peace. The antagonism continues to run deep. The fact that former president Trump still insists that the 2020 election was stolen fuels antagonisms.

A second key development in the US was the insurrection and mob attack on the Capitol Building in Washington D.C. on January 6, 2021. This event again deeply divided the US. It seems that most Mennonites, along with other Christians in the US and Canada, are fully engaged in the most emotion-laden political controversy of our times.

The third major development, a very recent one, is the humiliating collapse of the US military and political involvement in Afghanistan, along with the sudden demise of the pro-Western government of that country on August 16, 2021. Most Americans, including faith communities, conclude that 2,448 military deaths [Canada 148], 20,660 wounded military persons [Canada 2,150] and a massive expenditure in excess of $1 trillion [Canada about $20 million] have been largely for naught? Only time will tell. Have the Taliban really emerged as the victors over the US and its allies? In Afghanistan, at least in the short term, the answer is Yes. One fact cannot be denied. The termination of US military presence and the drawn-out and massive chaos and suffering in trying to extricate Americans, allied persons, and Afghan supporters fearing brutal retaliation from the Taliban, is one of the saddest chapters in US history. Although less involved, the Canadian and other allied countries also share in this tragedy. Many Christian folk, along with others, saw the US and Allied involvement in Afghanistan as an undertaking to counteract Muslim terrorists. What will be their response now?

John and Doris, on a Rhine River cruise, with valued friends and strong Stillwood and personal supporters, Henry and Linda Esau, 2019

My Spiritual Pilgrimage   2011 - 2021

The longer I live, soon four score years and ten, the more conscious I become that I am very much "an earthen vessel," as St. Paul puts it. My weaknesses and shortcomings are obvious. Looking back on past years, I increasingly realize the mistakes I made, the times I could have done better, and the Christian opportunities I have missed. But when I feel that I should have done more with the time and opportunities God graciously gave me, I also become deeply thankful for what, by God's grace and with his enablement, I have been able to do. Even more important, and I say it again, is the awareness that God is much more interested in who we are than in what we do.

Many important and for me fascinating questions still exist in my mind. They deal with the Genesis creation account, the reality of the dinosaurs and geology, the incomprehensible immensity of the universe, and many other matters. If a person has a naturally inquisitive mind and has been taught by wise professors to evaluate everything critically, then the cultivation of childlike faith can be challenging. Already long ago, fortunately, I concluded that the many truly perplexing questions will be answered only in heaven. I am at ease with unanswered questions. That reality provides adequate interim satisfaction.

I thank God that my faith commitment remains real and fundamentally important. Temptations and faith challenges remain with us as long as we live, but they do not negate simple trust in God's goodness, his love, and his salvation for all who believe. I thank God that he has granted me the opportunity and the reality of saving faith. By God's grace I have been granted the blessing not only to know about God but, albeit to a limited extent, also to know God.

God has given me a good life. As recounted in these chapters, at various times he has spared my life. That reality has frequently reminded me that God had a purpose for my life as he does for any person's life. I have been privileged and blessed beyond measure.

A Concluding Statement

I close this summary of my life thus far, with these expressions of gratitude. I thank God for my Christian parents and for my Christian heritage. I thank God that I was born in this sanguine, free, prosperous and privileged country. I thank God for granting me the faith to believe the Gospel. I thank God for the ministry and service opportunities he has allotted to me. I thank God for my loving, patient and altogether wonderful wife, Doris. I thank God for our four fine children - Wendy, Gary, Heather and Bonnie(Satya) - and, of course, the partners that some have. I thank God for our three dear grandchildren - David, Danielle, and Michelle - and the partners they have chosen or will yet choose. I thank God for our first great-grandchild, dear little Ada Grace, born to Danielle and Billy Wright, May 6, 2021.

Concerning the future, I am committed to try to move beyond hindrances, setbacks, and uninformed opposition to build on all that was and remains good, to spend the rest of my life serving God and others and living out and telling others of God's great redemptive and beneficial love for us all. A key verse for me is John 1:16: "From the fulness of his grace, we have all received one blessing after another."

Finally, let me say that I trust that all who have read this illustrated summary of my almost completed earthly pilgrimage will find it interesting and maybe even helpful.

Our Family

A happy family.
Back Row L to R: Heather, Wendy. Gary.
Front Row L to R: Bonnie, John, Doris.

Wendy and Craig Carmichael

Lee Ann Wills and Gary Redekop

Heather Harmony

Bonnie "Satya" Redekop

Great-granddaughter Ada Grace Wright.

Danielle Charbonneau, Billy Wright and Ada Grace

David Redekop and Rebecca Moore

Michelle Redekop

APPENDIX A

STATEMENTS BY OTHERS

1. The re-launch of the Evangelical Fellowship of Canada (EFC) was in part spurred on by the vision and unapologetic encouragement which John Redekop offered to the Council of the EFC at its winter 1983 meeting. The focus of that meeting was to recruit a new full-time leader and CEO for the EFC and my name had been raised as a possible candidate. With logic and passion, John stood and offered why this was the right time and why this was an opportunity that would fit my calling. It was personal and historic. However, John's enthusiasm and commitment did not end with his speech. It carried on in personal mentoring and eventually brought him to serve as chair, then called President, of the Council. His vision was all-embracing, allowing Canadian Evangelicals to gain identity and cohesion, with distinction from USA voices which at times were strident and ideological. I will always be grateful to John for his presence and inspiration, which helped change my life and renew this national fellowship of Evangelicals in Canada.

Brian C Stiller, *Global Ambassador, World Evangelical Alliance*

2. My earliest recollection of John was at a lecture he gave about Marxism and Christianity. Having obtained my doctorate from what has been called "the most Marxist Institution in Canada," I was attracted to a man who could "see through the fog," analyze reality, and propose insightful solutions. John's articulate academic skills may cause some to cautiously view him as having an above-average amount of confidence and knowledge. I served with John on the Mennonite Brethren Canadian Board of Faith and Life and at Trinity Western University. From my experience, I know that eighteen inches beneath that brilliance lies a heart committed to obeying and serving Jesus Christ — whatever the political climate. Thanks John.

James D. ("Jim") Cunningham, Ed.D.

3. Dr. Redekop was my instructor for *Introduction to Canadian Government and Politics* at Trinity Western University. I remember him being knowledgeable, inspiring and a wee bit terrifying – not a bad combination for a university prof! In addition to all the ins and outs of the Canadian government, Dr. Redekop taught me an important life lesson: a well-researched and clearly articulated argument is worthy of respect, even if one disagrees with the conclusions drawn. This lesson stayed with me throughout my many subsequent years of graduate education. Today, I have the privilege of teaching the current generation of Trinity students the same course he taught me. It is my hope that the same dedication to the subject matter and high standard for learning he modelled in the classroom so many years ago will be evident to my students today.

Leanne Smythe, Ph.D.

4. The Christian fellowship that Kim and I enjoyed with Prof. Dr. John and Doris Redekop at Bakerview Church went far beyond Sunday mornings. I recall Dr. Redekop as a fellow TWU faculty member, on our knees on wet parking lot gravel, helping a colleague with her flat tire. Symbolically, that moment summarized things to come. John and Doris were second to none in prayerfully supporting our desire to bring Glory to God through music. They brought guests to our events in the Orpheum and Chan Centre, always with kingdom-building objectives. John chaired multiple Canadian tour committee and board meetings as we laboured together "on our knees" in outreach to the former Soviet Union and across Canada. John's pure genius in intellect, planning, communication, attention to detail, commitment to excellence, integration of discipline and faith, and thoughtful thinking always inspire us – but his desire to be a Christ-follower and bring glory to God, are at the top of the list. In a sea of storms, foggy thinking and uncertainty, we consistently see John reflect the light of Christ. We love you John and Doris.

Wes Janzen, *Professor Emeritus, Trinity Western University*

5. I have had the privilege of knowing and reading John Redekop's insightful political discourses for more than 40 years. While so many Christian leaders and writers shy away from contemporary and controversial subjects such as abortion, capital punishment, euthanasia, civil disobedience, and political activism, Dr. Redekop faces them head-on, not as an abstract theoretical topic for debate, but as concerns that demand a well-researched and detailed Christian response. Whenever an issue emerges onto the political scene, I want to know what he thinks and advises on the subject, as do countless other Christians in this country. From years of personal experience in the federal political scene in Ottawa, I can attest to the profound influence that this intellectual giant has had on numerous political figures. My personal Christian hero has always been William Wilberforce and as a scholar and activist, John is a close second. Canada is so much better because of his influence and we need much more of it. In his personal life, he is the epitome of Micah 6:8.

Don Page, *former Academic Vice President, Trinity Western University*

6. John played important mentoring roles in my spiritual development and career path. His College and Career Sunday school class at Waterloo Mennonite Brethren, plus evenings when he and Doris opened their home to many students, were important in drawing me into the church community and adult baptism. John was privately skeptical when I got a high mark on an early assignment in his *Introduction to Political Science* class at WLU. After I did equally well on the mid-term exam, he singled me out for praise in front of several hundred students. That public recognition helped me get elected to the student union board a few months later, a cause of some grumbling by older students. As thesis advisor for my master's degree, John was generously supportive, and patient when my full-time job relegated thesis writing to weekends over several years. When work has taken me to BC occasionally, John has been a gracious host and tour guide.

Thank you John.

Mike Strathdee, *Ontario, editor of the Marketplace; formerly with Mennonite Foundation of Canada, now Abundance Canada*

7. My association with John Redekop began with my appointment as editor of the *MB Herald* in 1964. John was already writing columns before I arrived. But he literally stuck with me throughout my years as editor. Of course, many others also became columnists during my more than three decades with the *Herald* and later *ChristianWeek*. But no one lasted as long as John. The reasons aren't hard to understand. John has a fertile and retentive mind, and he never ran out of subjects to treat and vantage points from which to treat them. Since he was clearly anchored in a Christian worldview to which his readers could relate, the arguments he made seldom failed to resonate. The fact that he was well-read and knowledgeable meant that his readers could usually learn from his columns even if they disagreed.

John has an organized mind, and when he was making a case about an issue, you knew he would line up his arguments clearly. For most of my years with the *Herald*, his columns came handwritten, always the first draft, often in point form, and on one page. Because he also always had more ideas than space, the lines became tighter and the script smaller as he neared the bottom of the page. A questionnaire during those years called him the most trusted voice within the MB conference in Canada. The traits he displayed during my years at the *Herald* made it easy for me to invite him to write for *ChristianWeek* as well, where he found the same acceptance.

John is the kind of writer every editor welcomes. He wasn't defensive toward critics, his columns were always on time, and he remained a fountain of worthwhile ideas. He was the epitome of an engaged Christian.

Harold Jantz, *former Editor of the Mennonite Brethren Herald and ChristianWeek*

8. When I began attending WLU, undergrad courses in political science allowed me to experience John's talents as a dynamic and engaging professor. His subject matter was always interesting and his presentations and written materials were clear, logical and well-reasoned. I always appreciated that, despite our differences in age and experience, John treated me with respect. Later, at Waterloo MB Church, in a collegial and patient way, leading by example, he coached me on setting agendas, running effective committee meetings, and the skills needed to encourage, communicate and implement decisions. John was also the first person from whom I heard (and observed in practice!) the leadership maxim, "It's sometimes easier to ask for forgiveness than to ask for permission." I blame all my subsequent use of that learning on John. I also credit John for being intentional about identifying and developing the gifts of many younger persons like myself.

His initiative was instrumental in setting the foundation for my involvement with several charitable organizations and committees over the following decades, long after John and Doris moved on to BC. I therefore think of John Redekop as an important mentor in my early life.

Ted Dueck, *Barrister and Solicitor,*

9. Now retired after decades of active political life, including seven years' service in the Canadian Parliament, I retain warm admiration for my most significant mentor, Dr. John Redekop. As a WLU student from 1972 to 1974, I knew immediately there was something different about John, even if I couldn't consciously articulate it. It wasn't merely his authentically sincere concern for his students, although that was a very positive personal quality. With the benefit of life experience, it's easy to pinpoint now: John's rare gift is the ability to see the whole person rather than merely their presenting appearance. I confided my hopes and ambitions to John, unexpectedly for the reserved young man I was. I remember his wise advice, going beyond simply the courses he taught and infusing not only practical career advice but also insight into the spiritual significance of law and politics. His words were indelible. I have sought John's counsel in the years since, and have never been disappointed in his wisdom.

Stephen Woodworth, *former Member of Parliament, Barrister and Solicitor, Ontario*

10. It's a pleasant task to write a few words about my friend Dr. John Redekop. I have known him for my entire adult life. First, through his Personal Opinion column, which appeared in the *MB Herald* for multiple decades. My mother told me that her favourite piece in the *Herald* was Dr. John's column. That column and its longevity symbolizes the qualities of John which I much admire.

I admire his discipline and unmatched work ethic. He has mental capacity and he does not let it go to waste. Sharing his wisdom and insight with his church family has been high on his list of priorities all along.

I admire his commitment to excellence. Recently in a series of email exchanges with him, he could not resist refreshing my fading memory of Turabian's formatting rules. He believes in the biblical admonition "let everything be done decently and in order."

I admire his humility. Even as a highly acclaimed academic, he maintains an open circle of friendship. I fondly recall how he welcomed me into the wider MB church family. I was a newbie, unknown pastor from a small town in Saskatchewan when our paths crossed at a National Convention; yet, he was interested in me and took time to listen to my story.

I admire his ability to treat his adversaries with grace and dignity, it's incomprehensible how a person with such a record of success and blessing would have the soul-crushing pain of being temporarily cast aside from volunteer conference ministry. However, by enduring such treatment with perseverance, faith, hope, and love. John has proven to be a true Christ-follower.

John has been a teacher all his life and his autobiography has much to teach us. Thank you for sharing your story with us.

A friend and fellow servant, **Peter W. Nikkel***, retired pastor*

11. The word that comes to mind to describe Dr. John Redekop's many years of selfless service to church and community is "irrepressible." Those of us who have worked closely with John know that there is no task he undertakes that won't be meticulously planned and executed or to which an abundance of energy won't be applied. He simply won't accept "no" as an answer when work needs to be done! He and I had the privilege of serving together on Abbotsford's City Council under legendary Mayor George Ferguson, and even in that political arena, John brought his prodigious intellect to bear in guiding the affairs of our city.

Later, he had remarkable success in doing what he's done for so many other organizations, fundraising for me in the federal election of 2019 - something he accomplished with enthusiasm and without any thought of asking "What's in it for me?" I have often turned to John for sage advice on the pressing issues of the day. For as long as I've known him, John has applied his gifts to building community and promoting God's kingdom whenever called upon to do so. In so doing, he has epitomized what it means to be a servant leader.

Hon. Ed Fast*, Member of Parliament*

12. My late husband, Richard Unruh, was recruited to be John's first political science student at Fresno Pacific College in 1964. Over three years, Richard took every course John taught and fell in love with political science. It became his vocation as he succeeded John in teaching at FPC for 42 years. Richard always credited John for teaching him to write well. He took John's constructive criticism on each research paper very seriously and made sure that in the next paper he followed his professor's suggestions for improvement. Richard and John became colleagues and very close friends over the years and any trip to the Northwest would always include a visit to the Redekops in Abbotsford.

I enrolled in John's *Comparative Government* class in the spring of 1968. I was engaged to Richard Unruh, then a graduate student who had been hired to succeed John in the Political Science Department at Fresno Pacific College in the Fall. I needed that class to complete my Social Science minor and preferred not to take it the following year from my future husband. I was very determined to make a good impression on John and got right to work writing a term paper on apartheid. I thought I found a treasure trove of source materials in the pamphlet files of  the Hiebert Library. In my excitement I failed to notice that all the brochures were written or endorsed by the current South African Government. Not surprisingly, my term paper defended the apartheid policy and failed to criticize it. I don't remember my Grade, but John's comment on the paper spoke volumes to this naïve college sophomore: "You might want to read *Cry the Beloved Country* by Alan Patton to get a more balanced perspective."

Pat Unruh, *Retired Educator (Sadly Richard passed away on May 7, 2021.)*

13. As a very recent high school grad, I first became acquainted with the name John Redekop in 1956, when he was the guest speaker at a Sunday evening service in my home church in Chilliwack, B.C. He had recently traveled across Europe and North Africa on a motorcycle. His eloquent description of this adventure certainly ignited some personal ambitions. In the years that followed, I began to take note of John's name, as it appeared in various places, more and more frequently.

As I became more involved in the M B Conference, I soon became more acquainted with John. His gifted contribution as a leader, in both the MB denomination and in the larger Christian community was impossible to miss. He served tirelessly on numerous boards, often as chairman;

He was my mentor while I served as his assistant during his four-year term as moderator of our Canadian M B Conference. Notably, he also modelled faithfulness to his local church, where he assisted with the ministry of leading, teaching, and preaching.

One of Dr. Redekop's significant contributions also came through his provocative, insightful editorials and scholarly articles, which appeared in numerous newspapers and magazines. For 39 years he wrote a Personal Opinion column in the *M B Herald*. Many readers made this one of the first articles they turned to when that magazine arrived.

Through these many years, I have cherished the friendship and the privilege of serving with John Redekop on several boards. I have admired his commitment to Jesus as Lord and his firm adherence to the authority of the Bible. He has modelled boldness in advocating for justice and truth; He has fearlessly challenged the status quo, and he sacrificially served for the glory of God. As a result, the name, Dr. John Redekop, undoubtedly became one of the best-known names of M.B. leaders and also household names in the Canadian M B family. It was a worthy honour. With many others, I thank God for his friendship and example that has impacted my life.

Herb Neufeld, *former Canadian MB Conference Moderator, Retired Pastor*

14. I first met Dr. John H. Redekop when he chaired a search committee that interviewed me in January 1997, for the position of Executive Director of Columbia Bible Camp, now known as Stillwood Camp and Conference Centre.

It has been said that to really know people, you need to spend time with them in a confined space. My wife Gail and I had the privilege of travelling down the west coast by car from BC to Los Angeles over a period of 10 days with John and Doris. The purpose of our trip was to research conference facilities in a Christian setting. To say that the trip was enjoyable is a definite understatement, as John regaled us with stories of some of his life experiences from Moscow to the Sahara Desert and beyond. Having worked with John for more than 20 years in Christian ministry, he as board member, mostly as board chair, and I as CEO, I can honestly say that I have not met anyone more researched and ready for any project or who has put more effort into it than he. As a former pastor of John once told me, if you want a thorough job done, ask John to lead it.

Through 20-plus years of ministry together, we faced many challenges, some from within and many from without, and in every situation I can honestly say I was glad that John was a member of our team. I am delighted to call Dr. John H. Redekop, my friend.

Harry E Edwards, *former Executive Director, Stillwood Camp and Conference Centre*

15. It is with a great appreciation of Dr. John Redekop's inspiration, encouragement and support that I remember his presence and time in Waterloo. From the College and Careers class at Waterloo MB Church where he challenged so many bright students to a deeper personal inquiry, and continuing through his teaching at Wilfrid Laurier University, his guidance started me on the path of a deeper and more informed involvement with the world. An appreciation for intensive study and an ongoing love of learning — with politics, spirituality, and theology as essential building blocks — was born for me from his teaching. With many thanks and much enduring respect.

Philip Hiebert, *Barrister & Solicitor, Ontario*

16. My impression of John is of a man doing what he enjoys and is meant to do. During carpooling trips to board meetings at Stillwood, I learned what was important to him. At our meetings, each member was included in discussions and entreated to give impressions and ideas. To sit as Vice-Chair and then as Chair when John had to be absent set me on a firmer base. He hit a home run so that I could come in from third. He inspired confidence. His delight in progress and completed goals was catching. Ecclesiastes. 7:13a "Consider what God has done," would be his reflection. For hard times John faced, just plain slugging through a tough patch or being wrongfully accused, he faced adversity with kindness and humility.

"Meaningful lives shape legacies through which we are remembered, an essential endorsement of our character." *Richard G. Capen Jr.* Character is that combination of virtues that gives us a legacy to leave for others. John's influence and valued friendship have given me courage to face difficult times and people with kindness and a gentle spirit but resolve to see it through.

Faith Dahl, *Former Vice-Chair, Stillwood Board of Directors*

17. At 69 I am no longer a young man, by any stretch of the imagination, but John was of the generation of elder statesmen and women of the MB world that I have grown up with and that I love. John represents the best of the depth and diversity that bring life and vigour to a community in changing seasons.

Change, by its nature, brings anxiety and fear with it. The gift that John brings is a desperately needed combination of penetrating analytical analysis, courage to deal with the hard questions that change brings, and grace for those who hold differing opinions.

John and I share a deep world view formed out of our relationship to Jesus, and from that place have on a few occasions seen the world quite differently, but far from shaking our friendship, those differences, when they happened, only sharpened out friendship.

May you be blessed as you read the story of John's pilgrimage in following the Master we love.

James Toews, *retired Pastor after 33 years in Nanaimo, BC*

18. I have known John Redekop for many years. For a time, I served on the Canadian Mennonite Brethren Board of Faith and Life, a Board that John chaired at the time. For another period of time, I had the privilege of being John's pastor. During that time, John chaired the church council. I have also interviewed him on my daily radio program at *Back to the Bible Canada*. Furthermore, I have, on occasion, enjoyed having coffee with him and talking.

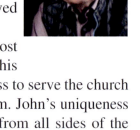

I can say without hesitation that John is among the most unique men I have ever known. His keen intellect, his activism, his organizational abilities and his willingness to serve the church and our common Savior have always drawn me to him. John's uniqueness consists in his ability to see a difference in opinion from all sides of the debate, and then form his own conclusions without bowing to peer pressure. I am honored for the friendship we have shared.

Dr. John Neufeld, *Radio Teacher, Back to the Bible Canada*

APPENDIX B PUBLICATIONS

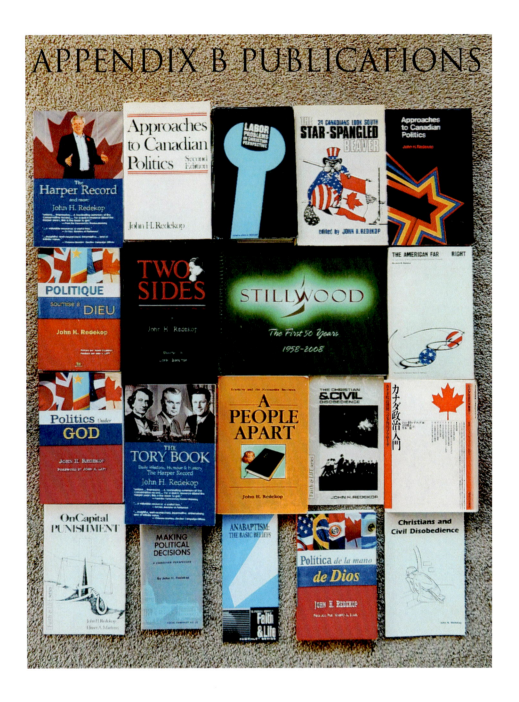

APPENDIX B

PUBLICATIONS

1. Books

The American Far Right (Grand Rapids, MI: Eerdmans, 1968). 240 pp. (author)

The Star-Spangled Beaver: Twenty-four Canadians Look South (Toronto: Peter Martin Associates, 1971). 253 pp. (editor and contributor) This volume was selected as a Book-of-the-Month by the Readers' Club of Canada in 1972.

Labour Problems in Christian Perspective (Grand Rapids, MI: Eerdmans, 1972). 364 pp. (editor and contributor)

Approaches to Canadian Politics (Scarborough, ON: Prentice-Hall, 1978). 377 pp. (editor and author of three chapters.) A second edition was published in 1983. 369 pp. This textbook was translated into Japanese by Kensei Yoshida and Toru Takemoto and published by Ochanimizu Press, Tokyo, 1989 as *Canada seiji nyumon, 319 pp.* It won a national prize in Japan for best work translated from English that year.

Two Sides: The Best of Personal Opinion, 1964-1984 (Winnipeg: Kindred Press, 1984). 306 pp. (author) This is a selection of columns published in the *Mennonite Brethren Herald* during a twenty-year period.

A People Apart: Ethnicity and the Mennonite Brethren (Winnipeg and Hillsboro, KS: Kindred Press, 1987). xi, 198 pp. (author)

Politics Under God (Waterloo, ON and Scottdale, PA: Herald Press, 2007). 224 pp. (author) This book was translated into French, *Politique soumise a Dieu*, 231 pp., and published by Editions Mukanda, Kinshasa, Democratic Republic of Congo, 2007. 220 pp. It was also translated into Spanish, *Politica de la mano de Dios and published* by Universidad Evangelica del Paraguay, 201) 227 pp.

Stillwood: The First 50 Years, 1958 - 2008 (Chilliwack, BC: Stillwood Publications, 2008). 186 pp. (editor and contributor)

The Tory Book (Abbotsford, BC: JHR Book Company, 2015). 344 pp. (author)

The Harper Record (Abbotsford, BC: JHR Book Company, 2015). 144 pp. (author)

The Church in Surrey & White Rock (Surrey, BC: SWR Publishing Company, 2018). xii, 213 pp. Editor with Lloyd Mackey and Neil Bramble. I wrote two chapters and co-authored the third chapter.

2. Chapters in books

"Party Structures and Decision-Making," co-authored with John McMenemy and Conrad Winn in J. McMenemy and C. Winn, eds., *Political Parties in Canada* (Toronto: McGraw-Hill Ryerson, 1976). pp. 167-190.

"The State and the Free Church," in John R. Burkholder and Calvin. Redekop, eds., *Kingdom, Cross and Community* (Scottdale, PA: Herald Press, 1976). pp. 179-195. This is a *Festschrift* for the American political scientist, Guy Franklin Hershberger.

"A Reinterpretation of Canadian-American Relations," in N. Nyiri and R. Preece, eds., *Unity in Diversity* (Waterloo, ON: WLU Press, 1977). pp. 243-259.

"Social Policy: The Role of the Governing Party," in Shankar Yelaja, ed., *Canadian Social Policy* (Waterloo, ON: WLU Press, 1978). pp. 243-259. This textbook was revised and printed as a second edition in 1987, my chapter is found on pp.288-309.

"Church and State in Canada: Co-operation and Confrontation," in Jarold K. Zeman and Walter Klaassen, eds., *The Believers Church in Canada* (Winnipeg: Baptist Federation of Canada and Mennonite Central Committee Canada, 1979). pp. 191-205.

"Reinhold Niebuhr, Christian Idealism and Political Realism," in J.C. Wenger, ed., *A Cloud of Witnesses: Profiles of Church Leaders* (Harrisonburg, VA: Eastern Mennonite Seminary Press, 1981). pp. 250-254.

"Roles of Church and Government," in Gerald Vandezande, ed., *Christians in the Crisis: Toward Responsible Citizenship* (Toronto: Anglican Book Centre, 1984). pp. 192-197.

"More Than Ethnic: Redefining Mennonite Identity," in Harry Loewen, ed., *Why I Am A Mennonite* (Scottdale, PA: Herald Press, 1988). pp. 212-224.

"A Reassessment of Some Traditional Anabaptist Church-State Perspectives," in Willard Swartley, ed., *Essays on Peace Theology and Witness* (Elkhart, IN: Institute of Mennonite Studies, 1988). pp. 61-72.

"Canada versus the United States," in Gregory S. Mahler and Roman R. March, eds., *Canadian Politics 91/92* (Guildford, CN: Dushkin Publishing Group, 1991). pp. 138-139.

"The Involvement of Canadian Mennonites with non-Mennonite National Religious Bodies," in Abe J. Dueck, ed., *Canadian Mennonites and the Challenge of Nationalism* (Winnipeg: Canadian Mennonite Historical Society and Christian Press, 1994). pp. 111-127.

"Decades of Transition: North American Mennonite Brethren in Politics," in Paul Toews, ed., *Bridging Troubled Waters; The Mennonite Brethren at Mid-Twentieth Century* (Winnipeg and Hillsboro, KS: Kindred Productions, 1995). pp. 19-84.

"The Meaning of it All," in Robert S. Kreider and Ronald J. Mathies, eds., *Unity Amidst Diversity; Mennonite Central Committee at 75* (Akron, PA: Mennonite Central Committee, 1996). pp. 151-157.

"Group Representation in Parliament Would be Dysfunctional for Canada," in Mark Charlton and Paul Barker, eds. *Contemporary Political Issues, Third Edition* (Toronto, etc. : Nelson, 1998). pp. 392-405. (Earlier versions appeared in the earlier editions.)

"Mennonite Brethren in a Changing Society," in Paul Toews and Kevin Enns-Rempel, eds., *For Everything a Season; Mennonite Brethren in North America, 1874 -2002* (Winnipeg, MB: The Christian Press, 2002}. pp.151-166.

"Urbanization, Religious Dispersion and Secularization," in Harvey Neufeldt, Ruth Derksen Siemens and Robert Martens, eds., *First Nations and First Settlers in the Fraser Valley (1890-1960)* (Kitchener, ON: Pandora Press, 2004). pp. 261-278.

"The Mennonite Contribution to Abbotsford," in *Being the Church in Abbotsford* (Abbotsford, BC: Abbotsford Christian Leaders Network, 2013). pp. 90-100.

"The Hungarians Come to Abbotsford," in Robert Martens, editor, *Abbotsford: A diverse Tapestry* (Abbotsford, BC: Abbotsford Historical Book Committee, 2021). pp. 129-140.

3. Articles in books

"Whose Anabaptist Heritage?" in Merle Good and Phyllis Pellman Good, eds, *What Mennonites Are Thinking, 1999* (Intercourse, PA: Good Books, 1999). 115-118.

"Buying Two Farms," in John H. Redekop, editor, *Stillwood: The First 50 Years, 1958 - 2008 (Chilliwack, BC: Stillwood Publications, 2008). pp. 117-118.*

"Building on God's Acres," in John H. Redekop, editor, *Stillwood: The First 50 Years, 1958 - 2008* (Chilliwack, BC: Stillwood Publications, 2008). pp. 176-177.

4. Articles in encyclopedias

Five articles in *Baker's Dictionary of Christian Ethics* (Grand Rapids, MI: Baker Book House, 1974). "Arbitration," p. 35; "Boycott," p. 68; "Guaranteed Income," pp. 277-278; "Labor Relations," pp. 374-376; "Strikes," pp. 649-650.

Three articles in *The Mennonite Encyclopedia*, Vol. 5 (Scottdale, PA: Herald Press, 1990). "Government," pp. 349-351; "Politics," pp. 711-714; "Labor Unions," pp. 502-503.

Three articles in Robert Banks and R. Paul Stevens, eds., *The Complete Book of Everyday Christianity* (Downers Grove, IL: InterVarsity Press, 1997). "Lobbying," pp. 591-593; "Pluralism," pp. 762-765; "Political Parties; Joining," pp. 765-768.

5. Articles in *Direction* (A refereed journal)

"Civil Religion in Canada," Vol. V, No. 3 (July 1976), pp. 10-14.
"The Interaction of Economics and Religion: The Case of the Mennonite Brethren in Canada," Vol. X, No. 3 (July 1981), pp. 48-68.

"The Christian in Politics: Some Basic Problems," Vol. XIV, No. 1 (Spring, 1985), pp. 34-41.

"Perspectives and Interpretations: the Influence of Rising Educational Levels," Vol. XIV, No. 2 (Fall, 1985), pp. 54-59.

"Ethnicity and the Mennonite Brethren: Issues and Responses," Vol. 17, No. 1 (Spring, 1988), pp. 3-16.

"The Politics of the Mennonite Central Committee," Vol.3, No. 2 (Fall, 1994), pp. 63-76.

"Being the Church in the Midst of Culture," Vol. 35, No. 2 (Fall, 2006), pp. 245-252.

"A Reflection of a Spiritual Pilgrimage" or "What UBC did to me and for me," Vol. 37, No 1 (Spring, 2008), pp. 50-59.

"Introduction to 'Faith and Learning,'" Vol. 37, No. 1 (Spring, 2008), pp. 3-6.

6. Articles in other refereed journals

"Billy James Hargis' Perception of the American Constitution, Government, and Society," *The Journal of Church and Society,* Vol. 1, No. 1 (Spring, 1965), pp. 43-64.

"Authors and Publishers: An Analysis of Textbook Selections in Canadian Departments of Political Science and Sociology," *Canadian Journal of Political Science,* Vol. IX, No. 1 (March 1976), pp. 107-120.

"A Re-interpretation of Canadian-American Relations," *Canadian Journal of Political Science*, Vol. IX, No. 2 (June 1976), pp. 227-243.

"Mennonites and Politics in Canada and the United States," *Journal of Mennonite Studies* Vol. 1, No. 1 (Summer, 1983), pp.79-105.

"Dilemmas of Nationalism and National Unity in Canada since 1945," *British Bulletin of Canadian Studies*, Vol. IX, No. 1 (Spring, 1985), pp. 5-24.

"The Roots of Nazi Support Among Canadian Mennonites, 1930 to 1939, A Case Study Based on a Major Mennonite Paper," *Journal of Mennonite Studies*, Vol. 14 (1996), pp. 81-95.

"An Assessment of the Citizens Assembly on Electoral Reform," *BC Studies*, No. 147 (Autumn, 2005), pp. 89-102.

7. Articles in other academic publication

"Religious Pressure Groups in the Canadian Political System, *WLU Research Paper Series No 8470,* (Fall, 1984), 27 pp. Co-editor with Nicolas Nyiri, "Uses and Abuses of Systems Theory," (Waterloo, ON: Wilfrid Laurier University Press, 1985), 96 pp. Occasional Paper 2, Interdisciplinary Research Seminar.

"God in Public: John Redekop to Scott Holland," *Conrad Grebel Review*, Vol. 4, No. 2 (Spring, 1986), pp. 156-158.

8. Introductions and Forewords in books

"Foreword," in Walter Klaassen, *What Have You To Do With Peace?* (Altona, MB: D. W. Friesen & Sons, 1969).

"Foreword," in Maria Foth, *Beyond the Border; Maria's Miraculous Pilgrimage* (Burlington, ON: G.R. Welch Company, 1981).

"Foreword," in Robert N. Thompson, *A House of Minorities* (Burlington, ON: G., R. Welch Publishing Company, 1990).

"Foreword," in James John Guy, 2nd edition, *People, Politics and Government* (Don Mills, ON: Collier Macmillan, 1990).

"Foreword," in Brian C. Stiller, *Critical Options for Evangelicals* (Markham, ON: Faith Today Publications, 1991).

"Foreword," in Walfried Goossen, *Anabaptism; A Dying Candle* (Winnipeg: Henderson Books, 1994).

"Foreword," in John R. Sutherland, ed., *Us and Them; Building a Just Workplace Community* (Mississauga, ON: Work Research Foundation, 1999).
"Introduction," in Jacob (Jack) Block, *Reflections* (Surrey, B.C: Coastline Mountain Press (1983) Ltd., 2002).

9. Papers published in Conference Proceedings

"Canadian-American Relations in the 1970s; Towards a Systemic Analysis" in *Proceedings,* Canadian Political Science Association, McGill University, 1972.
"A Subsystemic Interpretation of Canadian Politics" in *Proceedings,* Canadian Political Science Association, University of Alberta, 1975).

"The Role of Religious Pressure Groups in the Canadian Political System" in *Proceedings,* Canadian Political Science Association, University of Montreal, 1985).

10. **Miscellaneous Publications**

Making Political Decisions; a Christian Perspective (Scottdale, PA, 1972). 45 pp.

Leadership Handbook (Winnipeg: Kindred Press, 1984). 53 pp. This booklet was written jointly with Frank C. Peters.

"An Analysis of Capital Punishment" in *On Capital Punishment* by Elmer Martens and John H. Redekop (Winnipeg: Kindred Press, 1987). pp. 7-18. This booklet has gone into several printings. It has also been translated into French as *La Peine Capitale (*Winnipeg: Kindred Press, 1987). 32 pp.

The Christian and Civil Disobedience (Winnipeg: Kindred Press, 1990). 42 pp. This booklet has been translated into French as *Chretien et la Desobeissance Civile* (Winnipeg: Kindred Press, 1990). 44 pp.

Anabaptism: The Basic Beliefs (Winnipeg: Canadian Mennonite Brethren Conference Board of Faith and Life, 1993). Faith and Life Pamphlet Series. This pamphlet had been translated into German, French, Spanish, Portuguese, Telegu, Lithuanian, and Mandarin.

Christians and War (Winnipeg: Canadian Mennonite Brethren Conference Board of Faith and Life, 1993). Faith and Life Pamphlet Series. This pamphlet was written jointly with Henry Hubert.

Finding Fulfillment in Retiring: When Christians Retire (Winnipeg: Canadian Conference of Mennonite Brethren Board of Faith and Life, c. 1995). Faith and Life Pamphlet Series. This pamphlet was written jointly with Herbert Brandt.

Christians and Civil Disobedience (Markham, ON: The Religious Liberty Commission of the Evangelical Fellowship of Canada, 2002). 12 pp.

11. Publications in the popular press

The Mennonite Brethren Herald. Between January 1, 1964, and February 28, 2003, I wrote 870 *Personal Opinion* columns. In addition, between 1962 and 2020, I published about 30 other articles in this periodical.

ChristianWeek. Between 1987 and 1999, I wrote 142 columns for this newspaper.

The Canadian Mennonite. Between 1954 and 1969, I wrote approximately 85 columns and articles in this newspaper.

WLU Newsfeatures. Between 1974 and 1994, I wrote 66 *Newsfeature* columns, which were distributed to about 40 Ontario newspapers. Not all items appeared in all of the newspapers.

Kitchener-Waterloo Record. Between 1970 and 2019, I had about 35 articles published in this newspaper.

Christian Leader Between May 1962 and November 2004, I wrote 22 feature articles for this magazine.

BC Christian News. Between 1996 and 2009, I wrote 17 articles for this newspaper.

Abbotsford News. Between 1994 and 2021, I wrote at least 17 articles for this newspaper.

In addition to these publications, I had about 185 articles published in other newspapers, magazines, and other periodicals, including about 35 in major newspapers such as *Toronto Star, Toronto Globe and Mail, Vancouver Sun, Calgary Herald, St. John's Evening Telegram, Regina Leader-Post* and *Vancouver Province.*

Various articles were translated and published in French, German, Punjabi, and Chinese.

APPENDIX C

STILLWOOD DEVELOPMENT

A. New Buildings (33)
The Pool Bath-House
Ten Cottage Duplexes
The Open Storage Shed
The Dyck Dining Hall
Three Guest Lodges
The Red Barn Gymnasium
The Courtyard Gazebo
Four Tree Houses
Ambassador House
The Speaker's Cabin
The Tree House Viewing Tower
Stillwood Station Building
The Krahn Centre
The Dome Gymnasium
Stillwood Chapel
The Schmidt General Store
Two Bunkhouses
The electrical utility building

B. Major Renovations and additions (9)
Addition to the Executive Director's Residence
The Wiebe-Isaak Craft Building
Raised deck and staircase addition to the Maple Lodge Assembly Room
Renovation of the Maple Lodge Assembly Room
The Dueck Health Centre
Construction of Stillbuck's Coffee Shop in Maple Lodge
The Dogwood Lodge Renovation
Construction of the Founders and Pioneers Lounge in Dogwood Lodge
The Program Centre Building (Poplar)

C. Other Major Development Projects (12)
Purchase of the Eades property (10 acres)
Purchase of the Olsen property (30 acres)
Paving of main roads and walkways
The 25-metre Schroeder Junior Olympic-size Pool
Laying of 10,000 paving stones in the main courtyard and elsewhere
The outdoor paved basketball court
Four 40-foot climbing stations in the Red Barn Gymnasium
Major landscaping around Stillwood Station and the entrance area
Land exchange with BC Parks
The reconstruction and resodding of the main playing field
Construction of the chain-link fence
The second paving of lanes and parking areas

To fund these projects, John raised approximately $12,750,000 from about 200 donors located between Calgary and the BC coast. He also solicited about $400,000 worth of supplies and services from regional individuals and companies and, together with Executive Director Harry Edwards, recruited more than 5,000 person-days of donated labour. The latter number includes construction volunteers and retirees who served in maintenance and operations over the years as SOWERs (Servants On Wheels Ever Ready) or RVICS (Retired Volunteers In Christ's Service).

Red Barn Gymasium $2,650,000

Dyck Dining Hall $2,200,000

Stillwood Station (Administration Building) $700,000

Camper Cabin Duplex $50,000

A One-Day Store-Raising, at noon, $35,000

Stillwood Chapel $1,650,000

25-metre Junior Olympic-size Pool $600,000

Campers in Stillwood Pool

APPENDIX D

HONORARY DEGREE CITATIONS

A. The following statement was printed in the *Trinity Western University Commencement Exercises* Booklet, May 1, 1994. The event was held in the Sevenoaks Alliance Church in Abbotsford, BC.

John Harold Redekop is a friend of long-standing to the church, to Canada, to higher education, and to Trinity Western University.

His reputation as a man of God is such that he became the National Moderator of the Mennonite Brethren Churches of Canada. He has also served on the Boards of Mennonite Brethren Bible College, Mennonite Central Committee, the Evangelical Fellowship of Canada, and World Relief Canada.

Dr. John Redekop's scholarship has brought more than 100 invitations to lecture and to participate in scholarly conferences. He has also been awarded Canada Council Fellowships, the McKenzie King Travelling Scholarship, and many research grants from Wilfrid Laurier University, including WLU's Outstanding Teacher Award.

Often sought out by the media as an authoritative and articulate voice for evangelical Christians in Canada, his work has earned him the Leslie K. Tarr Award in recognition of outstanding contribution in the field of Christian writing and the Canadian Church Press Award of Excellence.

His areas of research have included government and politics in Canada, the U.S., and the Soviet Union; the relationship between church, religion and politics; political thought; Canadian Studies; and political socialization. Dr. Redekop is recognized as a scholar and a man of godly wisdom on the Canadian and international scene.

His coming here today is, in two senses, a coming home: in his early days as a high school teacher, Dr. Redekop taught in Langley and was president of the Langley Teachers' Association; and, of course, he has been an adjunct professor of Inter-Disciplinary Studies here at Trinity Western.

Trinity Western University is pleased to announce that Dr. John Redekop will be joining us in September 1994 as a Research Scholar in Residence. We are especially pleased at this time to confer upon Dr. Redekop the degree of Doctor of Humanities, *honoris causa*, and to ask him to share his current insights by addressing the Graduating Class and his many friends gathered here today.

B. This citation was read by Vice-President Donald Page at the awarding of the degree. It is reproduced here as it was later submitted to John. (Three minor corrections were made in this reproduction.)

DR. DON PAGE
THIS YEAR THE UNIVERSITY HAS CHOSEN TO HONOUR A DISTINGUISHED CHRISTIAN SCHOLAR WHO HAS USED HIS ABILITIES TO SERVE THOUSANDS OF YOUNG PEOPLE AND THE CHURCH OF JESUS CHRIST THROUGHOUT THE WORLD.
 I TAKE GREAT PLEASURE IN PRESENTING TO YOU JOHN HAROLD REDEKOP, A HUMBLE AND GIFTED SERVANT OF THE LORD JESUS CHRIST.
 IN UNIVERSITY CIRCLES, PROFESSOR REDEKOP IS WELL KNOWN FOR THE HIGH STANDARDS THAT HE HAS SET FOR TEACHING AND SCHOLARSHIP. HIS OWN CAREER WAS A MODEL FOR STUDENTS. HAVING OBTAINED HIS FOUR DEGREES, THREE WITH FIRST CLASS HONOURS FROM THE UNIVERSITIES OF BRITISH COLUMBIA, CALIFORNIA, AND WASHINGTON. HE HAS TAUGHT AT THE UNIVERSITY OF WASHINGTON, FRESNO PACIFIC COLLEGE, FRESNO STATE UNIVERSITY, AND SINCE 1968 AT WILFRID LAURIER UNIVERSITY. DURING THIS TIME HIS ACADEMIC PEERS HAVE HONOURED HIM WITH APPOINTMENTS AS CHAIR OF THE POLITICAL SCIENCE DEPARTMENT, PRESIDENT OF THE FACULTY ASSOCIATION AND THE FACULTY REPRESENTATIVE ON THE BOARD OF GOVERNORS.

 IN THE LAST TEN YEARS, HE HAS RECEIVED 13 RESEARCH GRANTS. THROUGHOUT HIS CAREER AS A SCHOLAR, HE HAS CONTRIBUTED CHAPTERS TO 10 BOOKS ON CANADIAN AND AMERICAN POLITICS, PUBLISHED 10 ARTICLES IN REFEREED JOURNALS, AND WRITTEN 6 BOOKS ON CANADIAN AND AMERICAN POLITICS, LABOUR RELATIONS, AND MENNONITE HISTORY. UNLIKE SO MANY OF HIS ACADEMIC PEERS, HOWEVER, PROFESSOR REDEKOP HAS AT THE SAME TIME EXCELLED AS A TEACHER, AND IN 1992, HE WON THE OUTSTANDING TEACHER AWARD AT WILFRID LAURIER UNIVERSITY.

TO MANY CANADIANS, DR. REDEKOP IS BEST KNOWN FOR THE THOUGHTFUL CHRISTIAN PERSPECTIVE ON TROUBLESOME ISSUES IN CONTEMPORARY SOCIETY, INCLUDING THE RESPONSIBILITY OF CHRISTIANS IN POLITICS AND ETHICAL ISSUES. READERS OF CHRISTIAN WEEK HAVE FOUND THEIR FAITH AND THEIR RESPONSIBILITIES AS CHRISTIAN CITIZENS ENHANCED BY HIS COMMON-SENSE APPROACH TO COMPLICATED ISSUES. IN 1989 HE WAS THE RECIPIENT OF THE LESLIE K TARR AWARD IN RECOGNITION OF HIS OUTSTANDING CONTRIBUTION IN THE FIELD OF CHRISTIAN WRITING.

HE HAS ALSO HAD HIS ARTICLES PUBLISHED IN 23 CANADIAN NEWSPAPERS, INCLUDING THE KINGSTON WHIG-STANDARD, THE HAMILTON SPECTATOR, THE PETERBOROUGH EXAMINER, THE CALGARY HERALD, AND THE ST. JOHN'S EVENING TELEGRAM, AND OVER 700 ARTICLES FOR POPULAR MAGAZINES. ON THE PUBLIC PLATFORM, HE HAS GIVEN NUMEROUS LECTURES, AVERAGING 50 PER YEAR FOR THE LAST 15 YEARS.

WE ALSO WISH TO ACKNOWLEDGE THE LEADERSHIP THAT HE HAS CONTRIBUTED TO THE BOARD OF DIRECTORS OF THE MENNONITE CENTRAL COMMITTEE AND HIS SERVICE AS NATIONAL MODERATOR OF THE CANADIAN CONFERENCE OF MENNONITE BRETHREN CHURCHES FROM 1983 TO 1987. HIS INFLUENCE GOES FAR BEYOND HIS DENOMINATION TO THE ENTIRE CANADIAN EVANGELICAL COMMUNITY. FROM 1985 TO 1991, HE SERVED AS THE VICE-PRESIDENT OF THE EVANGELICAL FELLOWSHIP OF CANADA AND FROM 1991 TO 1993 AS ITS PRESIDENT. DURING HIS TERM IN OFFICE, THE EFC HAS BECOME THE FOREMOST CHRISTIAN VOICE INFLUENCING OUR NATIONAL AFFAIRS.

THROUGHOUT HIS LIFE, DR. REDEKOP HAS BEEN RECOGNIZED FOR HIS CONTRIBUTION TO RAISING THE INTELLECTUAL AND MORAL LIFE OF THINKING ON PUBLIC AFFAIRS. WE ALSO HONOUR HIM FOR HIS WARM AND COMPASSIONATE HEART, A CHAMPION OF CHRISTIAN HIGHER EDUCATION, AND CANADA'S FOREMOST CHRISTIAN LEADER IN EXPOUNDING A CHRISTIAN WORLDVIEW ON CONTEMPORARY SOCIETY AND POLITICS

PRESIDENT SNIDER, I AM PLEASED TO PRESENT JOHN HAROLD REDEKOP FOR THE DEGREE OF DOCTOR OF HUMANITIES, *HONORIS CAUSA.*

DR. SNIDER
BY THE AUTHORITY OF THE BOARD OF GOVERNORS AND BY VIRTUE OF THE POWERS VESTED IN TRINITY WESTERN UNIVERSITY BY THE PROVINCE OF BRITISH COLUMBIA, I HEREBY CONFER UPON JOHN HAROLD REDEKOP THE DEGREE OF DOCTOR OF HUMANITIES, *HONORIS CAUSA.*

Stillwood Memories

The late Dr. Ken Dyck, a long-time friend and a long-term Stillwood supporter with John.

John, on the right, placing siding shingles with John Hamm.

John being dunked to raise funds at Stillwood.

INDEX

Bold font indicates importance or picture.
A People Apart: Ethnicity and the Mennonite Brethren 219-220
A & W Stillwood donation 297
A personal apology 64
Abbotsford, British Columbia 28, 30, 159
 a burgeoning city, 1994 259
 city councillor 303-304
 Mountain Drive home 259
 moving to Garden Park Tower 317
 population in 1994 259
Abbotsford Bible School (later Columbia Bible College) 27-30
 John as student 71-73
 Redekop, Jacob F. as teacher 27, 28, 29
Abbotsford City Council
 councillor, 199-202 303-304
  Fraser Valley Treaty Advisory Committee 303
  Fukagawa visit 303-304
  Sumas Energy Company, SE2 crisis 304-305
Abbotsford Symphony Orchestra 261
Acapulco family holiday **209**-210
Acceptance of Quebec Association of Mennonite Brethren Churches 1984 226-227
Afghanistan Crisis 350
Agricultural Land Commission 296
Aldergrove Secondary School 142, 145, 146
 improper report card 143
All-Union Council of Evangelical Christians-Baptists, Moscow 250
 Barclay's Commentary crisis 1984 240
Almand, Warren 230
Anabaptism: The Basic Beliefs 222
 many translations 222
Anabaptist-Mennonite Centre, Trinity Western University 292
Anabaptist sites in The Netherlands 130
Anabaptist theology 153
 report on **Anabaptists Four Centuries Later** 197
 and conference structure 198
apology to Japanese-Canadians 230-231
apology to Mennonite General Conference 227-**228**
Approaches to Canadian Politics 193
 second edition 219
 Japanese translation 219
Ascania, steamship to Europe 1955 90

Asperia, steamship to Beirut 1956 114
Aunt Katherine's miraculous vision 202
Bachelor of Arts 1954 **77**, 135
Baerg, Rudy 267, 288
Bakerview Church
 care group 320
 establishment of three distinct services 267-268
 gift of bicycles for India 280
 home church, 1994- 266
 meeting Michael and Edit Ellis 143
 moderator 268
Bakerview Sings! cassettes and CDs 266-**267**
Barclay's Commentary crisis, 1984 240
Basford, Skip. 291
Bauman, Ed, room-mate 1953-1954 76
BC Christian News 274
 two authors review each other's books 274
BCMB Conference of Churches
 elected to Youth Committee 151
 first assignment 147
 first English-language secretary 148
 member, Executive Committee 2007-2011 271
BCMB Conference Minister 326, 327
 closure meeting 330
 Covenant of Confidentiality 330
 forgiveness 331, 332
 persistent opposition 330, 334
  refusal to meet **328**
 relevant actions 331
BCMB Moderator
 closure meeting 330
 conditional acceptance of a new overture 330
 Covenant of Confidentiality **330**
 forgiveness 331, 332
 her letter rejecting the Leis Report 330
 refusal to meet 328
 relevant actions by the moderator 331
 unacceptable conditions for meeting 327-328
BCMB Executive Board
 forgiveness 331, 332
 halted Stillwood planning 326
 ignored the 1992 Transfer Agreement 326-327
 obstructive actions 331
 received David Leis's report 328
 report of an Executive Board member **328, 329**
 resignation of dissident Executive Board member 330

termination of all of John's ministry 326-327, 334
BCMB Youth Committee 151
  Youth Rally, 1958 151
  Clayburn Camp 151
BC School of Science and Matriculation 78
Berg, Steve 302
Berkeley, CA 155-156
Beriozka 240-241
Bethel Bible Institute 290
Bibby, Reginald 203
blasting stumps **6**
Bichkov, Alexie
  AUCECB General Secretary 246
  arranged meeting with the Commisar of Religious Affairs 250
bicycles for evangelists in India 280
  illiterate Elijah 280
Bishkek, Kyrgyzstan 278
  Ray of Hope Mission 278
Block, Arthur 229
Block, Ernie 290
  Ernie and Elfrieda 288
Block, Jack 151
  first camp director, 1958 151
Board of Higher Education (Canada)
  member, vice-chair 198
Board of Spiritual and Social Concerns (Canada)
  member 197, 198, 229
  publication of *A People Apart* 219-220
Board of Spiritual and Social Concerns (Ontario) 226
Boge, Jascha 311
Boschman, Merv 288, 299
box wagon **42**
  collecting buffalo bones 50
Brucks, Henry 227-229
Brunk Evangelistic Campaign 148-150
Butler Avenue Mennonite Brethren Church 176, 181
Canadian Charter of Rights and Freedoms 257
Canadian Conference of Mennonite Brethren Churches
  1968 structure 311
  2004 structural changes 311-313
  comments on the 1950s and 1960s 152-153
  critical evaluation, 2004 278
  critical evaluation, 2019 338
  a declining conference 312-313
  a financial crisis 312
  request for a report on labour unions 196
  the German language issue, 1963 168-169
  good years 198
Canadian Council of Mennonite and Brethren in Christ Moderators 231
Canadian Mennonite Brethren conventions
  John dropped on concrete, 1973 197-198
  support for the Evangelical Fellowship of Canada 203
Canadian Pacific Railway 18
  Settler's Car 28
  John as third cook 71-74, 76, 87
Canadian religious data 346-348
Care Group **220**
Carmichael, Craig **353**
Celebration of Praise, Columbia Bible College 290
  plans and reflections 288-291
Central Heights Church (formerly Abbotsford MB and McCallum Road MB) 289
  established, first pastors 67, 134, 136
  first preaching assignments 147
  MB Biblical Seminary celebration, 1999 283
  youth leader 148
Charbonneau, Danielle
  as young child **217, 318**
  with Billy Wright and Ada Grace 355
childhood chores, work 32, 53-55
  in British Columbia 64
  in Saskatchewan 31-32, 40-41, 53
China
  anti-Christian values 264
  civil war, 1949 70
China trip, 2007 263-265
  speaking in Hangchou church 263-**264**
  Tiananmen Square and Great Wall **264**
Citizens Assembly
  electoral brief submitted 2004 306
Christian Week columnist 222
  later columns 271
Christmas in Germany, 1955 95-97
  with other Canadian students 96-97
  with students in Burg Liebenzoll 97
  with the Schmidt family 95-96
Christian Leader
  early articles 171
  early criticisms of John 171
  political articles 182
church life; John's spiritual pilgrimage
  childhood years 48-50
  high school years 67-69
  faith formation 67-69
  faith formation at UBC 79-82
Clearbrook 25
Clearbrook issue of *The Canadian Mennonite* **146**-147
Clinton, Bill 314
Coghlan Bible School 290
  no tuition; no fees 290
College and Career Class, Waterloo Mennonite Brethren Church 188, 211
College Community Church, Clovis, CA 10
Collegium Academicum, Heidelberg

accepted as Collegiate 91-92
embarrassing moment 93-94
return from the long trip 128
Columbia Bible Camp
 conditions of transfer to BCMB Conference 325
Columbia Bible College 288-291
 1930 students in Yarrow 289
 a proposal for an alumni event 288
 alumni event 289-290
 Celebration of Worship and Praise 290
 planning committee 288
 plans for the present and the future 288-289
 Residence Planning Team 291
Communist Party of the Soviet Union 248
 deceived by a taxi driver 242
 Heinrich Abramovich Unger and others **246, 247**
Conference restructuring in Canada, 2004 311-313
convention presentations, 1981-1994 224-225
Congo (DRC) National Assembly
 Maleghi, Leonard, member 285
 addressing Assembly members 285-**286**
Congo visit (DRC) **287**
 an unusual flight 285
 Batela MB Church 285
 open-air church 285
 orphanage **284**
cooling food in pioneer times 37-38
Cooperative Commonwealth Federation (CCF) 47-48, 59
Country Guide 48, 55, 69
Covenant of Confidentiality 330
cross-Canada car trip, 2008 265
Cuban Missile Crisis, 1963 169-170
Cunningham, Jim 357
Current Issues Class presentations 267, 275
Czerkova, Lyuba
 tour guide, USSR, 1984 240
 translator 243
Dahl, Faith **365**
debate with David Noebel, 1968 184
debates with Marvin Glass, "Marxism vs. Christianity" 235-238
 Carleton University debate 235, **236**, 237
 Wilfrid Laurier University debate 237-238,**258**
 Trinity Western University debate 238
delirious in Damascus 116
detentions in the parlour 43
Deutsche Academische Austausch Dienst (German Academic Exchange Program) 136
 offer of scholarship 78
 expenses covered 89
Dick, Lorraine 298-299
Dirks, Sylvester 290

Doctor of Humanities conferred by Trinity Western University, 1994 255-256
 the citations 256, 383-386
Doerksen, Leonard 288
Doerksen, Lillian; Ramabai Mukti Mission 31
Dominican Republic holiday, 1991 214
Doris Redekop (nee Nikkel) 13, **88, 154**
 Bachelor of Arts 213-214
 "daily mail" from John 131
 early picture **134**
 early picture with John **135**
 Hawaiian holiday 309
 in Fresno **182**
 jam jars **318, 319**
 Nikkel family **133**
 postponing our wedding 78-79
 reunited, August 3, 1956 131
 rice-planting in Japan 304
 sang in a trio 211
 wedding 137
dropped on concrete by members of the Board of Management 197-198
Dueck, John room-mate 1954-1955 78
Dueck, Ted 361
Durksen, Carl and Mary
 Passion Play in Drumheller, Alberta 320
 travels **319, 320**
dust storm **38**, 39
Dyck, Calvin and Heather 267
Dyck, David (MBMSI) 279
Dyck, Harvey
 an unusual border crossing 127
 celebrating Christmas, 1955 96-97
 inspecting a destroyed tank 106
 leaving Heidelberg for Africa 99
 planning travel 96
Dyck, John and Edith, daughter Carol 296
 With RCMP officers 324
Dyck, Ken 296, **315**, 323, **386**
Dyck, Peter 59-60
Eades, Bob 297-299
Edwards, Harry 324, **364**
 fundraising 298-300
 gratitude 333
 prayer circle **298, 299**
 Stillwood executive director 294, **295**, 326
 with Harry and Gail for China trip 263
egg collection 41
engagement 135-136
Enns, Abram **245**-247, 248-251
Enns, Alvin 188,201
 with Alvin and Sue for China trip 2007 263
Enns, John and Elizabeth 294

Enns, Peter 269
Epp, Frank
  editor, *The Canadian Mennonite* 82-83
  led the delegation to Warren Almand, Ottawa 230
  special Clearbrook issue of *The Canadian Mennonite* **144**
Esau, Henry and Elizabeth
  executive director, Columbia Bible Camp 292-**295**, 325-326, **351**
  Henry and Linda, special gratitude 332 **351**
  invitation to John to help at camp 292-293
Esther, the MEI drama 61-62
  John as Mordecai **61**
Evangelical Fellowship of Canada 198
  elected president, 1991 232
  elected vice-president, 1985 232
  Social Action Commission chair, 200
Ewert, David 283
faith-formation 50
family activities
  devotions 33, 48-49
  good times 42, 43
  making music together **32**
  Saturday bath routines in early times 52
farming
  King Road, Abbotsford, BC 28
  Main Centre, Saskatchewan 28, 37-38
Fast, Ed **362**
  proposal for Borge Olsen 299
Ferndale home **187**
  buying the property 187-188
  family residence, 1972-1994 188
  sale 218
first book 179
first date 136
first winter in Abbotsford, BC 55
flour mills in Russia 16, 17
Franz, Jake **228**-229
Fraser River flood, 1948 65-66
Fraserview MB Church 292
Friesen, Abe, taxidermist 324
Friesen, Bill and Anne 298-299
Friesen, John D. 301
Friesen, Robert 227
Fresno, CA 171-178
Froese, David and Hilda
  prayer circle "claiming" property **298, 299**
  Stillwood donors 296-300
  the A & W donation 297
  the Eades property purchase 297-298
  with Borge Olsen **300**
Fukugawa, Twin City visit 302-304
fundraising
  hesitation 325
  joys and challenges 325

Mark Centre 302
Music Mission Kiev 341
Pacific Mennonite Children's Choir 301
reflections 323-325, 293-296
Stillwood 293-300, 323, **324, 325**
Stillwood anniversary book, 2008 269
The Tabor Home Society 343
Garden Park Journal 322
Garden Park Newsletter 322
Garden Park Tower 290, 317, 322
German language as church issue 168-169
Giesbrecht, David 267
Glass, Marvin 235-238, **236, 258**
Gosling house 139
grade seven 56
Government of Canada award, 1992 **254**
gramophone, selection and destruction of records 52
grandchildren **318**
  Danielle **217, 355**
  David **217, 356**
  Michelle **260, 356**
Great Depression 12, 37-38, 151
  relief provisions from government 39
guided to the wrong Y 117
Hargis, Billy James 164, 184
Harper, Stephen 311-312
Hatfield, Mark
  Foreword in *The American Far Right* 179
Hawaii 309
  Honolulu, 1996 292
  gift of a holiday **309**
health, health care, diets
  early years 37-39
  organic food 37
  Wonder Oil 38-39
health issues
  subdural hematoma, 2008 265-266
  Type 2 Diabetes, 2008 266
Heidebrecht, Harry 266
Heidelberg 89, 90-**91**, 92, 136
Heidelberg University 91
  courses 94
  examinations; examination results 85, 96
  second semester 128-131
  with Paul Froman teaching fellow students 98
Herbert Bible School 26, **27**-28, 35
Herbert, Saskatchewan 19, 23, 32, 35, 36
Hiebert, Philip **365**
Hiebert, Vic 184
  with Alyce as hosts 186, 187
high school at MEI 57-64
hog-butchering 52-53
homestead **23**, 27
honeymoon 138-139
hop-picking 64-65

hospital bed to committee meeting 212
House of Commons Standing Committee on
    Human Rights 305-306
    brief presented on same-sex unions 305-306
    Prime Minister Jean Chretien 305-306
house-buying in Fresno 171-172
Hungarian professors **143**
impasse at the Vienna Opera House 127
Ingwersen, Cornelius, call for help 68
InterVarsity Christian Fellowship
    at UBC 81
    university debates 235-238, **236**
    Waterloo Committee
Isaac, John room-mate 1952-1953 75-76
Jahnke Cattle Ranch 47
jam jars **318, 319**
Jantz, Harold 360
    ChristianWeek editor 222
    editor, *Leaders Who Shaped Us* 310
January 6, 2021 riot 350
Janzen, Bill 199-200
Janzen, Daniel
    late supper in the Janzen home 248
    Orenburg trip 245-246
    pastor. Donskoye Church 245
    visit to the Janzen home 248-249
    visit to Waterloo 246
Janzen, Leona 297
Janzen, Wes and Kim 342, **358**
Japan Mennonite Brethren Conference 281
Jewish spies? 108-109
Kamenskaya 16
Karaganda "escape" 252-253
Kennedy assassination, 1963 170
KGB (Soviet secret police)
    four KGB agents in church service 247
    a KGB agent as a dinner guest **248**
Kikwit 285
King Road farm 28
Kharchev, Konstatin
    Commissar Kharchev's response 250
    John's prepared statement 247
    Kremlin interview 248-250
    Soviet Commissar of Religious Affairs 248-250
Killarney Park MB Church 295-296
King, Martin Luther assassinated 182
Klassen, Peter 176
Kooy, Doug 301
Kopp, Herb 229
Korean War 70
    experiences during the NAZI era 94
    saying "Good-Bye," 1956 131
Krieg, Herman **94**
    Heidelberg room-mate 93-94
Labour Problems in Christian Perspective 192
Labrador 265
Langley Secondary School 141, 145-146

hired as teacher 141
briefly taught Girls Phys Ed 141
Model United Nations 143
Langley Teachers Association, president 145
language transition in churches 168-169, 204
Learning Plus 307, 343
Leis, David
    BCMB leaders reject the Leis Report 329
    hired by the Reconciliation Advocates as
        investigator **328, 329**
    vindication by David Leis 328, 329
Leningrad (St. Petersburg)
    Beriozka **240**
    "night tour" 241-242
Leslie K. Tarr Award 253
Letkemann, John 308-309
    John and Betty 298-299
Liberal Party of Canada 47, 306, 313
Liberdad Church, Asuncion 329-341, **340**
Lobetal School 45-47
Loewen, Art 298-299, 333
Lumeya, Maleghi Leonard 285
Lumeya, Nzash 284-286
Main Centre Mennonite Brethren Church 47,
    48, **49**, 50
    Missions Fest 50
Main Centre, Saskatchewan 25-27, 28, 35-36, 39
    100th Anniversary message 276
    Cooperative Commonwealth Federation 45
    farm 27, 32
    homestead **23**
    telephone system 51
    VE celebration 48
Mandelbaum Gate; the two-passport crossing 119
Mander, Linden
    dissertation advisor 104-165
    mentor 162-1
    the gift 166-167
Manning, Preston 334-335
Martin Luther King assassinated 182
Martin, Paul, legalized same-sex marriage 313
Martens, Menno
    choir director, 1987 Soviet Union trip 252
    detained a pursuing Soviet officer 252
Master of Arts, University of California 145, 155-157
    graduation ceremony **156**-157
Mathies, Helmut 292
    diagnosis of Henry H. Nikkel 210
    holiday travel, 2000 262
    hot weather in London, UK 213
    serious car problem 262
McCarthy, Joseph 70
Mennonite Brethren Bible College
    vice-chair of the board 197
Mennonite Brethren Biblical Seminary
    Abbotsford Centre 282
    board member, board chair 197

celebration at Central Heights Church, 1999 283
currency controversy, 1978 197-198
negotiations with ACTS at Trinity Western
    University 283
    researching the British Columbia options 282-283
Mennonite Brethren Church 21, 25
    weakened conference structure 348-349
    research report 277
Mennonite Brethren Herald
    closure 2019 312
    high readership of column 180
    last report of the Board of Faith and Life 281
    later column writing 271
    Personal Opinion column launched, 1984 169
    Personal Opinion columns 1968-1980 193
    Personal Opinion columns 1981-1994 223
    Personal Opinion columns 1994-2003 220-221
Mennonite Brethren Missions and Services
    board member 1996-1999 278
    trip to Russia, Kazakhstan, Kyrgyzstan, 1997 278-279
    trip to Indonesia, India, Pakistan, Japan, 1998- 199, 279-281
Mennonite Central Committee 198
    apology to Frst Nations 231
    apology to Japanese-Canadians 230-231
    evaluation reports 1999-2000
    member, 1988-1994 229-231
    session with Warren Almand 230
    William "Bill" Janzen 199
Mennonite Church in Russia 18
Mennonite Educational Institute, Abbotsford, BC
    57-64, 230
    closed for five weeks because of snow 66
    Evergreen yearbook, editor 61
    Sir Cecil's Gold 62-63
    Students' Call, editor 60
    student life 58
    teachers 58-59
Mennonite Faith and Learning Society 291-292
    at the University of the Fraser Valley 291- 292
    at Trinity Western University 292
Mennonite heritage 14, 151
Mennonite World Conference
    co-organizer of 1986 Soviet trip 244
Mennonites in Paraguay 338-339
minefield, sleeping in 107-108
mistaken by a hunter 87
moderator of the Canadian Conference of
    Mennonite Brethren Churches
    acceptance of Quebec Mennonite Brethren 226-227
    apology to Mennonite General Conference **227-228**
    assistant moderator 1980-1983 198, 226

moderator 1983-1987 226
moderator messages 226-227
moose hunting 72-73, **74**
Moscow 242
    Red Square **244**
Moscow Baptist Church
    preaching **243**
    Sunday service 242
    wedding ceremony 242-243
motorcycle items (in chronological order)
    buying the DKW **84, 99**
    leaving for Africa and the Middle East **100**
    sand-clogged speed-control 104-105
    sand-clogged gas filter 105
    stolen DKW 121-122
Mountain Drive home 259, 261
    view **259**
Mt. Baker climb **159, 160, 161**
Muria Synod, Indonesia 279
Music Mission Kiev 341-342
    financial challenges 342
    Janzen, Wes and Kim 342, **358**
    tours 342
Narcosli Creek School 85-86, 260
Nahkshon, Israeli freighter 123-**124**
Nazarene Church, Richmond, CA 156
Neuendorf 16
Neufeld, Herb **364**
    2021 overture to BCMB Conference leaders 330
    assistant moderator Canadian MB Conference 226-**227**
    successful intervener 332
Neufeld, John **366**
Ngoma, Zahedi, Cong (DRC)
    report to MBMSI board 287
    session with Zahedi Ngoma 286-**287**
Nickel, Helen 26
Nickel, Murray and Faith 287
Nickel, Evangeline 239
Nickel family **133**
Nickel, Henry H. 150, 152, 154
    Bible School teacher 71
    death 210
    family **133**
    founding pastor, Central Heights Church 68
    the only grandparent 187
    with Redekop grandchildren 186
Nickel, Maria 133, 144
    death 18
Nikkel, Peter **362**
    2021 overture to BCMB Conference leaders 330
    successful intervenor 332
Nikkel, Ruben 90, 131, 13
Nixon, Richard, Watergate Scandal 206
North American (General) Mennonite Brethren

Conference 196
  request for a report on labour unions 196
  member, Historical Commission 1994-2002 277
NOW TV 201
Obama, Barak 314
OCUFA Teaching Award 1993 255
Olsen, Borge 299, 300
On Capital Punishment 222
Orlov, Tatyana
  translator for the 1994 Kremlin session 249, 251
Osaka Bible Church 304
out of gas in Egypt
  incredible Good Samaritan 113-114
Ontario Task Force on Private Colleges and Seminaries 239
Pacific College (now Fresno Pacific University) 171-178
  medical "insurance" 173-174
  salary 172
  dedication of PORTAL yearbook 178
Pacific Mennonite Children's Choir 301
Page, Don 359
Parasailing, Doris **209**
Parkview Street duplex 145
Parliamentary prayer breakfast, Ottawa, 2009 276
Penner, Myron 292
Penner, Ron 291
Personal Opinion column 112
  puzzling letters 271, **272, 273**
  ran 1964-2003 270-271
  affirmation 310
  apology for an embarrassing column 194
  high readership 180
  launched, January, 1964 169
  personal reflections 271
Peters, Frank C. 178, 191
  advantageous salary adjustment 190
Peters, Jake 245-247, 248-251
Petrovka 16, 18, 25
Ph.D.
  dissertation **162, 164-165**
  dissertation defense 164-165
  exams 164
  graduation **166**
political activism among Mennonites 181, 205-206
Political Science Department affirmation 255
Politics Under God, 2007 268-269
  Chuck Colson's review 269
  French version, 2007, 2012 269
  Spanish version, 2010 269
poverty 37-40
  father's low salaries 29-30
  sharing one apple 37

crop failures 39
Prague Peace Conference 174-175
  cancelled 175
  East Germany 174-175
  Why the widow voted 174-175
prayer circle "claiming" property **298, 299**
Preaching
  Central Heights Church 147
  from the wrong Psalm 243-244
  in Hangchou, China **264**-265
  in Moscow Baptist Church **243**
  with KGB agents present 247-248
presentation of Genesis in the Letters Club 76
press conference in the Kremlin **251**
Prison Church in Asuncion, Paraguay 339-341, 340
professionalization of MB clergy 204
Professor Emeritus 308
Pyramid, Khufu (Cheops) **112**-113
Quebec 169
  separatism, FLQ 164, 204-205
  second referendum 257, 313
quilt, embroidered 31, **51**
racism in Oklahoma, 1965 174
radio programs monitored in early years 41
RCMP officers, 290, 324
Reconciliation Advocates
  a new overture 330
  hiring David Leis 328
  the investigation report 328
  the 12 accusations identified later 328
red barn, deck, and table set 214
Redekop, Agnes (nee Wiebe) 13, 22, **26**, **30-34**, 154
  accepted her children's support **150**-151
  as a widow 150
  death, February 25, 1965 173
  last Christmas, 1964 173
  multiple myeloma **173**
  personal comments 32-33
  talents and skills 30-31
  wedding and marriage **15**, 33
Redekop, Bonnie (later Satya) **202, 221, 355**
  a happy girl **185**
  Bachelor of Law 1997 **215**
  birth 185,
Redekop children making music in Main Centre **32**
Redekop clan Shuswap reunion 215-**216**
Redekop, Clara (Hoff, Anderson) 13
  memorial service for Don Anderson 261
  unknown speaking assignment 261-262
Redekop, David
  birth, young boy **217, 318**
  with Rebecca Moore **356**
Redekop, Ernest "Ernie" 36

buggy mishap 46-47
fighting the Fraser River flood, 1948 65-66
John writing love-card for Ernie 73
moose hunting with John 72-73
riding on the buggy back axle 49
stump blasting 65
Redekop family picture (c. 1941) **36 183**
Redekop, Gary 186, 187, **202,** 260
  birth **158**
  cheerful young boy **159**
  Gary and Lee Ann **354**
  graduated as Medical Doctor **210**
  regarding *Vancouver Sun* article 308
Redekop, Heather (now Heather Harmony) 186, 187, **221**
  birth **163, 354**
  thoughtful, happy girl **164**
  Master of Social Work **215**
Redekop, Jacob F. **15**, 25, **33**, 154
  as student 25, **26-27**
  assistant pastor 68
  Bible School teacher 26-**27, 149**
  father's death 149-150
  marriage **15**, 26
  migration from Russia 16
  personal comments 29-30
  the Brunk challenge 148
Redekop. John H. (selected pictures in chronological Order)
  as toddler with Sophie **33**
  family, c. 1941 **34**
  Bachelor of Arts, 1954 **73**
  viewing Heidelberg **87**
  on pyramid **106**
  wedding **137**
  with Hungarian professors **143**
  a happy couple **140**
  climbing Mt. Baker **160, 161**
  Master of Arts graduate **156**
  with Ph.D. defense committee **165**
  Ph.D. graduate **166**
  with family in Waterloo **183**
  25th wedding anniversary **207-208**
  with Marvin Glass in Marxist debates **236**
  preaching in Moscow **243**
  with Comrade Heinrich Abramovich Unger **246**
  at the Kremlin press conference **251**
  Government of Canada Award, 1992 **254**
  preaching in Hangchou, China, 2007 **264-265**
  with vice-president Zahedi Ngoma, Congo 287
  Stillwood **315, 386**
  60th wedding anniversary 321, **322**
  Betty Urqhart Award **346, 347**
Redekop, Michelle **260, 318, 356**
Redekop, Paul 150
  buggy mishap 46-47

  had to miss school 43
  operated the farm 26
  riding on the buggy axle 49
Redekop, Rosella (nee Siemens) 28
Redekop siblings; six couples **216**
Redekop, Sophie (later Toews)
  on a tire-less bicycle **41**
  USSR tour, 1984 239
  with pets **40**
  with young John **35**
Redekop, Wendy (now Wendy Carmichael) **154**, 186, 187, **202, 353**
  birth **144**
  young girl **145, 170**
  locked trunk **199**
  Master of Social Work 210, **211**
Redekopp, Anna (nee Wiebe, Berg) 18
Redekopp, Benjamin 18
Redekopp, Elizabeth (nee Friesen) **16**, 19
Redekopp, Franz B. 16-19
reflections and memories
  childhood years 50-54
  embroidering a quilt **51**
  early bath customs 52
  hog-butchering 52-53
  studying at UBC 79-82
  threshing time 53-**54**
Reform Party research 302
Regina Manifesto, criticism 59
Reimer, Colin 329
  gratitude 333
Rempel, Darrell 323
Richmond, CA 155
Saffold, Guy 283
Sahara Desert
  missing bridge **104**
  motorcycle troubles **104-105**
  Sahara Highway **103**
  sandstorm **104**-106
  taken for questioning in Libya 108-111
  the minefield 107
salaries
  high school teacher 145
  Pacific College, Fresno, CA 172, 178
  Waterloo Lutheran University 178
  WLU advantageous salary settlement 190
San Francisco Chronicle 179-180
Sandstorm
  missing bridge **104**
  sand-clogged fuel filter 105
  sand-clogged speed control 104-105
  sleeping in a minefield 107
  the Sahara Highway **103**
Sawatzky, Donna and Gerry 298-299
Schladewitz, Katherine 176-177
  anticipating a rental 176

negotiating rental 177
Schmidt, Henry 282, 283
Schmidt, Rosella first crafts director, 1958 151
scholarships (major)
    Deutsche Academische Austausch Dienst 78
    Christie Scholarship 153
    Canada Council 153
Schroeder, Henry 296, **316**
Seeley, David 300
Seattle 157, 166-167, 170
S.F. Coffmann Peace Lecture 195
shown an occupied hotel room 119-120
sixtieth wedding anniversary **321, 322**
Shuh, Robert 212
silver wedding anniversary **207-208**
Sir Cecile's Gold **62-63**
sleeping Yugoslav border officer 127
sleeping under the stars
    in Germany 130
    in the Sahara Desert 107
    in The Netherlands 92
Smythe, Leanne 358
social assistance
    Canada Pension Plan 181
    family allowance 48
    Old Age Security 70
South Abbotsford Church 133
    first preaching assignment 67
    junior choir 67
    youth group 67-68
Soviet Union, 1984 trip 239-244
    AUCECB 240
    Barclay's Commentary crisis 240
    Leningrad Night tour 241-242
    preaching in Moscow Baptist Church **243**
Soviet Union, 1986 trip 244-251
    four participants **245**
    Kremlin interview and press conference 248-251
Soviet Union 1987 trip 252-253
    a crowded Karaganda church 252
    pursued by an officer 252-253
Spiritual pilgrimage 40-50, 62, 67-69, 147-148, 151-152, 167, 351
Stiller, Brian 357
    first EFC executive secretary 232
    The Stiller Report 232-233
Stillwood Board 327
    received accusation against John 329
Stillwood Camp and Conference Centre (Columbia Bible Camp until 2000) **292-300, 316**, 329
    50th anniversary 269
    anniversary book **269**-270
    beginnings 151, 292
    Columbia Bible Camp history 325
    COVID-19 323

Development Commission 293
    fundraising 293-300, **324-325, 345**
    golf-cart with guests **323**
    later developments 323-334
    personal reflections and memories 333-334
    Phase Two 326
    termination of John's ministry 325, 326, 327
Stillwood Board, holiday gift 308-**309**
Stillwood – The first 50 Years, 1958-2008 269
stolen motorcycle 121-123
Strathdee, Mike **359**
Strumpski, Fred and Ella
    Stillwood donors 296
    funded Columbia Place 290
student ministries 301-302
Stuttgart and Rubble Mountain 131
Sumas Energy Company, SE2 304-305
    presentation to the National Energy Board 305
Tabor Home Society 342-343
teaching
    Columbia Bible College 261
    elementary school 85-87
    high school 141-147
    Hungarian professors 142-**143**
    Pacific College, Fresno 171-178
    MB Biblical Seminary 282
    Trinity Western University 260-261
    University of Washington, 1962-1964 162-163
    university teaching assistant 162
    Wilfrid Laurier University (formerly Waterloo Lutheran University) 190-192, 218
telephone service in Main Centre 51-52
termination of John's Stillwood ministry by the BCMB Executive Board 325-327, 328
    consequences 331
    forgiveness **331, 332**
    painful experiences **327, 329, 330**, 334
    reasons for reviewing the saga 331
    termination of plans for Phase Two 331
The Betty Urqhart Award, 2019 **346, 347**
    the citation 346
The Canadian Mennonite
    beginning of a writing career 82-83
    press card use in Cairo 113
    special Clearbrook issue 146-147
The Grouse Grind, 2006 262-263
The Harper Record 335
The Star-Spangled Beaver 192
The Stiller Report 232-**233**
The Tory Book 334
The Writers Guild awards 210, 346, 347
Thiessen, Arden 231
Thiessen, Isaac 227-229
threshing time 49-50

Todd, Douglas, *Vancouver Sun* article 308
Toews, James **366**
　statement of affirmation 310
Toews, Neil 144
　third room-mate 75, 76
　choir conductor, USSR trip, 1984 239
tour to the United Kingdom 212-213
　hot weather crisis 212-213
travel (selected trips in chronological sequence)
　across Canada, 1955 85-86
　across the Atlantic Ocean, 1955 86
　in northern Europe, 1955 87-88
　in Italy, 1956 96-97
　in Tunisia and Libya, 1956 98-104
　in Egypt, 1956 104-107
　in Lebanon and Jordan, 1956 108-112
　in Israel, 1956 112-116
　in Yugoslavia, Italy, Austria, 1956 116-120
　in the *Deutsche Demokratische Republik*, 1956 121
　to Prague, Czechoslovakia, 1965 174-175
　to the Soviet Union, 1984 239-244
　to the Soviet Union, 1986 244-251
　to the Soviet Union, 1987 252-253
　MBMSI missions trip to Russia, Kazakhstan, Kyrgyzstan, 1997 278
　MBMSI missions trip to Indonesia, India, Pakistan, 1999 279
　to Japan, 1998-1999 279-281
　to Japan 2002 303-304
　European tour, *Oberammergau* 2000 262
　to China, 2007 263-265
　to Congo (DRC), 2004 284-287
　t o Paraguay, 2011 338-341
Trinity Western University 218, 308
　honorary doctorate, D. Hum. 255-256
　part-time faculty, 1995-2016 260
　scholar in residence 260
　missed faculty meetings 260
Trudeau, Justin
　Medical Assistance In Dying 349-350
Trump, Donald 350
　Trinity Western University debate 260
Two Sides; The Best of Personal Opinion, 1964-1984 219
unintentionally inebriated 101
University of British Columbia 75-82
　rides to class 75
　joining the Letters Club 76
　debating team 76-77
　Teacher Training, 1954-1955 73
　Bachelor of Arts, 1954 77
　coach of the UBC debating team 78
　reflections 79-82
University of California, Berkeley 155-157, 177-178
University of the Fraser Valley 291-292

University of Washington 157-158, 162-167
　teaching assistant 162
　part-time faculty member 162-163
　dissertation 164
　dissertation defense 164-165
　graduation **166**
Unger, Heinrich Abramovich
　communist official **246, 247**
Unger, Peter 323
Unger, Wally tribute in *Mosaic of Grace* 345
Unruh, Richard and Pat **363**
US religious data 349
UNWRA refugee camp 117-118
Vancouver Sun Douglas Todd's affirmation 308
Vatican visit 101-102
Vietnam War, casualties, opposition 206
Vietnamese "Boat People" as guests **189**-190
Voth, Heinrich 278
Warkentin, Abe
　first 1996 camp donor 293
　loaned John his rifle to hunt moose 72
　loaned John $50, 1956 136
　old John his first car, 1956 136
Warkentin, Marvin 201
Wartman, Paul 288, 290-291
Waterloo, ON 183-192
　moving to 183
　decision to leave 218
Waterloo Mennonite Brethren Church 188, 189-**190, 313**
　pastors Alvin Enns and Marvin Warkentin 20
　moderator 211
　building dedication 212
Waterloo MB Church building committee 212
wedding 138
Wiebe, Aganeta (nee Martens) 20, **22**. 23, 24, 25, **34**
Wiebe, Arthur 176
Wiebe, Johann "John" P. 20, 22, 24, **34,** 276
　spiritual pilgrimage 21-22
　migration to Canada 22-24
　homestead **23**
　retirement 25
Wiebe, Katherine (nee Schellenberg) **20**
Wiebe, Paul 20, 21
Wiebe, Rudy 169
Wieler, Abraham 144, 21
　employed John part-time 76
　first camp dean, 1958 151
　preacher 65, 68
　Bible School teacher 71
Wiens, John and Verna **316**, 323
Wilfrid Laurier University
　1968 appointment 190
　advantageous salary adjustment 190
　courses taught 191

Marxism vs. Christianity debate 237, **258**
member, Board of Governors 191
member, Senate 191
Willowdale house **185**
Wills, Lee Ann **260, 354**
   graduated as Medical Doctor **210**
Winnipeg Free Press 48, 55, 69
WLU News Features
   launched, 1974 200
   sixty-six columns 234
WLU Outstanding Teacher Award, 1992 **255**
WLU president Lorna Marsden's affirmation 256
Woodworth, Stephen **361**
working as third cook on the CPR 73-74
World War II
   as taught in Heidelberg University 97-98
   better grain prices 42
   casualties 48
   destroyed tank and bridge in North Africa **104, 106**
   Hermann Krieg reports 94
   mines in North Africa **107-108**
   war began 55
Wollman, Harvey
   Mennonite, Democrat, governor of South Dakota 2005
World Evangelical Fellowship convention 1997 301
Wright, Ada Grace **355**
writing a love note for Ernie 73
writing Doris daily 89-90
youth rally, 1958 1522
youth leader, Central Heights Church 148-149
Yugoslavia
   a communist economy 135-126
   conversations with students 125-126
   price reduction or piety **126**

p. 337
p. 338 repeated